Wisdom of Buddha

The Saṁdhinirmocana Sūtra

Translated by
John Powers

Dharma  Publishing

TIBETAN TRANSLATION SERIES

1. *Calm and Clear*
2. *The Legend of the Great Stupa*
3. *Mind in Buddhist Psychology*
4. *Golden Zephyr* (Nāgārjuna)
5. *Kindly Bent to Ease Us, Parts 1–3*
6. *Elegant Sayings* (Nāgārjuna, Sakya Pandita)
7. *The Life and Liberation of Padmasambhava*
8. *Buddha's Lions: Lives of the 84 Siddhas*
9. *The Voice of the Buddha* (Lalitavistara Sūtra)
10. *The Marvelous Companion* (Jātakamālā)
11. *Mother of Knowledge: Enlightenment of Yeshe Tshogyal*
12. *The Dhammapada* (Teachings on 26 Topics)
13. *The Fortunate Aeon* (Bhadrakalpika Sūtra)
14. *Master of Wisdom* (Nāgārjuna)
15. *Joy for the World* (Candrakīrti)
16. *Wisdom of Buddha* (Saṁdhinirmocana Sūtra)

Library of Congress Cataloging-in-Publication Data

Tripiṭaka. Saṁdhinirmocanasūtra. English
Wisdom of Buddha : the Saṁdhinirmocana Sūtra / translated by John Powers.
p. cm. – (Tibetan translation series.)
Includes bibliographical references and index.
ISBN 0-89800-247-8. – ISBN 0-89800-246-X (pbk.)
I. Title. II. Series
BQ2092.E5 1994
294.3'85–dc20 94-25023 CIP

Frontispiece: Courtesy of the Metropolitan Museum of Art
Gift of Joseph H. Heil, 1970 (1970.298.1)

This publication was sponsored by a generous donation from Michael Gray.

Printed in the United States of America by Dharma Press
Typeset in ITC Zapf Book Light with WP Murray Hill initials

9 8 7 6 5 4 3 2 1

May this meritorious action
liberate all sentient beings from saṁsāra
and establish them on the Bodhisattva path

Contents

Preface

Buddhism teaches that life is precious. If we wish to use our limited time on earth to create a truly meaningful existence, there is no better foundation than the Dharma, the teachings of the Buddha.

The Buddha taught for almost fifty years, and although many of his teachings have been lost over the millennia, thousands of texts have been preserved in Sanskrit, Pāli, Tibetan, and Chinese, bringing the wisdom of the Dharma to many lands. Only a few hundred of these texts have been translated into Western languages. Each new translation reveals further aspects of the Buddha's realization, confirming the value of the Dharma and the depth and richness of the teachings.

With this publication, the Saṁdhinirmocana Sūtra becomes available in its entirety in English for the first time. Considered a Sūtra of definitive meaning, the Saṁdhinirmocana is among the extraordinary teachings that the Buddha gave to the advanced Bodhisattvas. Its brilliance illuminates ideas and practices of great depth and subtlety.

Vast in scope, the Saṁdhinirmocana is rich in profound meaning that cannot be fully fathomed in one reading. However, patient study, reflection, and rereading will evoke clear insight into the Buddha's awakened vision.

Conveying the deep and subtle meanings of a text such as the Saṁdhinirmocana into clear, readable English is a demanding task. Buddhist terminology and perspectives are still unfamiliar to the West, and the vocabulary available cannot always convey the ideas being expressed. In the eighth and ninth centuries, when the Dharma was being transmitted to Tibet, Indian paṇḍitas and Tibetan lotsāwas worked together to establish uniform standards of translation. As similar efforts are carried out in the West, the challenge of communicating the heart of the Dharma teachings will become easier and the results more accurate. I hope that the present translation will inspire efforts in this direction.

For over twenty years Dharma Publishing has been dedicated to producing Buddhist books and art of the highest quality. Although a work such as this has a very limited audience and is quite difficult to produce, I am confident that the immeasurable virtue of the wisdom that the text contains makes it infinitely worth the effort.

I would like to thank the translator, John Powers, for his careful work. My thanks go as well to the Dharma Publishing editors and production staff, especially Sylvia Gretchen, who worked closely with Dr. Powers to prepare the translation for publication. There is no doubt that the meritorious action of making this wonderful Sūtra available to the English-reading world will benefit many living beings.

Sarvaṁ Maṅgalam
Tarthang Tulku
September 1994

Introduction

One of the most influential texts in Indian Mahāyāna Buddhist literature, the Saṁdhinirmocana Sūtra presents a wealth of teachings central to all Buddhist practice and philosophy. Its explications of the meaning of the ultimate, the basis-consciousness (ālaya-vijñāna), and the doctrine of cognition-only (vijñapti-mātra) have had a major impact in every country where Mahāyāna Buddhism has flourished, including India, Tibet, Mongolia, China, Korea, and Japan.

The teachings of the Buddha demonstrate how our common modes of viewing reality and our habitual ways of living and relating to the world are fundamentally mistaken. While Christian philosophy traditionally identifies the root of our existential problems as original sin, the Buddha taught that ignorance is more fundamental than sin, for through ignorance we unwittingly commit actions that result in harm to ourselves and others. This ignorance clouds the continuum of each and every being who is not a Buddha, and can be overcome only through individual effort.

The Saṁdhinirmocana Sūtra tells us how the full force of our mental and physical faculties can be harnessed for this task. Comprehensive and multifaceted, the text details the world view, stages, and yogic practices necessary for transforming even the most subtle manifestations of ignorance.

The reader is guided on a path that leads to mental balance, insight into the nature of reality, and deep commitment to work selflessly for the benefit of other beings.

Summary of the Text

Like many Sūtras, the text recounts a series of questions and answers between the Buddha and his followers, or, in the case of chapter one, between two Bodhisattvas. Except for chapter four, where the Śrāvaka Subhūti questions the Buddha, all of the interlocutors are highly developed Bodhisattvas. Their questions and the Buddha's answers go to the very heart of the practice or issue being discussed, fully explicating profound and subtle meanings.

The setting in which the Buddha teaches the Sūtra is described as a vast celestial palace that fills countless worldly realms with its brilliance and surpasses all other dwellings. This wondrous palace reflects the supreme spiritual attainments of the Buddha, who created it, and the aspirations of all its inhabitants, who are Dharma practitioners of a high level of development.

The Sūtra may be divided into five main parts. The first four chapters present the ultimate and how it is to be understood by trainees. Chapter five is an analysis of consciousness; chapters six and seven discuss the relative character of phenomena and of teachings as they are illuminated by definitive understanding. The path to enlightenment is the subject of the eighth and ninth chapters, which focus on meditative practices and the methods for mastering the mental afflictions and obstacles that undermine progress on the path. Chapter ten is a discussion of the nature of a Buddha, the final goal of yogic practice.

The Bodhisattva Gambhīrārthasaṁdhinirmocana characterizes the ultimate as "ineffable and of a non-dual character" in chapter one. The ultimate pervades all reality but cannot be described in words or understood by conceptual thought. It is realized only by Āryas, those who have attained the path of seeing and are able to perceive the ultimate directly.

In chapter two the Bodhisattva Dharmodgata describes a debate on the ultimate character of phenomena that he witnessed among proponents of various Tīrthika systems. The Bodhisattva laments their divergent opinions, doubts, and misconceptions and marvels at the Buddha's realization and actualization of the ultimate, "whose character completely transcends all argumentation." In response, the Buddha teaches that the ultimate is realized individually, is signless, inexpressible, devoid of the conventional, and free from all dispute. Beings caught up in desire, discursiveness, and the conventions of seeing, hearing, differentiating, and perceiving, as well as beings engaged in dispute, cannot even imagine what the ultimate is like.

In chapter three, the Bodhisattva Suviśuddhamati points out that even Bodhisattvas disagree about the ultimate: Some believe the character of the ultimate and the character of the compounded are the same; others believe them to be different. Through a series of reasonings, the Buddha demonstrates that any attempt to categorize leads to error, for the ultimate is "profound and subtle, having a character completely transcending sameness and difference."

The ultimate must be sought through meditation that moves beyond all limiting and distorting categories. In chapter four the Buddha poses two questions to Subhūti: How many people communicate their spiritual understanding under the influence of conceit? How many communicate without conceit? Subhūti recounts a time when he witnessed a large gathering of monks, all advanced in training, who expressed their understanding based on "various forms of phenomena" such as the five aggregates, the six sense spheres, and the four noble truths. Since they did "not seek the ultimate whose character is all of one taste . . . therefore, these venerable persons have conceit." The Buddha explains that the ultimate, which pervades all phenomena and is undifferentiated in all compounded things, is "an object of observation for purification of the aggregates."

Using this discussion of the ultimate as a basis, chapter five provides an analysis of the nature of consciousness that indicates how we are able to progress from our present state of ignorance, desire, and hatred to the state of a Buddha. In response to questions by the Bodhisattva Viśālamati, the Buddha teaches that our present mental states and life situations result solely from our own past actions. Each action and thought creates a concordant predisposition that is deposited in our mental continuum. The Buddha points to a "basis-consciousness" which collects these predispositions and holds them until the time is ripe for them to give rise to their resultant effects. "Bodhisattvas are wise with respect to the secrets of mind, thought, and consciousness," not only because they understand the very subtle ways that consciousness functions, but also because they have transcended even the most subtle clinging to any object of perception.

In chapter six the Buddha teaches the Bodhisattva Guṇākara that phenomena exhibit a threefold character: the imputational (parikalpita), the other-dependent (paratantra), and the thoroughly established (pariniṣpanna). These characters are illustrated by compelling examples that remind us that the Buddha is not introducing abstract philosophical concepts, but is instructing us in how to reorient the mind toward enlightenment.

In chapter seven, the Bodhisattva Paramārthasamudgata asks the Buddha his intention in teaching that "All phenomena lack own-being; all phenomena are unproduced, unceasing, quiescent from the start, and naturally in a state of nirvāṇa." The Buddha's response further reveals the nature of phenomena and differentiates teachings of definitive meaning from those of interpretable meaning. Just as space pervades all form, teachings of definitive meaning pervade all Sūtras of interpretable meaning. Those who understand the intention behind the Buddha's teaching know that although beings are diverse, there is a "single purity" and "one vehicle."

In the eighth chapter the Bodhisattva Maitreya's questions focus on how to develop śamatha and vipaśyanā, two main bases of Buddhist meditation. Śamatha is the ability, developed through concentrated meditative practice, to focus one's mind on an object without distraction. This is essential for more advanced meditative practice, since it prevents the afflictions from arising. Vipaśyanā involves analyzing the object to determine its true nature. This practice recalls the teachings of the first four chapters, since the true nature of phenomena is the ultimate, which is equated with suchness and emptiness. Through developing vipaśyanā, one eradicates the basis of the afflictions and is able to perceive the ultimate directly. Here the Buddha teaches that the images of people and things that we observe are "cognition-only."

The ninth chapter maps the path to enlightenment, delineating the ten Bodhisattva stages, the levels through which Mahāyāna practitioners progress. Each stage represents a decisive advance in understanding and spiritual attainment. The questioner here is Avalokiteśvara, the embodiment of compassion. The main meditative practice is the six perfections—generosity, ethics, patience, effort, concentration, and wisdom—the essence of the Bodhisattva's training.

Compassion motivates Bodhisattvas to work tirelessly on the spiritual path for an unimaginably long period of time. The final fruition of their efforts is the state of a Buddha, the focus of chapter ten. It represents the apex of all spiritual qualities and the highest development of compassion and wisdom. Through the Buddha's answers to the Bodhisattva Mañjuśrī's questions, we learn that a Buddha's limitless compassionate action is accomplished without any manifest activity. There is no afflicted being who later becomes purified: "Afflicted phenomena and pure phenomena are all without activity and personhood." Hearing this, the aspiring Bodhisattva is again reminded that pursuing the ultimate goal of the path of yogic practice begins and ends with a proper understanding of the nature of the ultimate.

About This Translation

As this brief summary suggests, the Saṁdhinirmocana Sūtra is a complex and advanced text. Translating it has proven to be a demanding task which has taken many years. I first began work on the translation as a graduate student at the University of Virginia, where it became my doctoral thesis. Later much effort was devoted to refining the translation and preparing it for publication. Throughout, my goal has been to keep the English translation faithful to the structure of the Tibetan text and to translate technical terms conservatively and consistently. While this has sometimes resulted in awkward readings, I prefer this approach to being overly speculative about the meaning of the Sūtra's many difficult passages.

Although the original Sanskrit text was probably lost by the thirteenth century, numerous translations of this Sūtra exist today in Asian languages. I chose to base this translation on the Tibetan since I had access to a number of different Tibetan editions, and also because the Tibetans are especially noted for their accurate translations of canonical texts. In my studies, I have consulted ten different Tibetan editions, as well as three Chinese editions, and have noted their variant readings.

The Tibetan text presented here is reproduced from the canonical edition found in the sDe-dge bKa'-'gyur, which is highly esteemed by Tibetan scholars, and the English translation is based on this text. It is my hope that having the Tibetan text facing the English translation will encourage students and scholars to draw inspiration and clarity from both.

In preparing the translation and notes, I have also relied on the five commentaries found in the Tibetan Buddhist Canon, as well as on Tibetan exegetical materials (both written texts and oral instructions), and on Yogācāra texts that explain concepts presented in the Sūtra.

Most of the footnotes are drawn from the two most comprehensive commentaries in Tibetan. The larger of these is a three-volume work authored by Wonch'uk, a Korean student of the great Chinese scholar Hsüan-tsang. Since major sections of Wonch'uk's original Chinese text have been lost, the only complete version of the text available today is the Tibetan translation found in the Tibetan Buddhist Canon. The text is a masterpiece of traditional Buddhist scholarship that draws upon a vast range of Buddhist literature, cites many different opinions, raises important points about the thought of the Sūtra, and provides explanations of virtually every technical term and phrase.

The other major commentary, consisting of two volumes, is signed by "Byang-chub-rdzu-'phrul." Although there is some mystery surrounding the author's identity, most Tibetan scholars attribute this text to Cog-ro Klu'i-rgyal-mtshan, a renowned eighth-century Tibetan translator and scholar. The text provides insightful explications of most of the Sūtra.

Other sources consulted for the notes include the works of Asaṅga and his brother Vasubandhu (generally considered to be the main exponents and systematizers of the Yogācāra school); commentaries on their works by Sthiramati and Sumatiśīla; the commentary on the eighth chapter attributed to Jñānagarbha; the Legs-bshad-snying-po (which mainly focuses on the seventh chapter of the Sūtra) by Tsong-kha-pa, founder of the dGe-lugs-pa school of Tibetan Buddhism; its commentary by dPal-'byor-lhun-grub; and oral explanations from contemporary Tibetan scholars.

I am truly fortunate to have had access to such a wide range of secondary materials and explanations, for the meanings expressed in the Sūtra can be obscure. Each source has helped me greatly in understanding and translating the Sūtra. While the constraints of space have made it necessary to condense the notes prepared for my doctoral thesis, I hope that the notes included here will inspire readers to consider the many differing perspectives available and foster a deeper understanding of the Sūtra's meaning.

I have also had the great good fortune to have worked with Tibetan and Western scholars who generously shared their knowledge and understanding of this Sūtra with me. I would especially like to thank Geshe Jamphel Phandro, Geshe Palden Dragpa, Geshe Yeshe Thabkhe, Dr. Jeffrey Hopkins, Dr. Christian Lindtner, Dr. Ernst Steinkellner, and Dr. Helmut Eimer. I am also grateful to H. H. the Dalai Lama for his illuminating remarks on this Sūtra during a meeting in Dharamsala in 1988.

Taught by the Buddha as a skillful means, the Saṁdhinirmocana Sūtra is intended as a basis for meditative practice, a guide to a Bodhisattva's training for enlightenment. Bearing this in mind may encourage the reader to undertake the careful and sustained study, contemplation, and application in daily life that will ultimately help to reveal the full depth and scope of this profound work.

Wisdom of Buddha

Homage to the Tathāgata Buddha Śākyamuni

།དོན་ཟབ་དགོངས་པ་ངེས་པར་འགྲེལ་གྱི་ལེའུ་སྔེ་དང་པོ།

The Chapter of Gambhīrārthasaṁdhinirmocana

The Setting and Chapter One

༄༅། །རྒྱ་གར་སྐད་དུ། ཨཱརྱ་སནྡྷི་ནི་ར་མོ་ཙ་ན་ནཱ་མ་མ་ཧཱ་ཡཱ་ན་སཱུ་ཏྲ། བོད་སྐད་དུ། འཕགས་པ་དགོངས་པ་ངེས་པར་འགྲེལ་པ་ཞེས་བྱ་བ་ཐེག་པ་ཆེན་པོའི་མདོ། སངས་རྒྱས་དང་བྱང་ཆུབ་སེམས་དཔའ་ཐམས་ཅད་ལ་ཕྱག་འཚལ་ལོ། །འདི་སྐད་བདག་གིས་ཐོས་པ་དུས་གཅིག་ན། བཅོམ་ལྡན་འདས་གཞལ་མེད་ཁང་རིན་པོ་ཆེ་སྣ་བདུན་མཆོག་ཏུ་འབར་བ་བཀོད་པ། འཇིག་རྟེན་གྱི་ཁམས་དཔག་ཏུ་མེད་པ་རྒྱས་པར་འགེངས་པའི་འོད་ཟེར་ཆེན་པོ་ཤིན་ཏུ་མངའ་བ། གནས་ཀྱི་བྱེ་བྲག་ཤིན་ཏུ་རྣམ་པར་ཕྱེ་བ། མཐའ་ཡས་པ་རྣམ་པར་གཞག་པ། དཀྱིལ་འཁོར་ཡོངས་སུ་མཆད་པ། ཁམས་གསུམ་པ་ལས་ཡང་དག་པར་འདས་པའི་སྤྱོད་ཡུལ། འཇིག་རྟེན་ལས་འདས་པ་དེའི་བླ་མའི་དགེ་བའི་རྩ་བ་ལས་བྱུང་བ། དབང་སྒྱུར་བའི་རྣམ་པར་རིག་པ་ཤིན་ཏུ་རྣམ་པར་རིག་པའི་མཚན་ཉིད། དེ་བཞིན་གཤེགས་པའི་གནས། བྱང་ཆུབ་སེམས་དཔའ་དཔག་ཏུ་མེད་པའི་དགེ་འདུན་རྗེས་སུ་རྟེན་པ། ལྷ་དང་ཀླུ་དང་གནོད་སྦྱིན་དང་དྲི་ཟ་དང་ལྷ་མ་ཡིན་དང་ནམ་མཁའ་ལྡིང་དང་མིའམ་ཅི་དང་ལྟོ་འཕྱེ་ཆེན་པོ་དང་མི་དང་མི་མ་ཡིན་པ་མཐའ་ཡས་པ་རྣམ་པར་རྒྱུ་བ། ཆོས་ཀྱི་རོའི་དགའ་བ་དང་བདེ་བ་ཆེན་པོས་བརྟན་པ། སེམས་ཅན་ཐམས་ཅད་ཀྱི་དོན་ཐམས་ཅད་ཡང་དག་པར་ཐོབ་པར་མཛད་པས་ཉེ་བར་གནས་པ། ཉོན་མོངས་པའི་དྲི་མའི་གནོད་པ་ཐམས་ཅད་དང་བྲལ་བ། བདུད་ཐམས་ཅད་ཡོངས་སུ་སྤངས་པ། ཐམས་ཅད་ཀྱི་བཀོད་པ་ལས་ལྷག་པ། དེ་བཞིན་གཤེགས་པའི་བྱིན་གྱི་རླབས་ཀྱིས་བཀོད་པ། དྲན་པ་དང་བློ་གྲོས་དང་། རྟོགས་པ་ཆེན་པོས་ངེས་པར་འབྱུང་བ། ཞི

Homage to all Buddhas and Bodhisattvas!

Thus have I heard at one time: The Bhagavan was dwelling in an immeasurable palace arrayed with the supreme brilliance of the seven precious substances,[1] emanating great rays of light that suffused innumerable universes.

Well-apportioned into distinctive sections, it was limitless in reach;[2] an unimpeded mandala; a sphere of activity completely transcending the three worldly realms; arisen from the root of supreme virtue that transcends the world.[3] It was characterized by perfect knowledge, the knowledge of one who has mastery.[4]

Abode of the Tathāgata, attended by a community of innumerable Bodhisattvas,[5] it was alive with unlimited numbers of devas, nāgas, yakṣas, gandharvas, asuras, garuḍas, kiṁnaras, mahoragas, humans, and non-humans.[6] Steadfast due to great bliss and joy in the taste of the Dharma; enduring in order to bring about the welfare of all sentient beings; free from the harm of the defilements of the afflictions; completely free from all demons;[7] surpassing all patterns; arranged through the blessing of the Tathāgata; emancipated through great mindfulness, intelligence, and realization; support of the great state of peace and penetrating awareness; entered through the great doors of liberation—emptiness, signlessness, and wishlessness—this pattern was adorned with

གནས་དང་ལྷག་མཐོང་ཆེན་པོ་བཞོན་པ་ཡིན་པ། རྣམ་པར་ཐར་པའི་སྒོ་ཆེན་པོ་སྐོང་པ་ཉིད་
དང་མཚན་མ་མེད་པ་དང་། སྨོན་པ་མེད་པ་ནས་འཇུག་པ། རིན་པོ་ཆེའི་པདྨའི་རྒྱལ་པོ་
ཆེན་པོ་ཡོན་ཏན་གྱི་ཚོགས་མཐའ་ཡས་པས་བརྒྱན་པའི་བཀོད་པ་ལ་བརྟེན་པ་ན་བཞུགས་ཏེ།
བཅོམ་ལྡན་འདས་ལེགས་པར་ཐུགས་སུ་ཆུད་པའི་བློ་དང་ལྡན་པ། ཀུན་ཏུ་སྤྱོད་པ།
གཉིས་མི་མངའ་བ། མཚན་ཉིད་མེད་པའི་ཆོས་ལ་མཆོག་ཏུ་གཞོལ་བར་མཛད་པ།
སངས་རྒྱས་ཀྱི་གནས་པས་གནས་པ། སངས་རྒྱས་ཐམས་ཅད་དང་མཉམ་པ་ཉིད་བརྙེས་
པ༑ སྒྲིབ་པ་མེད་པའི་རྟོགས་པ་ཐུགས་སུ་ཆུད་པ། ཕྱིར་མི་ལྡོག་པའི་ཆོས་དང་ལྡན་པ།
སྤྱོད་ཡུལ་གྱིས་མི་འཕྲོགས་པ། བསམ་གྱིས་མི་ཁྱབ་པ་རྣམ་པར་འཇོག་པ། དུས་
གསུམ་ལ་མཉམ་པ་ཉིད་ཚར་ཕྱིན་པ། འཇིག་རྟེན་གྱི་ཁམས་ཐམས་ཅད་དུ་ཞུགས་པའི་སྐུ་
ལྷུ་དང་ལྡན་པ། ཆོས་ཐམས་ཅད་ལ་ཐེ་ཚོམ་མེད་པའི་མཁྱེན་པ་མངའ་བ། སྤྱོད་པ་ཐམས་
ཅད་དང་ལྡན་པའི་བློ་མངའ་བ། ཆོས་ཤེས་པ་ལ་ནེམ་ནུར་མི་མངའ་བ། རྣམ་པར་མ་
བརྟགས་པའི་སྐུ་མངའ་བ། བྱང་ཆུབ་སེམས་དཔའ་ཐམས་ཅད་ཀྱིས་ཡེ་ཤེས་ཡང་དག་
པར་བླངས་པ། སངས་རྒྱས་ཀྱི་གནས་པ་གཉིས་སུ་མེད་པ། དམ་པའི་ཕ་རོལ་ཏུ་ཕྱིན་པ།
དེ་བཞིན་གཤེགས་པ་མ་འདྲེས་པའི་རྣམ་པར་ཐར་པར་མཛད་པའི་ཡེ་ཤེས་ཀྱི་མཐར་ཕྱིན་པ།
མཐའ་དང་དབུས་མེད་པའི་སངས་རྒྱས་ཀྱིས་མཉམ་པ་ཉིད་ཐུགས་སུ་ཆུད་པ། ཆོས་ཀྱི་
དབྱིངས་ཀྱིས་ཀླས་པ། ནམ་མཁའི་ཁམས་ཀྱི་མཐས་གཏུགས་པ་དེ། ཉན་ཐོས་ཀྱི་དགེ་
འདུན་ཚད་མེད་པ་ཐམས་ཅད་ཀྱང་། ཅང་ཤེས་པ། སངས་རྒྱས་ཀྱི་སྲས། སེམས་ཤིན་

boundless masses of excellent qualities, and with great kingly jeweled lotuses.[8]

The Bhagavan was endowed with a mind of good understanding and did not possess the two [negative] behaviors.[9] Perfectly absorbed in the teaching of signlessness, abiding in the way that a Buddha abides,[10] having attained sameness with all Buddhas, having full realization without obscurations, he was endowed with irreversible qualities.[11] Not captivated by objects of activity, positing [doctrines] inconceivably,[12] thoroughly penetrating the sameness of the three times, the [Bhagavan] was endowed with the five [types of] embodiments that abide in every worldly realm.

Having attained the knowledge that has no doubts regarding all phenomena, having attained intelligence possessing all capabilities, he was unperplexed with respect to knowledge of the Dharma. Endowed with an unimaginable embodiment,[13] having fully given rise to the wisdom of all the Bodhisattvas, endowed with the non-dual abiding of a Buddha[14] and the supreme perfections, he had reached the limit of the uniquely liberating and exalted wisdom of a Tathāgata. He had realized full equality with the state of a Buddha without ends or middle, wholly permeated by the Dharmadhātu, extending to the limit of the realm of space.[15]

He was also accompanied by a measureless assembly of Śrāvakas, all very knowledgeable sons of the Buddha, with liberated minds,[16] very liberated wisdom, and completely

ཏུ་རྣམ་པར་གྲོལ་བ། ཤེས་རབ་ཤིན་ཏུ་རྣམ་པར་གྲོལ་བ། ཚུལ་ཁྲིམས་ཤིན་ཏུ་རྣམ་པར
དག་པ། ཆོས་འདོད་པ་རྣམས་དང་བདེ་བར་ཕྲད་པ། མང་དུ་ཐོས་པ། ཐོས་པ་འཛིན
པ། ཐོས་པ་བསྒྲུགས་པ། ལེགས་པར་བསམ་པ་སེམས་པ། ལེགས་པར་སྨྲ་བརྗོད
པ། ལེགས་པར་བྱ་བའི་ལས་བྱེད་པ། ཤེས་རབ་མྱུར་བ། ཤེས་རབ་མགྱོགས་པ།
ཤེས་རབ་རྣོ་བ། ངེས་པར་འབྱུང་བའི་ཤེས་རབ་ཅན། ངེས་པར་རྟོགས་པའི་ཤེས་རབ
ཅན། ཤེས་རབ་ཆེ་བ། ཤེས་རབ་ཡངས་པ། ཤེས་རབ་ཟབ་པ། ཤེས་རབ་མཉམ
པ་མེད་པ། ཤེས་རབ་རིན་པོ་ཆེ་དང་ལྡན་པ། རིག་པ་གསུམ་དང་ལྡན་པ། ཚེ་འདི་ལ
བདེ་བར་གནས་པའི་མཆོག་ཐོབ་པ། ཡོངས་སུ་སྦྱོང་བ་ཆེན་པོ། སྤྱོད་ལམ་རབ་ཏུ་ཞི་བ
ཕུན་སུམ་ཚོགས་པ། བཟོད་པ་དང་ངེས་པ་ཆེན་པོ་དང་ལྡན་པ། དེ་བཞིན་གཤེགས
པའི་བཀའ་ལ་ཤིན་ཏུ་ཞུགས་པ་ཤ་སྟག་དང་། སངས་རྒྱས་ཀྱི་ཞིང་ཐ་དད་པ་ནས་འདུས
པའི་བྱང་ཆུབ་སེམས་དཔའ་དཔག་ཏུ་མེད་པ་ཐམས་ཅད་ཀྱང་གནས་ཆེན་པོ་ལ་གནས་ཤིང
ཡང་དག་པར་ཞུགས་པ། ཐེག་པ་ཆེན་པོའི་ཆོས་ཀྱིས་ངེས་པར་འབྱུང་བ། སེམས་ཅན
ཐམས་ཅད་ལ་སེམས་མཉམ་པ། རྟོག་པ་དང་། རྣམ་པར་རྟོག་པ་དང་། ཡོངས་སུ་རྟོག
པ་ཐམས་ཅད་བྲལ་བ། བདུད་དང་ཕྱིར་རྒོལ་བ་ཐམས་ཅད་བཅོམ་པ། ཉན་ཐོས་དང
རང་སངས་རྒྱས་ཀྱི་ཡིད་ལ་བྱེད་པ་ཐམས་ཅད་ལས་རིང་དུ་གྱུར་པ། ཆོས་ཀྱི་རོའི་དགའ་བ
དང་། བདེ་བ་ཆེན་པོས་བརྟན་པ། འཇིགས་པ་ཆེན་པོ་ལྔ་ལས་ཡང་དག་པར་འདས་པ།
ཕྱིར་མི་ལྡོག་པའི་ས་བགྲོད་པ་གཅིག་པར་གྱུར་བ། སེམས་ཅན་ཐམས་ཅད་ཀྱི་གནོད་པ

pure ethics. They happily associated with those who yearn for the teaching. They were very learned, bearing in mind what they had learned, accumulating learning, intent on good contemplations, speaking good words, and doing good deeds. They had agile wisdom, quick wisdom, sharp wisdom, the wisdom of renunciation, the wisdom of certain realization, great wisdom, extensive wisdom, profound wisdom, wisdom without equal. Endowed with the precious jewel of wisdom, they possessed the three knowledges[17] and had obtained supremely blissful abiding in this life and great purity. They had fully developed a completely peaceful way of acting, were endowed with great patience and determination, and were wholly engaged in the Tathāgata's teaching.

Also in attendance were innumerable Bodhisattvas who assembled from various Buddha lands, all of them fully engaged and abiding in the great state [of the Mahāyāna].[18] They had renounced cyclic existence through the teaching of the Great Vehicle, were even-minded toward all beings, and were free from all imputations, ideations, and mental constructions. They had conquered all demons and opponents and were removed from all the mental tendencies of the Śrāvakas and Pratyekabuddhas. They were steadfast through great bliss and joy in the taste of the Dharma. They had completely transcended the five great fears[19] and had progressed solely to the irreversible stages.[20] They had actualized those stages which bring to rest all harms to all sentient beings.

ཐམས་ཅད་རབ་ཏུ་ཞི་བར་བྱེད་པའི་ས་མངོན་དུ་གྱུར་པ་ཤ་སྟག་ལ་འདི་ལྟ་སྟེ། བྱང་ཆུབ་སེམས་དཔའ་སེམས་དཔའ་ཆེན་པོ་དོན་ཟབ་དགོངས་པ་ངེས་པར་འགྲེལ་དང་། ཚུལ་བཞིན་ཀུན་འདྲི་དང་། ཆོས་འཕགས་དང་། བློ་གྲོས་ཤིན་ཏུ་རྣམ་དག་དང་། བློ་གྲོས་ཡངས་པ་དང་། ཡོན་ཏན་འབྱུང་གནས་དང་། དོན་དམ་ཡང་དག་འཕགས་དང་། འཕགས་པ་སྤྱན་རས་གཟིགས་དབང་ཕྱུག་དང་། བྱམས་པ་དང་། བྱང་ཆུབ་སེམས་དཔའ་སེམས་དཔའ་ཆེན་པོ་འཇམ་དཔལ་ལ་སོགས་པ་དང་ཐབས་ཅིག་གོ། དེ་ནས་བྱང་ཆུབ་སེམས་དཔའ་ཚུལ་བཞིན་ཀུན་འདྲིས་ཀྱིས་བརྗོད་དུ་མེད་པ་དང་། གཉིས་སུ་མེད་པའི་མཚན་ཉིད་དོན་དམ་པ་ལས་བརྩམས་ཏེ། བྱང་ཆུབ་སེམས་དཔའ་དོན་ཟབ་དགོངས་པ་ངེས་པར་འགྲེལ་པ་ལ་དྲི་བ་དྲིས་པ། ཀྱེ་རྒྱལ་བའི་སྲས་ཆོས་ཐམས་ཅད་གཉིས་སུ་མེད་པ་ཆོས་ཐམས་ཅད་གཉིས་སུ་མེད་པ་ཞེས་བྱ་ན། ཆོས་ཐམས་ཅད་ནི་གང་། ཇི་ལྟར་ན་གཉིས་སུ་མེད་པ་ཡིན། རིགས་ཀྱི་བུ་ཆོས་ཐམས་ཅད་ཆོས་ཐམས་ཅད་ཅེས་བྱ་བ་ནི་གཉིས་ཇི་ཙམ་པ་སྟེ། འདུས་བྱས་དང་། འདུས་མ་བྱས་སོ། །དེ་ལ་འདུས་བྱས་ནི་འདུས་བྱས་ཀྱང་མ་ཡིན། འདུས་མ་བྱས་ཀྱང་མ་ཡིན་ནོ། །འདུས་མ་བྱས་ནི་འདུས་མ་བྱས་ཀྱང་མ་ཡིན། འདུས་བྱས་ཀྱང་མ་ཡིན་ནོ། །སྨྲས་པ། ཀྱེ་རྒྱལ་བའི་སྲས་ཇི་ལྟར་ན་འདུས་བྱས་ནི་འདུས་བྱས་ཀྱང་མ་ཡིན། འདུས་མ་བྱས་ཀྱང་མ་ཡིན་ལ། འདུས་མ་བྱས་ཀྱང་འདུས་མ་བྱས་ཀྱང་མ་ཡིན། འདུས་བྱས་ཀྱང་མ་ཡིན། རིགས་ཀྱི་བུ་འདུས་བྱས་ཞེས་བྱ་བ་དེ་ནི་སྟོན་པས་བཏགས་པའི་ཚིག་ཡིན་ཏེ། སྟོན་པས་བཏགས་པའི་ཚིག་གང་ཡིན་པ་དེ་ནི།

Among them were the Bodhisattvas, the Mahāsattvas, Gambhīrārthasaṁdhinirmocana and Vidhivatparipṛcchaka, Dharmodgata, Suviśuddhamati, Viśālamati and Guṇākara, Paramārthasamudgata and Āryāvalokiteśvara, Maitreya and Mañjuśrī, all abiding together.

At that time, Bodhisattva Vidhivatparipṛcchaka questioned the Bodhisattva Gambhīrārthasaṁdhinirmocana[21] about the ultimate whose character is inexpressible and non-dual. "O Son of the Conqueror, when it is said, 'All phenomena are non-dual, all phenomena are non-dual,' how is it that all phenomena are non-dual?"

"Son of good lineage, with respect to all phenomena, 'all phenomena' are of just two kinds: compounded and uncompounded.[22] The compounded is not compounded, nor is it uncompounded. The uncompounded is not uncompounded, nor is it compounded."

"O son of the Conqueror, why is the compounded neither compounded nor uncompounded? Why is the uncompounded neither uncompounded nor compounded?"

"Son of good lineage, 'compounded' is a term designated by the Teacher. This term designated by the Teacher is a conventional expression arisen from mental construction.

ཀུན་ཏུ་རྟོག་པ་ལས་བྱུང་བ་ཐ་སྙད་དུ་བརྗོད་པ་ཡིན་ལ། ཀུན་ཏུ་རྟོག་པ་ལས་བྱུང་བ་ཐ་སྙད་དུ་བརྗོད་པ་གང་ཡིན་པ་དེ་ནི། ཀུན་ཏུ་རྟོག་པ་སྣ་ཚོགས་ཀྱི་ཐ་སྙད་དུ་བརྗོད་པ་གཞན་ཡོངས་སུ་མ་གྲུབ་པའི་ཕྱིར་འདུས་བྱས་མ་ཡིན་ནོ། །རིགས་ཀྱི་བུ་འདུས་མ་བྱས་ཞེས་བྱ་བ་དེ་ཡང་ཐ་སྙད་ཀྱི་ཁོངས་སུ་གཏོགས་པ་ཡིན་ལ། འདུས་བྱས་དང་འདུས་མ་བྱས་སུ་མ་གཏོགས་པ་གང་ཅི་བརྗོད་ཀྱང་དེ་ཡང་དེ་དང་འདྲ་བ་ཉིད་དུ་གྱུར། དེ་ཡང་དེ་དང་འདྲ་བ་ཉིད་དུ་འགྱུར་རོ། །བརྗོད་པ་ནི་དངོས་པོ་མེད་པ་ཅན་ཡང་མ་ཡིན་ཏེ། དངོས་པོ་དེ་ཡང་གང་ཞེ་ན། འཕགས་པ་རྣམས་ཀྱི་འཕགས་པའི་ཤེས་པ་དང་། འཕགས་པའི་མཐོང་བས་བརྗོད་དུ་མེད་པར་མངོན་པར་རྫོགས་པར་སངས་རྒྱས་པ་གང་ཡིན་པ་སྟེ། བརྗོད་དུ་མེད་པའི་ཆོས་ཉིད་དེ་ཉིད་མངོན་པར་རྫོགས་པར་རྟོགས་པར་བྱ་བའི་ཕྱིར་འདུས་བྱས་ཞེས་མིང་དུ་བཏགས་སོ། །རིགས་ཀྱི་བུ་འདུས་མ་བྱས་ཞེས་བྱ་བ་དེ་ཡང་སྟོན་པས་བཏགས་པའི་ཚིག་ཡིན་ཏེ། སྟོན་པས་བཏགས་པའི་ཚིག་གང་ཡིན་པ་དེ་ནི་ཀུན་ཏུ་རྟོག་པ་ལས་བྱུང་བ་ཐ་སྙད་དུ་བརྗོད་པ་ཡིན་ལ། ཀུན་ཏུ་རྟོག་པ་ལས་བྱུང་བ་ཐ་སྙད་དུ་བརྗོད་པ་གང་ཡིན་པ་དེ་ནི་ཀུན་ཏུ་རྟོག་པ་སྣ་ཚོགས་ཀྱི་ཐ་སྙད་དུ་བརྗོད་པ་གཞན་ཡོངས་སུ་མ་གྲུབ་པའི་ཕྱིར་འདུས་མ་བྱས་མ་ཡིན་ནོ། །རིགས་ཀྱི་བུ་འདུས་བྱས་ཞེས་བྱ་བ་དེ་ཡང་ཐ་སྙད་ཀྱི་ཁོངས་སུ་གཏོགས་པ་ཡིན་ལ། འདུས་བྱས་དང་འདུས་མ་བྱས་སུ་མ་གཏོགས་པ་གང་ཅི་བརྗོད་ཀྱང་དེ་ཡང་དེ་དང་འདྲ་བ་ཉིད་དུ་གྱུར། དེ་ཡང་དེ་དང་འདྲ་བ་ཉིད་དུ་འགྱུར་རོ། །བརྗོད་པ་ནི་དངོས་པོ་མེད་པ་ཅན་ཡང་མ་ཡིན་ཏེ། དངོས་པོ་དེ་ཡང་གང་ཞེ་ན།

Because a conventional expression arisen from mental construction is a conventional expression of various mental constructions, it is not established. Therefore, it is [said to be] not compounded.

"Son of good lineage, 'uncompounded' is also included within the conventional. Even if something were expressed that is not included within the compounded or uncompounded it would be just the same as this. It would be just like this. An expression is also not without thingness. What is a thing? It is that to which the Āryas completely and perfectly awaken without explanation, through their exalted wisdom and exalted vision.[23] Because they have completely and perfectly realized that very reality which is inexpressible, they designate the name 'compounded'.

"Son of good lineage, 'uncompounded' is also a term designated by the Teacher. This term designated by the Teacher is a conventional expression arisen from mental construction. Because a conventional expression arisen from mental construction is a conventional expression of various mental constructions, it is not established. Therefore, it is [said to be] not uncompounded.

"Son of good lineage, 'compounded' is also included within the conventional. Even if something were expressed that is not included within the compounded or uncompounded it would be just the same as this. It would be just like this. An

འཕགས་པ་རྣམས་ཀྱིས་འཕགས་པའི་ཤེས་པ་དང་། འཕགས་པའི་མཐོང་བས་བརྗོད་དུ་མེད་པར་མངོན་པར་རྫོགས་པར་སངས་རྒྱས་པ་གང་ཡིན་པ་སྟེ། བརྗོད་དུ་མེད་པའི་ཆོས་ཉིད་དེ་ཉིད་མངོན་པར་རྫོགས་པར་རྟོགས་པར་བྱ་བའི་ཕྱིར་འདུས་མ་བྱས་ཞེས་མིང་དུ་བཏགས་སོ། །ཀྱེ་རྒྱལ་བའི་སྲས་ཇི་ལྟར་ན་འཕགས་པ་རྣམས་ཀྱིས་དངོས་པོ་དེ་འཕགས་པའི་ཤེས་པ་དང་། འཕགས་པའི་མཐོང་བས་བརྗོད་དུ་མེད་པར་མངོན་པར་རྫོགས་པར་སངས་རྒྱས་ཤིང་བརྗོད་དུ་མེད་པའི་ཆོས་ཉིད་དེ་ཉིད་མངོན་པར་རྫོགས་པར་རྟོགས་པར་བྱ་བའི་ཕྱིར་འདུས་བྱས་དང་འདུས་མ་བྱས་ཞེས་མིང་དུ་བཏགས་པ་ཡིན་ནོ། །རིགས་ཀྱི་བུ་འདི་ལྟ་སྟེ་དཔེར་ན། སྒྱུ་མ་མཁན་ནམ་སྒྱུ་མ་མཁན་གྱི་སློབ་མ་མཁས་པ་ཞིག་ལམ་པོ་ཆེའི་བཞི་མདོར་འདུག་སྟེ། རྩྭ་དག་གམ། ལོ་མ་དག་གམ། ཤིང་དག་གམ། གསེག་མ་དག་གམ། གྲོ་དུམ་དག་གཅིག་ཏུ་བསྡུས་ནས་སྒྱུ་མའི་ལས་རྣམ་པ་སྣ་ཚོགས་འདི་ལྟ་སྟེ། གླང་པོ་ཆེའི་ཚོགས་དང་རྟ་པའི་ཚོགས་དང་ཤིང་རྟའི་ཚོགས་དང་དཔུང་བུ་ཆུང་གི་ཚོགས་དང་། ནོར་བུ་དང་། མུ་ཏིག་དང་། བཻཌཱུརྻ་དང་། དུང་དང་། མན་ཤེལ་དང་། བྱི་རུའི་ཚོགས་དང་། ནོར་དང་འབྲུ་དང་མཛོད་དང་བང་བའི་ཚོགས་རྣམ་པར་བསྟན་ན། དེ་ལ་སེམས་ཅན་གང་དག་བྱིས་པའི་རང་བཞིན་ཅན། རྨོངས་པའི་རང་བཞིན་ཅན། ཤེས་རབ་འཆལ་པའི་རང་བཞིན་ཅན། རྩྭ་དང་ལོ་མ་དང་ཤིང་དང་གསེག་མ་དང་། གྲོ་དུམ་དེ་དག་མི་ཤེས་པ་དེ་དག་ནི་དེ་མཐོང་ངམ་ཐོས་ན་འདི་སྙམ་དུ་སེམས་ཏེ། གླང་པོ་ཆེའི་ཚོགས་སྣང་བ་གང་ཡིན་པ་དེ་ནི་ཡོད་དོ། །རྟའི་ཚོགས་དང་ཤིང་རྟའི་ཚོགས་དང་དཔུང་བུ་ཆུང་

expression is also not without thingness. What is a thing? It is that to which the Āryas completely and perfectly awaken without explanation, through their exalted wisdom and exalted vision. Because they have completely and perfectly realized that very reality which is inexpressible, they designate the name 'uncompounded'."

"O son of the Conqueror, how is it that the Āryas, through their exalted wisdom and exalted vision completely and perfectly realize things without explanation, and completely and perfectly realize that very reality which is inexpressible and therefore designate the names 'compounded' and 'uncompounded'?"

"Son of good lineage, for example, a magician or a magician's able student, standing at the crossing of four great roads, after gathering grasses, leaves, twigs, pebbles or stones, displays various magical forms, such as a herd of elephants, a cavalry, chariots, and infantry; collections of gems, pearls, lapis lazuli, conch-shells, crystal, and coral; collections of wealth, grain, treasuries, and granaries.[24]

"When those sentient beings who have childish natures, foolish natures, or confused natures—who do not realize that these are grasses, leaves, twigs, pebbles, and stones—see or hear these things, they think: 'This herd of elephants that appears, exists; these cavalry, chariots, infantry, gems, pearls,

གི་ཚོགས་དང་ནོར་བུ་དང་མུ་ཏིག་དང་བཻཌཱུརྱ་དང་དུང་དང་མན་ཤེལ་དང་བྱི་རུའི་ཚོགས་དང་ནོར་དང་འབྲུ་དང་མཛོད་དང་བང་བའི་ཚོགས་སྣང་བ་གང་ཡིན་པ་འདི་ནི་ཡོད་དོ་སྙམ་དུ་སེམས་ཤིང་། དེ་དག་ཇི་ལྟར་མཐོང་བ་དང་། ཇི་ལྟར་ཐོས་པ་བཞིན་དུ། དེ་ལ་ནན་གྱིས་མཆོག་ཏུ་བཟུང་ཞིང་མངོན་པར་ཞེན་ནས། འདི་ནི་བདེན་གྱི་གཞན་ནི་བརྫུན་པའོ་ཞེས་རྗེས་སུ་ཐ་སྙད་འདོགས་པར་ཡང་བྱེད་དེ། དེ་ནི་དེ་དག་གིས་ཕྱིས་ཉེ་བར་བརྟག་པར་བྱ་དགོས་པ་ཡིན་ནོ། །དེ་ལ་སེམས་ཅན་གང་དག་བྱིས་པའི་རང་བཞིན་ཅན་མ་ཡིན་པ། རྨོངས་པའི་རང་བཞིན་ཅན་མ་ཡིན་པ། ཤེས་རབ་དང་ལྡན་པའི་རང་བཞིན་ཅན་རྩྭ་དང་ལོ་མ་དང་ཤིང་དང་གསེག་མ་དང་གྱོ་དུམ་དེ་དག་ཤེས་པ་དེ་དག་ནི་དེ་མཐོང་ངམ་ཐོས་ན་འདི་སྙམ་དུ་སེམས་ཏེ། གླང་པོ་ཆེའི་ཚོགས་སྣང་བ་གང་ཡིན་པ་འདི་ནི་མེད་དོ། །རྟ་པའི་ཚོགས་དང་ཤིང་རྟའི་ཚོགས་དང་དཔུང་བུ་ཆུང་གི་ཚོགས་དང་། ནོར་བུ་དང་མུ་ཏིག་དང་བཻཌཱུརྱ་དང་དུང་དང་མན་ཤེལ་དང་བྱི་རུའི་ཚོགས་དང་། ནོར་དང་། འབྲུ་དང་མཛོད་དང་བང་བའི་ཚོགས་སྣང་བ་གང་ཡིན་པ་འདི་ནི་མེད་ཀྱི། གང་ལ་གླང་པོ་ཆེའི་ཚོགས་ཀྱི་འདུ་ཤེས་དང་། གླང་པོ་ཆེའི་ཚོགས་ཀྱི་རྣམ་གྲངས་ཀྱི་འདུ་ཤེས་འབྱུང་བ་དང་། ནོར་དང་འབྲུ་དང་མཛོད་དང་བང་བའི་ཚོགས་ཀྱི་བར་གྱི་འདུ་ཤེས་དང་། དེ་དག་གི་རྣམ་གྲངས་ཀྱི་འདུ་ཤེས་འབྱུང་བ་སྒྱུ་མ་བྱས་པ་འདི་ནི་ཡོད། མིག་སླུ་བར་བྱེད་པ་འདི་ནི་ཡོད་དོ་སྙམ་དུ་སེམས་ཤིང་། དེ་དག་ཇི་ལྟར་མཐོང་བ་དང་ཇི་ལྟར་ཐོས་པ་བཞིན་དུ་དེ་ལ་ནན་གྱིས་མཆོག་ཏུ་བཟུང་ཞིང་མངོན་པར་ཞེན་ནས་འདི་ནི་བདེན་གྱི་གཞན་ནི་བརྫུན་པའོ་ཞེས་རྗེས་སུ་ཐ་སྙད

lapis lazuli, conch-shells, crystal, coral, wealth, grain, treasuries, and granaries that appear, exist.'

"Having thought this, they emphatically apprehend and emphatically assert in accordance with how they see and hear. Subsequently they make the conventional designations: 'This is true, the other is false.' Later they must closely examine these things.

"When those sentient beings who do not have childish or foolish natures, who have natures endowed with wisdom—who recognize that these are grasses, twigs, pebbles, and stones—hear and see these things, they think: 'This herd of elephants that appears does not exist. These cavalry, chariots, infantry, gems, pearls, lapis lazuli, conch-shells, crystal, coral, wealth, grain, treasuries, and granaries that appear do not exist. But, in regard to them there arises the perception of a herd of elephants and the perception of the attributes of a herd of elephants, the perception of wealth, grain, treasuries, and granaries and the perception of their attributes. These magical illusions exist.'

"Having thought, 'These visual deceptions exist,' they emphatically apprehend and emphatically assert in accordance with how they see and hear. Subsequently they do not make the conventional designations: 'This is true, the other is false.' They make conventional designations because they fully know the object in this way. Later, they will not need to closely examine these things.

མི་འདོགས་ཀྱི། འདི་ལྟར་དོན་རྣམ་པར་རིག་པར་བྱ་བའི་ཕྱིར་རྗེས་སུ་ཐ་སྙད་འདོགས་པར
བྱེད་དེ། དེ་ནི་དེ་དག་གིས་ཕྱིས་ཉེ་བར་བརྟག་པར་བྱ་མི་དགོས་པ་ཡིན་ནོ། །དེ་བཞིན
དུ་སེམས་ཅན་གང་དག་བྱིས་པའི་རང་བཞིན་ཅན་སོ་སོའི་སྐྱེ་བོར་གྱུར་པ། ཤེས་རབ
འཕགས་པ་འཇིག་རྟེན་ལས་འདས་པ་མ་ཐོབ་པ། ཆོས་ཐམས་ཅད་ཀྱི་བརྗོད་དུ་མེད་པའི
ཆོས་ཉིད་མངོན་པར་མི་ཤེས་པ་དེ་དག་ནི་འདུས་བྱས་དང་། འདུས་མ་བྱས་ཏེ་མཐོང་ངམ
ཐོས་ན། འདི་སྙམ་དུ་སེམས་ཏེ། འདུས་བྱས་དང་འདུས་མ་བྱས་སྣང་བ་གང་ཡིན་པ་འདི
ནི་ཡོད་དོ་སྙམ་དུ་སེམས་ཤིང་། དེ་དག་ཇི་ལྟར་མཐོང་བ་དང་། ཇི་ལྟར་ཐོས་པ་བཞིན་དུ
དེ་ལ་ནན་གྱིས་མཆོག་ཏུ་བཟུང་ཞིང་མངོན་པར་ཞེན་ནས་འདི་ནི་བདེན་གྱི་གཞན་ནི་བརྫུན
པའོ་ཞེས་རྗེས་སུ་ཐ་སྙད་འདོགས་པར་ཡང་བྱེད་དེ། དེ་ནི་དེ་དག་གིས་ཕྱིས་ཉེ་བར་བརྟག
པར་བྱ་དགོས་པ་ཡིན་ནོ། །དེ་ལ་སེམས་ཅན་གང་དག་བྱིས་པའི་རང་བཞིན་ཅན་མ་ཡིན
པ༑ བདེན་པ་མཐོང་བ། ཤེས་རབ་འཕགས་པ་འཇིག་རྟེན་ལས་འདས་པ་ཐོབ་པ།
ཆོས་ཐམས་ཅད་ཀྱི་བརྗོད་དུ་མེད་པའི་ཆོས་ཉིད་མངོན་པར་ཤེས་པ་དེ་དག་ནི། འདུས་བྱས
དང༑ འདུས་མ་བྱས་དེ་མཐོང་ངམ། ཐོས་ན་འདི་སྙམ་དུ་སེམས་ཏེ། འདུས་བྱས་དང་།
འདུས་མ་བྱས་སྣང་བ་གང་ཡིན་པ་འདི་ནི་མེད་ཀྱི། གང་ལ་འདུས་བྱས་དང་། འདུས་མ
བྱས་ཀྱི་འདུ་ཤེས་དང་། འདུས་བྱས་དང་། འདུས་མ་བྱས་ཀྱི་རྣམ་གྲངས་ཀྱི་འདུ་ཤེས
འབྱུང་བ། རྣམ་པར་རྟོག་པ་ལས་བྱུང་བ། འདུ་བྱེད་ཀྱི་མཚན་མ་སྒྱུ་མ་ལྟ་བུ་འདི་ནི་ཡོད།
བློ་རྣམ་པར་སྔོངས་པར་བྱེད་པ་འདི་ནི་ཡོད་དོ་སྙམ་དུ་སེམས་ཤིང་དེ་དག་ཇི་ལྟར་མཐོང་བ

"Similarly, when sentient beings who are ordinary beings with childish natures—who have not attained the supramundane wisdom of Āryas, who do not manifestly recognize the inexpressible reality of all phenomena—see and hear these compounded and uncompounded things, they think: 'These compounded and uncompounded things which appear, exist.' They emphatically apprehend and emphatically assert in accordance with how they see and hear. Subsequently they make the conventional designations: 'This is true, the other is false.' Later they must closely examine these things.

"When those sentient beings who do not have childish natures—who see the truth, who have attained the supramundane wisdom of the Āryas, who manifestly recognize the inexpressible reality of all phenomena—see and hear these compounded and uncompounded things, they think: 'These compounded and uncompounded things that appear do not exist.' With regard to them there arises a perception of what is compounded and uncompounded and a perception of the attributes of the compounded and the uncompounded.

"Thinking that, 'The compositional signs that arise from mental constructions exist like a magician's illusions; these obscurations of the mind exist,' they emphatically apprehend and emphatically assert in accordance with how they see and how they hear. But they do not subsequently make the conventional designations: 'This is true, the other is false.' They make conventional designations because they fully know the

དང་། དེ་ལྟར་ཐོས་པ་བཞིན་དུ་དེ་ལ་ནན་གྱིས་མཆོག་ཏུ་བརྣད་ཞིང་མངོན་པར་ཞེན་ནས་འདི་ནི་བདེན་གྱི་གཞན་ནི་བརྫུན་པའོ་ཞེས་རྗེས་སུ་ཐ་སྙད་མི་འདོགས་ཀྱི། འདི་ལྟར་དོན་རྣམ་པར་རིག་པར་བྱ་བའི་ཕྱིར་རྗེས་སུ་ཐ་སྙད་འདོགས་པར་བྱེད་དེ། དེ་ནི་དེ་དག་གིས་ཕྱིས་ཉེ་བར་བརྟག་པར་བྱ་མི་དགོས་པ་ཡིན་ནོ། །རིགས་ཀྱི་བུ་དེ་ལྟར་ན་འཕགས་པ་རྣམས་ཀྱིས་དངོས་པོ་དེ་འཕགས་པའི་ཤེས་པ་དང་། འཕགས་པའི་མཐོང་བས་བརྗོད་དུ་མེད་པར་སངས་རྒྱས་ཤིང་བརྗོད་དུ་མེད་པའི་ཆོས་ཉིད་དེ་ཉིད་མངོན་པར་རྫོགས་པར་རྟོགས་པར་བྱ་བའི་ཕྱིར་འདུས་བྱས་དང་། འདུས་མ་བྱས་ཞེས་མིང་དུ་བཏགས་པ་ཡིན་ནོ། །

དེ་ནས་བྱང་ཆུབ་སེམས་དཔའ་དོན་ཟབ་དགོངས་པ་ངེས་པར་འགྲེལ་གྱིས་དེའི་ཚེ་ཚིགས་སུ་བཅད་པ་འདི་དག་སྨྲས་སོ། །ཟབ་མོ་བྱིས་པའི་སྤྱོད་ཡུལ་མ་ཡིན་པ། །བརྗོད་མེད་གཉིས་མིན་རྒྱལ་བས་བསྟན་མཛད་ཀྱང་། །བྱིས་པ་གཏི་མུག་རྨོངས་པ་འདི་དག་ནི། །སྨྲ་བའི་སྤྲོས་ལ་དགའ་ཞིང་གཉིས་ལ་གནས། །མ་རྟོགས་པའམ་ལོག་པར་རྟོགས་པ་དག །ལུག་དང་བ་ལང་དག་ཏུ་ཡང་སྐྱེ་ཞིང་། །དེ་དག་ཤེས་པའི་སྨྲ་བ་དེ་བོར་ནས། །ཤིན་ཏུ་ཡུན་རིང་འཁོར་བ་འདིར་འཁོར་འགྱུར། །དོན་ཟབ་དགོངས་པ་ངེས་པར་འགྲེལ་གྱི་ལེའུ་སྟེ་དང་པོའོ།། །།

object in this way. Later, they will not need to closely examine these things.

"Son of good lineage, in that way the Āryas, through exalted wisdom and exalted vision, completely and perfectly realize things without explanation. Because they completely and perfectly realize that very reality which is inexpressible, they nominally designate the names 'compounded' and 'uncompounded'."

Then Bodhisattva Gambhīrārthasaṁdhinirmocana spoke these verses:

"The Conquerors taught that the profound,
inexpressible and non-dual, is not the domain of children,
but childish ones, obscured by ignorance,
delight in elaborations of speech and abide in duality.[25]

"Those who do not realize this or who understand it wrongly
will be reborn as sheep or oxen.
Having abandoned the speech of the wise,
they cycle in saṁsāra for a very long time."

This completes the first chapter of the Bodhisattva Gambhīrārthasaṁdhinirmocana.

Homage to the Tathāgata Buddha Śākyamuni

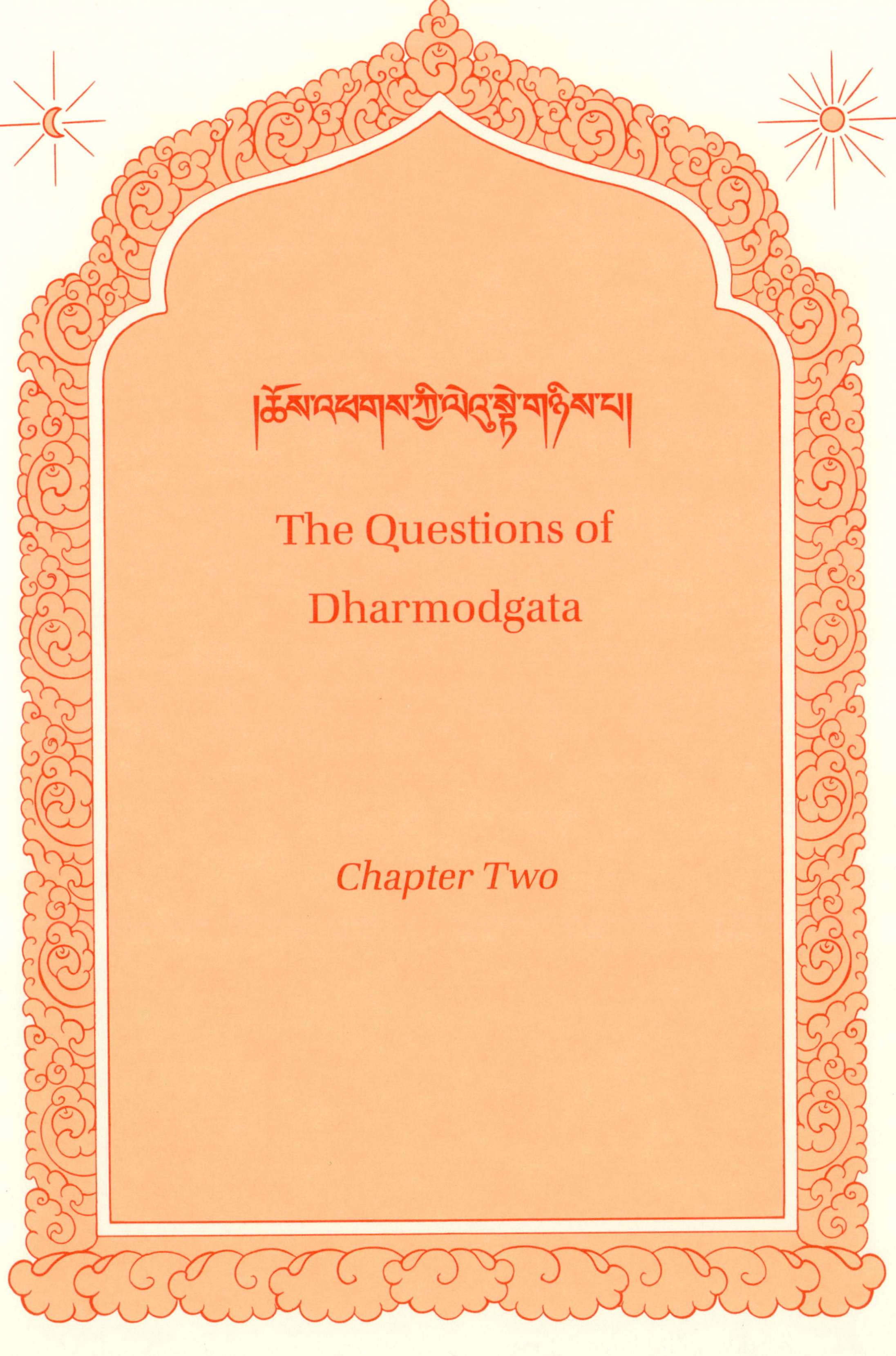
།ཆོས་འཕགས་ཀྱི་ལེའུ་སྟེ་གཉིས་པ།
The Questions of
Dharmodgata
Chapter Two

༄༅། །དེ་ནས་བཅོམ་ལྡན་འདས་ལ་བྱང་ཆུབ་སེམས་དཔའ་ཆོས་འཕགས་ཀྱིས་འདི་
སྐད་ཅེས་གསོལ་ཏོ། །བཅོམ་ལྡན་འདས་སྔོན་གྱི་དུས་རྣམས་ཀྱི་ཤིན་ཏུ་སྔ་མ་ཞིག་ན།
འདི་ནས་འཇིག་རྟེན་གྱི་ཁམས་གང་གཱའི་ཀླུང་བདུན་ཅུ་རྩ་བདུན་གྱི་བྱེ་མ་སྙེད་འདས་པ་ན།
དེ་བཞིན་གཤེགས་པ་གྲགས་པ་རྒྱ་ཆེན་གྱི་སངས་རྒྱས་ཀྱི་ཞིང་འཇིག་རྟེན་གྱི་ཁམས་གྲགས་
པ་ཅན་ཞེས་བགྱི་བ་དེར་བདག་མཆིས་པའི་ཚེ། དེ་ན་བདག་གིས་མུ་སྟེགས་ཅན་རང་རང་
གི་སྟོན་པ་ལ་སོགས་པ་འབུམ་ཕྲག་བདུན་ཅུ་རྩ་བདུན་འདི་ལྟ་སྟེ། ཆོས་རྣམས་ཀྱི་དོན་དམ་
པའི་མཚན་ཉིད་བསམ་པ་ལས་བརྩམས་ནས་ས་ཕྱོགས་ཞིག་ན་མཆིས་ཤིང་འདུས་ནས་དེ་
དག་ཆོས་རྣམས་ཀྱི་དོན་དམ་པའི་མཚན་ཉིད་སེམས་པར་བགྱིད། འཇལ་བར་བགྱིད།
ཉེ་བར་རྟོག་པར་བགྱིད། ཡོངས་སུ་ཚོལ་བར་བགྱིད་ཀྱང་མ་རྟོགས་ནས་བློ་གྲོས་ཐ་དད་པ་
ཡིད་གཉིས་ཅན། བློ་གྲོས་ངན་པ། རྩོད་པ་དང་འགྱེད་པར་གྱུར་པ་དག་གཅིག་ལ་
གཅིག་ཁ་སྐྱོབས་ཀྱིས་གནོན་པ་བགྱིས། ཞེར་འདེབས་པ་བགྱིས། གབ་གབ་བགྱིས།
མནན་པ་བགྱིས། ཚར་གཅད་པ་བགྱིས་ཏེ་སོ་སོར་མཆིས་པ་དག་ཅིག་མཐོང་ནས།
བཅོམ་ལྡན་འདས་བདག་འདི་སྙམ་བགྱིད་དོ། །ཀྱེ་མ་དེ་བཞིན་གཤེགས་པ་རྣམས་འཇིག་
རྟེན་དུ་འབྱུང་ཞིང་དེ་དག་བྱུང་བས་དོན་དམ་པ་རྟོག་གེ་ཐམས་ཅད་ལས་ཡང་དག་པར་
འདས་པའི་མཚན་ཉིད་འདི་ལྟ་བུ་རྟོགས་པ་དང་། མངོན་སུམ་དུ་བགྱི་བ་མཆིས་པ་ནི་ངོ་
མཚར་རྨད་དུ་བྱུང་བ་ལགས་སོ་སྙམ་བགྱིད་ལགས་སོ། །དེ་སྐད་ཅེས་གསོལ་བ་དང་།
བཅོམ་ལྡན་འདས་ཀྱིས་བྱང་ཆུབ་སེམས་དཔའ་ཆོས་འཕགས་ལ་འདི་སྐད་ཅེས་བཀའ་སྩལ་

Then Bodhisattva Dharmodgata[1] spoke to the Bhagavan: "Bhagavan, in a distant epoch of ancient times, passing beyond this world system as many world systems as there are grains of sand in seventy-seven Ganges rivers, I lived in the world system Kīrtimat, Buddha Land of the Tathāgata Viśālakīrti. While there, I saw 7,700,000 teachers and others of various Tīrthika systems.[2]

"They had gathered together at a certain place to begin considering the ultimate character of phenomena. Although they contemplated, weighed, closely examined, and sought the ultimate character of phenomena, they had not realized it. They had divergent opinions, doubts, and misconceptions. They debated and quarreled; they insulted each other with harsh words; they were abusive, deceitful, and overbearing; they attacked one another.

"Having seen them so divided, Bhagavan, I thought: 'Alas! Tathāgatas arise in the world and through their arising the realization and actualization of the ultimate, whose character completely transcends all argumentation, is indeed marvelous and astonishing!'"

The Bhagavan replied to the Bodhisattva Dharmodgata: "So it is! Dharmodgata, so it is! I have fully and perfectly realized the ultimate whose character completely transcends all argumentation.[3] Having fully and perfectly realized this, I have

ཏོ། །ཆོས་འཕགས་དེ་དེ་བཞིན་ནོ། །དེ་དེ་བཞིན་ཏེ། ངས་ནི་དོན་དམ་པ་རྟོག་གེ་
ཐམས་ཅད་ལས་ཡང་དག་པར་འདས་པའི་མཚན་ཉིད་མངོན་པར་རྫོགས་པར་སངས་རྒྱས་
ཏེ། མངོན་པར་རྫོགས་པར་སངས་རྒྱས་ནས་ཀྱང་བསྙད་ཅིང་གསལ་བར་བྱས། རྣམ་
པར་ཕྱེ། གདགས་པར་བྱས། རབ་ཏུ་བསྟན་ཏོ། །དེ་ཅིའི་ཕྱིར་ཞེ་ན། དོན་དམ་པ་ནི་
འཕགས་པ་རྣམས་ཀྱི་སོ་སོ་རང་གི་རིག་པ་ཡིན་པར་ངས་བཤད་ལ། སོ་སོའི་སྐྱེ་བོ་རྣམས་
ཀྱི་ཕན་ཚུན་རིག་པར་བྱ་བ་ནི། རྟོག་གེའི་སྤྱོད་ཡུལ་ཡིན་པའི་ཕྱིར་ཏེ། ཆོས་འཕགས་
དེའི་ཕྱིར་རྣམ་གྲངས་དེས་ཁྱོད་ཀྱིས་འདི་ལྟར་རྟོག་གེ་ཐམས་ཅད་ལས་ཡང་དག་པར་འདས་
པའི་མཚན་ཉིད་གང་ཡིན་པ་ནི་དོན་དམ་པ་ཡིན་པར་རིག་པར་བྱའོ། །ཆོས་འཕགས་
གཞན་ཡང་དོན་དམ་པ་ནི་མཚན་མ་མེད་པའི་སྤྱོད་ཡུལ་ཡིན་པར་ངས་བཤད་ལ། རྟོག་
གེ་ནི་མཚན་མའི་སྤྱོད་ཡུལ་ཡིན་ཏེ། ཆོས་འཕགས་དེའི་ཕྱིར་རྣམ་གྲངས་དེས་ཀྱང་ཁྱོད་
ཀྱིས་འདི་ལྟར་རྟོག་གེ་ཐམས་ཅད་ལས་ཡང་དག་པར་འདས་པའི་མཚན་ཉིད་གང་ཡིན་པ་ནི་
དོན་དམ་པ་ཡིན་པར་རིག་པར་བྱའོ། །ཆོས་འཕགས་གཞན་ཡང་དོན་དམ་པ་ནི་བརྗོད་དུ་
མེད་པ་ཡིན་པར་ངས་བཤད་ལ། རྟོག་གེ་ནི་བརྗོད་པའི་སྤྱོད་ཡུལ་ཡིན་ཏེ། ཆོས་
འཕགས་དེའི་ཕྱིར་རྣམ་གྲངས་དེས་ཀྱང་ཁྱོད་ཀྱིས་འདི་ལྟར་རྟོག་གེ་ཐམས་ཅད་ལས་ཡང་
དག་པར་འདས་པའི་མཚན་ཉིད་གང་ཡིན་པ་ནི། དོན་དམ་པ་ཡིན་པར་རིག་པར་བྱའོ། །
ཆོས་འཕགས་གཞན་ཡང་དོན་དམ་པ་ནི་ཐ་སྙད་ཐམས་ཅད་ཡང་དག་པར་ཆད་པ་ཡིན་པར་
ངས་བཤད་ལ། རྟོག་གེ་ནི་ཐ་སྙད་ཀྱི་སྤྱོད་ཡུལ་ཡིན་ཏེ། ཆོས་འཕགས་དེའི་ཕྱིར་རྣམ་

proclaimed it and made it clear, opened it up and systematized it, and taught it comprehensively.

"Why is this? I have explained that the ultimate is realized individually by the Āryas,[4] while objects collectively known by ordinary beings [belong to] the realm of argumentation. Thus, Dharmodgata, by this form of explanation know that whatever has a character completely transcending all argumentation is the ultimate.

"Moreover, Dharmodgata, I have explained that the ultimate belongs to the signless realm, while argumentation belongs to the realm of signs. Thus, Dharmodgata, by this form of explanation also know that whatever has a character completely transcending all argumentation is the ultimate.

"Moreover, Dharmodgata, I have explained that the ultimate is inexpressible, while argumentation belongs to the realm of expression. Thus, Dharmodgata, by this form of explanation also know that whatever has a character completely transcending all argumentation is the ultimate.

"Moreover, Dharmodgata, I have explained that the ultimate is devoid of conventions, while argumentation belongs to the realm of conventions.[5] Thus, Dharmodgata, by this form of explanation also know that whatever has a character completely transcending all argumentation is the ultimate.

གྲངས་དེས་ཀྱང་ཁྱོད་ཀྱིས་འདི་ལྟར་རྟོག་གེ་ཐམས་ཅད་ལས་ཡང་དག་པར་འདས་པའི་མཚན་ཉིད་གང་ཡིན་པ་ནི་དོན་དམ་པ་ཡིན་པར་རིག་པར་བྱའོ། །ཆོས་འཕགས་གཞན་ཡང་དོན་དམ་པ་ནི་རྩོད་པ་ཐམས་ཅད་ཡང་དག་པར་ཆད་པ་ཡིན་པར་ངས་བཤད་ལ། རྟོག་གེ་ནི་རྩོད་པའི་སྤྱོད་ཡུལ་ཡིན་ཏེ། ཆོས་འཕགས་དེའི་ཕྱིར་རྣམ་གྲངས་དེས་ཀྱང་ཁྱོད་ཀྱིས་འདི་ལྟར་རྟོག་གེ་ཐམས་ཅད་ལས་ཡང་དག་པར་འདས་པའི་མཚན་ཉིད་གང་ཡིན་པ་ནི་དོན་དམ་པ་ཡིན་པར་རིག་པར་བྱའོ། །ཆོས་འཕགས་འདི་ལྟ་སྟེ་དཔེར་ན། སྐྱེས་བུ་གང་ཟག་ཇི་སྲིད་འཚོ་བའི་བར་དུ་ཚ་བ་དང་ཁ་བའི་རོ་སྐྱེན་སྐྱེན་པས་ནི་སྦྲང་རྩིའི་རོ་འམ། ཤ་ཁ་རའི་རོ་ལ་བརྟག་པའམ། རྗེས་སུ་དཔག་པའམ། མོས་པར་མི་ནུས་སོ། །ཡུན་རིང་པོ་ནས་འདོད་པའི་འདོད་ཆགས་ལ་མོས་པ། འདོད་པའི་ཡོངས་སུ་གདུང་བ་དག་གིས་ཡོངས་སུ་གདུངས་པ་ནི་ནང་གི་རབ་ཏུ་དབེན་པའི་བདེ་བ་གཟུགས་དང་། སྒྲ་དང་། དྲི་དང་། རོ་དང་། རེག་བྱའི་མཚན་མ་ཐམས་ཅད་དང་བྲལ་བ་ལ་བརྟག་པའམ། རྗེས་སུ་དཔག་པའམ། མོས་པར་མི་ནུས་སོ། །ཡུན་རིང་པོ་ནས་ཀུན་ཏུ་སྨྲ་བ་ལ་མོས་པ་ཀུན་ཏུ་སྨྲ་བ་ལ་མངོན་པར་དགའ་བས་ནི་ནང་གི་མི་སྨྲ་བ་འཕགས་པའི་བདེ་བ་ལ་བརྟག་པའམ། རྗེས་སུ་དཔག་པའམ། མོས་པར་མི་ནུས་སོ། །ཡུན་རིང་པོ་ནས་མཐོང་བ་དང་ཐོས་པ་དང་བྱེ་བྲག་ཕྱེད་པ་དང་། རྣམ་པར་ཤེས་པའི་ཐ་སྙད་ལ་མོས་པ། ཐ་སྙད་ལ་མངོན་པར་དགའ་བས་ནི་ཐ་སྙད་ཐམས་ཅད་ཡང་དག་པར་ཆད་པ། འཇིག་ཚོགས་འགོག་པའི་མྱ་ངན་ལས་འདས་པ་ལ་བརྟག་པའམ། རྗེས་སུ་དཔག་པའམ། མོས་པར་

"Moreover, Dharmodgata, I have explained that the ultimate is completely devoid of all dispute, while argumentation belongs to the realm of controversy. Thus, Dharmodgata, by this form of explanation also know that whatever has a character completely transcending argumentation is the ultimate.

"Dharmodgata, for example,[6] beings acquainted only with hot and bitter tastes for their entire lives would be unable to imagine, infer, or appreciate the sweet taste of honey or the taste of sugar.

"Beings who have been engaged in passionate desire for a long time, who have been utterly tormented by the pangs of desire, are unable to imagine, infer, or appreciate the happiness of inner solitude free from all the signs of form, sound, smell, taste, or touch.

"Because beings have been engaged in discursiveness for a long time, manifestly delighting in discursiveness, they are unable to imagine, infer, or appreciate the inner non-discursive joy of the Āryas.

"Because beings have been engaged in the conventions of seeing, hearing, differentiating, and perceiving for a long time, manifestly delighting in these conventions, they are unable to imagine, infer, or appreciate nirvāṇa, which is the cessation of [belief in] true personhood,[7] the complete elimination of all conventions.

མི་ནུས་སོ། །ཆོས་འཕགས་འདི་ལྟ་སྟེ་དཔེར་ན། ཡུན་རིང་པོ་ནས་བདག་གི་ཡོངས་སུ
འཛིན་པ་ཉིད་ཀྱིས་རྩོད་པ་ལ་བརྩོན་པ་རྩོད་པ་ལ་མངོན་པར་དགའ་བས་ནི་བྱུང་གི་སྦྲ་མི
སྙན་པ་དག་གི་བདག་གིར་ཡོངས་སུ་འཛིན་པ་མེད་པ་ཉིད་དང་། རྩོད་པ་མེད་པ་ཉིད་ལ
བརྟག་པའམ། རྗེས་སུ་དཔག་པའམ། མོས་པར་མི་ནུས་སོ། །ཆོས་འཕགས་དེ
བཞིན་དུ་རྟོག་གེ་པ་ཐམས་ཅད་ཀྱིས་ཀྱང་དོན་དམ་པ་རྟོག་གེ་ཐམས་ཅད་ལས་ཡང་དག་པར
འདས་པའི་མཚན་ཉིད་བརྟག་པའམ། རྗེས་སུ་དཔག་པའམ། མོས་པར་མི་ནུས་སོ། །
དེ་ནས་བཅོམ་ལྡན་འདས་ཀྱིས་དེའི་ཚེ་ཚིགས་སུ་བཅད་པ་འདི་དག་བཀའ་སྩལ་ཏོ། །སོ
སོ་རང་རིག་མཚན་ཉིད་སྤྱོད་ཡུལ་ཏེ། །བརྗོད་དུ་མེད་ཅིང་ཐ་སྙད་ཡོངས་ཆད་པ། །
རྩོད་དང་བྲལ་བ་དོན་དམ་ཆོས་ཡིན་ཏེ། །དེ་ནི་རྟོག་གེ་ཀུན་ལས་འདས་མཚན་ཉིད། །
ཆོས་འཕགས་ཀྱི་ལེའུ་སྟེ་གཉིས་པའོ།། ༎

"Dharmodgata, for instance, because beings have devoted their energy to dispute for a long time through strongly holding onto 'mine', manifestly delighting in dispute, they are unable to imagine, infer, or appreciate the absence of dispute or the absence of strongly holding onto 'mine' [like those who dwell] in Uttarakuru.[8]

"Accordingly, Dharmodgata, all disputants are unable to imagine, infer, or appreciate the ultimate whose characteristic completely transcends all argumentation."

Then the Bhagavan spoke this verse:

"The realm with an individually realized character
is ineffable and devoid of conventions.
Ultimate reality is free from dispute,
a character that transcends all argument."

This completes the second chapter of Dharmodgata.

Homage to the Tathāgata Buddha Śākyamuni

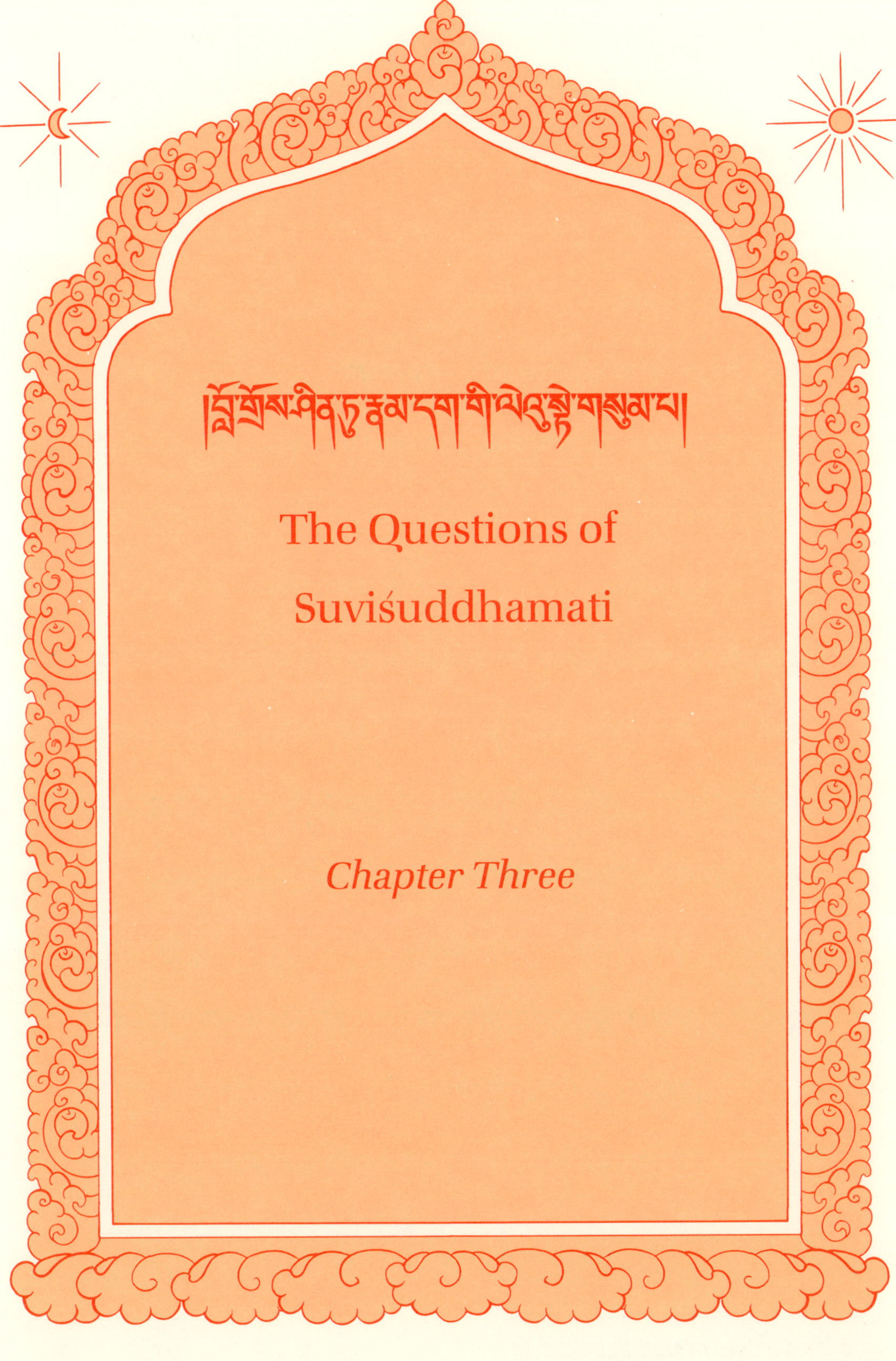

།བློ་གྲོས་ཤིན་ཏུ་རྣམ་དག་གི་ལེའུ་སྟེ་གསུམ་པ།

The Questions of Suviśuddhamati

Chapter Three

༄༅། །དེ་ནས་བཅོམ་ལྡན་འདས་ལ་བྱང་ཆུབ་སེམས་དཔའ་བློ་གྲོས་ཤིན་ཏུ་རྣམ་དག་གིས་འདི་སྐད་ཅེས་གསོལ་ཏོ། །བཅོམ་ལྡན་འདས་བཅོམ་ལྡན་འདས་ཀྱིས་གང་གི་སླད་དུ་འདི་སྐད་ཅེས་དོན་དམ་པ་ནི་ཕྲ་བ། ཟབ་པ་ཐ་དད་པ་དང་ཐ་དད་པ་མ་ཡིན་པ་ཉིད་ལས་ཡང་དག་པར་འདས་པའི་མཚན་ཉིད་རྟོགས་པར་དཀའ་བ་ཡིན་ནོ་ཞེས་བཀའ་སྩལ་ཏེ། ཇི་ཙམ་དུ་བཅོམ་ལྡན་འདས་ཀྱིས་ལེགས་པར་གསུངས་པ་དེ་ནི་ངོ་མཚར་ལགས་སོ། །བཅོམ་ལྡན་འདས་འདི་ལ་བདག་གིས་ས་ཕྱོགས་ཞིག་ན། བྱང་ཆུབ་སེམས་དཔའ་མོས་པས་སྤྱོད་པའི་ས་ལ་ཞུགས་པ་རབ་ཏུ་མང་པོ་དག་ཅིག །འདི་ལྟ་སྟེ། འདུ་བྱེད་རྣམས་དང་། དོན་དམ་པ་ཐ་དད་པ་དང་། ཐ་དད་པ་མ་ལགས་པ་ཉིད་ལས་བརྩམས་ཏེ། ཕན་ཚུན་ནས་མཆིས་ཤིང་མཆིས་ནས་འདུས་ཏེ་མཆིས་ནས་དེ་ན་བྱང་ཆུབ་སེམས་དཔའ་ཁ་ཅིག་འདི་སྐད་ཅེས་འདུ་བྱེད་ཀྱི་མཚན་ཉིད་དང་། དོན་དམ་པའི་མཚན་ཉིད་ཐ་དད་པ་མ་ལགས་སོ་ཞེས་མཆི། ཁ་ཅིག་ནི་འདི་སྐད་འདུ་བྱེད་ཀྱི་མཚན་ཉིད་དང་། དོན་དམ་པའི་མཚན་ཉིད་ཐ་དད་པ་མ་ལགས་པ་མ་ལགས་ཀྱི། འདུ་བྱེད་ཀྱི་མཚན་ཉིད་དང་། དོན་དམ་པའི་མཚན་ཉིད་ཐ་དད་པ་ལགས་སོ་ཞེས་མཆི། ཐེ་ཚོམ་དུ་གྱུར་པའི་བློ་གྲོས་ཅན། ཡིད་གཉིས་སུ་གྱུར་པ་ཁ་ཅིག་ནི་འདི་སྐད་དུ་གང་དག་དེ་སྐད་ཅེས་འདུ་བྱེད་ཀྱི་མཚན་ཉིད་དང་། དོན་དམ་པའི་མཚན་ཉིད་ཐ་དད་པ་ལགས་སོ། །ཞེས་མཆི་བ་དང་། གང་དག་དེ་སྐད་ཅེས་འདུ་བྱེད་ཀྱི་མཚན་ཉིད་དང་། དོན་དམ་པའི་མཚན་ཉིད་ཐ་དད་པ་མ་ལགས་སོ་ཞེས་མཆིས་པའི་བྱང་ཆུབ་སེམས་དཔའ་དེ་དག་ལས་གང་ནི་བདེན་པར་མཆི་བ་ལགས།

Then Bodhisattva Suviśuddhamati[1] spoke to the Bhagavan: "Bhagavan, regarding what the Bhagavan formerly said: 'The ultimate, profound and subtle, having a character completely transcending sameness and difference, is difficult to realize.' What the Bhagavan has spoken so eloquently in this way is truly wondrous.

"Bhagavan, concerning this, once at a certain place I saw a great many Bodhisattvas who had entered the stage of engagement through conviction.[2] They had gathered together to set about considering the difference or non-difference of the compounded and the ultimate.

"Once they had assembled, a certain Bodhisattva said, 'The character of the compounded and the character of the ultimate are not different.'

"Another said, 'It is not the case that the character of the compounded and the character of the ultimate are not different: The character of the compounded and the character of the ultimate are different.'

"Another became uncertain and full of doubts and said, 'There are those who say, "The character of the compounded and the character of the ultimate are different," and those who say, "The character of the compounded and the character of the ultimate are not different." Which of these Bodhisattvas is

གང་ནི་ཤོབ་བེ་མཆིས་ལགས། གང་ནི་ཚུལ་བཞིན་དུ་ཞུགས་པ་ལགས། གང་ནི་ཚུལ་བཞིན་དུ་མ་ལགས་པར་ཞུགས་པ་ལགས་ཞེས་མཆི་བ་དག་ཅིག་མཆིས་ལགས་སོ། །བཅོམ་ལྡན་འདས་བདག་འདི་སྙམ་བགྱིད་དེ། རིགས་ཀྱི་བུ་འདི་དག་ཐམས་ཅད་ནི་འདི་ལྟར་དོན་དམ་པ་འདུ་བྱེད་རྣམས་དང་། ཐ་དད་པ་དང་། ཐ་དད་པ་མ་ལགས་པ་ཉིད་ལས་ཡང་དག་པར་འདས་པའི་མཚན་ཉིད་ཕྲ་བ་མ་འཚལ་བ། བྱིས་པ་རྨོངས་པ་མི་གསལ་བ། མི་མཁས་པ། ཚུལ་བཞིན་མ་ལགས་པར་ཞུགས་པ་ཤ་སྟག་ལགས་སོ་སྙམ་བགྱིད་ལགས་སོ། །དེ་སྐད་ཅེས་གསོལ་པ་དང་། བཅོམ་ལྡན་འདས་ཀྱིས་བྱང་ཆུབ་སེམས་དཔའ་བློ་གྲོས་ཤིན་ཏུ་རྣམ་པར་དག་པ་ལ་འདི་སྐད་ཅེས་བཀའ་སྩལ་ཏོ། །བློ་གྲོས་ཤིན་ཏུ་རྣམ་པར་དག་པ་དེ་དེ་བཞིན་ནོ། །དེ་དེ་བཞིན་ཏེ། རིགས་ཀྱི་བུ་དེ་དག་ཐམས་ཅད་ནི་འདི་ལྟར་དོན་དམ་པ་འདུ་བྱེད་རྣམས་དང་ཐ་དད་པ་དང་། ཐ་དད་པ་མ་ཡིན་པ་ཉིད་ལས་ཡང་དག་པར་འདས་པའི་མཚན་ཉིད་ཕྲ་བ་མི་ཤེས་པ། བྱིས་པ་རྨོངས་པ། མི་གསལ་བ། མི་མཁས་པ། ཚུལ་བཞིན་མ་ཡིན་པར་ཞུགས་པ་ཤ་སྟག་ཡིན་ནོ། །དེ་ཅིའི་ཕྱིར་ཞེ་ན། བློ་གྲོས་ཤིན་ཏུ་རྣམ་དག་འདུ་བྱེད་རྣམས་ལ་དེ་ལྟར་སོ་སོར་རྟོག་པ་དག་ནི་དོན་དམ་པ་རྟོགས་པའམ། དོན་དམ་པ་མངོན་སུམ་དུ་བྱེད་པ་མ་ཡིན་པའི་ཕྱིར་རོ། །དེ་ཅིའི་ཕྱིར་ཞེ་ན། བློ་གྲོས་ཤིན་ཏུ་རྣམ་དག་གལ་ཏེ་འདུ་བྱེད་ཀྱི་མཚན་ཉིད་དང་། དོན་དམ་པའི་མཚན་ཉིད་ཐ་དད་པ་མ་ཡིན་པར་གྱུར་ན་ནི་དེས་ན་བྱིས་པ་སོ་སོའི་སྐྱེ་བོ་ཐམས་ཅད་བདེན་པ་མཐོང་བ་ཡིན་པར་ཡང་འགྱུར། སོ་སོའི་སྐྱེ་བོ་ཁོ་ནར་གྱུར་བཞིན་དུ་གྲུབ་པ་དང་།

truthful, which is mistaken? Which is properly oriented, which is improperly oriented?'

"Bhagavan, having seen these things, I thought this: 'All these sons and daughters of good lineage have not sought out the ultimate, the subtle character completely transcending difference or non-difference from compounded things. They are all childish, obscured, unclear, unskilled, and they are not properly oriented.'"[3]

The Bhagavan replied to the Bodhisattva Suviśuddhamati: "So it is! Suviśuddhamati, so it is! All these sons and daughters of good lineage do not understand the ultimate, the subtle character completely transcending difference or non-difference from compounded things. They are all childish, obscured, unclear, unskilled, and not properly oriented.

"Why is this? Suviśuddhamati, it is because those who investigate the compounded in that way neither realize the ultimate nor do they manifest the ultimate.

"Why is this? Suviśuddhamati, if the character of the compounded and the character of the ultimate were not different, then, because of that, even all ordinary childish beings would see the truth and, while still mere ordinary beings, would attain [the highest achievement] and would even achieve the

བདེ་བ་བླ་ན་མེད་པའི་མྱ་ངན་ལས་འདས་པ་འཐོབ་པར་ཡང་འགྱུར། བླ་ན་མེད་པ་ཡང་
དག་པར་རྫོགས་པའི་བྱང་ཆུབ་མངོན་པར་རྫོགས་པར་འཚང་རྒྱ་བར་ཡང་འགྱུར་རོ། །
གལ་ཏེ་འདུ་བྱེད་ཀྱི་མཚན་ཉིད་དང་། དོན་དམ་པའི་མཚན་ཉིད་ཐ་དད་པ་ཡིན་པར་གྱུར
ན་ནི། དེས་ན་བདེན་པ་མཐོང་བ་རྣམས་ཀྱང་འདུ་བྱེད་ཀྱི་མཚན་མ་དང་མ་བྲལ་བར་འགྱུར།
འདུ་བྱེད་ཀྱི་མཚན་མ་དང་མ་བྲལ་བའི་ཕྱིར་བདེན་པ་མཐོང་བ། མཚན་མའི་འཆིང་བ
ལས་རྣམ་པར་འགྲོལ་བར་ཡང་མི་འགྱུར། མཚན་མའི་འཆིང་བ་ལས་རྣམ་པར་མ་གྲོལ
ན། གནས་ངན་ལེན་གྱི་འཆིང་བ་ལས་ཀྱང་རྣམ་པར་མ་གྲོལ་བར་འགྱུར། འཆིང་བ་དེ
གཉིས་ལས་མ་གྲོལ་ན་བདེན་པ་མཐོང་བས་གྲུབ་པ་དང་། བདེ་བ་བླ་ན་མེད་པའི་མྱ་ངན
ལས་འདས་པ་ཐོབ་པར་ཡང་མི་འགྱུར། བླ་ན་མེད་པ་ཡང་དག་པར་རྫོགས་པའི་བྱང་ཆུབ
མངོན་པར་རྫོགས་པར་འཚང་རྒྱ་བར་ཡང་མི་འགྱུར་རོ། །བློ་གྲོས་ཤིན་ཏུ་རྣམ་དག་གང
གི་ཕྱིར་སོ་སོའི་སྐྱེ་བོ་བདེན་པ་མཐོང་བ་མ་ཡིན། སོ་སོའི་སྐྱེ་བོ་ཁོ་ནར་གྱུར་བཞིན་དུ་གྲུབ
པ་དང་། བདེ་བ་བླ་ན་མེད་པའི་མྱ་ངན་ལས་འདས་པ་འཐོབ་པར་ཡང་མི་འགྱུར། བླ་ན
མེད་པ་ཡང་དག་པར་རྫོགས་པའི་བྱང་ཆུབ་མངོན་པར་རྫོགས་པར་འཚང་རྒྱ་བར་མི་
འགྱུར་བ་དེའི་ཕྱིར་འདུ་བྱེད་ཀྱི་མཚན་ཉིད་དང་། དོན་དམ་པའི་མཚན་ཉིད་ཐ་དད་པ་མ
ཡིན་ཞེས་བྱ་བར་མི་རུང་སྟེ། དེ་ལ་གང་དག་དེ་སྐད་ཅེས་འདུ་བྱེད་ཀྱི་མཚན་ཉིད་དང་།
དོན་དམ་པའི་མཚན་ཉིད་ཐ་དད་པ་མ་ཡིན་ཞེས་ཟེར་བ་དེ་དག་ནི་རྣམ་གྲངས་དེས་ན་ཁྱོད
ཀྱིས་འདི་ལྟར་ཚུལ་བཞིན་མ་ཡིན་པར་ཞུགས་པ་ཡིན་གྱི། ཚུལ་བཞིན་དུ་ཞུགས་པ་མ

highest bliss of nirvāṇa. Moreover, they would completely and perfectly realize unsurpassed, perfect enlightenment.

"If the character of the compounded and the character of the ultimate were different, then, because of that, even those who see the truth would not be free from the signs of the compounded.

"Since they would not be free from the signs of the compounded, even those who see the truth would not be liberated from the bondage of signs. If they were not liberated from the bondage of signs, then they would also not be liberated from the bondage of errant tendencies.[4] If they were not liberated from these two bonds, then those who see the truth would not attain [the highest achievement], and would not achieve the highest bliss of nirvāṇa. Furthermore, they would not completely and perfectly realize unsurpassed, perfect enlightenment.

"Suviśuddhamati, since ordinary beings are not seers of truth, they are merely ordinary beings. They have not attained [the highest achievement], nor have they achieved the highest bliss of nirvāṇa. Further, they have not completely and perfectly realized unsurpassed, perfect enlightenment. Therefore, it is not suitable to say, 'The character of the compounded and the character of the ultimate are not different.' Know by this form of explanation that those who say, 'The character of the compounded and the character of the

ཡིན་པར་རིག་པར་བྱའོ། །བློ་གྲོས་ཤིན་ཏུ་རྣམ་དག་གང་གི་ཕྱིར་བདེན་པ་མཐོང་བ་རྣམས་འདུ་བྱེད་ཀྱི་མཚན་མ་དང་བྲལ་བ་མ་ཡིན་གྱི། བྲལ་བ་ཁོ་ན་ཡིན་པ་དང་། བདེན་པ་མཐོང་བ་མཚན་མའི་འཆིང་བ་ལས་རྣམ་པར་གྲོལ་བ་མ་ཡིན་གྱི། རྣམ་པར་གྲོལ་བ་ཡིན་པ་དང་། བདེན་པ་མཐོང་བ་གནས་ངན་ལེན་གྱི་འཆིང་བ་ལས་རྣམ་པར་གྲོལ་བ་མ་ཡིན་གྱི། རྣམ་པར་གྲོལ་བ་དང་། འཆིང་བ་དེ་གཉིས་ལས་རྣམ་པར་གྲོལ་ན་གྲུབ་པ་དང་། བདེ་བ་བླ་ན་མེད་པའི་ཕྱིར་མྱ་ངན་ལས་འདས་པ་འཐོབ་པར་འགྱུར་བ་དང་། བླ་ན་མེད་པ་ཡང་དག་པར་རྫོགས་པའི་བྱང་ཆུབ་མངོན་པར་རྫོགས་པར་འཚང་རྒྱ་བར་ཡང་འགྱུར་བ་དེའི་ཕྱིར་འདུ་བྱེད་ཀྱི་མཚན་ཉིད་དང་། དོན་དམ་པའི་མཚན་ཉིད་ཐ་དད་པ་ཞེས་བྱར་མི་རུང་ངོ༑ དེ་ལ་གང་དག་དེ་སྐད་ཅེས་འདུ་བྱེད་ཀྱི་མཚན་ཉིད་དང་། དོན་དམ་པའི་མཚན་ཉིད་ཐ་དད་པ་ཞེས་ཟེར་བ་དེ་དག་ནི་རྣམ་གྲངས་དེས་ན་ཁྱོད་ཀྱིས་འདི་ལྟར་ཚུལ་བཞིན་མ་ཡིན་པར་ཞུགས་པ་ཡིན་གྱི། ཚུལ་བཞིན་དུ་ཞུགས་པ་མ་ཡིན་པར་རིག་པར་བྱའོ། །བློ་གྲོས་ཤིན་ཏུ་རྣམ་དག་གཞན་ཡང་གལ་ཏེ་འདུ་བྱེད་ཀྱི་མཚན་ཉིད་དང་། དོན་དམ་པའི་མཚན་ཉིད་ཐ་དད་པ་མ་ཡིན་པར་གྱུར་ན་ནི། དེས་ན་ཇི་ལྟར་འདུ་བྱེད་ཀྱི་མཚན་ཉིད་ཀུན་ནས་ཉོན་མོངས་པའི་མཚན་ཉིད་དུ་གཏོགས་པ་དེ་བཞིན་དུ་དོན་དམ་པའི་མཚན་ཉིད་ཀྱང་ཀུན་ནས་ཉོན་མོངས་པའི་མཚན་ཉིད་དུ་གཏོགས་པར་འགྱུར་རོ། །བློ་གྲོས་ཤིན་ཏུ་རྣམ་དག་གལ་ཏེ་འདུ་བྱེད་ཀྱི་མཚན་ཉིད་དང་། དོན་དམ་པའི་མཚན་ཉིད་ཐ་དད་པ་ཡིན་པར་གྱུར་ན་ཡང་། དེས་ན་འདུ་བྱེད་ཀྱི་མཚན་ཉིད་ཐམས་ཅད་ལ་དོན་དམ་པའི་མཚན་ཉིད་སྤྱིའི་

ultimate are not different' are improperly oriented; their orientation is incorrect.

"Suviśuddhamati, it is not the case that seers of truth are free from the signs of the compounded; they are simply free. Moreover, seers of truth are not liberated from the bondage of signs, but they are liberated. Seers of truth are not liberated from the bondage of errant tendencies, but they are liberated.

"Since they are liberated from these two bonds, they attain the highest achievement. With unexcelled bliss they attain nirvāṇa and also completely and perfectly realize unsurpassed enlightenment. Therefore, it is not suitable to say, 'The character of the compounded and the character of the ultimate are different.'

"Know by this form of explanation that those who say, 'The character of the compounded and the character of the ultimate are different' are improperly oriented; their orientation is incorrect.

"Moreover, Suviśuddhamati, if the character of the compounded and the character of the ultimate were not different, then just as the character of the compounded would be included in the afflicted character, the character of the ultimate would also be included in the afflicted character.

"Suviśuddhamati, if the character of the compounded and the character of the ultimate were different, then the ultimate

མཚན་ཉིད་དུ་གྱུར་པ་མ་ཡིན་པར་འགྱུར་རོ། །བློ་གྲོས་ཤིན་ཏུ་རྣམ་དག་གང་གི་ཕྱིར་དོན་དམ་པའི་མཚན་ཉིད་ཀུན་ནས་ཉོན་མོངས་པའི་མཚན་ཉིད་དུ་གཏོགས་པ་མ་ཡིན་པ་དང་། འདུ་བྱེད་ཀྱི་མཚན་ཉིད་ཐམས་ཅད་ལ་དོན་དམ་པའི་མཚན་ཉིད་སྤྱིའི་མཚན་ཉིད་དུ་གྱུར་པ་ཡིན་པ་དེའི་ཕྱིར་འདུ་བྱེད་ཀྱི་མཚན་ཉིད་དང་། དོན་དམ་པའི་མཚན་ཉིད་ཐ་དད་པ་མ་ཡིན་ཞེས་བྱ་བར་ཡང་མི་རུང་ལ། དོན་དམ་པའི་མཚན་ཉིད་ཐ་དད་པ་ཞེས་བྱར་ཡང་མི་རུང་སྟེ། དེ་ལ་གང་དག་དེ་སྐད་ཅེས་འདུ་བྱེད་ཀྱི་མཚན་ཉིད་དང་། དོན་དམ་པའི་མཚན་ཉིད་ཐ་དད་པ་མ་ཡིན་པ་ཞེས་ཟེར་བ་དང་། དོན་དམ་པའི་མཚན་ཉིད་ཐ་དད་པ་ཞེས་ཟེར་བ་དེ་དག་ནི། རྣམ་གྲངས་དེས་ན་ཁྱོད་ཀྱིས་འདི་ལྟར་ཚུལ་བཞིན་མ་ཡིན་པར་ཞུགས་པ་ཡིན་གྱི། ཚུལ་བཞིན་དུ་ཞུགས་པ་མ་ཡིན་པར་རིག་པར་བྱའོ། །བློ་གྲོས་ཤིན་ཏུ་རྣམ་དག་གཞན་ཡང་གལ་ཏེ་འདུ་བྱེད་ཀྱི་མཚན་ཉིད་དང་། དོན་དམ་པའི་མཚན་ཉིད་ཐ་དད་པ་མ་ཡིན་པར་གྱུར་ན་ནི། དེས་ན་ཇི་ལྟར་དོན་དམ་པའི་མཚན་ཉིད་འདུ་བྱེད་ཀྱི་མཚན་ཉིད་ཐམས་ཅད་ལ་བྱེ་བྲག་མེད་པ་དེ་བཞིན་དུ་འདུ་བྱེད་ཀྱི་མཚན་ཉིད་ཐམས་ཅད་ཀྱང་བྱེ་བྲག་མེད་པ་དང་། རྣལ་འབྱོར་པ་དག་འདུ་བྱེད་རྣམས་ལ་ཇི་ལྟར་མཐོང་བ་དང་ཇི་ལྟར་ཐོས་པ་དང་ཇི་ལྟར་བྱེ་བྲག་ཕྱེད་པ་དང་ཇི་ལྟར་རྣམ་པར་ཤེས་པ་ལས་གོང་དུ་དོན་དམ་པ་ཡོངས་སུ་འཚོལ་བར་ཡང་མི་འགྱུར་རོ། །གལ་ཏེ་འདུ་བྱེད་ཀྱི་མཚན་ཉིད་དང་། དོན་དམ་པའི་མཚན་ཉིད་ཐ་དད་པ་ཡིན་པར་གྱུར་ན་ནི། དེས་ན་འདུ་བྱེད་རྣམས་ཀྱི་བདག་མེད་པ་ཙམ་དང་། ངོ་བོ་ཉིད་མེད་པ་ཙམ་ཉིད་དོན་དམ་པའི་མཚན་ཉིད་ཡིན་པར་ཡང་མི་འགྱུར། ཀུན་ནས་ཉོན་

character within all characters of compounded things would not be their general character.

"Suviśuddhamati, since the character of the ultimate is not included in the character of the afflicted, and the ultimate character in all characters of compounded things is their general character, it is neither suitable to say, 'The character of the compounded and the character of the ultimate are not different,' nor is it suitable to say, 'The character of the ultimate is different.'

"Know by this form of explanation that those who say, 'The character of the compounded and the character of the ultimate are not different' and those who say, 'The character of the ultimate is different' are improperly oriented; their orientation is incorrect.

"Moreover, Suviśuddhamati, if the character of the compounded and the character of the ultimate were not different, then just as the ultimate character does not differ within all characters of compounded things, so also all the characters of compounded things would not differ. Even yogis would not search for an ultimate beyond compounded things as they are seen, heard, differentiated, and known.

"If the character of the compounded and the character of the ultimate were different, then just the absence of self and just the absence of an own-being of compounded things would not be the ultimate character [of those phenomena].

མོངས་པའི་མཚན་ཉིད་དང་། རྣམ་པར་བྱང་བའི་མཚན་ཉིད་ཀྱང་དུས་གཅིག་ཏུ་མཚན་
ཉིད་ཐ་དད་དུ་གྲུབ་པར་འགྱུར་རོ། །བློ་གྲོས་ཤིན་ཏུ་རྣམ་དག་གང་གི་ཕྱིར་འདུ་བྱེད་ཀྱི་
མཚན་ཉིད་རྣམས་ནི་བྱེ་བྲག་ཡོད་པ་ཡིན་ཏེ། བྱེ་བྲག་མེད་པམ་ཡིན་པ་དང་། རྣལ་
འབྱོར་པ་དག་འདུ་བྱེད་རྣམས་ལ་ཇི་ལྟར་མཐོང་བ་དང་། ཐོས་པ་དང་། བྱེ་བྲག་ཕྱེད་པ་
དང་། རྣམ་པར་ཤེས་པ་ལས་གོང་དུ་དོན་དམ་པ་ཡོངས་སུ་ཚོལ་བར་བྱེད་པ་དང་། དོན་
དམ་པ་ནི་འདུ་བྱེད་རྣམས་ཀྱི་བདག་མེད་པས་རབ་ཏུ་ཕྱེ་བ་ཡིན་པ་དང་། ཀུན་ནས་ཉོན་
མོངས་པ་དང་། རྣམ་པར་བྱང་བའི་མཚན་ཉིད་ཀྱང་དུས་གཅིག་ཏུ་མཚན་ཉིད་ཐ་དད་དུ་
གྲུབ་པ་མེད་པ་དེའི་ཕྱིར་འདུ་བྱེད་ཀྱི་མཚན་ཉིད་དང་། དོན་དམ་པའི་མཚན་ཉིད་ཐ་དད་
པམ་ཡིན་པའམ། ཐ་དད་པ་ཞེས་བྱར་མི་རུང་ངོ་། །དེ་ལ་གང་དག་དེ་སྐད་ཅེས་འདུ་བྱེད་
ཀྱི་མཚན་ཉིད་དང་། དོན་དམ་པའི་མཚན་ཉིད་ཐ་དད་པམ་ཡིན་པའམ། ཐ་དད་པ་ཞེས་
ཟེར་བ་དེ་དག་ནི་རྣམ་གྲངས་དེས་ན། ཁྱོད་ཀྱིས་འདི་ལྟར་ཚུལ་བཞིན་མ་ཡིན་པར་ཞུགས་
པ་ཡིན་གྱི། ཚུལ་བཞིན་དུ་ཞུགས་པམ་ཡིན་པར་རིག་པར་བྱའོ། །བློ་གྲོས་ཤིན་ཏུ་རྣམ་
དག་འདི་ལྟ་སྟེ་དཔེར་ན། དུང་གི་དཀར་པོ་ཉིད་ནི། དུང་དང་མཚན་ཉིད་ཐ་དད་པམ་
ཡིན་པའམ། མཚན་ཉིད་ཐ་དད་དུ་གདགས་པར་སླ་བམ་ཡིན་ནོ། །དུང་གི་དཀར་པོ་
ཉིད་ཇི་ལྟ་བ་བཞིན་དུ་གསེར་གྱི་སེར་པོ་ཉིད་ཀྱང་དེ་བཞིན་ནོ། །པི་བང་གི་སྒྲའི་སྙན་པ་
ཉིད་ཀྱང་པི་བང་གི་སྒྲ་དང་མཚན་ཉིད་ཐ་དད་པམ་ཡིན་པའམ། མཚན་ཉིད་ཐ་དད་པར་
གདགས་པར་སླ་བམ་ཡིན་ནོ། །ཨ་ག་རུ་ནག་པོའི་དྲི་ཞིམ་པ་ཉིད་ཀྱང་ཨ་ག་རུ་ནག་པོ་

The afflicted character and the purified character would also be established as simultaneously having different characters.

"Suviśuddhamati, since the characters of the compounded both differ and do not differ, yogis search for an ultimate beyond all compounded things as they are seen, heard, differentiated, and known. The ultimate is distinguished by being the selflessness of compounded things. Further, the afflicted character and the purified character are not established as simultaneously having different characters. Therefore, it is not suitable to say that the character of the compounded and the character of the ultimate are either 'not-different' or 'different'.

"Also know by this form of explanation that those who say, 'The character of the compounded and the character of the ultimate are not different,' and those who say, 'They are different' are improperly oriented; their orientation is incorrect.

"Suviśuddhamati, for instance, it is not easy to designate the whiteness of a conch as being a character that is different from the conch or as being a character that is not different from it.[5] As it is with the whiteness of a conch, so it is with the yellowness of gold.

"It is also not easy to designate the melodiousness of the sound of the vīṇā[6] as being either a character that is not different from the sound of the vīṇā or as being a character that is different [from it]. It is also not easy to designate the

དང་མཚན་ཉིད་ཐ་དད་པ་མ་ཡིན་པའམ། མཚན་ཉིད་ཐ་དད་དུ་གདགས་པར་སླ་བ་མ
ཡིན་ནོ། །ན་ལེ་ཤམ་གྱི་ཚ་བ་ཉིད་ཀྱང་ན་ལེ་ཤམ་དང་མཚན་ཉིད་ཐ་དད་པ་མ་ཡིན་པའམ།
མཚན་ཉིད་ཐ་དད་དུ་གདགས་པར་སླ་བ་མ་ཡིན་ནོ། །ན་ལེ་ཤམ་གྱི་ཚ་བ་ཉིད་ཇི་ལྟ་བ
བཞིན་ཨ་རུ་རའི་བསྐ་བ་ཉིད་ཀྱང་དེ་བཞིན་ནོ། །འདི་ལྟ་སྟེ་དཔེར་ན། ཤིང་བལ་གྱི་འདའ་
བའི་འཇམ་པ་ཉིད་ཀྱང་ཤིང་བལ་གྱི་འདའ་བ་དང་མཚན་ཉིད་ཐ་དད་པ་མ་ཡིན་པའམ།
མཚན་ཉིད་ཐ་དད་དུ་གདགས་པར་སླ་བ་མ་ཡིན་ནོ། །འདི་ལྟ་སྟེ་དཔེར་ན། མར་ལ་མར་
གྱི་སྙིང་ཁུ་ཡང་མར་དང་མཚན་ཉིད་ཐ་དད་པ་མ་ཡིན་པའམ། མཚན་ཉིད་ཐ་དད་དུ
གདགས་པར་སླ་བ་མ་ཡིན་ནོ། །འདི་ལྟ་སྟེ་དཔེར་ན། འདུ་བྱེད་ཐམས་ཅད་ལ་མི་རྟག་པ
ཉིད་དང་། ཟག་པ་དང་བཅས་པ་ཐམས་ཅད་ལ་སྡུག་བསྔལ་བ་ཉིད་དང་། ཆོས་ཐམས
ཅད་ལ་གང་ཟག་བདག་མེད་པ་ཉིད་ཀྱང་དེ་དག་དང་མཚན་ཉིད་ཐ་དད་པ་མ་ཡིན་པའམ།
མཚན་ཉིད་ཐ་དད་དུ་གདགས་པར་སླ་བ་མ་ཡིན་ནོ། །བློ་གྲོས་ཤིན་ཏུ་རྣམ་དག་འདི་ལྟ་སྟེ
དཔེར་ན་འདོད་ཆགས་ཀྱི་མ་ཞི་བའི་མཚན་ཉིད་དང་། ཀུན་ནས་ཉོན་མོངས་པའི་མཚན
ཉིད་ཀྱང་འདོད་ཆགས་དང་མཚན་ཉིད་ཐ་དད་པ་མ་ཡིན་པའམ། མཚན་ཉིད་ཐ་དད་དུ
གདགས་པར་སླ་བ་མ་ཡིན་པ་དང་། འདོད་ཆགས་ཀྱི་ཇི་ལྟ་བ་བཞིན་དུ་ཞེ་སྡང་དང་གཏི
མུག་གི་ཡང་དེ་བཞིན་དུ་རིག་པར་བྱའོ། །བློ་གྲོས་ཤིན་ཏུ་རྣམ་དག་དེ་བཞིན་དུ་འདུ་བྱེད་ཀྱི
མཚན་ཉིད་དང་། དོན་དམ་པའི་མཚན་ཉིད་ཀྱང་མཚན་ཉིད་ཐ་དད་པ་མ་ཡིན་པའམ།
མཚན་ཉིད་ཐ་དད་དུ་གདགས་པར་མི་བཟོད་དོ། །བློ་གྲོས་ཤིན་ཏུ་རྣམ་དག་ངས་ནི་དེ་ལྟར

fragrant smell of the black agaru tree[7] as being a character that is not different from the black agaru tree or as being a character that is different from it.

"Similarly, it is not easy to designate the heat of pepper as being a character that is not different from pepper or as being a character that is different [from it]. As it is with the heat of pepper, so it is also with the astringency of myrobalan arjuna.[8]

"For instance, it is not easy to designate the softness of cotton as being either a character that is not different from the cotton or a character that is different [from it]. For instance, it is not easy to designate clarified butter as being either a character that is not different from butter or a character that is different from it. For instance, it is not easy to designate the impermanence in all compounded things, or the suffering in all contaminated things, or the selflessness in all phenomena as being characters that are not different from those things or characters that are different from them.

"Suviśuddhamati, for instance, it is not easy to designate the agitating character of desire and the character of affliction as being a character that is not different from desire or a character that is different [from it]. Know that just as it is with desire, so it is with hatred and also obscuration.

"Similarly, Suviśuddhamati, it is not appropriate to designate the character of the compounded and the character of the ultimate as being either characters that are not-different or characters that are different.

དོན་དམ་པ་ཟབ་པ་མཆོག་ཏུ་ཟབ་པ། མཆོག་ཏུ་ཟབ་པ། རྟོགས་པར་དཀའ་བ། མཆོག་ཏུ་དཀའ་བ། ཐ་དད་པ་དང་། ཐ་དད་པ་མ་ཡིན་པ་ཉིད་ལས་ཡང་དག་པར་འདས་པའི་མཚན་ཉིད་མངོན་པར་རྫོགས་པར་སངས་རྒྱས་ཏེ། མངོན་པར་རྫོགས་པར་སངས་རྒྱས་ནས་ཀྱང་བསྐྱང་ཅིང་གསལ་བར་བྱས། རྣམ་པར་ཕྱེ། གདགས་པ་བྱས། རབ་ཏུ་བསྟན་ཏོ། །དེ་ནས་བཅོམ་ལྡན་འདས་ཀྱིས་དེ་ཡི་ཚེ་ཚིགས་སུ་བཅད་པ་འདི་དག་བཀའ་སྩལ་ཏོ། །འདུ་བྱེད་ཁམས་དང་དོན་དམ་མཚན་ཉིད་ནི། །གཅིག་དང་ཐ་དད་བྲལ་བའི་མཚན་ཉིད་དེ། །གཅིག་དང་ཐ་དད་དུ་ཡང་གང་རྟོག་པ། །དེ་དག་ཚུལ་བཞིན་མ་ཡིན་ཞུགས་པ་ཡིན། །སྐྱེ་བོ་ཡིས་ལྷག་མཐོང་དང་། །ཞི་གནས་གོམས་པར་བྱས་ནས་ནི། །གནས་ངན་ལེན་གྱི་འཆིང་བ་དང་། །མཚན་མའི་འཆིང་ལས་རྣམ་གྲོལ་འགྱུར། །བློ་གྲོས་ཤིན་ཏུ་རྣམ་དག་གི་ལེའུ་སྟེ་གསུམ་པའོ།། །།

"Suviśuddhamati, in that way I have completely and perfectly realized the ultimate, which is subtle, supremely subtle, supremely profound, difficult to realize, supremely difficult to realize, and which is a character that completely transcends difference and non-difference. Having completely and perfectly realized this, I have proclaimed it and made it clear, opened it up, systematized it, and taught it comprehensively."

Then the Bhagavan spoke these verses:

"The character of the compounded realm and of the ultimate
is a character devoid of sameness and difference.
Those who impute sameness and difference
are improperly oriented.

"Cultivating śamatha and vipaśyanā,
beings will be liberated from
the bonds of errant tendencies
and the bonds of signs."

This completes the third chapter of Suviśuddhamati.

Homage to the great Arhat Subhūti

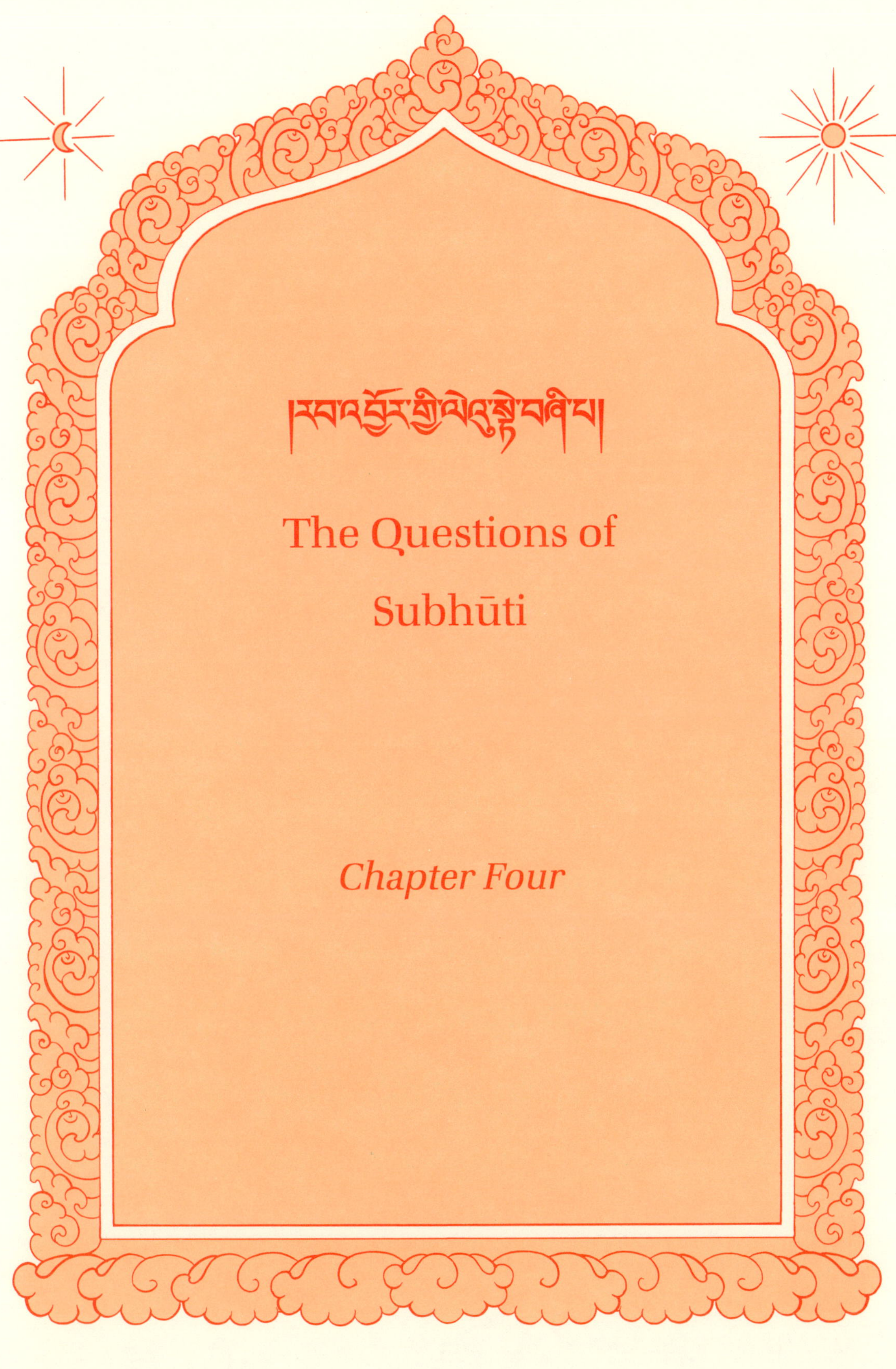

།རབ་འབྱོར་གྱི་ལེའུ་སྟེ་བཞི་པ།

The Questions of Subhūti

Chapter Four

༄༅། །དེ་ནས་བཅོམ་ལྡན་འདས་ཀྱིས་ཚེ་དང་ལྡན་པ་རབ་འབྱོར་ལ་བཀའ་སྩལ་པ། རབ་འབྱོར་ཁྱོད་ཀྱིས་སེམས་ཅན་གྱི་ཁམས་ན་གང་དག་མངོན་པའི་ང་རྒྱལ་གྱིས་མངོན་དུ་ཞེན་ཅིང་ཤེས་པ་བརྗོད་པར་བྱེད་པའི་སེམས་ཅན་ནི་ཇི་ཙམ་ཞིག་ཡོད་པར་ཤེས། ཁྱོད་ཀྱིས་སེམས་ཅན་གྱི་ཁམས་ན་གང་དག་མངོན་པའི་ང་རྒྱལ་མེད་པར་ཤེས་པ་བརྗོད་པར་བྱེད་པའི་སེམས་ཅན་ནི་ཇི་ཙམ་ཞིག་ཡོད་པར་ཤེས། རབ་འབྱོར་གྱིས་གསོལ་པ། བཅོམ་ལྡན་འདས་བདག་ནི་སེམས་ཅན་གྱི་ཁམས་ན་གང་དག་མངོན་པའི་ང་རྒྱལ་མ་མཆིས་པར་ཤེས་པ་བརྗོད་པར་བགྱིད་པའི་སེམས་ཅན་ནི་ཉུང་ཤས་ཤིག་མཆིས་པར་འཚལ་ལགས་ཀྱི༑ བཅོམ་ལྡན་འདས་བདག་གིས་སེམས་ཅན་གྱི་ཁམས་ན་གང་དག་མངོན་པའི་ང་རྒྱལ་གྱིས་མངོན་དུ་ཞེན་ཅིང་ཤེས་པ་བརྗོད་པར་བགྱིད་པའི་སེམས་ཅན་ནི་ཚད་མ་མཆིས་གྲངས་མ་མཆིས། བརྗོད་དུ་མ་མཆིས་པར་འཚལ་ལགས་ཏེ། བཅོམ་ལྡན་འདས་བདག་དུས་གཅིག་ཅིག་ན། དགོན་པ་ནགས་ཁྲོད་ཆེན་པོ་ཞིག་ན་མཆིས་པའི་ཚེ། དེ་ན་བདག་གི་ཉེ་འཁོར་ན་དགེ་སློང་རབ་ཏུ་མང་པོ་དག་ཅིག་ཀྱང་དགོན་པ་ནགས་ཁྲོད་ཆེན་པོ་ན་རྟེན་ཅིང་གནས་ལགས་ཏེ། བདག་གིས་སྔ་དྲོའི་དུས་ཀྱི་ཚེ་དགེ་སློང་ཕན་ཚུན་ནས་མཆིས་ཤིང་མཇལ་ནས། ཆོས་རྣམ་པ་སྣ་ཚོགས་དམིགས་པའི་མངོན་པར་རྟོགས་པ་སྟོན་པས་ཤེས་པ་བརྗོད་པར་བགྱིད་དེ། དེ་ན་ཁ་ཅིག་ནི་ཕུང་པོ་དམིགས་པ་དང་། ཕུང་པོའི་མཚན་མ་དམིགས་པ་དང་། ཕུང་པོའི་སྐྱེ་བ་དམིགས་པ་དང་། ཕུང་པོའི་འཇིག་པ་དམིགས་པ་དང༑ ཕུང་པོ་འགོག་པ་དམིགས་པ་དང་། ཕུང་པོ་འགོག་པ་མངོན་དུ་བགྱིད་པ

Then the Bhagavan spoke to the venerable Subhūti:[1] "Subhūti, in the realms of sentient beings, how many sentient beings do you think there are who communicate their understanding under the influence of conceit? In the realms of sentient beings, how many sentient beings do you think there are who communicate their understanding without conceit?"[2]

Subhūti replied: "Bhagavan, I think that in the realms of sentient beings, those sentient beings who communicate their understanding without conceit are few. Bhagavan, I think that in the realms of sentient beings, sentient beings who communicate their understanding under the influence of conceit are immeasurable, countless, and inexpressible [in number].

"Bhagavan, at one time I lived in a great forest hermitage. Dwelling with me in that great forest hermitage were numerous monks. Early one morning, I saw the monks gather together. At that time, they communicated their understanding by describing what they had manifestly realized through observing the various forms of phenomena. One communicated his understanding based on observing the [five] aggregates: observing the signs of the aggregates, observing the arising of the aggregates, observing the disintegration of the aggregates, observing the cessation of the aggregates, and observing the actualization of the cessation of the aggregates.[3]

"Just as this one communicated his understanding based upon observing the aggregates, another did so based upon

དམིགས་པས་ཤེས་པ་བརྡ་སྤྲོད་པར་བགྱིད། ཁ་ཅིག་ཕུང་པོ་དམིགས་པས་ཇི་ལྟ་བ་དེ་བཞིན་དུ་ཁ་ཅིག་ནི་སྐྱེ་མཆེད་དམིགས་པས། ཁ་ཅིག་རྟེན་ཅིང་འབྲེལ་བར་འབྱུང་བ་དམིགས་པས་ཤེས་པ་བརྡ་སྤྲོད་པར་བགྱིད། ཁ་ཅིག་ནི་ཟས་དམིགས་པ་དང་། ཟས་ཀྱི་མཚན་མ་དམིགས་པ་དང་། ཟས་ཀྱི་སྐྱེ་བ་དམིགས་པ་དང་། ཟས་ཀྱི་འཇིག་པ་དམིགས་པ་དང་། ཟས་འགོག་པ་དམིགས་པ་དང་། ཟས་འགོག་པ་མངོན་དུ་བགྱི་བ་དམིགས་པས་ཤེས་པ་བརྡ་སྤྲོད་པར་བགྱིད། ཁ་ཅིག་ནི་བདེན་པ་དམིགས་པ་དང་། བདེན་པའི་མཚན་ཉིད་དམིགས་པ་དང་། བདེན་པ་ཡོངས་སུ་ཤེས་པ་དམིགས་པ་དང་། བདེན་པ་སྤངས་པ་དམིགས་པ་དང་། བདེན་པ་མངོན་དུ་བགྱི་བ་དམིགས་པ་དང་། བདེན་པ་སྒོམ་པ་དམིགས་པས་ཤེས་པ་བརྡ་སྤྲོད་པར་བགྱིད། ཁ་ཅིག་ནི་ཁམས་ཀྱི་དམིགས་པ་དང་། ཁམས་ཀྱི་མཚན་མ་དམིགས་པ་དང་། ཁམས་སྣ་ཚོགས་པ་ཉིད་དམིགས་པ་དང་། ཁམས་དུ་མ་དམིགས་པ་དང་། ཁམས་འགོག་པ་དམིགས་པ་དང་། ཁམས་འགོག་པ་མངོན་དུ་བགྱི་བ་དམིགས་པས་ཤེས་པ་བརྡ་སྤྲོད་པར་བགྱིད། ཁ་ཅིག་ནི་དྲན་པ་ཉེ་བར་གཞག་པ་དམིགས་པ་དང་། དྲན་པ་ཉེ་བར་གཞག་པའི་མཚན་མ་དམིགས་པ་དང་། དྲན་པ་ཉེ་བར་གཞག་པའི་མི་འཐུན་པའི་ཕྱོགས་དང་། གཉེན་པོ་དམིགས་པ་དང་། དྲན་པ་ཉེ་བར་གཞག་པ་བསྒོམ་པ་དམིགས་པ་དང་། དྲན་པ་ཉེ་བར་གཞག་པ་མ་སྐྱེས་པ་སྐྱེ་བར་དམིགས་པ་དང་། དྲན་པ་ཉེ་བར་གཞག་པ་སྐྱེས་པ་གནས་པ་དང་། མི་བསྙུད་པ་དང་། སླར་ཞིང་འབྱུང་བ་དང་། འཕེལ་ཞིང་རྒྱས་པ་དམིགས་

observing the sense spheres. Another did so based on observing dependent origination. Another communicated his understanding based on observing the [four] sustenances: observing the signs of the sustenances, observing the arising of the sustenances, observing the disintegration of the sustenances, observing the cessation of the sustenances, and observing the actualization of the cessation of the sustenances.[4]

"Another communicated his understanding based on observing the [four] truths: observing the signs of the truths, observing realization of the truth [of suffering], observing the truth of the abandonment [of the source of suffering], observing actualization of the truth [of the cessation of suffering], and observing meditative cultivation of the truth [of the path].[5]

"Another communicated his understanding based on observing the constituents: observing the signs of the constituents, observing the various constituents, observing the manifold constituents, observing the cessation of the constituents, and observing the actualization of the cessation of the constituents.[6]

"Another communicated his understanding based on observing the [four] mindful establishments: observing the signs of the mindful establishments, observing the discordances to the mindful establishments and the antidotes, observing the meditative cultivation of the mindful establishments, observing the arising of the mindful establishments that have not yet arisen, and observing the abiding, non-forgetting, continued

པས་ཤེས་པ་བརྗོད་པར་བགྱིད། ཁ་ཅིག་ནི་དྲན་པ་ཉེ་བར་གཞག་པ་རྣམས་ཇི་ལྟ་བ་དེ་བཞིན་དུ། ཁ་ཅིག་ནི་ཡང་དག་པར་སྤོང་བ་རྣམས་དང་། རྫུ་འཕྲུལ་གྱི་རྐང་པ་རྣམས་དང་། དབང་པོ་རྣམས་དང་། སྟོབས་རྣམས་དང་། བྱང་ཆུབ་ཀྱི་ཡན་ལག་རྣམས་དང་། ཁ་ཅིག་ནི་འཕགས་པའི་ལམ་ཡན་ལག་བརྒྱད་པ་དམིགས་པ་དང་། འཕགས་པའི་ལམ་ཡན་ལག་བརྒྱད་པའི་མཚན་མ་དམིགས་པ་དང་། འཕགས་པའི་ལམ་ཡན་ལག་བརྒྱད་པའི་མི་འཐུན་པའི་ཕྱོགས་ཀྱི་གཉེན་པོ་དམིགས་པ་དང་། འཕགས་པའི་ལམ་ཡན་ལག་བརྒྱད་པ་བསྒོམ་པ་དམིགས་པ་དང་། འཕགས་པའི་ལམ་ཡན་ལག་བརྒྱད་པ་མ་སྐྱེས་པ་སྐྱེ་བ་དམིགས་པ་དང་། འཕགས་པའི་ལམ་ཡན་ལག་བརྒྱད་པ་སྐྱེས་པ་གནས་པ་དང་། མི་བསྐྱུད་པ་དང་། སླར་ཞིང་འབྱུང་བ་དང་། འཕེལ་ཞིང་རྒྱས་པར་དམིགས་པས་ཤེས་པ་བརྗོད་པར་བགྱིད་པ་དག་མཐོང་ལགས་སོ། །མཐོང་ནས་ཀྱང་བདག་འདི་སྙམ་བགྱིད་དེ། ཚེ་དང་ལྡན་པ་འདི་དག་ནི་ཆོས་རྣམ་པ་སྣ་ཚོགས་པའི་མངོན་པར་རྟོགས་པ་སྟོན་པས་ཤེས་པ་བརྗོད་པར་བགྱིད་ཅིང་འདི་ལྟར་དོན་དམ་པ་ཐམས་ཅད་དུ་རོ་གཅིག་པའི་མཚན་ཉིད་མ་འཚལ་བས། ཚེ་དང་ལྡན་པ་འདི་དག་ནི་མངོན་པའི་ང་རྒྱལ་ཅན་མངོན་པའི་ང་རྒྱལ་གྱིས་མངོན་དུ་ཟིན་ཅིང་ཤེས་པ་བརྗོད་པར་བགྱིད་པ་ཤ་སྟག་ལགས་སོ་སྙམ་བགྱིད་ལགས་སོ། །བཅོམ་ལྡན་འདས་བཅོམ་ལྡན་འདས་ཀྱི་གང་གི་སྐད་དུ་འདི་སྐད་ཅེས་དོན་དམ་པ་ནི་ཕྲ་བ། ཟབ་པ་རྟོགས་པར་དཀའ་བ། མཆོག་ཏུ་རྟོགས་པར་དཀའ་བ། ཐམས་ཅད་དུ་རོ་གཅིག་པའི་མཚན་ཉིད་ཡིན་ནོ་ཞེས་བཀའ་སྩལ་པ་ཇི་ཙམ་དུ་བཅོམ་ལྡན་

arising, and increasing and extending of the mindful establishments that have arisen.[7]

"Just as that one [observed] the mindful establishments, others [observed] the [four] correct abandonings, the [four] bases of magical abilities, the [five] powers, the [five] forces, and the [seven] branches of enlightenment. Another one communicated his understanding based on observing the eight branches of the path of the Āryas: observing the signs of the eight branches of the path of the Āryas, observing the antidotes to the discordances to the eight branches of the path of the Āryas, observing the meditative cultivation of the eight branches of the path of Āryas, observing the arising of the eight branches of the path of Āryas that have not yet arisen, and observing the abiding, non-forgetting, continued arising, and increasing and extending of the eight branches of the path of the Āryas that have arisen.[8]

"Having seen them, I thought: 'These venerable persons communicate their understandings by describing their manifest realization of the various forms of phenomena, and, in this way, they do not seek the ultimate whose character is all of one taste.[9] Therefore, these venerable persons have conceit; they can only communicate their understanding under the influence of conceit.'

"Bhagavan, regarding what the Bhagavan formerly said: 'The ultimate is profound and subtle, very difficult to realize,

འདས་ཀྱིས་ལེགས་པར་གསུངས་པ་དེ་ནི་ངོ་མཚར་ལགས་ཏེ། བཅོམ་ལྡན་འདས་དོན་དམ་པ་ཐམས་ཅད་དུ་རོ་གཅིག་པའི་མཚན་ཉིད་ནི་བཅོམ་ལྡན་འདས་ཀྱིས་བསྟན་པ་འདི་ཉིད་ལ་ཞུགས་པ། དགེ་སློང་དུ་གྱུར་པའི་སེམས་ཅན་རྣམས་ཀྱིས་ཀྱང་དེ་ལྟར་རྟོགས་པར་དཀའ་བ་ལགས་ན། འདི་ལས་ཕྱིར་རོལ་པའི་མུ་སྟེགས་ཅན་རྣམས་ཀྱིས་ལྟ་སྨོས་ཀྱང་ཅི་འཚལ། བཅོམ་ལྡན་འདས་ཀྱིས་བཀའ་སྩལ་པ། རབ་འབྱོར་དེ་དེ་བཞིན་ནོ། །དེ་དེ་བཞིན་ཏེ། ངས་ནི་དོན་དམ་པ་ཐམས་ཅད་དུ་རོ་གཅིག་པའི་མཚན་ཉིད་ཕྲ་བ། མཆོག་ཏུ་ཕྲ་བ། ཟབ་པ་མཆོག་ཏུ་ཟབ་པ། རྟོགས་པར་དཀའ་བ། མཆོག་ཏུ་རྟོགས་པར་དཀའ་བ། མངོན་པར་རྫོགས་པར་སངས་རྒྱས་ཏེ། མངོན་པར་རྫོགས་པར་སངས་རྒྱས་ནས་ཀྱང་བསྙད་ཅིང་གསལ་བར་བྱས། རྣམ་པར་ཕྱེ་གདགས་པར་བྱས་རབ་ཏུ་བསྟན་ནོ།། དེ་ཅིའི་ཕྱིར་ཞེ་ན། རབ་འབྱོར་ཕུང་པོ་རྣམས་ལ་རྣམ་པར་དག་པའི་དམིགས་པ་གང་ཡིན་པ་དེ་ནི་ངས་དོན་དམ་པ་ཡིན་པར་ཡོངས་སུ་བསྟན་ཅིང་། རབ་འབྱོར་སྐྱེ་མཆེད་རྣམས་དང་། རྟེན་ཅིང་འབྲེལ་བར་འབྱུང་བ་དང་། ཟས་རྣམས་དང་། བདེན་པ་རྣམས་དང་། ཁམས་རྣམས་དང་། དྲན་པ་ཉེ་བར་གཞག་པ་རྣམས་དང་། ཡང་དག་པར་སྤོང་བ་རྣམས་དང་། རྫུ་འཕྲུལ་གྱི་རྐང་པ་རྣམས་དང་། དབང་པོ་རྣམས་དང་། སྟོབས་རྣམས་དང་། བྱང་ཆུབ་ཀྱི་ཡན་ལག་རྣམས་དང་། རབ་འབྱོར་འཕགས་པའི་ལམ་ཡན་ལག་བརྒྱད་པ་ལ་རྣམ་པར་དག་པའི་དམིགས་པ་གང་ཡིན་པ་དེ་ནི་དོན་དམ་པ་ཡིན་པར་ཡོངས་སུ་བསྟན་པའི་ཕྱིར་རོ། །ཕུང་པོ་རྣམས་ལ་རྣམ་པར་དག་པའི་དམིགས་པ་དེ་ཡང་ཐམས་ཅད་དུ་རོ

supremely difficult to realize, and it is of a character that is all of one taste.' What the Bhagavan said so eloquently in this way is wondrous.

"Bhagavan, regarding those who have entered into this very teaching by the Bhagavan that the ultimate is of a character that is everywhere of one taste: Since those sentient beings who are monks have difficulty in understanding in this way, what need is there to mention Tīrthikas who are outside of this [teaching]?"

The Bhagavan replied: "So it is! Subhūti, so it is! I have perfectly and completely realized the ultimate having a character that is all of one taste, which is subtle, supremely subtle, profound, supremely profound, difficult to realize, supremely difficult to realize. Having perfectly and manifestly realized this, I have proclaimed it and made it clear, opened it up and systematized it, and taught it comprehensively.

"Why is this so? Subhūti, I teach that the object of observation for purification of the aggregates is the 'ultimate'.[10] Also, Subhūti, I teach that the ultimate is an object of observation for purification of the sense spheres, dependent origination, the sustenances, the truths, the constituents, the mindful establishments, the correct abandonings, the bases of magical abilities, the powers, the forces, the branches of enlightenment, and, Subhūti, the eight branches of the path of the Āryas. That which is an object of observation for purification of the aggregates is all of one taste; its character does not differ.

གཅིག་པ་སྟེ། མཚན་ཉིད་ཐ་དད་པ་མ་ཡིན་ནོ། །ཕུང་པོ་རྣམས་ལ་ཇི་ལྟ་བ་དེ་བཞིན་དུ་སྐྱེ་མཆེད་རྣམས་ནས། འཕགས་པའི་ལམ་ཡན་ལག་བརྒྱད་པའི་བར་ལ་རྣམ་པར་དག་པའི་དམིགས་པ་དེ་ཡང་ཐམས་ཅད་དུ་རོ་གཅིག་པ་སྟེ། མཚན་ཉིད་ཐ་དད་པ་མ་ཡིན་ནོ། །རབ་འབྱོར་རྣམ་གྲངས་དེས་ན་ཁྱོད་ཀྱིས་འདི་ལྟར་ཐམས་ཅད་དུ་རོ་གཅིག་པའི་མཚན་ཉིད་གང་ཡིན་པ་དེ་ནི་དོན་དམ་པ་ཡིན་པར་རིག་པར་བྱའོ། །རབ་འབྱོར་གཞན་ཡང་དགེ་སློང་རྣལ་འབྱོར་སྤྱོད་པ་ནི་ཕུང་པོ་གཅིག་གི་དེ་བཞིན་ཉིད་དོན་དམ་པའི་ཆོས་བདག་མེད་པ་རབ་ཏུ་རྟོགས་ནས་ཡང་དེ་ལས་གཞན་པའི་ཕུང་པོ་རྣམས་དང་། ཁམས་རྣམས་དང་། སྐྱེ་མཆེད་རྣམས་དང་། རྟེན་ཅིང་འབྲེལ་བར་འབྱུང་བ་དང་། ཟས་རྣམས་དང་། བདེན་པ་རྣམས་དང་། དྲན་པ་ཉེ་བར་གཞག་པ་རྣམས་དང་། ཡང་དག་པར་སྤོང་བ་རྣམས་དང་། རྫུ་འཕྲུལ་གྱི་རྐང་པ་རྣམས་དང་། དབང་པོ་རྣམས་དང་། སྟོབས་རྣམས་དང་། བྱང་ཆུབ་ཀྱི་ཡན་ལག་རྣམས་སོ་སོ་དང་། འཕགས་པའི་ལམ་ཡན་ལག་བརྒྱད་པ་སོ་སོ་ལ་དེ་བཞིན་ཉིད་དོན་དམ་པ་བདག་མེད་པ་ཡོངས་སུ་ཚོལ་བར་མི་བྱེད་ཀྱི་དེ་བཞིན་ཉིད་ཀྱི་རྗེས་སུ་འབྲང་བ་གཉིས་མེད་པའི་ཤེས་པ་ལ་རྟེན་པ་དེ་ཉིད་ཀྱིས་དོན་དམ་པ་ཐམས་ཅད་དུ་རོ་གཅིག་པའི་མཚན་ཉིད་ངེས་པར་འཛིན་པ་དང་། མངོན་པར་རྟོགས་པ་ཕོ་ནར་བྱེད་དེ། རབ་འབྱོར་རྣམ་གྲངས་དེས་ཀྱང་ཁྱོད་ཀྱིས་འདི་ལྟར་ཐམས་ཅད་དུ་རོ་གཅིག་པའི་མཚན་ཉིད་གང་ཡིན་པ་དེ་དོན་དམ་པ་ཡིན་པར་རིག་པར་བྱའོ། །རབ་འབྱོར་གཞན་ཡང་ཇི་ལྟར་ཕུང་པོ་དང་། སྐྱེ་མཆེད་དང་། རྟེན་ཅིང་འབྲེལ་བར་འབྱུང་བ་དང་། ཟས་དང་། བདེན་པ

"Just as it is with the aggregates, so also that which is the object of observation for purification of [phenomena] ranging from the sense spheres up to the eight branches of the path of the Āryas is all of one taste: Its character does not differ. Therefore, Subhūti, know by this form of explanation that whatever is of a character that is all of one taste is the ultimate.

"Moreover, Subhūti, monks who practice yoga, having completely realized the suchness of one aggregate, the selflessness of phenomena that is the ultimate, do not have to seek further for suchness, for the ultimate, and for selflessness in each of the other aggregates, or in the constituents, the sense spheres, dependent origination, in the sustenances, the truths, the mindful establishments, in the correct abandonings, the bases of magical abilities, in the powers, the forces, the branches of enlightenment, or in each of the eight branches of the path of the Āryas.

"They rely on the non-dual understanding that follows suchness. Through just that, they definitely apprehend and manifestly realize the ultimate which is of a character that is all of one taste. Therefore, Subhūti, also know by this form of explanation that whatever is of a character that is all of one taste is the ultimate.

"Furthermore, Subhūti, the aggregates, sense spheres, dependent origination, sustenances, truths, constituents,

དང་། ཁམས་དང་། དྲན་པ་ཉེ་བར་གཞག་པ་དང་། ཡང་དག་པར་སྤོང་བ་དང་། རྫུ་འཕྲུལ་གྱི་རྐང་པ་དང་། དབང་པོ་དང་། སྟོབས་དང་། བྱང་ཆུབ་ཀྱི་ཡན་ལག་འདི་དག་ཕན་ཚུན་མཚན་ཉིད་ཐ་དད་པ་དང་། དེ་ལྟར་འཕགས་པའི་ལམ་ཡན་ལག་བརྒྱད་པ་ཕན་ཚུན་མཚན་ཉིད་ཐ་དད་པ་ཡིན་པ་དེ་བཞིན་དུ་གལ་ཏེ་ཆོས་དེ་དག་གི་དེ་བཞིན་ཉིད་དོན་དམ་པ་ཆོས་བདག་མེད་པ་ཡང་མཚན་ཉིད་ཐ་དད་པ་ཡིན་པར་གྱུར་ན་ནི། དེས་ན་དེ་བཞིན་ཉིད་དོན་དམ་པ་ཆོས་བདག་མེད་པ་ཡང་རྒྱུ་དང་བཅས་པ་ཡིན་ཞིང་རྒྱུ་ལས་བྱུང་བ་ཡིན་པར་འགྱུར་རོ། །རྒྱུ་ལས་བྱུང་བ་ཉིད་ཡིན་ན་ནི་འདུས་བྱས་ཡིན་པར་འགྱུར་རོ། །འདུས་བྱས་ཉིད་ཡིན་ན་ནི་དོན་དམ་པ་ཡིན་པར་མི་འགྱུར་རོ། །དོན་དམ་པ་མ་ཡིན་ན་ནི་དོན་དམ་པ་གཞན་ཞིག་ཡོངས་སུ་བཙལ་དགོས་པར་འགྱུར་རོ། །རབ་འབྱོར་གང་གི་ཕྱིར་དོན་དམ་པ་ཆོས་བདག་མེད་པ་རྒྱུ་ལས་བྱུང་བ་མ་ཡིན་པ་དང་། འདུས་བྱས་མ་ཡིན་པ་དང་། དོན་དམ་པ་མ་ཡིན་པ་མ་ཡིན་པ་དང་། དོན་དམ་པ་དེའི་དོན་དམ་པ་གཞན་ཡོངས་སུ་བཙལ་བར་བྱ་མི་དགོས་ཀྱི་དེ་བཞིན་གཤེགས་པ་རྣམས་བྱུང་ཡང་རུང་མ་བྱུང་ཡང་རུང་སྟེ། རྟག་པ་རྟག་པའི་དུས་དང་། ཐེར་ཟུག་ཐེར་ཟུག་གི་དུས་སུ་ཆོས་གནས་པར་བྱ་བའི་ཕྱིར་ཆོས་རྣམས་ཀྱི་ཆོས་ཉིད་དབྱིངས་དེ་ནི་རྣམ་པར་གནས་པ་ཁོ་ན་ཡིན་པ་དེའི་ཕྱིར། རབ་འབྱོར་རྣམ་གྲངས་དེས་ཀྱང་ཁྱོད་ཀྱིས་འདི་ལྟར་ཐམས་ཅད་དུ་རོ་གཅིག་པའི་མཚན་ཉིད་གང་ཡིན་པ་ནི་དོན་དམ་པ་ཡིན་པར་རིག་པར་བྱའོ། །རབ་འབྱོར་འདི་ལྟ་སྟེ་དཔེར་ན། ནམ་མཁའ་ནི་གཟུགས་ཀྱི་རྣམ་པ་སྣ་ཚོགས་དུ་མ་མཚན་ཉིད་

mindful establishments, correct abandonings, bases of magical abilities, powers, forces, and branches of enlightenment are of mutually different characters, just as the eight branches of the path of the Āryas are of mutually different characters. If, in the same way, the suchness of these phenomena, the ultimate, the selflessness of phenomena were also of different characters, then suchness, the ultimate, the selflessness of phenomena would also be associated with causes and would be produced from causes. If it were produced from causes, it would be compounded. If it were compounded, it would not be the ultimate. If it were not the ultimate it would be necessary to search for another ultimate.

"Therefore, Subhūti, the ultimate, the selflessness of phenomena, is not produced from causes and is not compounded. It is not that which is not the ultimate, and it is not necessary to search for an ultimate other than that ultimate.

"Whether Tathāgatas arise or do not arise, because phenomena abide in permanent, permanent time and in everlasting, everlasting time, the sphere of reality of phenomena alone abides.[11] Therefore, Subhūti, know by this form of explanation that whatever is of a character that is all of one taste is the ultimate.

"Subhūti, for example, with respect to the differing signs, the manifold various aspects of form, space is signless, nonconceptual, and unchanging. It is of a character that is all of

ཐ་དད་པ་ལ་མཚན་མ་མེད་པ་རྣམ་པར་རྟོག་པ་མེད་པ་འགྱུར་བ་མེད་པ་སྟེ། ཐམས་ཅད་དུ་རོ་གཅིག་པའི་མཚན་ཉིད་ཡིན་ནོ། །རབ་འབྱོར་དེ་བཞིན་དུ་དོན་དམ་པ་ཡང་མཚན་ཉིད་ཐ་དད་པའི་ཆོས་རྣམས་ལ་ཐམས་ཅད་དུ་རོ་གཅིག་པའི་མཚན་ཉིད་ཡིན་པར་བལྟ་བར་བྱའོ། །དེ་ནས་བཅོམ་ལྡན་འདས་ཀྱིས་དེའི་ཚེ་ཚིགས་སུ་བཅད་པ་འདི་དག་བཀའ་སྩལ་ཏོ། །དོན་དམ་དེ་ནི་ཐ་དད་མ་ཡིན་ཏེ། །ཀུན་ཏུ་རོ་གཅིག་མཚན་ཉིད་སངས་རྒྱས་གསུང་། །དེ་ལ་གང་དག་ཐ་དད་ཀུན་རྟོག་པ། །དེ་དག་ང་རྒྱལ་གནས་པ་རྨོངས་པ་ཡིན། །རབ་འབྱོར་གྱི་ལེའུ་སྟེ་བཞི་པའོ།། ༎

one taste. Similarly, Subhūti, with respect to phenomena that are of different characters, the ultimate is also to be viewed as being of a character that is all of one taste."[12]

Then the Bhagavan spoke this verse:

"Buddhas teach that the ultimate is undifferentiated
and is of a character all of one taste.
Those who conceptualize difference within it
abide in conceit and are obscured."

This completes the fourth chapter of Subhūti.

Homage to the Tathāgata Buddha Śākyamuni

།བློ་གྲོས་ཡངས་པའི་ལེའུ་སྟེ་ལྔ་པ།

The Questions of Viśālamati

Chapter Five

༄༅། །དེ་ནས་བཅོམ་ལྡན་འདས་ལ་བྱང་ཆུབ་སེམས་དཔའ་བློ་གྲོས་ཡངས་པས་ཞུ་བ་ཞུས་པ། བཅོམ་ལྡན་འདས་བྱང་ཆུབ་སེམས་དཔའ་སེམས་དང་ཡིད་དང་རྣམ་པར་ཤེས་པའི་གསང་བ་ལ་མཁས་པ། བྱང་ཆུབ་སེམས་དཔའ་སེམས་དང་ཡིད་དང་རྣམ་པར་ཤེས་པའི་གསང་བ་ལ་མཁས་པ་ཞེས་བགྱི་ན། བཅོམ་ལྡན་འདས་ཇི་ཙམ་གྱིས་ན་བྱང་ཆུབ་སེམས་དཔའ་སེམས་དང་ཡིད་དང་རྣམ་པར་ཤེས་པའི་གསང་བ་ལ་མཁས་པ་ལགས། དེ་བཞིན་གཤེགས་པ་བྱང་ཆུབ་སེམས་དཔའ་སེམས་དང་ཡིད་དང་རྣམ་པར་ཤེས་པའི་གསང་བ་ལ་མཁས་པར་འདོགས་ན་ཡང་ཇི་ཙམ་གྱིས་འདོགས་ལགས། དེ་སྐད་ཅེས་གསོལ་པ་དང་། བཅོམ་ལྡན་འདས་ཀྱིས་བྱང་ཆུབ་སེམས་དཔའ་བློ་གྲོས་ཡངས་པ་ལ་འདི་སྐད་ཅེས་བཀའ་སྩལ་ཏོ། །བློ་གྲོས་ཡངས་པ་ཁྱོད་དེ་ལྟར་སྐྱེ་བོ་མང་པོ་ལ་ཕན་པ་དང་། སྐྱེ་བོ་མང་པོ་ལ་བདེ་བ་དང་། འཇིག་རྟེན་ལ་སྙིང་བརྩེ་བ་དང་། ལྷ་དང་མིར་བཅས་པའི་སྐྱེ་དགུའི་དོན་དང་ཕན་པ་དང་བདེ་བའི་ཕྱིར་ཞུགས་ཏེ། དེ་བཞིན་གཤེགས་པ་ལ་ཁྱོད་དོན་འདི་ཉིད་འདྲི་བར་སེམས་པ་ནི་ལེགས་སོ་ལེགས་སོ། །བློ་གྲོས་ཡངས་པ་དེའི་ཕྱིར་ཉོན་ཅིག་དང་། སེམས་དང་ཡིད་དང་རྣམ་པར་ཤེས་པའི་གསང་བ་ལ་མཁས་པ་ཁྱོད་ལ་བཤད་པར་བྱའོ། །བློ་གྲོས་ཡངས་པ་འགྲོ་བ་དྲུག་གི་འཁོར་བ་འདི་ན་སེམས་ཅན་གང་དང་གང་དག་སེམས་ཅན་གྱི་རིས་གང་དང་གང་དུ་ཡང་སྒོང་ནས་སྐྱེ་བའི་སྐྱེ་གནས་སམ། ཡང་ན་མངལ་ནས་སྐྱེ་བའམ། ཡང་ན་དྲོད་གཤེར་ལས་སྐྱེ་བའམ། ཡང་ན་རྫུས་ཏེ་སྐྱེ་བའི་སྐྱེ་གནས་སུ་ལུས་མངོན་པར་འགྲུབ་ཅིང་འབྱུང་བར་འགྱུར་བ་དེར་དང་པོར་འདི་ལྟར་ལེན་པ

Then Bodhisattva Viśālamati[1] questioned the Bhagavan: "Bhagavan, when you say, 'Bodhisattvas are wise with respect to the secrets of mind, thought, and consciousness; Bodhisattvas are wise with respect to the secrets of mind, thought, and consciousness,' Bhagavan, just how are Bodhisattvas wise with respect to the secrets of mind, thought, and consciousness?[2] For what reason does the Tathāgata designate a Bodhisattva as wise with respect to the secrets of mind, thought, and consciousness?"

The Bhagavan replied to the Bodhisattva Viśālamati: "Viśālamati, you are involved in [asking] this in order to benefit many beings, to bring happiness to many beings, out of sympathy for the world, and for the sake of the welfare, benefit, and happiness of many beings, including gods and humans. Your intention in questioning the Tathāgata about this subject is good. It is good! Therefore, Viśālamati, listen well and I will describe for you the way [Bodhisattvas] are wise with respect to the secrets of mind, thought, and consciousness.

"Viśālamati, whatever type of sentient being there may be in this cyclic existence with its six kinds of beings, those sentient beings manifest a body and arise within states of birth such as egg-born, or womb-born, or moisture-born, or spontaneously-born.[3]

"Initially, in dependence upon two types of appropriation—the appropriation of the physical sense powers associated

རྣམ་པ་གཉིས་པོ་རྟེན་དང་བཅས་པའི་དབང་པོ་གཟུགས་ཅན་ཡིན་པ་དང་། མཚན་མ་དང་མིང་དང་རྣམ་པར་རྟོག་པ་ལ་ཐ་སྙད་འདོགས་པའི་སྤྲོས་པའི་བག་ཆགས་ཡིན་པ་ལ་རྟེན་ནས། ས་བོན་ཐམས་ཅད་པའི་སེམས་རྣམ་པར་སྨིན་ཅིང་འཇུག་ལ་རྒྱས་ཤིང་འཕེལ་བ་དང་ཡངས་པར་འགྱུར་རོ། །དེ་ལ་གཟུགས་ཅན་གྱི་ཁམས་ན་ནི་ལེན་པ་གཉིག་ཡོད་ལ། གཟུགས་ཅན་མ་ཡིན་པའི་ཁམས་ན་ནི་ལེན་པ་གཉིས་སུ་མེད་དོ། །བློ་གྲོས་ཡངས་པ་རྣམ་པར་ཤེས་པ་དེ་ནི་ལེན་པའི་རྣམ་པར་ཤེས་པ་ཞེས་ཀྱང་བྱ་སྟེ། འདི་ལྟར་དེས་ལུས་འདི་བཟུང་ཞིང་བླངས་པའི་ཕྱིར་རོ། །ཀུན་གཞི་རྣམ་པར་ཤེས་པ་ཞེས་ཀྱང་བྱ་སྟེ། འདི་ལྟར་དེ་ལུས་འདི་ལ་སྦྲུབ་པ་དང་བདེ་བ་གཅིག་པའི་དོན་གྱིས་ཀུན་ཏུ་སྦྱོར་བ་དང་རབ་ཏུ་སྦྱོར་བར་བྱེད་པའི་ཕྱིར་རོ། །སེམས་ཞེས་ཀྱང་བྱ་སྟེ། འདི་ལྟར་དེ་ནི་གཟུགས་དང་སྒྲ་དང་དྲི་དང་རོ་དང་རེག་བྱ་དང་ཆོས་ཀུན་ཏུ་བསྟུགས་པ་དང་ཉེ་བར་བསྟུགས་པ་ཡིན་པའི་ཕྱིར་རོ། །བློ་གྲོས་ཡངས་པ་ལེན་པའི་རྣམ་པར་ཤེས་པ་དེ་ལ་རྟེན་ཅིང་གནས་ནས་རྣམ་པར་ཤེས་པའི་ཚོགས་དྲུག་པོ་འདི་ལྟ་སྟེ། མིག་གི་རྣམ་པར་ཤེས་པ་དང་། རྣ་བ་དང་སྣ་དང་ལྕེ་དང་ལུས་དང་ཡིད་ཀྱི་རྣམ་པར་ཤེས་པ་དག་འབྱུང་ངོ། །དེ་ལ་རྣམ་པར་ཤེས་པ་དང་བཅས་པའི་མིག་དང་གཟུགས་རྣམས་ལ་བརྟེན་ནས། མིག་གི་རྣམ་པར་ཤེས་པ་འབྱུང་སྟེ། མིག་གི་རྣམ་པར་ཤེས་པ་དེ་དང་ལྷན་ཅིག་རྗེས་སུ་འཇུག་པ། དུས་མཚུངས་པ། སྤྱོད་ཡུལ་མཚུངས་པ། རྣམ་པར་རྟོག་པའི་ཡིད་ཀྱི་རྣམ་པར་ཤེས་པ་ཡང་འབྱུང་ངོ། །བློ་གྲོས་ཡངས་པ་དེ་ལ་རྣམ་པར་ཤེས་པ་དང་བཅས་པའི་རྣ་བ་དང་སྣ་དང་ལྕེ་དང་རྣམ་པར་ཤེས་པ

with a support and the appropriation of predispositions which proliferate conventional designations with respect to signs, names, and concepts—the mind which has all seeds ripens; it develops, increases, and expands in its operations.[4] Although two types of appropriation exist in the form realm, appropriation is not twofold in the formless realm.[5]

"Viśālamati, consciousness is also called the 'appropriating consciousness' because it holds and appropriates the body in that way.[6] It is called the 'basis-consciousness' because there is the same establishment and abiding within those bodies.[7] Thus they are wholly connected and thoroughly connected. It is called 'mind' because it collects and accumulates forms, sounds, smells, tastes, and tangible objects.[8]

"Viśālamati, the sixfold collection of consciousness—the eye consciousness, ear consciousness, nose consciousness, tongue consciousness, body consciousness, and mind consciousness—arises depending upon and abiding in that appropriating consciousness. An eye consciousness arises depending on an eye and a form in association with consciousness. Functioning together with that eye consciousness, a conceptual mental consciousness arises at the same time, having the same objective reference.

"Viśālamati, [an ear consciousness, a nose consciousness, a tongue consciousness, and] a bodily consciousness arise depending on an ear, a nose, a tongue, and a body in association

དང་བཅས་པའི་ལུས་དང་རེག་བྱ་རྣམས་ལ་བརྟེན་ནས་ལུས་ཀྱི་རྣམ་པར་ཤེས་པ་འབྱུང་སྟེ།
ལུས་ཀྱི་རྣམ་པར་ཤེས་པ་དེ་དང་ལྷན་ཅིག་རྗེས་སུ་འཇུག་པ། དུས་མཚུངས་པ། སྤྱོད་
ཡུལ་མཚུངས་པ། རྣམ་པར་རྟོག་པའི་ཡིད་ཀྱི་རྣམ་པར་ཤེས་པ་ཡང་འབྱུང་ངོ་། །གལ་
ཏེ་མིག་གི་རྣམ་པར་ཤེས་པ་གཅིག་ལྷན་ཅིག་འབྱུང་ན་ནི་མིག་གི་རྣམ་པར་ཤེས་པ་དང་སྤྱོད་
ཡུལ་མཚུངས་པ། རྣམ་པར་རྟོག་པའི་ཡིད་ཀྱི་རྣམ་པར་ཤེས་པ་གཅིག་པོ་ན་ལྷན་ཅིག་
འབྱུང་ངོ་། །གལ་ཏེ་རྣམ་པར་ཤེས་པའི་ཚོགས་གཉིས་སམ། གསུམ་མམ་བཞི་ལྷན་
ཅིག་གམ། ལྔ་ཅར་ལྷན་ཅིག་འབྱུང་ན་ཡང་དེར་རྣམ་པར་ཤེས་པའི་ཚོགས་ལྔ་པོ་དག་དང་།
སྤྱོད་ཡུལ་མཚུངས་པ་རྣམ་པར་རྟོག་པའི་ཡིད་ཀྱི་རྣམ་པར་ཤེས་པ་ཡང་གཅིག་པོ་ན་ལྷན་
ཅིག་འབྱུང་ངོ་། །བློ་གྲོས་ཡངས་པ་འདི་ལྟ་སྟེ་དཔེར་ན། ཆུའི་ཀླུང་ཆེན་པོ་འབབ་པ་ལ་
གལ་ཏེ་རླབས་ཅིག་འབྱུང་བའི་རྐྱེན་ཉེ་བར་གནས་པར་གྱུར་ན་རླབས་ཀྱང་གཅིག་པོ་ན་
འབྱུང་ངོ་། །གལ་ཏེ་རླབས་གཉིས་སམ། གལ་ཏེ་རབ་ཏུ་མང་པོ་དག་འབྱུང་བའི་རྐྱེན་ཉེ་
བར་གནས་པར་གྱུར་ན་རླབས་རབ་ཏུ་མང་པོ་དག་འབྱུང་ཞིང་ཆུའི་ཀླུང་དེ་རང་གི་རྒྱུན་གྱིས་
རྒྱུན་འཆད་པར་ཡང་མི་འགྱུར་ལ། ཡོངས་སུ་ཟད་པར་ཡང་མི་འགྱུར་རོ། །མེ་ལོང་གི་
དཀྱིལ་འཁོར་ཤིན་ཏུ་ཡོངས་སུ་དག་པ་ལ་ཡང་གལ་ཏེ་གཟུགས་བརྙན་གཅིག་འབྱུང་བའི་
རྐྱེན་ཉེ་བར་གནས་པར་གྱུར་ན། གཟུགས་བརྙན་ཡང་གཅིག་པོ་ན་འབྱུང་ངོ་། །གལ་ཏེ་
གཟུགས་བརྙན་གཉིས་སམ། གལ་ཏེ་རབ་ཏུ་མང་པོ་དག་འབྱུང་བའི་རྐྱེན་ཉེ་བར་གནས་
པར་གྱུར་ན། གཟུགས་བརྙན་རབ་ཏུ་མང་པོ་དག་འབྱུང་ཞིང་མེ་ལོང་གི་དཀྱིལ་འཁོར་དེ་

with consciousness and [sound, smell, taste, and] tangibles. Functioning together with [nose, ear, tongue, and bodily] consciousness, a conceptual mental consciousness arises at the same time, having the same objective reference.

"If there arises one eye consciousness, there arises together with it only one mental consciousness, which has the same object of activity as the eye consciousness. Likewise, if two, three, four, or five consciousnesses arise together, then there still arises, together with them, only one conceptual mental consciousness, which has the same object of activity as the fivefold collection of consciousness.

"Viśālamati, for example, if the causal conditions for the arising of one wave in a great flowing river are present, then just one wave will arise. If the causal conditions for two waves or many waves are present, then multiple waves will arise. But the river's own continuity will not be broken; it will never be entirely stopped.

"If the causal conditions for the arising of a single image in a perfectly clear round mirror are present, then just one image will arise. If the causal conditions for the arising of two images or of many images are present, then multiple images will arise. However, that round mirror will not be transformed into the nature of the image; they will never be fully linked.

"Viśālamati, just as it is with the water and the mirror, if, depending upon and abiding in the appropriating conscious-

གཟུགས་བརྙན་གྱི་དངོས་པོར་ཡོངས་སུ་འགྱུར་བ་ཡང་མ་ཡིན་ལ་ཡོངས་སུ་སྐྱུར་བར་ཡང་མི་མཐོང་ངོ། །བློ་གྲོས་ཡངས་པ་དེ་བཞིན་དུ་ཆུ་ཀླུང་ལྟ་བུ་དང་། མེ་ལོང་ལྟ་བུའི་ལེན་པའི་རྣམ་པར་ཤེས་པ་དེ་ལ་རྟེན་ཅིང་གནས་ནས། གལ་ཏེ་མིག་གི་རྣམ་པར་ཤེས་པ་གཅིག་ལན་ཅིག་འབྱུང་བའི་རྐྱེན་ཉེ་བར་གནས་པར་གྱུར་ན་ཡང་མིག་གི་རྣམ་པར་ཤེས་པ་གཅིག་ཁོ་ན་ལན་ཅིག་འབྱུང་ངོ། །གལ་ཏེ་རྣམ་པར་ཤེས་པའི་ཚོགས་ལྔ་ཅར་གྱི་བར་དག་ལན་ཅིག་འབྱུང་བའི་རྐྱེན་ཉེ་བར་གནས་པར་གྱུར་ན་ཡང་རྣམ་པར་ཤེས་པའི་ཚོགས་ལྔ་ཅར་ལན་ཅིག་འབྱུང་ངོ། །བློ་གྲོས་ཡངས་པ་དེ་ལྟར་བྱང་ཆུབ་སེམས་དཔའ་ཆོས་ཀྱི་ལུགས་ཤེས་པ་ལ་བརྟེན་ཅིང་ཆོས་ཀྱི་ལུགས་ཤེས་པ་ལ་གནས་ནས། སེམས་དང་ཡིད་དང་རྣམ་པར་ཤེས་པའི་གསང་བ་ལ་མཁས་པ་ཡིན་ཡང་དེ་བཞིན་གཤེགས་པ་ནི་བྱང་ཆུབ་སེམས་དཔའ་སེམས་དང་ཡིད་དང་རྣམ་པར་ཤེས་པའི་གསང་བ་ལ་མཁས་པར་འདོགས་ན་དེ་ཙམ་གྱིས་ཐམས་ཅད་ཀྱི་ཐམས་ཅད་དུ་མི་འདོགས་སོ། །བློ་གྲོས་ཡངས་པ་གང་གི་ཕྱིར་བྱང་ཆུབ་སེམས་དཔའ་ནང་གི་སོ་སོ་ནང་གི་ལེན་པ་མི་མཐོང་། ལེན་པའི་རྣམ་པར་ཤེས་པ་ཡང་མི་མཐོང་ལ། དེ་ཡང་ཡང་དག་པ་ཇི་ལྟ་བ་བཞིན་དུ་ཡིན་པ་དང་། ཀུན་གཞི་ཡང་མི་མཐོང་ཀུན་གཞི་རྣམ་པར་ཤེས་པ་ཡང་མི་མཐོང་། བསྐུགས་པ་ཡང་མི་མཐོང་། སེམས་ཀྱང་མི་མཐོང་། མིག་ཀྱང་མི་མཐོང་། གཟུགས་ཀྱང་མི་མཐོང་། མིག་གི་རྣམ་པར་ཤེས་པ་ཡང་མི་མཐོང་། རྣ་བ་ཡང་མི་མཐོང་། སྒྲ་ཡང་མི་མཐོང་། རྣ་བའི་རྣམ་པར་ཤེས་པ་ཡང་མི་མཐོང་། སྣ་ཡང་མི་མཐོང་། དྲི་ཡང་མི་མཐོང་། སྣའི་རྣམ་པར་ཤེས་པ

ness, the causal conditions for the simultaneous arising of one eye consciousness are present, then just one eye consciousness will arise one time. If the causal conditions for the single arising of up to the fivefold assemblage of consciousness are present, then up to that fivefold assemblage of consciousness will also arise one time.

"Viśālamati, it is like this: Bodhisattvas who rely on knowledge of the system of doctrine and abide in knowledge of the system of doctrine are wise with respect to the secrets of mind, thought, and consciousness. However, when the Tathāgata designates Bodhisattvas as being wise with respect to the secrets of mind, thought, and consciousness, it is not only because of this that he designates those Bodhisattvas as being [wise] in all ways.[9]

"Viśālamati, those Bodhisattvas [wise in all ways] do not perceive their own internal appropriators; they also do not perceive an appropriating consciousness, but they are in accord with reality. They also do not perceive a basis, nor do they perceive a basis-consciousness. They do not perceive accumulations, nor do they perceive mind. They do not perceive an eye, nor do they perceive form, nor do they perceive an eye-consciousness. They do not perceive an ear, nor do they perceive a sound, nor do they perceive an ear-consciousness. They do not perceive a nose, nor do they perceive a smell, nor do they perceive a nose-consciousness. They do not perceive a tongue, nor do they perceive a taste, nor do they

ཡང་མི་མཐོང་། ལྕེའང་མི་མཐོང་། རོ་ཡང་མི་མཐོང་། ལྕེའི་རྣམ་པར་ཤེས་པ་ཡང་མི་
མཐོང་། ལུས་ཀྱང་མི་མཐོང་། རེག་བྱ་ཡང་མི་མཐོང་། ལུས་ཀྱི་རྣམ་པར་ཤེས་པ་ཡང་
མི་མཐོང་། བློ་གྲོས་ཡངས་པ་གང་གི་ཕྱིར་བྱང་ཆུབ་སེམས་དཔའ་ནང་གི་སོ་སོ་རང་གི་
ཡིད་ཀྱང་མི་མཐོང་། ཆོས་རྣམས་ཀྱང་མི་མཐོང་། ཡིད་ཀྱི་རྣམ་པར་ཤེས་པ་ཡང་མི་མཐོང་
ལ། དེ་ཡང་ཡང་དག་པ་ཇི་ལྟ་བ་བཞིན་དུ་ཡིན་པ་དེ་ནི། བྱང་ཆུབ་སེམས་དཔའ་དོན་
དམ་པ་ལ་མཁས་པ་ཞེས་བྱ་སྟེ། དེ་བཞིན་གཤེགས་པ་ཡང་བྱང་ཆུབ་སེམས་དཔའ་དོན་
དམ་པ་ལ་མཁས་པ་ནི་སེམས་དང་ཡིད་དང་། རྣམ་པར་ཤེས་པའི་གསང་བ་ལ་མཁས་པ་
ཡིན་པར་འདོགས་སོ། །བློ་གྲོས་ཡངས་པ་དེ་ཙམ་གྱིས་ན་བྱང་ཆུབ་སེམས་དཔའ་སེམས་
དང་ཡིད་དང་རྣམ་པར་ཤེས་པའི་གསང་བ་ལ་མཁས་པ་ཡིན་ལ། དེ་བཞིན་གཤེགས་པ་
བྱང་ཆུབ་སེམས་དཔའ་སེམས་དང་ཡིད་དང་རྣམ་པར་ཤེས་པའི་གསང་བ་ལ་མཁས་པར་
འདོགས་ན་ཡང་དེ་ཙམ་གྱིས་འདོགས་སོ། །དེ་ནས་བཅོམ་ལྡན་འདས་ཀྱིས་དེའི་ཚེ་ཚིགས་
སུ་བཅད་པ་འདི་དག་བཀའ་སྩལ་ཏོ། །ལེན་པའི་རྣམ་པར་ཤེས་པ་ཟབ་ཅིང་ཕྲ། །ས་
བོན་ཐམས་ཅད་ཆུ་བོའི་ཀླུང་ལྟར་འབབ། །བདག་ཏུ་རྟོག་པར་གྱུར་ན་མི་རུང་ཞེས། །བྱིས་
པ་རྣམས་ལ་ངས་ནི་དེ་མ་བསྟན། །བློ་གྲོས་ཡངས་པའི་ལེའུ་སྟེ་ལྔ་པའོ།། ||

perceive a tongue consciousness. They do not perceive a body, nor do they perceive a tangible object, nor do they perceive a bodily consciousness. Viśālamati, these Bodhisattvas do not perceive their own particular thoughts, nor do they perceive phenomena, nor do they perceive a mental consciousness, but they are in accord with reality. These Bodhisattvas are said to be 'wise with respect to the ultimate'. The Tathāgata designates Bodhisattvas who are wise with respect to the ultimate as also being 'wise with respect to the secrets of mind, thought, and consciousness'.

"Viśālamati, this is how Bodhisattvas are wise with respect to the secrets of mind, thought, and consciousness. When the Tathāgata designates Bodhisattvas as being 'wise with respect to the secrets of mind, thought, and consciousness', he designates them as such for this very reason."

Then the Bhagavan spoke this verse:

"If the appropriating consciousness, deep and subtle,
all its seeds flowing like a river,
were conceived as a self, that would not be right.
Thus I have not taught this to children."[10]

This completes the fifth chapter of Viśālamati.

Homage to the Tathāgata Buddha Śākyamuni

།ཡོན་ཏན་འབྱུང་གནས་ཀྱི་ལེའུ་སྟེ་དྲུག་པ།
The Questions of
Guṇākara
Chapter Six

༄༅། །དེ་ནས་བཅོམ་ལྡན་འདས་ལ་བྱང་ཆུབ་སེམས་དཔའ་ཡོན་ཏན་འབྱུང་གནས
ཀྱིས་ཞུ་བ་ཞུས་པ། བཅོམ་ལྡན་འདས་བྱང་ཆུབ་སེམས་དཔའ་ཆོས་རྣམས་ཀྱི་མཚན་ཉིད
ལ་མཁས་པ། བྱང་ཆུབ་སེམས་དཔའ་ཆོས་རྣམས་ཀྱི་མཚན་ཉིད་ལ་མཁས་པ་ཞེས་བགྱི
ན།། བཅོམ་ལྡན་འདས་ཇི་ཙམ་གྱིས་ན་བྱང་ཆུབ་སེམས་དཔའ་ཆོས་རྣམས་ཀྱི་མཚན་ཉིད
ལ་མཁས་པ་ལགས། དེ་བཞིན་གཤེགས་པ་བྱང་ཆུབ་སེམས་དཔའ་ཆོས་རྣམས་ཀྱི་
མཚན་ཉིད་ལ་མཁས་པར་འདོགས་ན་ཡང་ཇི་ཙམ་གྱིས་འདོགས་ལགས། དེ་སྐད་ཅེས
གསོལ་པ་དང་། བཅོམ་ལྡན་འདས་ཀྱིས་བྱང་ཆུབ་སེམས་དཔའ་ཡོན་ཏན་འབྱུང་གནས
ལ་འདི་སྐད་ཅེས་བཀའ་སྩལ་ཏོ། །ཡོན་ཏན་འབྱུང་གནས་ཁྱོད་དེ་ལྟར་སྐྱེ་བོ་མང་པོ་ལ་
ཕན་པ་དང་། སྐྱེ་བོ་མང་པོ་ལ་བདེ་བ་དང་། འཇིག་རྟེན་ལ་སྙིང་བརྩེ་བ་དང་། ལྷ་དང་
མིར་བཅས་པའི་སྐྱེ་དགུའི་དོན་དང་། ཕན་པ་དང་བདེ་བའི་ཕྱིར་ཞུགས་ཏེ། དེ་བཞིན་
གཤེགས་པ་ལ་ཁྱོད་དོན་འདི་ཉིད་འདྲི་བར་སེམས་པ་ནི་ལེགས་སོ་ལེགས་སོ། །ཡོན་ཏན་
འབྱུང་གནས་དེའི་ཕྱིར་ཉོན་ཅིག་དང་། ཆོས་རྣམས་ཀྱི་མཚན་ཉིད་ལ་མཁས་པ་ཁྱོད་ལ་
བཤད་པར་བྱའོ། །ཡོན་ཏན་འབྱུང་གནས་ཆོས་རྣམས་ཀྱི་མཚན་ཉིད་ནི་གསུམ་པོ་འདི་
དག་ཡིན་ཏེ། གསུམ་གང་ཞེ་ན། ཀུན་བརྟགས་པའི་མཚན་ཉིད་དང་། གཞན་གྱི་
དབང་གི་མཚན་ཉིད་དང་། ཡོངས་སུ་གྲུབ་པའི་མཚན་ཉིད་དོ།། །ཡོན་ཏན་འབྱུང་
གནས་དེ་ལ་ཆོས་རྣམས་ཀྱི་ཀུན་བརྟགས་པའི་མཚན་ཉིད་གང་ཞེ་ན། ཇི་ཙམ་དུ་རྗེས་སུ་ཐ
སྙད་གདགས་པའི་ཕྱིར་ཆོས་རྣམས་ཀྱི་ངོ་བོ་ཉིད་དམ་བྱེ་བྲག་ཏུ་མིང་དང་བརྡར་རྣམ་པར

Then Bodhisattva Guṇākara[1] questioned the Bhagavan: "Bhagavan, when you say 'Bodhisattvas are wise with respect to the character of phenomena; Bodhisattvas are wise with respect to the character of phenomena,' Bhagavan, just how are Bodhisattvas wise with respect to the character of phenomena? For what reason does the Tathāgata designate a Bodhisattva as being wise with respect to the character of phenomena?"

The Bhagavan replied to the Bodhisattva Guṇākara: "Guṇākara, you are involved in [asking] this in order to benefit many beings, to bring happiness to many beings, out of sympathy for the world, and for the sake of the welfare, benefit, and happiness of many beings, including gods and humans. Your intention in questioning the Tathāgata about this subject is good! It is good! Therefore, Guṇākara, listen well and I will describe for you how [Bodhisattvas] are wise with respect to the character of phenomena.

"Guṇākara, there are three characteristics of phenomena. What are these three? They are the imputational character, the other-dependent character, and the thoroughly established character.

"Guṇākara, what is the imputational character of phenomena?[2] It is that which is imputed as a name or symbol in terms of the own-being or attributes of phenomena in order to subsequently designate any convention whatsoever.

གཞན་པ་གང་ཡིན་པའོ། །ཡོན་ཏན་འབྱུང་གནས་ཆོས་རྣམས་ཀྱི་གཞན་གྱི་དབང་གི་མཚན་ཉིད་གང་ཞེ་ན། ཆོས་རྣམས་ཀྱི་རྟེན་ཅིང་འབྲེལ་བར་འབྱུང་བ་ཉིད་དེ། འདི་ལྟ་སྟེ་འདི་ཡོད་པས་འདི་འབྱུང་ལ། འདི་སྐྱེས་པའི་ཕྱིར་འདི་སྐྱེ་བ་འདི་ལྟ་སྟེ། མ་རིག་པའི་རྐྱེན་གྱིས་འདུ་བྱེད་རྣམས་ཞེས་བྱ་བ་ནས། དེ་ལྟར་ན་སྡུག་བསྔལ་གྱི་ཕུང་པོ་ཆེན་པོ་འདི་འབའ་ཞིག་པོ་འདི་འབྱུང་བར་འགྱུར་རོ་ཞེས་བྱ་བའི་བར་གང་ཡིན་པའོ། །ཡོན་ཏན་འབྱུང་གནས་ཆོས་རྣམས་ཀྱི་ཡོངས་སུ་གྲུབ་པའི་མཚན་ཉིད་གང་ཞེ་ན། ཆོས་རྣམས་ཀྱི་དེ་བཞིན་ཉིད་གང་ཡིན་པ་སྟེ། བྱང་ཆུབ་སེམས་དཔའ་རྣམས་ཀྱིས་རྟུན་པའི་རྒྱུ་དང་། ལེགས་པར་ཚུལ་བཞིན་ཡིད་ལ་བྱས་པའི་རྒྱུས་དེ་རྟོགས་ཤིང་དེ་རྟོགས་པ་གོམས་པར་བྱས་པ་ཡང་དག་པར་གྲུབ་པས་ཀྱང་བླ་ན་མེད་པ་ཡང་དག་པར་རྫོགས་པའི་བྱང་ཆུབ་ཀྱི་བར་དུ་ཡང་དག་པར་འགྲུབ་པ་གང་ཡིན་པའོ། །ཡོན་ཏན་འབྱུང་གནས་འདི་ལྟ་སྟེ་དཔེར་ན། སྐྱེས་བུ་གང་ཟག་རབ་རིབ་ཅན་གྱི་མིག་ལ་རབ་རིབ་ཀྱི་སྐྱོན་ཆགས་པ་དེ་ལྟ་བུར་ནི་ཀུན་བརྟགས་པའི་མཚན་ཉིད་དུ་བལྟ་བར་བྱའོ། །ཡོན་ཏན་འབྱུང་གནས་འདི་ལྟ་སྟེ་དཔེར་ན། དེ་ཉིད་ལ་རབ་རིབ་ཀྱི་མཚན་མ་སྐྲ་ཤད་འཛིངས་པ་འམ། སྦྲང་མ་འམ། ཏིལ་གྱི་འབྲུ་འམ། སྔོན་པོའི་མཚན་མ་འམ། སེར་པོའི་མཚན་མ་འམ། དམར་པོའི་མཚན་མ་འམ། དཀར་པོའི་མཚན་མ་སྣང་བར་གྱུར་པ་དེ་ལྟ་བུར་ནི་གཞན་གྱི་དབང་གི་མཚན་ཉིད་དུ་བལྟ་བར་བྱའོ། །ཡོན་ཏན་འབྱུང་གནས་འདི་ལྟ་སྟེ་དཔེར་ན། སྐྱེས་བུ་གང་ཟག་དེ་ཉིད་ཀྱི་མིག་ཡོངས་སུ་དག་ཅིང་མིག་ལ་རབ་རིབ་ཀྱི་སྐྱོན་ཆགས་པ་དང་བྲལ་བར་གྱུར་པ་ན། མིག་དེ

"Guṇākara, what is the other-dependent character of phenomena? It is simply the dependent origination of phenomena. It is like this: Because this exists, that arises; because this is produced, that is produced. It ranges from: 'Due to the condition of ignorance, compositional factors [arise],' up to: 'In this way, the whole great assemblage of suffering arises.'[3]

"Guṇākara, what is the thoroughly established character of phenomena? It is the suchness of phenomena. Through diligence and through proper mental application, Bodhisattvas establish realization and cultivate realization of [the thoroughly established character]. Thus it is what establishes [all the stages] up to unsurpassed, complete, perfect enlightenment.[4]

"Guṇākara, for example, the imputational character should be viewed as being like the defects of clouded vision[5] in the eyes of a person with clouded vision. Guṇākara, for example, the other-dependent character should be viewed as being like the appearance of the manifestations of clouded vision in that very [person], manifestations which appear as a net of hairs, or as insects, or as sesame seeds; or as a blue manifestation, or a yellow manifestation, or a red manifestation, or a white manifestation.

"Guṇākara, for example, the thoroughly established character should be viewed as being like the unerring objective reference, the natural objective reference of the eyes when that person's eyes have become pure and free from the defects of clouded vision.

ཉིད་ཀྱི་རང་བཞིན་གྱི་སྤྱོད་ཡུལ་མ་ནོར་བའི་སྤྱོད་ཡུལ་དེ་ལྟ་བུར་ནི་ཡོངས་སུ་གྲུབ་པའི་མཚན་ཉིད་དུ་བལྟ་བར་བྱའོ། །ཡོན་ཏན་འབྱུང་གནས་འདི་ལྟ་སྟེ་དཔེར་ན། ཤེལ་ཤིན་ཏུ་གསལ་བ་ནི་གང་གི་ཚེ་ཚོན་སྔོན་པོ་དང་ཕྲད་པར་གྱུར་པ་དེའི་ཚེ་ནི་ནོར་བུ་རིན་པོ་ཆེ་ཨིན་དནཱི་ལ་དང་། མཐོན་ཀ་ཆེན་པོ་ལྟ་བུར་སྣང་བར་འགྱུར་ཞིང་། ནོར་བུ་རིན་པོ་ཆེ་ཨིན་དྣཱི་ལ་དང་མཐོན་ཀ་ཆེན་པོར་ཡོག་པར་འཛིན་པས་ཀྱང་སེམས་ཅན་རྣམས་རྣམ་པར་རྨོངས་པར་བྱེད་དོ། །གང་གི་ཚེ་ཚོན་དམར་པོ་དང་ཕྲད་པར་གྱུར་པ་དེའི་ཚེ་ནི་ནོར་བུ་རིན་པོ་ཆེ་པདྨ་རཱ་ག་ལྟ་བུར་སྣང་བར་འགྱུར་ཞིང་། ནོར་བུ་རིན་པོ་ཆེ་པདྨ་རཱ་ག་ཏུ་ཡོག་པར་འཛིན་པས་སེམས་ཅན་རྣམས་རྣམ་པར་རྨོངས་པར་བྱེད་དོ། །གང་གི་ཚོན་ཚོན་ལྗང་ཁུ་དང་ཕྲད་པར་གྱུར་པ་དེའི་ཚེ་ནི་ནོར་བུ་རིན་པོ་ཆེ་མརྒད་ལྟ་བུར་སྣང་བར་འགྱུར་ཞིང་། ནོར་བུ་རིན་པོ་ཆེ་མརྒད་དུ་ཡོག་པར་འཛིན་པས་ཀྱང་སེམས་ཅན་རྣམས་རྣམ་པར་རྨོངས་པར་བྱེད་དོ། །གང་གི་ཚེ་ཚོན་སེར་པོ་དང་ཕྲད་པར་གྱུར་པ་དེའི་ཚེ་ནི་གསེར་ལྟ་བུར་སྣང་བར་འགྱུར་ཞིང་། གསེར་དུ་ཡོག་པར་འཛིན་པས་ཀྱང་སེམས་ཅན་རྣམས་རྣམ་པར་རྨོངས་པར་བྱེད་དོ། །ཡོན་ཏན་འབྱུང་གནས་འདི་ལྟ་སྟེ་དཔེར་ན། ཤེལ་ཤིན་ཏུ་གསལ་བ་ཚོན་དང་ཕྲད་པ་དེ་ལྟ་བུར་ནི་གཞན་གྱི་དབང་གི་མཚན་ཉིད་ལ་ཀུན་བརྟགས་པའི་མཚན་ཉིད་ཀྱི་ཐ་སྙད་ཀྱི་བག་ཆགས་སུ་བལྟ་བར་བྱའོ། །འདི་ལྟ་སྟེ་དཔེར་ན། ཤེལ་ཤིན་ཏུ་གསལ་བ་ལ་ནོར་བུ་རིན་པོ་ཆེ་ཨིན་དྣཱི་ལ་དང་། མཐོན་ཀ་ཆེན་པོ་དང་། པདྨ་རཱ་ག་དང་། མརྒད་དང་། གསེར་དུ་ཡོག་པར་འཛིན་པ་ལྟ་བུར་ནི་གཞན་གྱི་དབང་གི་མཚན་ཉིད་ལ་ཀུན་བརྟགས་པའི

"Guṇākara, for example, when a very clear crystal comes in contact with the color blue, it then appears as a precious gem, such as a sapphire or a mahānīla.[6] Further, by mistaking it for a precious gem such as a sapphire or a mahānīla, sentient beings are deluded.

"When it comes in contact with the color red, it then appears as a precious gem such as a ruby and, by mistaking it for a precious gem such as a ruby, sentient beings are deluded. When it comes in contact with the color green, it then appears as a precious gem such as an emerald and, further, by mistaking it for a precious gem such as an emerald, sentient beings are deluded. When it comes in contact with the color gold, it then appears as gold and, further, by mistaking it for gold, sentient beings are deluded.

"Guṇākara, for example, you should see that in the same way as a very clear crystal comes in contact with a color, the other-dependent character comes in contact with the predispositions for conventional designations that are the imputational character. For example, in the same way as a very clear crystal is mistaken for a precious substance such as a sapphire, a mahānīla, a ruby, an emerald, or gold, see how the other-dependent character is apprehended as the imputational character.

"Guṇākara, for example, you should see that the other-dependent nature is like that of very clear crystal. For example, a clear crystal is not thoroughly established in permanent,

མཚན་ཉིད་དུ་འཛིན་པར་བལྟ་བར་བྱའོ། །ཡོན་ཏན་འབྱུང་གནས་འདི་ལྟ་སྟེ་དཔེར་ན།
ཤེལ་ཤིན་ཏུ་གསལ་བ་དེ་ཉིད་ལྟ་བུར་ནི་གཞན་གྱི་དབང་གི་མཚན་ཉིད་བལྟ་བར་བྱའོ། །
འདི་ལྟ་སྟེ་དཔེར་ན། ཤེལ་ཤིན་ཏུ་གསལ་བ་ཉིད་ནོར་བུ་རིན་པོ་ཆེ་ཨིན་ད་ནཱི་ལ་དང་།
མཐོན་ཀ་ཆེན་པོ་དང་པདྨ་རཱ་ག་དང་། མརྐད་དང་། གསེར་གྱི་མཚན་ཉིད་དེར་རྟག་པ
རྟག་པའི་དུས་དང་། ཕྱིར་ཟླུག་ཕྱིར་ཟླུག་གི་དུས་སུ་ཡོངས་སུ་མ་གྲུབ་ཅིང་ངོ་བོ་ཉིད་མེད་པ
དེ་ལྟ་བུར་ནི་གཞན་གྱི་དབང་གི་མཚན་ཉིད་དེ། ཀུན་བརྟགས་པའི་མཚན་ཉིད་དེར་རྟག
པ་རྟག་པའི་དུས་དང་། ཕྱིར་ཟླུག་ཕྱིར་ཟླུག་གི་དུས་སུ་ཡོངས་སུ་མ་གྲུབ་ཅིང་ངོ་བོ་ཉིད་མེད
པ་ཉིད་ཀྱིས་ཡོངས་སུ་གྲུབ་པའི་མཚན་ཉིད་བལྟ་བར་བྱའོ། །ཡོན་ཏན་འབྱུང་གནས་དེ་ལ
མཚན་མ་དང་འབྲེལ་བའི་མིང་ལ་བརྟེན་ནས་ནི་ཀུན་བརྟགས་པའི་མཚན་ཉིད་རབ་ཏུ་ཤེས
སོ། །གཞན་གྱི་དབང་གི་མཚན་ཉིད་ལ་ཀུན་བརྟགས་པའི་མཚན་ཉིད་དུ་མངོན་པར་ཞེན
པ་ལ་བརྟེན་ནས་ནི་གཞན་གྱི་དབང་གི་མཚན་ཉིད་རབ་ཏུ་ཤེས་སོ། །གཞན་གྱི་དབང་གི
མཚན་ཉིད་ལ་ཀུན་བརྟགས་པའི་མཚན་ཉིད་དུ་མངོན་པར་ཞེན་པ་མེད་པ་ལ་བརྟེན་ནས་ནི
ཡོངས་སུ་གྲུབ་པའི་མཚན་ཉིད་རབ་ཏུ་ཤེས་སོ། །ཡོན་ཏན་འབྱུང་གནས་དེ་ལ་བྱང་ཆུབ
སེམས་དཔའ་ཆོས་རྣམས་ཀྱི་གཞན་གྱི་དབང་གི་མཚན་ཉིད་ལ་ཀུན་བརྟགས་པའི་མཚན
ཉིད་ཡང་དག་པ་ཇི་ལྟ་བ་བཞིན་དུ་རབ་ཏུ་ཤེས་ན་མཚན་ཉིད་མེད་པའི་ཆོས་ཡང་དག་པ་ཇི
ལྟ་བ་བཞིན་དུ་རབ་ཏུ་ཤེས་སོ། །ཡོན་ཏན་འབྱུང་གནས་དེ་ལ་བྱང་ཆུབ་སེམས་དཔའི
གཞན་གྱི་དབང་གི་མཚན་ཉིད་ཡང་དག་པ་ཇི་ལྟ་བ་བཞིན་དུ་རབ་ཏུ་ཤེས་ན། ཀུན་ནས

permanent time or in everlasting, everlasting time as having the character of a precious substance like a sapphire, a mahānīla, a ruby, an emerald, or gold, and is without the natures [of such things].

"In the same way, you should see that since the other-dependent character is not thoroughly established in permanent, permanent time, or in everlasting, everlasting time as being the imputational character, and is without its nature, it is the thoroughly established character.

"Guṇākara, in dependence upon names that are connected with signs, the imputational character is known. In dependence upon strongly adhering to the other-dependent character as being the imputational character, the other-dependent character is known. In dependence upon absence of strong adherence to the other-dependent character as being the imputational character, the thoroughly established character is known.[7]

"Guṇākara, when Bodhisattvas know the imputational character as it really is with respect to the other-dependent character of phenomena, then they know characterless phenomena as they really are.

"Guṇākara, when Bodhisattvas know the other-dependent character as it really is, then they know the phenomena of afflicted character as they really are.

ཉོན་མོངས་པའི་མཚན་ཉིད་ཀྱི་ཆོས་ཡང་དག་པ་ཇི་ལྟ་བ་བཞིན་དུ་རབ་ཏུ་ཤེས་སོ། །ཡོན་ཏན་འབྱུང་གནས་དེ་ལ་བྱང་ཆུབ་སེམས་དཔས་ཡོངས་སུ་གྲུབ་པའི་མཚན་ཉིད་ཡང་དག་པ་ཇི་ལྟ་བ་བཞིན་དུ་རབ་ཏུ་ཤེས་ན། རྣམ་པར་བྱང་བའི་མཚན་ཉིད་ཀྱི་ཆོས་ཡང་དག་པ་ཇི་ལྟ་བ་བཞིན་དུ་རབ་ཏུ་ཤེས་སོ། །ཡོན་ཏན་འབྱུང་གནས་དེ་ལ་བྱང་ཆུབ་སེམས་དཔས་གཞན་གྱི་དབང་གི་མཚན་ཉིད་ལ་མཚན་ཉིད་མེད་པའི་ཆོས་ཡང་དག་པ་ཇི་ལྟ་བ་བཞིན་དུ་རབ་ཏུ་ཤེས་ན། ཀུན་ནས་ཉོན་མོངས་པའི་མཚན་ཉིད་ཀྱི་ཆོས་རབ་ཏུ་སྤོང་ངོ། །ཀུན་ནས་ཉོན་མོངས་པའི་མཚན་ཉིད་ཀྱི་ཆོས་རབ་ཏུ་སྤངས་ན་རྣམ་པར་བྱང་བའི་མཚན་ཉིད་ཀྱི་ཆོས་ཐོབ་པར་འགྱུར་ཏེ། ཡོན་ཏན་འབྱུང་གནས་གང་གི་ཕྱིར་བྱང་ཆུབ་སེམས་དཔས་དེ་ལྟར་ཆོས་རྣམས་ཀུན་བརྟགས་པའི་མཚན་ཉིད་དང་གཞན་གྱི་དབང་གི་མཚན་ཉིད་དང་ཡོངས་སུ་གྲུབ་པའི་མཚན་ཉིད་ཡང་དག་པ་ཇི་ལྟ་བ་བཞིན་དུ་རབ་ཏུ་ཤེས་ཤིང་མཚན་ཉིད་མེད་པ་དང་། ཀུན་ནས་ཉོན་མོངས་པའི་མཚན་ཉིད་དང་། རྣམ་པར་བྱང་བའི་མཚན་ཉིད་ཡང་དག་པ་ཇི་ལྟ་བ་བཞིན་དུ་རབ་ཏུ་ཤེས་ལ། མཚན་ཉིད་མེད་པའི་ཆོས་ཡང་དག་པ་ཇི་ལྟ་བ་བཞིན་དུ་རབ་ཏུ་ཤེས་ནས། ཀུན་ནས་ཉོན་མོངས་པའི་མཚན་ཉིད་ཀྱི་ཆོས་རབ་ཏུ་སྤོང་ཞིང་ཀུན་ནས་ཉོན་མོངས་པའི་མཚན་ཉིད་ཀྱི་ཆོས་རབ་ཏུ་སྤངས་ན་རྣམ་པར་བྱང་བའི་མཚན་ཉིད་ཀྱི་ཆོས་འཐོབ་པར་འགྱུར་བ་དེ་ཙམ་གྱིས་ན། བྱང་ཆུབ་སེམས་དཔའ་ཆོས་རྣམས་ཀྱི་མཚན་ཉིད་ལ་མཁས་པ་ཡིན་ལ། དེ་བཞིན་གཤེགས་པ་བྱང་ཆུབ་སེམས་དཔའ་ཆོས་རྣམས་ཀྱི་མཚན་ཉིད་ལ་མཁས་པར་འདོགས་ན་ཡང་དེ་ཙམ་གྱིས་འདོགས་སོ། །དེ་ནས

"Guṇākara, when Bodhisattvas know the thoroughly established character as it really is, then they know the phenomena of purified character as they really are.

"Guṇākara, when Bodhisattvas know characterless phenomena as they really are with respect to the other-dependent character, then they completely abandon phenomena of afflicted character. When they have completely abandoned phenomena of afflicted character, they realize phenomena of purified character.

"Therefore, Guṇākara, Bodhisattvas know the imputational character of phenomena, the other-dependent character, and the thoroughly established character of phenomena as they really are. Once they know characterlessness, the thoroughly afflicted character, and the purified character as they really are, then they know characterless phenomena as they really are. They completely abandon the phenomena of afflicted character, and when they have completely abandoned phenomena of afflicted character, then they realize phenomena of purified character.

"This is how Bodhisattvas are wise with respect to the character of phenomena. When the Tathāgata designates Bodhisattvas as being wise with respect to the character of phenomena, he designates them as such for this very reason."

Then the Bhagavan spoke these verses:

བཅོམ་ལྡན་འདས་ཀྱིས་དེའི་ཚེ་ཚིགས་སུ་བཅད་པ་འདི་དག་བཀའ་སྩལ་ཏོ། །མཚན་ཉིད་མེད་པའི་ཆོས་ནི་རབ་ཤེས་ན། །ཀུན་ནས་ཉོན་མོངས་མཚན་ཉིད་ཆོས་སྤོང་འགྱུར། །ཀུན་ནས་ཉོན་མོངས་ཆོས་ནི་རབ་སྤངས་ན། །ཤིན་ཏུ་རྣམ་དག་མཚན་ཉིད་ཆོས་ཐོབ་འགྱུར། །སྐྱེ་བོ་བག་མེད་ཉེས་བཅོམ་ལེ་ལོ་ཅན། །འདུ་བྱེད་སྐྱོན་ལ་རྟོག་པར་མི་བྱེད་པ། །བརྟན་མེད་གཡོ་བ་ཡོད་པའི་ཆོས་རྣམས་ལ། །རབ་ཏུ་ཉམས་པས་སྙིང་བརྩེར་བྱ་བ་ཡིན། །ཡོན་ཏན་འབྱུང་གནས་ཀྱི་ལེའུ་སྟེ་དྲུག་པའོ།། །།

"When one knows characterless phenomena,
one abandons phenomena of afflicted character.
When one abandons phenomena of afflicted character,
one attains phenomena of pure character.

"Heedless beings, overcome by faults and lazy,
do not consider the faults of compounded phenomena.
Weak regarding stable and fluctuating phenomena,
they are objects of compassion."

This completes the sixth chapter of Guṇākara.

Homage to the Tathāgata Buddha Śākyamuni

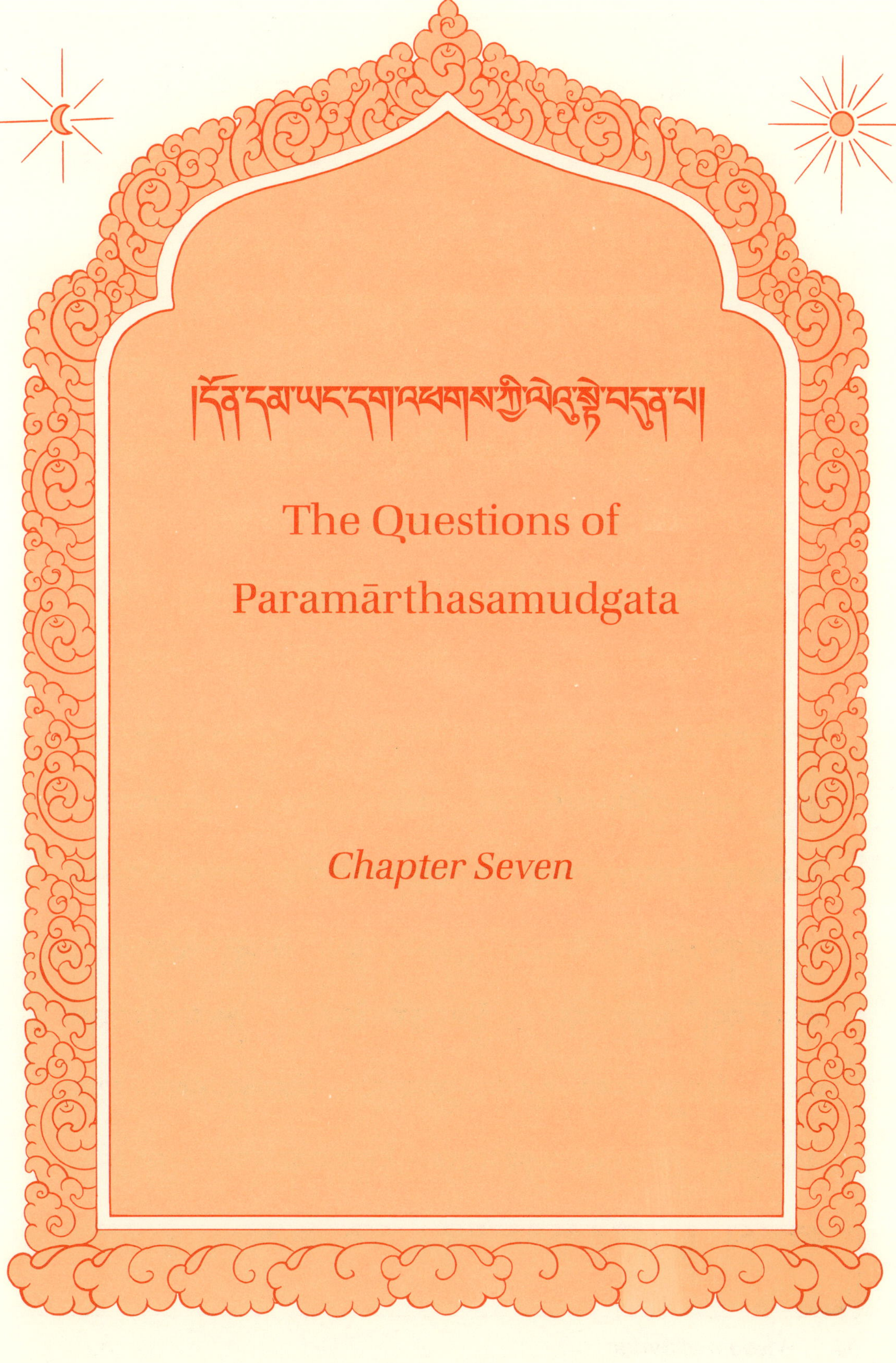

།དོན་དམ་ཡང་དག་འཕགས་ཀྱི་ལེའུ་སྟེ་བདུན་པ།

The Questions of Paramārthasamudgata

Chapter Seven

༄༅། །དེ་ནས་བཅོམ་ལྡན་འདས་ལ་བྱང་ཆུབ་སེམས་དཔའ་དོན་དམ་ཡང་དག
འཕགས་ཀྱིས་འདི་སྐད་ཅེས་གསོལ་ཏོ། །བཅོམ་ལྡན་འདས་འདི་ན་བདག་གཅིག་པུ
དབེན་པ་ཞིག་ན་མཆིས་པའི་ཚེ། སེམས་ཀྱི་ཡོངས་སུ་རྟོག་པ་འདི་ལྟ་བུ་སྐྱེས་ལགས་ཏེ།
བཅོམ་ལྡན་འདས་ཀྱིས་རྣམ་གྲངས་དུ་མར་ཕུང་པོ་རྣམས་ཀྱི་རང་གི་མཚན་ཉིད་ཀྱང་བཀའ
སྩལ། སྐྱེ་བའི་མཚན་ཉིད་དང་། འཇིག་པའི་མཚན་ཉིད་དང་། སྤང་བ་དང་ཡོངས་སུ
ཤེས་པ་ཡང་བཀའ་སྩལ། ཕུང་པོ་རྣམས་ཀྱི་ཇི་ལྟ་བ་བཞིན་དུ་སྐྱེ་མཆེད་རྣམས་དང་།
རྟེན་ཅིང་འབྲེལ་བར་འབྱུང་བ་དང་། ཟས་རྣམས་ཀྱི་ཡང་བཀའ་སྩལ། བཅོམ་ལྡན
འདས་ཀྱིས་རྣམ་གྲངས་དུ་མར་བདེན་པ་རྣམས་ཀྱི་མཚན་ཉིད་ཀྱང་བཀའ་སྩལ། ཡོངས་སུ
ཤེས་པ་དང་། སྤང་བ་དང་། མངོན་དུ་བྱ་བ་དང་། བསྒོམ་པ་ཡང་བཀའ་སྩལ།
བཅོམ་ལྡན་འདས་ཀྱིས་རྣམ་གྲངས་དུ་མར་ཁམས་རྣམས་ཀྱི་རང་གི་མཚན་ཉིད་ཀྱང་བཀའ
སྩལ། ཁམས་སྣ་ཚོགས་པ་ཉིད་དང་། ཁམས་དུ་མ་ཉིད་དང་། སྤང་བ་དང་།
ཡོངས་སུ་ཤེས་པ་ཡང་བཀའ་སྩལ། བཅོམ་ལྡན་འདས་ཀྱིས་རྣམ་གྲངས་དུ་མར་དྲན་པ་ཉེ
བར་གཞག་པ་རྣམས་ཀྱི་རང་གི་མཚན་ཉིད་ཀྱང་བཀའ་སྩལ། མི་མཐུན་པའི་ཕྱོགས་དང་།
གཉེན་པོ་དང་། བསྒོམ་པ་དང་། མ་སྐྱེས་པ་རྣམས་སྐྱེ་བ་དང་། སྐྱེས་པ་རྣམས་གནས
པ་དང་། མི་བསྐྱུད་པ་དང་། སླར་ཞིང་འབྱུང་བ་དང་། འཕེལ་ཞིང་ཡངས་པ་ཉིད་ཀྱང
བཀའ་སྩལ། དྲན་པ་ཉེ་བར་གཞག་པ་རྣམས་ཀྱི་ཇི་ལྟ་བ་བཞིན་དུ་ཡང་དག་པར་སྤོང་བ
རྣམས་དང་། རྫུ་འཕྲུལ་གྱི་རྐང་པ་རྣམས་དང་། དབང་པོ་རྣམས་དང་། སྟོབས་རྣམས

Then Bodhisattva Paramārthasamudgata[1] questioned the Bhagavan: "Bhagavan, when I was in seclusion there arose this thought: 'The Bhagavan has spoken in many ways of the own-character of the aggregates and further spoken of their character of production, their character of disintegration, and their abandonment and realization. Just as he has spoken of the aggregates, he has also spoken of the sense spheres, dependent origination, and the sustenances.

"'The Bhagavan has also spoken in many ways of the [own-] character of the [four] truths and further spoken of the realization [of suffering], abandonment [of the source of suffering], actualization [of the cessation of suffering], and meditative cultivation [of the path].

"'The Bhagavan has also spoken in many ways of the own-character of the constituents and has further spoken of the various constituents, the manifold constituents, and of their abandonment and realization.

"'The Bhagavan has also spoken in many ways of the own-character of the mindful establishments and further spoken of their discordances and antidotes, their meditative cultivation, the production of [the mindful establishments] that have not yet arisen, the abiding of those that have arisen, their non-forgetting, continued arising, increasing, and extending.

"'Just as he spoke of the mindful establishments, he has also spoken of the correct abandonings, the bases of magical

དང༌། བྱང་ཆུབ་ཀྱི་ཡན་ལག་རྣམས་ཀྱི་ཡང་བཀའ་སྩལ། བཅོམ་ལྡན་འདས་ཀྱིས་རྣམ
གྲངས་དུ་མར་འཕགས་པའི་ལམ་ཡན་ལག་བརྒྱད་པའི་རང་གི་མཚན་ཉིད་ཀྱང་བཀའ
སྩལ། མི་འཐུན་པའི་ཕྱོགས་དང༌། གཉེན་པོ་དང༌། བསྒོམ་པ་དང༌། མ་སྐྱེས་པ
རྣམས་སྐྱེ་བ་དང༌། སྐྱེས་པ་རྣམས་གནས་པ་དང༌། མི་བསྐྱུད་པ་དང༌། སླར་ཞིང་འབྱུང
བ་དང༌། འཕེལ་ཞིང་ཡངས་པ་ཉིད་ཀྱང་བཀའ་སྩལ་ལ། བཅོམ་ལྡན་འདས་ཀྱིས
ཐམས་ཅད་ངོ་བོ་ཉིད་མ་མཆིས་པ། ཆོས་ཐམས་ཅད་མ་སྐྱེས་པ། མ་འགགས་པ།
གཟོད་མ་ནས་ཞི་བ། རང་བཞིན་གྱིས་ཡོངས་སུ་མྱ་ངན་ལས་འདས་པ་ཞེས་ཀྱང་བཀའ
སྩལ་ལགས་ན། བཅོམ་ལྡན་འདས་ཀྱིས་ཇི་ལྟར་དགོངས་ནས་ཆོས་ཐམས་ཅད་ངོ་བོ་ཉིད་མ
མཆིས་པ། ཆོས་ཐམས་ཅད་མ་སྐྱེས་པ། མ་འགགས་པ། གཟོད་མ་ནས་ཞི་བ། རང
བཞིན་གྱིས་ཡོངས་སུ་མྱ་ངན་ལས་འདས་པ་ཞེས་བཀའ་སྩལ་སྙམ་བགྱིད་ལགས་ཏེ།
བཅོམ་ལྡན་འདས་ཀྱིས་ཅི་ལ་དགོངས་ནས་ཆོས་ཐམས་ཅད་ངོ་བོ་ཉིད་མ་མཆིས་པ། ཆོས
ཐམས་ཅད་མ་སྐྱེས་པ། མ་འགགས་པ། གཟོད་མ་ནས་ཞི་བ། རང་བཞིན་གྱིས་ཡོངས
སུ་མྱ་ངན་ལས་འདས་པ་ཞེས་བཀའ་སྩལ་པའི་དོན་དེ་ཉིད་བཅོམ་ལྡན་འདས་ལ་བདག
ཡོངས་སུ་ཞུ་ལགས་སོ། །དེ་སྐད་ཅེས་གསོལ་པ་དང༌། བཅོམ་ལྡན་འདས་ཀྱིས་བྱང
ཆུབ་སེམས་དཔའ་དོན་དམ་ཡང་དག་འཕགས་ལ་འདི་སྐད་ཅེས་བཀའ་སྩལ་ཏོ། །དོན
དམ་ཡང་དག་འཕགས་ཁྱོད་ཀྱི་སེམས་ཀྱི་ཡོངས་སུ་རྟོག་པ། དགེ་བ་ཚུལ་བཞིན་སྐྱེས་པ
ལེགས་སོ་ལེགས་སོ། །དོན་དམ་ཡང་དག་འཕགས་ཁྱོད་དེ་ལྟར་སྐྱེ་བོ་མང་པོ་ལ་ཕན་པ

abilities, the powers, the forces, and the branches of enlightenment. The Bhagavan has also spoken in many ways of the own-character of the eight branches of the path of the Āryas and further spoken of their discordances and antidotes, their meditative cultivation, the production of those that have not yet arisen, the abiding of those that have arisen, their non-forgetting, continued arising, increasing, and extending.

"'The Bhagavan has also said that all phenomena lack own-being, that all phenomena are unproduced, unceasing, quiescent from the start, and naturally in a state of nirvāṇa.'

"Then I thought, 'Of what was the Bhagavan thinking when he said, "All phenomena lack own-being; all phenomena are unproduced, unceasing, quiescent from the start, and naturally in a state of nirvāṇa?"

"'Why was the Bhagavan thinking, "All phenomena lack own-being; all phenomena are unproduced, unceasing, quiescent from the start, and naturally in a state of nirvāṇa?"' I ask the Bhagavan the meaning of this."[2]

The Bhagavan replied to Bodhisattva Paramārthasamudgata: "Paramārthasamudgata, your thought, virtuously arisen, is good! It is good! Paramārthasamudgata, you are involved [in asking] this in order to benefit many beings, to bring happiness to many beings, out of sympathy for the world, and for the sake of the welfare, benefit, and happiness of beings,

དང་། སྐྱེ་བོ་མང་པོ་ལ་བདེ་བ་དང་། འཇིག་རྟེན་ལ་སྙིང་བརྩེ་བ་དང་། ལྷ་དང་མིར་
བཅས་པའི་སྐྱེ་དགུའི་དོན་དང་། ཕན་པ་དང་བདེ་བའི་ཕྱིར་ཞུགས་ཏེ། དེ་བཞིན་
གཤེགས་པ་ལ་དོན་འདི་ཉིད་འདྲི་བར་སེམས་པ་ནི་ཡང་ཁྱོད་ལེགས་སོ། །དོན་དམ་ཡང་
དག་འཕགས་དེའི་ཕྱིར་ཉོན་ཅིག་དང་། ངས་ཅི་ལས་དགོངས་ནས་ཆོས་ཐམས་ཅད་ངོ་བོ་
ཉིད་མེད་པ། ཆོས་ཐམས་ཅད་མ་སྐྱེས་པ། མ་འགགས་པ། གཟོད་མ་ནས་ཞི་བ།
རང་བཞིན་གྱིས་ཡོངས་སུ་མྱ་ངན་ལས་འདས་པ་ཞེས་གསུངས་པ་ཁྱོད་ལ་བཤད་པར་བྱའོ། །
དོན་དམ་ཡང་དག་འཕགས་ངས་ཆོས་རྣམས་ཀྱི་ངོ་བོ་ཉིད་མེད་པ་ཉིད་རྣམ་པ་གསུམ་པོ་འདི་
ལྟ་སྟེ། མཚན་ཉིད་ངོ་བོ་ཉིད་མེད་པ་ཉིད་དང་། སྐྱེ་བ་ངོ་བོ་ཉིད་མེད་པ་ཉིད་དང་། དོན་
དམ་པ་ངོ་བོ་ཉིད་མེད་པ་ཉིད་ལས་དགོངས་ནས་ཆོས་ཐམས་ཅད་ངོ་བོ་ཉིད་མེད་པའོ་ཞེས་
བསྟན་ཏོ། །དོན་དམ་ཡང་དག་འཕགས་དེ་ལ་ཆོས་རྣམས་ཀྱི་མཚན་ཉིད་ངོ་བོ་ཉིད་མེད་
པ་ཉིད་གང་ཞེ་ན། ཀུན་བརྟགས་པའི་མཚན་ཉིད་གང་ཡིན་པའོ། །དེ་ཅིའི་ཕྱིར་ཞེ་ན།
འདི་ལྟར་དེ་ནི་མིང་དང་བརྡར་རྣམ་པར་གཞག་པའི་མཚན་ཉིད་ཡིན་གྱི། རང་གི་མཚན་
ཉིད་ཀྱིས་རྣམ་པར་གནས་པ་ནི་མ་ཡིན་པས་དེའི་ཕྱིར་དེ་ནི་མཚན་ཉིད་ངོ་བོ་ཉིད་མེད་པ་ཉིད་
ཅེས་བྱའོ། །དོན་དམ་ཡང་དག་འཕགས་ཆོས་རྣམས་ཀྱི་སྐྱེ་བ་ངོ་བོ་ཉིད་མེད་པ་ཉིད་གང་
ཞེ་ན། ཆོས་རྣམས་ཀྱི་གཞན་གྱི་དབང་གི་མཚན་ཉིད་གང་ཡིན་པའོ། །དེ་ཅིའི་ཕྱིར་ཞེ་ན།
འདི་ལྟར་དེ་ནི་རྐྱེན་གཞན་གྱི་སྟོབས་ཀྱིས་བྱུང་བ་ཡིན་གྱི། བདག་ཉིད་ཀྱིས་ནི་མ་ཡིན་པས
དེའི་ཕྱིར་སྐྱེ་བ་ངོ་བོ་ཉིད་མེད་པ་ཉིད་ཅེས་བྱའོ། །དོན་དམ་ཡང་དག་འཕགས་ཆོས་རྣམས

including gods and humans. Your intention in questioning the Tathāgata about this subject is good! Therefore, Paramārthasamudgata, listen well and I will explain to you what I was thinking when I said: 'All phenomena lack an own-being; all phenomena are unproduced, unceasing, quiescent from the start, and naturally in a state of nirvāṇa.'

"Paramārthasamudgata, thinking of the three types of lack of own-being of phenomena—the lack of own-being in terms of character, the lack of own-being in terms of production, and an ultimate lack of own-being—I taught, 'All phenomena lack own-being.'

"Paramārthasamudgata, what is the lack of own-being in terms of character of phenomena? It is the imputational character. Why is this? The [imputational character] is a character posited as names and symbols, but it does not subsist by way of its own character. Therefore, it is the 'lack of own-being in terms of character'.

"Paramārthasamudgata, what is the lack of own-being in terms of production of phenomena? It is the other-dependent character of phenomena. Why is this? The [other-dependent character] arises through the force of other conditions and not by itself. Therefore, it is the 'lack of own-being in terms of production'.

"Paramārthasamudgata, what is an ultimate lack of own-being of phenomena? Phenomena that are dependently

གྱི་དོན་དམ་པ་ངོ་བོ་ཉིད་མེད་པ་ཉིད་གང་ཞེ་ན། རྟེན་ཅིང་འབྲེལ་བར་འབྱུང་བའི་ཆོས་གང་དག་སྐྱེ་བ་ངོ་བོ་ཉིད་མེད་པ་ཉིད་ཀྱིས་ངོ་བོ་ཉིད་མེད་པ་དེ་དག་ནི་དོན་དམ་པའི་ངོ་བོ་ཉིད་མེད་པ་ཉིད་ཀྱིས་ངོ་བོ་ཉིད་མེད་པ་ཡང་ཡིན་ནོ། །དེ་ཅིའི་ཕྱིར་ཞེ་ན། དོན་དམ་ཡང་དག་འཕགས་ཆོས་རྣམས་ལ་རྣམ་པར་དག་པའི་དམིགས་པ་གང་ཡིན་པ་དེ་ནི་ངས་དོན་དམ་པ་ཡིན་པར་ཡོངས་སུ་བསྟན་ལ། གཞན་གྱི་དབང་གི་མཚན་ཉིད་དེ་ནི་རྣམ་པར་དག་པའི་དམིགས་པ་མ་ཡིན་པས་དེའི་ཕྱིར་དོན་དམ་པའི་ངོ་བོ་ཉིད་མེད་པ་ཉིད་ཅེས་བྱའོ། །དོན་དམ་ཡང་དག་འཕགས་གཞན་ཡང་ཆོས་རྣམས་ཀྱི་ཡོངས་སུ་གྲུབ་པའི་མཚན་ཉིད་གང་ཡིན་པ་དེ་ཡང་དོན་དམ་པ་ངོ་བོ་ཉིད་མེད་པ་ཉིད་ཅེས་བྱའོ། །དེ་ཅིའི་ཕྱིར་ཞེ་ན། དོན་དམ་ཡང་དག་འཕགས་ཆོས་རྣམས་ཀྱི་ཆོས་བདག་མེད་པ་གང་ཡིན་པ་དེ་ནི། དེ་དག་གི་ངོ་བོ་ཉིད་མེད་པ་ཉིད་ཅེས་བྱ་སྟེ། དེ་ནི་དོན་དམ་པ་ཡིན་ལ། དོན་དམ་པ་ནི་ཆོས་ཐམས་ཅད་ཀྱི་ངོ་བོ་ཉིད་མེད་པ་ཉིད་ཀྱིས་རབ་ཏུ་ཕྱེ་བ་ཡིན་པས་དེའི་ཕྱིར་དོན་དམ་པ་ངོ་བོ་ཉིད་མེད་པ་ཉིད་ཅེས་བྱའོ། །དོན་དམ་ཡང་དག་འཕགས་དེ་ལ་འདི་ལྟ་སྟེ་དཔེར་ན། ནམ་མཁའི་མེ་ཏོག་ཇི་ལྟ་བ་དེ་ལྟ་བུར་ནི་མཚན་ཉིད་ངོ་བོ་ཉིད་མེད་པ་ཉིད་བལྟ་བར་བྱའོ། །དོན་དམ་ཡང་དག་འཕགས་དེ་ལ་འདི་ལྟ་སྟེ་དཔེར་ན། སྒྱུ་མ་བྱས་པ་ཇི་ལྟ་བ་དེ་ལྟ་བུར་ནི་སྐྱེ་བ་ངོ་བོ་ཉིད་མེད་པ་ཉིད་ཀྱང་བལྟ་བར་བྱ། དོན་དམ་པ་ངོ་བོ་ཉིད་མེད་པ་ཉིད་དེ་ལས་གཅིག་ཀྱང་བལྟ་བར་བྱའོ། །དོན་དམ་ཡང་དག་འཕགས་དེ་ལ་འདི་ལྟ་སྟེ་དཔེར་ན། ནམ་མཁའི་གཟུགས་ཀྱི་ངོ་བོ་ཉིད་མེད་པ་ཉིད་ཙམ་གྱིས་རབ་ཏུ་ཕྱེ་བ་དང་། ཐམས་ཅད་དུ

originated lack an own-being due to the lack of own-being in terms of production. They also lack own-being due to an ultimate lack of own-being. Why is this? Paramārthasamudgata, I teach that whatever is an object of observation for purification of phenomena is the ultimate.[3] Since the other-dependent character is not an object of observation for purification, it is an 'ultimate lack of own-being'.

"Moreover, Paramārthasamudgata, the thoroughly established character of phenomena is also 'an ultimate lack of own-being'. Why is this? Paramārthasamudgata, that which is the 'selflessness of phenomena' of phenomena is known as their 'lack of own-being'. That is the ultimate. Since the ultimate is distinguished as the lack of own-being of all phenomena, it is an 'ultimate lack of own-being'.

"Paramārthasamudgata, for example, you should view lack of own-being in terms of character as being like a sky-flower.[4] For example, Paramārthasamudgata, you should also view the lack of own-being in terms of production as being like a magical apparition.

"The ultimate lack of own-being should be viewed as being something other than those [first two characters]. For example, Paramārthasamudgata, just as [space] is distinguished by being just the lack of own-being of forms in space and as pervading everywhere, in the same way the ultimate lack of

སོང་བ་ཇི་ལྟ་བ་དེ་ལྟ་བུར་ནི་དོན་དམ་པ་ངོ་བོ་ཉིད་མེད་པ་ཉིད་ལས་ཆོས་བདག་མེད་པས་རབ་ཏུ་ཕྱེ་བ་དང་ཐམས་ཅད་དུ་སོང་བ་གཅིག་བལྟ་བར་བྱ་སྟེ། དོན་དམ་ཡང་དག་འཕགས་རས་ངོ་བོ་ཉིད་མེད་པ་ཉིད་རྣམ་པ་གསུམ་པོ་དེ་དག་ལས་དགོངས་ནས་ཆོས་ཐམས་ཅད་ངོ་བོ་ཉིད་མེད་པའོ་ཞེས་བསྟན་ཏོ། །དོན་དམ་ཡང་དག་འཕགས་དེ་ལ་མཚན་ཉིད་ངོ་བོ་ཉིད་མེད་པ་ཉིད་ལས་དགོངས་ནས། ངས་ཆོས་ཐམས་ཅད་མ་སྐྱེས་པ། མ་འགགས་པ། གཟོད་མ་ནས་ཞི་བ། རང་བཞིན་གྱིས་ཡོངས་སུ་མྱ་ངན་ལས་འདས་པའོ་ཞེས་བསྟན་ཏོ། །དེ་ཅིའི་ཕྱིར་ཞེ་ན། དོན་དམ་ཡང་དག་འཕགས་འདི་ལྟར་རང་གི་མཚན་ཉིད་ཀྱིས་མེད་པ་གང་ཡིན་པ་དེ་ནི་མ་སྐྱེས་པ་ཡིན། མ་སྐྱེས་པ་གང་ཡིན་པ་དེ་ནི་མ་འགགས་པ་ཡིན། མ་སྐྱེས་པ་དང་མ་འགགས་པ་གང་ཡིན་པ་དེ་ནི། གཟོད་མ་ནས་ཞི་བ་ཡིན། གཟོད་མ་ནས་ཞི་བ་གང་ཡིན་པ་དེ་ནི་རང་བཞིན་གྱིས་ཡོངས་སུ་མྱ་ངན་ལས་འདས་པ་ཡིན། རང་བཞིན་གྱིས་ཡོངས་སུ་མྱ་ངན་ལས་འདས་པ་གང་ཡིན་པ་དེ་ལ་ནི། ཡོངས་སུ་མྱ་ངན་ལས་བཟླ་བར་བྱ་བ་ཅུང་ཟད་ཀྱང་མེད་དེ། དེའི་ཕྱིར་མཚན་ཉིད་ངོ་བོ་ཉིད་མེད་པ་ཉིད་ལ་དགོངས་ནས་ངས་ཆོས་ཐམས་ཅད་མ་སྐྱེས་པ། མ་འགགས་པ། གཟོད་མ་ནས་ཞི་བ། རང་བཞིན་གྱིས་ཡོངས་སུ་མྱ་ངན་ལས་འདས་པའོ་ཞེས་བསྟན་ཏོ། །དོན་དམ་ཡང་དག་འཕགས་ཡང་དོན་དམ་པ་ངོ་བོ་ཉིད་མེད་པ་ཉིད་ཆོས་བདག་མེད་པས་རབ་ཏུ་ཕྱེ་བ་ལས་དགོངས་ནས་ངས་ཆོས་ཐམས་ཅད་མ་སྐྱེས་པ། མ་འགགས་པ། གཟོད་མ་ནས་ཞི་བ། རང་བཞིན་གྱིས་ཡོངས་སུ་མྱ་ངན་ལས་འདས་པའོ་ཞེས་བསྟན་ཏོ། །

own-being is distinguished by being the selflessness of phenomena and should be viewed as all-pervasive and unitary.

"Paramārthasamudgata, thinking of those three types of lack of own-being, I taught, 'All phenomena lack own-being.'

"Paramārthasamudgata, thinking of lack of own-being in terms of character, I taught: 'All phenomena are unproduced, unceasing, quiescent from the start, and naturally in a state of nirvāṇa.' Why is this?

"Paramārthasamudgata, that which does not exist by way of its own character is not produced. That which is not produced does not cease. That which is not produced and does not cease is quiescent from the start. That which is quiescent from the start is naturally in a state of nirvāṇa. That which is naturally in a state of nirvāṇa does not have even the slightest remainder that could pass beyond sorrow. Therefore, thinking of lack of own-being in terms of character, I taught, 'All phenomena are unproduced, unceasing, quiescent from the start, and naturally in a state of nirvāṇa.'[5]

"Moreover, Paramārthasamudgata, thinking of an ultimate lack of own-being that is distinguished by being the selflessness of phenomena, I taught: 'All phenomena are unproduced, unceasing, quiescent from the start, and naturally in a state of nirvāṇa.' Why is this?

"An ultimate lack of own-being, distinguished by being the selflessness of phenomena, abides solely in permanent,

དེ་ཅིའི་ཕྱིར་ཞེ་ན། འདི་ལྟར་དོན་དམ་པ་ངོ་བོ་ཉིད་མེད་པ་ཉིད་ཆོས་བདག་མེད་པས་རབ་ཏུ་ཕྱེ་བ་ནི་རྟག་པ་རྟག་པའི་དུས་དང་། ཐེར་ཟུག་ཐེར་ཟུག་གི་དུས་སུ་རྣམ་པར་གནས་པ་ཁོ་ན་ཡིན་ལ། དེ་ནི་ཆོས་རྣམས་ཀྱི་ཆོས་ཉིད་དུ་འདུས་མ་བྱས་པ་ཉོན་མོངས་པ་ཐམས་ཅད་དང་བྲལ་བ་ཡིན་ཏེ། རྟག་པ་རྟག་པའི་དུས་དང་། ཐེར་ཟུག་ཐེར་ཟུག་གི་དུས་སུ་ཆོས་ཉིད་དེ་ཉིད་ཀྱིས་རྣམ་པར་གནས་པ་འདུས་མ་བྱས་པ་གང་ཡིན་པ་དེ་ནི་འདུས་མ་བྱས་པའི་ཕྱིར་མ་སྐྱེས་པ་དང་མ་འགགས་པ་ཡིན་ལ། དེ་ནི་ཉོན་མོངས་པ་ཐམས་ཅད་དང་བྲལ་བའི་ཕྱིར་གཟོད་མ་ནས་ཞི་བ་དང་། རང་བཞིན་གྱིས་ཡོངས་སུ་མྱ་ངན་ལས་འདས་པ་ཡིན་ཏེ། དེའི་ཕྱིར་དོན་དམ་པ་ངོ་བོ་ཉིད་མེད་པ་ཉིད་ཆོས་བདག་མེད་པས་རབ་ཏུ་ཕྱེ་བ་ལས་དགོངས་ནས་ངས་ཆོས་ཐམས་ཅད་མ་སྐྱེས་མ་འགགས་པ། གཟོད་མ་ནས་ཞི་བ། རང་བཞིན་གྱིས་ཡོངས་སུ་མྱ་ངན་ལས་འདས་པའོ་ཞེས་བསྟན་ཏོ། །དོན་དམ་ཡང་དག་འཕགས་ངས་ནི་སེམས་ཅན་གྱི་ཁམས་ན་སེམས་ཅན་རྣམས་ཀྱིས་ཀུན་བརྟགས་པའི་ངོ་བོ་ཉིད་ངོ་བོ་ཉིད་ཀྱིས་ཐ་དད་པར་མཐོང་ཞིང་གཞན་གྱི་དབང་གི་ངོ་བོ་ཉིད་དང་། ཡོངས་སུ་གྲུབ་པའི་ངོ་བོ་ཉིད་ཀྱང་ངོ་བོ་ཉིད་ཀྱིས་ཐ་དད་པར་མཐོང་ན། དེའི་ཕྱིར་ངོ་བོ་ཉིད་མེད་པ་ཉིད་རྣམ་པ་གསུམ་མི་འདོགས་ཀྱི། སེམས་ཅན་རྣམས་གཞན་གྱི་དབང་དང་། ཡོངས་སུ་གྲུབ་པའི་ངོ་བོ་ཉིད་ལ་ཀུན་བརྟགས་པའི་ངོ་བོ་ཉིད་དུ་སྒྲོ་བཏགས་ནས། གཞན་གྱི་དབང་དང་། ཡོངས་སུ་གྲུབ་པའི་ངོ་བོ་ཉིད་ལ་ཀུན་བརྟགས་པའི་ངོ་བོ་ཉིད་ཀྱི་མཚན་ཉིད་རྗེས་སུ་ཐ་སྙད་འདོགས་ཏེ། ཇི་ལྟ་ཇི་ལྟར་རྗེས་སུ་ཐ་སྙད་འདོགས་པ་དེ་ལྟ་དེ་ལྟར་ཐ་སྙད་བཏགས་པས

permanent time and everlasting, everlasting time. That uncompounded reality of phenomena is free from all afflictions. That which is uncompounded, which abides in permanent, permanent time and everlasting, everlasting time due to being this very reality, is uncompounded. Therefore, it is unproduced and unceasing. Because it is free from all afflictions, it is quiescent from the start and is naturally in a state of nirvāṇa. Therefore, thinking of an ultimate lack of own-being that is distinguished by being the selflessness of phenomena, I taught, 'All phenomena are unproduced, unceasing, quiescent from the start, and naturally in a state of nirvāṇa.'

"Paramārthasamudgata, I do not designate the three types of lack of own-being because sentient beings in the realms of sentient beings view the own-being of the imputational as distinct [from the other-dependent and the thoroughly established character] in terms of own-being; or because they view the other-dependent and the thoroughly established as distinct in terms of own-being. Superimposing the own-being of the imputational onto the own-being of the other-dependent and the thoroughly established, sentient beings subsequently attribute conventions of the character of the own-being of the imputational to the own-being of the other-dependent and the thoroughly established.

"To the extent that they subsequently attribute such conventions, their minds are infused with conventional designations. Thereafter, because of being bound to conventional

ཡོངས་སུ་བསྒོས་པའི་སེམས་ཐ་སྙད་བཏགས་པ་དང་རྗེས་སུ་འབྲེལ་བའམ། ཐ་སྙད་བཏགས་པ་བག་ལ་ཉལ་གྱིས་གཞན་གྱི་དབང་དང་ཡོངས་སུ་གྲུབ་པའི་ངོ་བོ་ཉིད་ལ་ཀུན་བརྟགས་པའི་ངོ་བོ་ཉིད་ཀྱི་མཚན་ཉིད་དུ་མངོན་པར་ཞེན་ནོ། །ཇི་ལྟ་ཇི་ལྟར་མངོན་པར་ཞེན་པ་དེ་ལྟ་དེ་ལྟར་གཞན་གྱི་དབང་གི་ངོ་བོ་ཉིད་ལ་ཀུན་བརྟགས་པའི་ངོ་བོ་ཉིད་དུ་མངོན་པར་ཞེན་པའི་རྒྱུ་དེ་དང་། རྐྱེན་དེས་ཕྱི་མ་ལ་གཞན་གྱི་དབང་གི་ངོ་བོ་ཉིད་ཀུན་ཏུ་བསྐྱེད་དེ། གཞི་དེས་ན། ཉོན་མོངས་པའི་ཀུན་ནས་ཉོན་མོངས་པས་ཀྱང་ཀུན་ནས་ཉོན་མོངས་པར་འགྱུར། ལས་ཀྱི་ཀུན་ནས་ཉོན་མོངས་པ་དང་སྐྱེ་བའི་ཀུན་ནས་ཉོན་མོངས་པས་ཀྱང་ཀུན་ནས་ཉོན་མོངས་པར་འགྱུར་ཞིང་། ཡུན་རིང་པོར་ཡང་ན་སེམས་ཅན་དམྱལ་བ་རྣམས་དང་། ཡང་ན་དུད་འགྲོ་རྣམས་སམ། ཡང་ན་ཡི་དྭགས་རྣམས་སམ། ཡང་ན་ལྷ་རྣམས་སམ། ཡང་ན་ལྷ་མ་ཡིན་རྣམས་སམ། ཡང་ན་མི་རྣམས་ཀྱི་ནང་དུ་ཀུན་ཏུ་རྒྱུག་ཅིང་འཁོར་བར་འགྱུར་ཏེ། འཁོར་བ་ལས་མི་འདའ་བའི་ཕྱིར་རོ། །དོན་དམ་ཡང་དག་འཕགས་དེ་ལ་སེམས་ཅན་གང་དག་དང་པོ་ཉིད་ནས་དགེ་བའི་རྩ་བ་མ་བསྐྱེད་པ། སྒྲིབ་པ་ཡོངས་སུ་མ་དག་པ་རྒྱུད་ཡོངས་སུ་མ་སྨིན་པ་མོས་པ་མི་མང་བ། བསོད་ནམས་དང་ཡེ་ཤེས་ཀྱི་ཚོགས་ཡང་དག་པར་མ་གྲུབ་པ་དེ་དག་ལ་ནི་ང་སྐྱེ་བ་ངོ་བོ་ཉིད་མེད་པ་ཉིད་ལས་བརྩམས་ནས་ཆོས་སྟོན་ཏེ། དེ་དག་གིས་ཆོས་དེ་ཐོས་ནས་རྟེན་ཅིང་འབྲེལ་བར་འབྱུང་བའི་འདུ་བྱེད་རྣམས་ལ་མི་རྟག་པ་ཉིད་དུ་ཤེས་ཤིང་མི་བརྟན་པ་ཉིད་དང་། ཡིད་བརྟན་དུ་མི་རུང་བ་ཉིད་དང་། འགྱུར་བའི་ཆོས་ཉིད་དུ་ཤེས་ནས། འདུ་བྱེད་ཐམས་ཅད་ལས་ཡིད་སྐྱོ་བར་བྱེད་

designations or due to predispositions toward conventional designations, they strongly adhere to the character of the own-being of the imputational as the own-being of the other-dependent and the thoroughly established.

"To the extent that they strongly adhere [to this], they strongly adhere to the own-being of the imputational as the own-being of the other-dependent. Due to these causes and conditions, in the future [this view of] the own-being of the other-dependent proliferates. Based on this, the afflictive afflictions give rise to further afflictions.

"The afflictions of actions and the afflictions of birth give rise to further afflictions. For a long time sentient beings will wander, transmigrating among hell beings, or animals, or hungry ghosts, or gods, or asuras, or humans. They will not pass beyond cyclic existence.

"Paramārthasamudgata, I initially teach doctrines starting with the lack of own-being in terms of production to those beings who have not generated roots of virtue, who have not purified obstructions, who have not ripened their continuums, who do not have much conviction, and who have not completed the accumulations of merit and wisdom. When they hear those doctrines, they understand dependently originated compounded phenomena as being impermanent. They know them to be phenomena that are unstable, unworthy of confidence, and changeable, whereupon they develop aversion and antipathy toward all compounded phenomena.

སྐྱོ་བར་བྱེད་དོ། །ཡིད་སྡང་བར་བྱས། སྐྱོ་བར་བྱས་ནས་སྡིག་པ་ལས་ཕྱིར་ལྡོག་སྟེ། དེ་དག་སྡིག་པ་གང་ཡིན་པ་དེ་མི་བྱེད་ཅིང་དགེ་བ་ལ་སྟེན་པར་བྱེད་དོ། །དགེ་བ་ལ་བསྟེན་པའི་རྒྱུས་དགེ་བའི་རྩ་བ་མ་བསྐྱེད་པ་རྣམས་ནི་སྐྱེད་དོ། །སྒྲིབ་པ་ཡོངས་སུ་མ་བྱང་བ་རྣམས་ཀྱང་ཡོངས་སུ་སྦྱོང་ངོ་། །རྒྱུད་ཡོངས་སུ་མ་སྨིན་པ་ཡང་ཡོངས་སུ་སྨིན་པར་བྱེད་དོ། །གཞི་དེས་མོས་པ་མང་ཞིང་བསོད་ནམས་དང་ཡེ་ཤེས་ཀྱི་ཚོགས་ཡང་དག་པར་གྲུབ་པར་འགྱུར་རོ། །དེ་དག་དེ་ལྟར་དགེ་བའི་རྩ་བ་བསྐྱེད་པ་ནས་བསོད་ནམས་དང་ཡེ་ཤེས་ཀྱི་ཚོགས་ཀྱི་བར་དུ་ཡང་དག་པར་འགྲུབ་མོད་ཀྱི། འོན་ཀྱང་སྐྱེ་བ་ངོ་བོ་ཉིད་མེད་པ་ཉིད་དེ་ལ་མཚན་ཉིད་ངོ་བོ་ཉིད་མེད་པ་ཉིད་དང་། དོན་དམ་པ་ངོ་བོ་ཉིད་མེད་པ་ཉིད་རྣམ་པ་གཉིས་ཡང་དག་པ་ཇི་ལྟ་བ་བཞིན་དུ་མི་ཤེས་པས། འདུ་བྱེད་ཐམས་ཅད་ལས་ཡང་དག་པར་སྐྱོ་བར་མི་འགྱུར། ཡང་དག་པར་འདོད་ཆགས་དང་བྲལ་བར་མི་འགྱུར། ཡང་དག་པར་རྣམ་པར་གྲོལ་བར་མི་འགྱུར་ཞིང་། ཉོན་མོངས་པའི་ཀུན་ནས་ཉོན་མོངས་པ་ལས་ཀྱང་ཡོངས་སུ་གྲོལ་བར་མི་འགྱུར། ལས་ཀྱི་ཀུན་ནས་ཉོན་མོངས་པ་ལས་ཀྱང་ཡོངས་སུ་གྲོལ་བར་མི་འགྱུར། སྐྱེ་བའི་ཀུན་ནས་ཉོན་མོངས་པ་ལས་ཀྱང་ཡོངས་སུ་གྲོལ་བར་མི་འགྱུར་བས། ཡང་དེ་བཞིན་གཤེགས་པ་དེ་དག་ལ་འདི་ལྟ་སྟེ། མཚན་ཉིད་ངོ་བོ་ཉིད་མེད་པ་ཉིད་དང་། དོན་དམ་པ་ངོ་བོ་ཉིད་མེད་པ་ཉིད་ལས་བརྩམས་ནས་འདི་ལྟར་འདུ་བྱེད་ཐམས་ཅད་ལས་ཡང་དག་པར་སྐྱོ་བར་བྱ་བ་དང་། འདོད་ཆགས་དང་བྲལ་བར་བྱ་བ་དང་། རྣམ་པར་གྲོལ་བར་བྱ་བ་དང་། ཉོན་མོངས་པའི་ཀུན་ནས་ཉོན་མོངས་པ་ལས

"Having developed aversion and antipathy, they turn away from wrong-doing. They do not commit any wrong-doing, and they adhere to virtue. Because of adhering to virtue, they generate roots of virtue that were not previously generated. They also purify obscurations that were not previously purified. They also ripen their continuums, which were not previously ripened. On that basis, they have great conviction, and they complete the accumulations of merit and wisdom.

"In that way they complete everything from the generation of roots of virtue up to the accumulation of merit and wisdom. However, because they do not understand, as they are, the two aspects pertaining to lack of own-being in terms of production—lack of own-being in terms of character and ultimate lack of own-being—they do not become wholly averse toward all compounded phenomena. They do not become separated from attachment. They do not become fully liberated. They do not become fully liberated from the afflictive afflictions nor fully liberated from the afflictions of actions nor fully liberated from the afflictions of birth.

"The Tathāgatha further teaches them doctrines beginning with lack of own-being in terms of character and ultimate lack of own-being. Thus they become wholly averse toward all compounded phenomena, separated from attachment, and liberated; they pass beyond the afflictive afflictions, pass beyond the afflictions of actions, and pass beyond the afflictions of birth.

ཡང་དག་པར་བཟླ་བ་དང་། ལས་ཀྱི་ཀུན་ནས་ཉོན་མོངས་པ་ལས་ཡང་དག་པར་བཟླ་བ
དང་། སྐྱེ་བའི་ཀུན་ནས་ཉོན་མོངས་པ་ལས་ཡང་དག་པར་བཟླ་བའི་ཕྱིར་ཆོས་སྟོན་ཏོ། །
དེ་དག་གིས་ཆོས་དེ་ཐོས་ནས་གཞན་གྱི་དབང་གི་ངོ་བོ་ཉིད་ལ་ཀུན་བརྟགས་པའི་ངོ་བོ་ཉིད
ཀྱི་མཚན་ཉིད་དུ་མངོན་པར་ཞེན་པ་མེད་པས་སྐྱེ་བ་ངོ་བོ་ཉིད་མེད་པ་ཉིད་དང་། དེ་ལ་མཚན
ཉིད་ངོ་བོ་ཉིད་མེད་པ་ཉིད་དུ་དོན་དམ་པ་ངོ་བོ་ཉིད་མེད་པ་ཉིད་དུ་མོས་པར་བྱེད། རབ་ཏུ
རྣམ་པར་འབྱེད་པར་བྱེད། ཇི་ལྟ་བ་བཞིན་དུ་རྟོགས་པར་བྱེད་ཅིང་འདི་ལྟ་སྟེ། ཐ་སྙད
བཏགས་པས་ཡོངས་སུ་མ་བསྒོས་པའི་ཤེས་པ་ཐ་སྙད་བཏགས་པ་དང་རྗེས་སུ་འབྲེལ་བ
མེད་ཅིང་ཐ་སྙད་བག་ལ་ཉལ་མེད་པའི་ཤེས་པས་གཞན་གྱི་དབང་གི་མཚན་ཉིད་དེ། ཚེ
འདི་ལ་ཤེས་པའི་སྟོབས་བསྐྱེད་པ་དང་། ཕྱི་མ་ལ་རྒྱུད་ཡང་དག་པར་ཆད་པས་འགོག
པར་བྱེད་དེ། གཞི་དེས་འདུ་བྱེད་ཐམས་ཅད་ལས་ཡང་དག་པར་སྐྱོ་བ་དང་། ཡང་དག
པར་འདོད་ཆགས་དང་བྲལ་བ་དང་། ཡང་དག་པར་རྣམ་པར་གྲོལ་བར་འགྱུར་ཞིང་ཉོན
མོངས་པའི་ཀུན་ནས་ཉོན་མོངས་པ་དང་། ལས་ཀྱི་ཀུན་ནས་ཉོན་མོངས་པ་དང་། སྐྱེ་བའི
ཀུན་ནས་ཉོན་མོངས་པ་ལས་ཀྱང་ཡོངས་སུ་གྲོལ་བར་འགྱུར་རོ། །དོན་དམ་ཡང་དག
འཕགས་དེ་ལ་སེམས་ཅན་ཉན་ཐོས་ཀྱི་ཐེག་པའི་རིགས་ཅན་རྣམས་ཀྱིས་ཀྱང་ལམ་འདི་ཉིད
དང་སྒྲུབ་པ་འདི་ཉིད་ཀྱིས་གྲུབ་པ་དང་། བདེ་བ་བླ་ན་མེད་པའི་མྱ་ངན་ལས་འདས་པ
འཐོབ་པར་འགྱུར་ལ། སེམས་ཅན་རང་སངས་རྒྱས་ཀྱི་ཐེག་པའི་རིགས་ཅན་རྣམས་དང་།
དེ་བཞིན་གཤེགས་པའི་རིགས་ཅན་རྣམས་ཀྱིས་ཀྱང་ལམ་འདི་ཉིད་དང་སྒྲུབ་པ་འདི་ཉིད

"Hearing these doctrines, they do not strongly adhere to the own-being of the other-dependent as being of the character of the own-being of the imputational. Further, they become confident that the lack of own-being in terms of production does not exist as an ultimate own-being in the sense that it is just an absence of own-being in terms of character with respect to those [phenomena]. They fully distinguish this. They realize it as it is and, in this way, their understanding is not infused with conventional designations. Thereafter, because they are not bound to conventional designations and because their understanding is free from predispositions toward conventions, in this lifetime they produce the ability to understand the other-dependent character. In future lives they achieve cessation through cutting off the continuum.

"Based on this, they become wholly averse toward all compounded phenomena, free from attachment, and liberated. They become fully liberated from the afflictive afflictions, the afflictions of actions, and the afflictions of birth.

"Paramārthasamudgata, through just this path and through just this attainment, even sentient beings of the Śrāvaka lineage attain the establishment and abiding of unsurpassed nirvāṇa. Through just this path and through just this attainment, sentient beings of the Pratyekabuddha lineage and sentient beings of the Tathāgata lineage also attain the establishment and abiding of unsurpassed nirvāṇa. Thus, there is a

གྱིས་གྲུབ་པ་དང་བདེ་བ་བླ་ན་མེད་པའི་མྱ་ངན་ལས་འདས་པ་ཐོབ་པར་འགྱུར་བས་འདི་ནི་ཉན་ཐོས་དང་རང་སངས་རྒྱས་དང་བྱང་ཆུབ་སེམས་དཔའ་རྣམས་ཀྱི་རྣམ་པར་དག་པའི་ལམ་གཅིག་པ་ཡིན་ལ། རྣམ་པར་དག་པ་གཅིག་སྟེ། གཉིས་པ་གང་ཡང་མེད་པས་ངས་དེ་ལས་དགོངས་ནས་ཐེག་པ་གཅིག་པུ་བསྟན་ཏོ། སེམས་ཅན་གྱི་ཁམས་ན་སེམས་ཅན་རང་བཞིན་གྱིས་དབང་པོ་རྟུལ་པོ་རྣམས་དང་། དབང་པོ་འབྲིང་རྣམས་དང་། དབང་པོ་རྣོན་པོ་རྣམས་ཀྱི་སེམས་ཅན་གྱི་རིགས་སྣ་ཚོགས་དག་ཀྱང་མེད་པ་མ་ཡིན་ནོ། །དོན་དམ་ཡང་དག་འཕགས་ཉན་ཐོས་ཀྱི་རིགས་ཅན་གང་ཟག་ཞི་བའི་བགྲོད་པ་གཅིག་པུ་པ་ནི་སངས་རྒྱས་ཐམས་ཅད་བརྩོན་པ་དང་ལྡན་པར་གྱུར་ཀྱང་བྱང་ཆུབ་ཀྱི་སྙིང་པོ་ལ་བཞག་སྟེ། བླ་ན་མེད་པ་ཡང་དག་པར་རྫོགས་པའི་བྱང་ཆུབ་ཐོབ་པར་བྱར་མི་ནུས་སོ། །དེ་ཅིའི་ཕྱིར་ཞེ་ན། འདི་ལྟར་དེ་ནི་སྙིང་རྗེ་ཤིན་ཏུ་ཆུང་བ་དང་། སྡུག་བསྔལ་གྱིས་ཤིན་ཏུ་འཇིགས་པའི་ཕྱིར་རང་བཞིན་གྱིས་རིགས་དམན་པ་ཁོ་ན་ཡིན་པའི་ཕྱིར་རོ། །དེ་ཇི་ལྟར་སྙིང་རྗེ་ཤིན་ཏུ་ཆུང་བ་དེ་བཞིན་དུ་སེམས་ཅན་གྱི་དོན་བྱ་བ་ལ་ཤིན་ཏུ་མི་ཕྱོགས་པར་འགྱུར་རོ། །ཇི་ལྟར་སྡུག་བསྔལ་གྱིས་ཤིན་ཏུ་འཇིགས་པ་དེ་བཞིན་དུ་འདུ་བྱེད་མངོན་པར་འདུ་བྱ་བ་ཐམས་ཅད་ལ་ཤིན་ཏུ་མི་ཕྱོགས་པར་འགྱུར་རོ། །སེམས་ཅན་གྱི་དོན་བྱ་བ་ལ་ཤིན་ཏུ་མི་ཕྱོགས་པ་དང་། འདུ་བྱེད་མངོན་པར་འདུ་བྱ་བ་ཐམས་ཅད་ལ་ཤིན་ཏུ་མི་ཕྱོགས་པ་ནི་བླ་ན་མེད་པ་ཡང་དག་པར་རྫོགས་པའི་བྱང་ཆུབ་ཏུ་ངས་མ་བསྟན་ཏོ། །དེའི་ཕྱིར་ཞི་བའི་བགྲོད་པ་གཅིག་པུ་པ་ཞེས་བྱའོ། །ཉན་ཐོས་བྱང་ཆུབ་ཏུ་ཡོངས་སུ་འགྱུར་བ་གང་ཡིན་པ་དེ་ནི་ངས

single path of purification for Śrāvakas, Pratyekabuddhas, and Bodhisattvas, and there is a single purification. There is no other. Thinking of that, therefore, I have taught that there is a single vehicle. Yet in the realms of sentient beings, there are various types of sentient beings, such as those who are naturally of weak faculties, or naturally of middling faculties, or naturally of sharp faculties.

"Paramārthasamudgata, even if all the Buddhas were to attempt to establish someone having the Śrāvaka lineage, who proceeds solely towards peacefulness, in the heart of enlightenment, that person would be unable to attain unsurpassed, perfect enlightenment.[6] Why is this? Due to extremely limited compassion and great fear of suffering, that one is simply by nature of an inferior lineage. Just as his compassion is extremely limited, so he turns away from the welfare of sentient beings. Just as he is extremely afraid of suffering, so he turns away from all the activities of compounded phenomena.

"I do not describe those who turn away from the welfare of sentient beings and who turn away from all the activities of compounded existence as unsurpassably, perfectly enlightened. They are 'those who seek peace for themselves alone'.

"[However] I teach that Śrāvakas who evolve with respect to enlightenment are a type of Bodhisattva.[7] It is like this: Having become liberated from the afflictive obstructions, they

རྣམ་གྲངས་ཀྱིས་བྱང་ཆུབ་སེམས་དཔའ་ཡིན་པར་བསྟན་ཏེ། འདི་ལྟར་དེ་ནི་ཉོན་མོངས་པའི་སྒྲིབ་པ་ལས་རྣམ་པར་གྲོལ་ནས། དེ་བཞིན་གཤེགས་པ་རྣམས་ཀྱིས་བསྐུལ་ན། ཤེས་བྱའི་སྒྲིབ་པ་ལས་སེམས་རྣམ་པར་གྲོལ་བར་བྱེད་པའི་ཕྱིར་རོ། །དེ་ནི་དང་པོར་བདག་གི་དོན་ལ་སྦྱོར་བའི་རྣམ་པས་ཉོན་མོངས་པའི་སྒྲིབ་པ་ལས་རྣམ་པར་གྲོལ་ཏེ། དེའི་ཕྱིར་དེ་བཞིན་གཤེགས་པས་དེ་ཉན་ཐོས་ཀྱི་རིགས་སུ་འདོགས་སོ། །དོན་དམ་ཡང་དག་འཕགས་འདི་ལྟར་ངའི་ཆོས་འདུལ་བ་ལེགས་པར་གསུངས་པ་ཤིན་ཏུ་བྲུ་ནོམ་པ་བསམ་པ་ཤིན་ཏུ་རྣམ་པར་དག་པ་སྟོན་པ། ཆོས་ལེགས་པར་བསྟན་པ་ལ་ནི་སེམས་ཅན་རྣམས་ཀྱི་མོས་པའི་རིམ་པ་ཡང་སྣང་སྟེ། དོན་དམ་ཡང་དག་འཕགས་འདི་ལ་དེ་བཞིན་གཤེགས་པ་ནི་ངོ་བོ་ཉིད་མེད་པ་ཉིད་རྣམ་པ་གསུམ་པོ་དེ་དག་ཉིད་ལས་དགོངས་ནས་དྲང་བའི་དོན་གྱི་མདོ་བརྗོད་པའི་རྣམ་པས་འདི་ལྟ་སྟེ། ཆོས་ཐམས་ཅད་ངོ་བོ་ཉིད་མེད་པ། ཆོས་ཐམས་ཅད་མ་སྐྱེས་པ། མ་འགགས་པ། གཟོད་མ་ནས་ཞི་བ། རང་བཞིན་གྱིས་ཡོངས་སུ་མྱ་ངན་ལས་འདས་པའོ་ཞེས་ཆོས་སྟོན་ཏོ། །དེ་ལ་སེམས་ཅན་གང་དག་དགེ་བའི་རྩ་བ་ཆེན་པོ་བསྐྱེད་པ་དང་། སྒྲིབ་པ་ཡོངས་སུ་དག་པ། རྒྱུད་ཡོངས་སུ་སྨིན་པ། མོས་པ་མང་བ། བསོད་ནམས་དང་ཡེ་ཤེས་ཀྱི་ཚོགས་ཆེན་པོ་ཡང་དག་པར་གྲུབ་པ་དེ་དག་གིས་ནི་ཆོས་དེ་ཐོས་ན་ངའི་དགོངས་ཏེ་བཤད་པ་ཡང་དག་པ་ཇི་ལྟ་བ་བཞིན་དུ་རབ་ཏུ་ཤེས་ཤིང་། ཆོས་དེ་ལ་ཡང་ཆོས་ཤེས་པར་འགྱུར་ལ། དོན་དེ་ཡང་ཤེས་རབ་ཀྱིས་ཡང་དག་པ་ཇི་ལྟ་བ་བཞིན་དུ་རྟོགས་པར་འགྱུར་ཞིང་། དེ་རྟོགས་པ་བསྒོམས་པས་ཀྱང་མྱུར་བ་མྱུར་བ་གོ་ནར་ཤིན་ཏུ

liberate their minds from the obstructions to omniscience when they are encouraged by the Tathāgatas. Thus, the Tathāgata designates those who initially work for their own benefit and are freed from the afflictive obstructions as being of the Śrāvaka lineage.[8]

"Paramārthasamudgata, it is like this: My disciplinary doctrine is explained well, is complete, and is taught with a very pure thought. With respect to this well-taught doctrine, degrees of conviction appear among sentient beings.[9]

"Paramārthasamudgata, thinking of just these three types of lack of own-being, through the teachings that are Sūtras of interpretable meaning, the Tathāgata taught such doctrines as: 'All phenomena lack own-being; all phenomena are unproduced, unceasing, quiescent from the start, and naturally in a state of nirvāṇa.'

"When those sentient beings who have generated great roots of virtue, purified the obstructions, ripened their continuums, who have great conviction and have completed the great accumulations of merit and wisdom[10] hear those doctrines, they understand the teaching just as it is in accordance with my thought.[11] They further understand those doctrines to be doctrine. Through wisdom they also realize the meaning just as it is. Through cultivating realization of that [meaning], they rapidly attain the final state. Regarding [these doctrines],

མཐར་ཐུག་པ་ཉིད་རྗེས་སུ་འཐོབ་པར་འགྱུར་ཏེ། དེ་ལ་ཡང་ཨ་ལ་ལ་བཅོམ་ལྡན་འདས་དེ
ནི་ཡང་དག་པར་རྫོགས་པའི་སངས་རྒྱས་ཡིན་ཏེ། དེས་ནི་ཆོས་ཐམས་ཅད་ལེགས་པར
མངོན་པར་རྫོགས་པར་སངས་རྒྱས་སོ་ཞེས་དད་པ་ཐོབ་པར་འགྱུར་རོ། །དེ་ལ་སེམས་ཅན
གང་དག་དགེ་བའི་རྩ་བ་མ་བསྐྱེད་པ་དང་། སྒྲིབ་པ་ཡོངས་སུ་མ་དག་པ་དང་། རྒྱུད
ཡོངས་སུ་མ་སྨིན་པ་དང་། མོས་པ་ཆེན་པོ་མ་ཡིན་པ། བསོད་ནམས་དང་ཡེ་ཤེས་ཀྱི
ཚོགས་ཆེན་པོ་ཡང་དག་པར་མ་གྲུབ་པ། དྲང་པོ་དང་དྲང་པོའི་རང་བཞིན་ཅན། རྟོག་པ
དང་སེལ་མི་ནུས་པ། རང་གི་ལྟ་བ་མཆོག་ཏུ་འཛིན་པར་མི་གནས་པ་དེ་དག་གིས་ནི་ཆོས
དེ་ཐོས་ན་དའི་དགོངས་ཏེ་བཤད་པ་ཡང་ཡང་དག་པ་ཇི་ལྟ་བ་བཞིན་དུ་རབ་ཏུ་མི་ཤེས་མོད
ཀྱི། འོན་ཀྱང་ཆོས་དེ་ལ་མོས་པར་བྱེད་ཅིང་དད་པ་ཡང་འཐོབ་སྟེ། མདོ་སྡེ་འདི་དག་ནི
དེ་བཞིན་གཤེགས་པས་གསུངས་པ་ཟབ་པ་ཟབ་པར་སྣང་བ། སྟོང་པ་ཉིད་དང་ལྡན་པ
མཐོང་བར་དཀའ་བ། རྟོགས་པར་དཀའ་བ། བརྟག་མི་ནུས་པ། རྟོག་གེའི་སྤྱོད་ཡུལ
མ་ཡིན་པ། ཞིབ་མོ་བརྟགས་པའི་མཁས་པ་མཛངས་པས་རིག་པ་ཡིན་ནོ་ཞེས་མོས་པར
བྱེད་དོ། །མདོ་སྡེ་དེ་དག་གི་དོན་བསྟན་པ་དག་གི་དོན་བསྟན་པ་དག་ལ་བདག་མི་ཤེས
སོ་སྙམ་ནས་འདུག་སྟེ། འདི་སྐད་ཅེས་སངས་རྒྱས་ཀྱི་བྱང་ཆུབ་ནི་ཟབ་ཆོས་རྣམས་ཀྱི་ཆོས
ཉིད་ཀྱང་ཟབ་སྟེ། དེ་བཞིན་གཤེགས་པ་ཉིད་ཀྱིས་མཁྱེན་གྱི་བདག་ཅག་གིས་ནི་མི་ཤེས
སོ། །དེ་བཞིན་གཤེགས་པ་རྣམས་ཀྱི་ཆོས་བསྟན་པ་ནི་སེམས་ཅན་རྣམས་ལ་མོས་པ་སྣ
ཚོགས་ཀྱིས་འཇུག་པ་ཡིན་ཏེ། དེ་བཞིན་གཤེགས་པ་རྣམས་ནི་མཁྱེན་པ་དང་གཟིགས

they develop faith, [thinking], 'Ah! The Bhagavan is completely and perfectly enlightened. He is completely and perfectly enlightened with respect to all phenomena.'

"When sentient beings who have not generated great roots of virtue, have not purified the obstructions, have not ripened their continuums, do not have great conviction, and have not completed the great accumulations of merit and wisdom, who are honest and have an honest nature, who are unable to remove conceptuality, who are not fixated on holding their own view to be supreme, [when such beings] hear those doctrines, they do not understand the teaching just as it is in accordance with my thought.

"Still, [these beings] develop conviction and also attain faith in these doctrines. They are convinced that: 'These Sūtras taught by the Tathāgata are profound, brilliantly profound, are endowed with emptiness, are difficult to perceive, difficult to understand, unanalyzable, not subject to dispute, and are known by the wise capable of fine discernment and by the astute.'

"They think: 'We do not understand the meaning of those Sūtras or the meaning of those teachings.' They think: 'The enlightenment of the Buddha is profound. The reality of phenomena is also profound. The Tathāgata alone knows; we do not understand. The doctrinal teaching of Tathāgatas influences sentient beings according to their diverse beliefs. The Tathāgatas' wisdom and perception are infinite, whereas our

པ་མཐའ་ཡས་པ་ཡིན་གྱི། བདག་ཅག་གི་ཤེས་པ་དང་མཐོང་བ་ནི་བ་ལང་གི་རྗེས་ཙམ་མོ
སྙམ་ནས། དེ་དག་མདོ་སྡེ་དེ་རྣམས་ལ་གུས་པར་བྱས་ཏེ་ཡི་གེར་འདྲི་བར་ཡང་བྱེད།
ཡི་གེར་བྲིས་ནས་འཆང་བར་ཡང་བྱེད། ཀློག་པར་ཡང་བྱེད། ཡང་དག་པར་འགོད
པར་ཡང་བྱེད། མཆོད་པར་ཡང་བྱེད། ལུང་ནོད་པར་ཡང་བྱེད། འདོན་པར་ཡང
བྱེད། ཁ་ཏོན་དུ་ཡང་བྱེད་མོད་ཀྱི། འདི་ལྟར་ངའི་དགོངས་ཏེ་བཤད་པ་ཟབ་མོ་འདི་མ
རྟོགས་པའི་ཕྱིར་བསྒོམ་པའི་རྣམ་པས་སྦྱོར་བར་མི་ནུས་སོ། །དེ་དག་གཞི་དེས་ན་བསོད
ནམས་ཀྱི་ཚོགས་ཀྱིས་ཀྱང་འཕེལ་བར་འགྱུར། ཡེ་ཤེས་ཀྱི་ཚོགས་ཀྱིས་ཀྱང་འཕེལ་བར
འགྱུར་ལ། གོང་དུ་ཡང་རྒྱུད་ཡོངས་སུ་མ་སྨིན་པ་དག་ཀྱང་ཡོངས་སུ་སྨིན་པར་བྱེད་དོ། །
ཅི་སྟེ་སེམས་ཅན་དེ་དག་ལས་སེམས་ཅན་གང་དག་བསོད་ནམས་དང་ཡེ་ཤེས་ཀྱི་ཚོགས
ཆེན་པོའི་བར་དུ་ཡང་དག་པར་གྲུབ་པ་མ་ཡིན་ཡང་དྲང་པོ་དང་དྲང་པོའི་རང་བཞིན་ཅན་མ
ཡིན་ལ། རྟོག་པ་དང་སེལ་ནུས་ལ། རང་གི་ལྟ་བ་མཆོག་ཏུ་འཛིན་པར་གནས་པ་དེ་དག
གིས་ནི་ཆོས་དེ་ཐོས་ན་ངའི་དགོངས་ཏེ་བཤད་པ་ཟབ་མོ་ཡང་དག་པ་ཇི་ལྟ་བ་བཞིན་མི་ཤེས
ཏེ། ཆོས་དེ་ལ་མོས་ཀྱང་ཆོས་འདི་དག་ཐམས་ཅད་ནི་ངོ་བོ་ཉིད་མེད་པ་ཁོ་ན་ཡིན་ནོ། །
ཆོས་འདི་དག་ཐམས་ཅད་ནི་མ་སྐྱེས་པ་ཁོ་ནའོ། །མ་འགགས་པ་ཁོ་ནའོ། །གཟོད་མ
ནས་ཞི་བ་ཁོ་ནའོ། །རང་བཞིན་གྱིས་ཡོངས་སུ་མྱ་ངན་ལས་འདས་པ་ཁོ་ནའོ་ཞེས་ཆོས་ཀྱི
དོན་ལ་སྒྲ་ཇི་བཞིན་ཁོ་ནར་མངོན་པར་ཞེན་པར་བྱེད་དེ། དེ་དག་གཞི་དེས་ན་ཆོས་ཐམས
ཅད་ལ་མེད་པར་ལྟ་བ་དང་། མཚན་ཉིད་མེད་པར་ལྟ་བ་འཐོབ་པར་འགྱུར་ཏེ། མེད་པར

understanding and perception are like mere cowprints.' With reverence toward these Sūtras, they copy the letters. Having copied them, they also memorize them, read them, propagate them, venerate them, receive their oral transmission, recite them, and repeat them to others. However, because they do not understand these profound teachings in accordance with my thought, they are unable to apply themselves to the types of meditative cultivation. Based on that, they progress due to the accumulation of merit; they also progress due to the accumulation of wisdom. They also progressively ripen their continuums which were not previously ripened.

"When other sentient beings who have not completed [the stages of the path] up to the great accumulations of merit and wisdom, who are not honest and do not have an honest nature, who are able to remove conceptuality, but who are fixated on holding their own view to be supreme[12] hear these doctrines, they do not understand this profound explanation just as it is, in accordance with my thought.

"Although they believe in the doctrine, they strongly adhere just to the literal meaning of the doctrine, [thinking], 'All phenomena just lack own-being; all phenomena are just unproduced, just unceasing, just quiescent from the start, just naturally in a state of nirvāṇa.' Based on this, they adopt the view that all phenomena do not exist and that character does not exist.[13] Having adopted the view of non-existence and the

ལྟ་བ་དང༌། མཚན་ཉིད་མེད་པར་ལྟ་བ་ཐོབ་ནས་ཀྱང་ཐམས་ཅད་ལ་མཚན་ཉིད་ཐམས་ཅད
གྱིས་སྐུར་བ་འདེབས་ཏེ། ཆོས་རྣམས་ཀྱི་ཀུན་བརྟགས་པའི་མཚན་ཉིད་ལ་སྐུར་བ་
འདེབས། ཆོས་རྣམས་ཀྱི་གཞན་གྱི་དབང་གི་མཚན་ཉིད་དང༌། ཡོངས་སུ་གྲུབ་པའི
མཚན་ཉིད་ལ་ཡང་སྐུར་བ་འདེབས་སོ། །དེ་ཅིའི་ཕྱིར་ཞེ་ན། དོན་དམ་ཡང་དག་
འཕགས་འདི་ལྟར་གཞན་གྱི་དབང་ཉིད་དང༌། ཡོངས་སུ་གྲུབ་པའི་མཚན་ཉིད་ཡོད་ན་ནི།
ཀུན་བརྟགས་པའི་མཚན་ཉིད་ཀྱང་རབ་ཏུ་ཤེས་པར་འགྱུར་ན། དེ་ལ་གང་དག་གཞན་གྱི་
དབང་གི་མཚན་ཉིད་དང༌། ཡོངས་སུ་གྲུབ་པའི་མཚན་ཉིད་ལ་མཚན་ཉིད་མེད་པར་
མཐོང་བ་དེ་དག་གིས་ནི་ཀུན་བརྟགས་པའི་མཚན་ཉིད་ལ་ཡང་སྐུར་བ་བཏབ་པ་ཡིན་པའི
ཕྱིར་ཏེ། དེ་ལྟ་བས་ན་དེ་དག་ནི་མཚན་ཉིད་རྣམ་པ་གསུམ་ཆར་ལ་ཡང་སྐུར་བ་འདེབས
པ་ཞེས་བྱའོ། །དེ་དག་ནི་ངའི་ཆོས་ལ་ཆོས་སུ་འདུ་ཤེས་པ་དང་དོན་མ་ཡིན་པ་ལ་དོན་དུ
འདུ་ཤེས་པ་ཡིན་ཏེ། ངའི་ཆོས་ལ་ཆོས་སུ་འདུ་ཤེས་པ་དང༌། དོན་མ་ཡིན་པ་ལ་དོན་དུ
འདུ་ཤེས་པ་དེ་དག་ཆོས་ལ་ཡང་ཆོས་སུ་འཛིན། དོན་མ་ཡིན་པ་ལ་ཡང་དོན་དུ་འཛིན་ཏོ། །
དེ་དག་ཆོས་ལ་མོས་པས་དགེ་བའི་ཆོས་རྣམས་ཀྱིས་འཕེལ་མོད་ཀྱི། འོན་ཀྱང་དོན་མ
ཡིན་པ་ལ་མངོན་པར་ཞེན་པས་ཤེས་རབ་ལས་ཡོངས་སུ་ཉམས་པར་འགྱུར་ཏེ། ཤེས་རབ
ལས་ཡོངས་སུ་ཉམས་ན་དགེ་བའི་ཆོས་ཤིན་ཏུ་རྒྱ་ཆེ་བ་དང༌། ཤིན་ཏུ་དཔག་ཏུ་མེད་པ
རྣམས་ལས་ཀྱང་ཡོངས་སུ་ཉམས་པར་འགྱུར་རོ། །དེ་དག་ལས་གཞན་དག་གིས་ཆོས་ལ
ཆོས་སུ་དང༌། དོན་མ་ཡིན་པ་ལ་དོན་དུ་ཐོས་ནས་གང་དག་ལྟ་བ་ལ་དགའ་བར་བྱེད་པ་དེ

view that character does not exist, they also deprecate everything through [deprecating] all characters. Because they deprecate the imputational character of phenomena, they also deprecate the other-dependent character of phenomena and the thoroughly established character.

"Why is this? Paramārthasamudgata, if the other-dependent and thoroughly established characters exist, then the imputational character is also understood.[14] However, those who see the other-dependent character and the thoroughly established character as non-existent also deprecate the imputational character. Therefore, they also 'deprecate all three types of character'. They perceive my doctrine to be doctrine, but they perceive what is not the meaning to be the meaning.

"Those who perceive my doctrine to be doctrine but perceive what is not the meaning to be the meaning also understand the doctrine to be doctrine. They also understand what is not the meaning to be the meaning. Due to belief in the doctrine, they progress by means of virtuous qualities. But, due to strongly adhering to what is not the meaning, they fall away from wisdom. When they fall away from wisdom, they also fall away from vast and immeasurable virtuous qualities.

"Others, having heard from them that the doctrine is the doctrine, but that what is not the meaning is the meaning, delight in that view. Because they conceive the doctrine to be doctrine and conceive what is not the meaning to be the

དག་ནི་ཆོས་ལ་ཆོས་སུ་འདུ་ཤེས་པ་དང་། དོན་མ་ཡིན་པ་ལ་དོན་དུ་འདུ་ཤེས་པས་ཆོས་ལ་ཆོས་སུ་དང་། དོན་མ་ཡིན་པ་ལ་དོན་དུ་མངོན་པར་ཞེན་པར་འགྱུར་ཏེ། དེ་དག་གཞི་དེས་ན་དེ་བཞིན་དུ་དགེ་བའི་ཆོས་ལས་ཉམས་པར་རིག་པར་བྱའོ། །གང་དག་ལྟ་བ་ལ་དགའ་བར་མི་བྱེད་པ་དེ་དག་ནི་དེ་དག་ལས་ཆོས་རྣམས་ཀྱི་ངོ་བོ་ཉིད་མེད་པ་ཉིད་ཐོས་ཤིང་ཆོས་རྣམས་ཀྱི་སྐྱེ་བ་མེད་པ་དང་། འགག་པ་མེད་པ་དང་། གཟོད་མ་ནས་ཞི་བ་དང་། རང་བཞིན་གྱིས་ཡོངས་སུ་མྱ་ངན་ལས་འདས་པ་ཐོས་ནས་སྐྲག་ཅིང་དངང་ལ་ཀུན་ཏུ་དངང་བར་འགྱུར་ཞིང་འདི་སྐད་ཅེས་འདི་ནི་སངས་རྒྱས་ཀྱི་བཀའ་མ་ཡིན་གྱི། འདི་ནི་བདུད་ཀྱིས་སྨྲས་པ་ཡིན་ནོ་ཞེས་ཀྱང་ཟེར་ཞིང་དེ་ལྟར་རིག་ནས་མདོ་སྡེ་དེ་དག་ལ་སྐུར་བ་འདེབས་པར་བྱེད། སྤོང་བར་བྱེད། མི་བསྔགས་པ་བརྗོད་པར་བྱེད། ངན་དུ་རྗོད་པར་བྱེད། གཞི་དེས་ན་ཕོངས་པ་ཆེན་པོ་འཐོབ་པར་འགྱུར་ཞིང་ལས་ཀྱི་སྒྲིབ་པ་ཆེན་པོས་ཀྱང་རེག་པར་འགྱུར་རོ། །གཞི་དེས་ཀྱང་གང་དག་སྐྱེ་བོ་ཕལ་པོ་ཆེ་ལ་ལས་ཀྱི་སྒྲིབ་པ་ཆེན་པོ་འཐོབ་པས་སླུ་བར་བྱེད་པ། མཚན་ཉིད་ཐམས་ཅད་མེད་པར་ལྟ་ཞིང་དོན་མ་ཡིན་པ་དོན་དུ་སྟོན་པར་བྱེད་པ་དེ་དག་ནི་ལས་ཀྱི་སྒྲིབ་པ་ཆེན་པོ་དང་ལྡན་པར་ང་སྨྲོ། །དོན་དམ་ཡང་དག་འཕགས་དེ་ལ་སེམས་ཅན་གང་དག་དགེ་བའི་རྩ་བ་མ་བསྐྱེད། སྒྲིབ་པ་ཡོངས་སུ་མ་དག །རྒྱུད་ཡོངས་སུ་མ་སྨིན། མོས་པ་མི་མང་། བསོད་ནམས་དང་ཡེ་ཤེས་ཀྱི་ཚོགས་ཡང་དག་པར་མ་གྲུབ་ཅིང་། དྲང་པོ་དང་དྲང་པོའི་རང་བཞིན་ཅན་མ་ཡིན་ལ་རྟོག་པ་དང་སེལ་མི་ནུས་ལ། རང་གི་ལྟ་བ་མཆོག་ཏུ་འཛིན་པར་གནས་པ་དེ་དག་གིས་ནི་ཆོས་དེ་ཐོས་ན། ངའི་དགོངས

meaning, they strongly adhere to doctrine as being doctrine and to what is not the meaning as being the meaning. Know that based on this they also fall away from virtuous qualities.

"When people who do not delight in such views hear from others that phenomena lack an own-being and hear that phenomena are unproduced, unceasing, quiescent from the start, and naturally in a state of nirvāṇa, they become fearful and develop misgivings, saying, 'This is not the word of the Buddha. This is a statement from Māra!' Thinking in this way they also deprecate these Sūtras. They reject them, condemn them, and speak badly of them.

"Based on this, they earn great misfortune, and they also meet with great karmic obstructions. Also based on this, since they cause many beings to meet with great obstructions, they deceive them. I state that those who view all characters as non-existent and who teach what is not the meaning to be the meaning possess great karmic obstructions.

"Paramārthasamudgata, when those sentient beings who have not produced roots of virtue, have not purified the obstructions, have not ripened their continuums, do not have great conviction, have not completed the accumulations of merit and wisdom, who are not honest and do not have an honest nature, and who are unable to remove conceptuality and who are fixated on holding their own view to be supreme hear these doctrines, they do not understand the teaching

ཏེ་བ་ཤད་པ་ཡང་ཡང་དག་པ་ཇི་ལྟ་བ་བཞིན་དུ་རབ་ཏུ་མི་ཤེས་ཤིང་ཆོས་དེ་ལ་མོས་པར་ཡང་མི་འགྱུར་བ། དེ་དག་ཆོས་ལ་ཆོས་མ་ཡིན་པར་འདུ་ཤེས་ཤིང་། དོན་ལ་དོན་མ་ཡིན་པར་འདུ་ཤེས་ལ། ཆོས་ལ་ཡང་ཆོས་མ་ཡིན་པ་དང་། དོན་ལ་ཡང་དོན་མ་ཡིན་པར་མངོན་པར་ཞེན་ནས་འདི་སྐད་ཅེས་འདི་ནི་སངས་རྒྱས་ཀྱི་བཀའ་མ་ཡིན་གྱི། འདི་ནི་བདུད་ཀྱིས་སྨྲས་པ་ཡིན་ནོ་ཞེས་ཀྱང་ཟེར་ཞིང་དེ་ལྟར་རིག་ནས་མདོ་སྡེ་དག་ལ་སྐུར་བ་འདེབས་པར་བྱེད། སྤོང་བར་བྱེད། མི་བསྔགས་པ་བརྗོད་པར་བྱེད། ངན་དུ་བརྗོད་པར་བྱེད་ཅིང་ལྷད་ཀྱང་འཇིག་པར་བྱེད་དེ། རྣམ་གྲངས་དུ་མར་མདོ་སྡེ་དེ་དག་སྤང་བ་དང་། ཆུད་གཟན་པ་དང་། རྣམ་པར་གཞིག་པའི་ཕྱིར་ཞུགས་ཤིང་དེ་ལ་མོས་པའི་གང་ཟག་རྣམས་ལ་ཡང་དགྲར་འདུ་ཤེས་པར་འགྱུར་རོ། །དེ་དག་ནི་དང་པོ་ཉིད་ནས་ཀྱང་ལས་ཀྱི་སྒྲིབ་པས་བསྒྲིབས་པ་ཡིན་ལ། གཞི་དེས་ཀྱང་ཡང་ལས་ཀྱི་སྒྲིབ་པ་དེ་ལྟ་བུས་སྒྲིབ་པར་བྱེད་དེ། ལས་ཀྱི་སྒྲིབ་པ་དེའི་དང་པོ་ནི་གདགས་པར་སླའི། བསྐལ་པ་བྱེ་བ་ཁྲག་ཁྲིག་འབུམ་ཕྲག་འདི་སྙེད་ཀྱི་བར་གྱིས་འབྱུང་བར་འགྱུར་རོ་ཞེས་གདགས་པར་ནི་དཀའོ། །དོན་དམ་ཡང་དག་འཕགས་དེ་ལྟར་ན་ངའི་ཆོས་འདུལ་བ་ལེགས་པར་གསུངས་པ། ཤིན་ཏུ་བྱ་ནོམ་པ། བསམ་པ་ཤིན་ཏུ་རྣམ་པར་དག་པ་སྟོན་པ་ཆོས་ལེགས་པར་བསྟན་པ་ལ་སེམས་ཅན་རྣམས་ཀྱི་མོས་པའི་རིམ་པ་དེ་ལྟ་བུ་དག་ཀྱང་སྣང་ངོ། །དེ་ནས་བཅོམ་ལྡན་འདས་ཀྱིས་དེའི་ཚེ་ཚིགས་སུ་བཅད་པ་འདི་དག་བཀའ་སྩལ་ཏོ། །ཆོས་རྣམས་ངོ་བོ་ཉིད་མེད་ཆོས་རྣམས་མ་སྐྱེས་དང་། །ཆོས་རྣམས་མ་འགགས་ཆོས་རྣམས་གཟོད་ནས་ཞི་བ་དང་། །ཆོས་རྣམས

just as it is in accordance with my thought. They also do not develop belief in this doctrine; they perceive the doctrine as non-doctrine and perceive the meaning to be what is not the meaning. Strongly adhering to the doctrine as non-doctrine and to the meaning as not being the meaning, they say: 'This is not the word of the Buddha. This is a statement from Māra!' Thinking in this way, they deprecate these Sūtras. They reject them, condemn them, speak badly of them, and also engage in interpolation. In many ways they are involved with these Sūtras in order to reject, undermine, and eradicate them. They also perceive people who believe in these [Sūtras] to be enemies. From the very beginning, they are obstructed by karmic obstructions. Based on that, they continue to be obstructed by similar karmic obstructions. It is easy to designate the beginning of these karmic obstructions; it is difficult to designate during how many hundred thousands of millions of epochs they will continue to arise.

"Paramārthasamudgata, in that way, degrees of conviction appear among sentient beings with respect to this well-taught doctrine, my disciplinary instruction which is explained well, is complete, and is taught with a very pure thought."

Then the Bhagavan spoke these verses:

"What sage would propound, without a thought behind it,
that dharmas lack own-being; dharmas are unproduced;
dharmas are unceasing; dharmas are quiescent from the start;
that all dharmas are naturally in a state of nirvāṇa?

ཐམས་ཅད་རང་བཞིན་མྱ་ངན་འདས་པར་ནི། །དགོངས་པ་མེད་པར་མཁས་པ་སུ་ཞིག་སྨྲ
བར་བྱེད། །མཚན་ཉིད་ངོ་བོ་ཉིད་མེད་སྐྱེ་བ་ངོ་བོ་མེད། །དོན་དམ་ངོ་བོ་ཉིད་མེད་ངོ་
ཞེས་ངས་བཤད་དེ། །འདི་ལ་མཁས་པ་གང་ཞིག་དགོངས་པ་ཤེས་པ་ནི། །རབ་ཏུ
ཉམས་པར་འགྱུར་བའི་ལམ་དུ་དེ་མི་འགྲོ། །ཀུན་གྱི་རྣམ་དག་ལམ་ནི་གཅིག་པུ་འདི་ཡིན
ཏེ༑ ༑རྣམ་པར་དག་པའང་གཅིག་སྟེ་གཉིས་པ་གང་ཡང་མེད། །དེ་ཕྱིར་ཐེག་པ
གཅིག་པ་འདི་ནི་འདོགས་བྱེད་ཀྱང་། །སེམས་ཅན་རིགས་ནི་རྣམ་པ་སྣ་ཚོགས་མེད་མ
ཡིན༑ ༑སེམས་ཅན་ཁམས་འདི་ན་ནི་གང་བདག་གཅིག་པུ་པ། །མྱ་ངན་འདའ་བར
བྱེད་པའི་སེམས་ཅན་དཔག་ཏུ་མེད། །གང་དག་མྱ་ངན་འདས་ཀྱང་སེམས་ཅན་མི་གཏོང
བའི༑ ༑བརྟན་པ་སྙིང་རྗེ་ལྡན་པ་དེ་དག་ཤིན་ཏུ་དཀོན། །གང་གྲོལ་དེ་དག་རྣམས་ཀྱི
ཟག་པ་མེད་པའི་དབྱིངས། །ཕྲ་ཞིང་བསམ་གྱིས་མི་ཁྱབ་མཉམ་ཞིང་བྱེ་བྲག་མེད། །
ཐམས་ཅད་དོན་གྲུབ་སྡུག་བསྔལ་ཉོན་མོངས་སྤངས་པ་སྟེ། །གཉིས་སུ་བརྗོད་པ་མ་ཡིན
བདེ་ཞིང་བརྟན་པ་ཡིན། །དེ་ནས་དེའི་ཚེ་བཅོམ་ལྡན་འདས་ལ་བྱང་ཆུབ་སེམས་དཔའ་དོན
དམ་ཡང་དག་འཕགས་ཀྱིས་འདི་སྐད་ཅེས་གསོལ་ཏོ། །བཅོམ་ལྡན་འདས་ཇི་ཙམ་དུ
སངས་རྒྱས་བཅོམ་ལྡན་འདས་རྣམས་ཀྱི་དགོངས་ཏེ་གསུངས་པ་ཟབ་བ། མཆོག་ཏུ་ཟབ་བ
ཟབ་པ། མཆོག་ཏུ་ཟབ་པ། རྟོགས་པར་དཀའ་བ། མཆོག་ཏུ་རྟོགས་པར་དཀའ་བ
ནི་ངོ་མཚར་རྨད་དུ་བྱུང་བ་ལགས་སོ། །བཅོམ་ལྡན་འདས་བཅོམ་ལྡན་འདས་ཀྱིས་བཀའ
སྩལ་པའི་དོན་བདག་གིས་འདི་ལྟར་འཚལ་ཏེ། རྣམ་པར་རྟོག་པའི་སྤྱོད་ཡུལ་ཀུན···

"I explain lack of own-being in terms of character,
in terms of production, and in terms of the ultimate.
Whatever sage understands the thought behind this
will not travel a path of degeneration.

"The path of purity is this alone;
there is one purity; there is no other.
Thus this one vehicle is designated,
although there are various types of beings.

"In the realms of beings, innumerable beings
seek nirvāṇa for themselves alone.
Those who, steadfast and compassionate,
attain nirvāṇa without abandoning beings are very rare.

"The uncontaminated realm of those who are liberated
is subtle, inconceivable, equal, and undifferentiated,
all-beneficial, free from suffering and affliction,
inexpressible in dualistic terms, blissful and stable."

Then the Bodhisattva Paramārthasamudgata said to the Bhagavan: "Bhagavan, since [your] teaching, having the thought of the Buddhas and the Bhagavans, is subtle, is supremely subtle, profound, supremely profound, difficult to realize, supremely difficult to realize, it is amazing and wondrous.

"Bhagavan, I understand the meaning of that which the Bhagavan said in this way: The imputational character consists of [first] those things that are posited in terms of names

བརྟགས་པའི་མཚན་ཉིད་ཀྱི་གནས་འདུ་བྱེད་ཀྱི་མཚན་མ་ལ། གཟུགས་ཀྱི་ཕུང་པོ་ཞེས་ངོ་བོ་ཉིད་ཀྱི་མཚན་ཉིད་དམ། བྱེ་བྲག་གི་མཚན་ཉིད་དུ་མིང་དང་བརྡར་རྣམ་པར་གཞག་པ་དང་། གཟུགས་ཀྱི་ཕུང་པོ་སྐྱེ་འོ་ཞེའམ། འགག་གོ་ཞེའམ། གཟུགས་ཀྱི་ཕུང་པོ་སྤང་བ་དང་། ཡོངས་སུ་ཤེས་པ་ཞེས་ངོ་བོ་ཉིད་ཀྱི་མཚན་ཉིད་དམ། བྱེ་བྲག་གི་མཚན་ཉིད་དུ་མིང་དང་བརྡར་རྣམ་པར་གཞག་པ་གང་ལགས་པ་དེ་ནི་ཀུན་བརྟགས་པའི་མཚན་ཉིད་ལགས་ཏེ། དེ་ལ་བརྟེན་ནས་བཅོམ་ལྡན་འདས་ཆོས་རྣམས་ཀྱི་མཚན་ཉིད་ངོ་བོ་ཉིད་མ་མཆིས་པ་ཉིད་འདོགས་པར་མཛད་ལགས་སོ། །རྣམ་པར་རྟོག་པའི་སྤྱོད་ཡུལ་ཀུན་བརྟགས་པའི་མཚན་ཉིད་ཀྱི་གནས་འདུ་བྱེད་ཀྱི་མཚན་མ་གང་ལགས་པ་དེ་ནི་གཞན་གྱི་དབང་གི་མཚན་ཉིད་ལགས་ཏེ། དེ་ལ་བརྟེན་ནས་བཅོམ་ལྡན་འདས་ཆོས་རྣམས་ཀྱི་སྐྱེ་བ་ངོ་བོ་ཉིད་མ་མཆིས་པ་ཉིད་དང་། དོན་དམ་པ་ངོ་བོ་ཉིད་མ་མཆིས་པ་དེ་ཉིད་ལས་གཅིག་ཀྱང་འདོགས་པར་མཛད་ལགས་སོ། །བཅོམ་ལྡན་འདས་བཅོམ་ལྡན་འདས་ཀྱིས་བཀའ་སྩལ་པའི་དོན་བདག་གིས་འདི་ལྟར་འཚལ་ཏེ། རྣམ་པར་རྟོག་པའི་སྤྱོད་ཡུལ་ཀུན་··· བརྟགས་པའི་མཚན་ཉིད་ཀྱི་གནས་འདུ་བྱེད་ཀྱི་མཚན་མ་དེ་ཉིད་ཀུན་བརྟགས་པའི་མཚན་ཉིད་དེར་ཡོངས་སུ་མ་གྲུབ་ཅིང་ངོ་བོ་ཉིད་མེད། དེ་ཁོ་ནས་ངོ་བོ་ཉིད་མ་མཆིས་པ་ཉིད་ཆོས་བདག་མ་མཆིས་པ་དེ་བཞིན་ཉིད་རྣམ་པར་དག་པའི་དམིགས་པ་གང་ལགས་པ་དེ་ནི་ཡོངས་སུ་གྲུབ་པའི་མཚན་ཉིད་ལགས་ཏེ། དེ་ལ་བརྟེན་ནས་བཅོམ་ལྡན་འདས་ཆོས་རྣམས་ཀྱི་དོན་དམ་པའི་ངོ་བོ་ཉིད་མ་མཆིས་པ་དེ་ཉིད་ལས་གཅིག་འདོགས་པར་མཛད་

and symbols—the objects of conceptual activity, the bases of the imputational character, the signs of compounded phenomena—as the character of the own-being or as the character of attributes of 'the form aggregate'; and [second], those things that are posited in terms of names and symbols as the character of own-being or the character of attributes of 'the production of a form aggregate', or its 'cessation', or the 'abandonment and realization of a form aggregate'. In dependence upon that, the Bhagavan designated the lack of own-being in terms of character of phenomena.

"Those things that are the objects of conceptual activity, the bases of the imputational character, the signs of compounded phenomena, are the other-dependent character. In dependence upon that, the Bhagavan designated the lack of own-being in terms of production of phenomena and, additionally, an ultimate lack of own-being.

"Bhagavan, I understand the meaning of the Bhagavan's teaching in this way: Those very objects of conceptual activity, the bases of the imputational character, and the signs of compounded phenomena are not established as being that imputational character, and they lack own-being. Because of just that, the lack of own-being, selflessness of phenomena, suchness, and object of observation for purification are the thoroughly established character. In dependence upon that, the Bhagavan additionally designated the ultimate lack of own-being of phenomena.

བཏགས་པའི་མཚན་ཉིད་ཀྱི་གནས་འདུ་བྱེད་ཀྱི་མཚན་མ་ལ། གཟུགས་ཀྱི་ཕུང་པོ་ཞེས་ངོ་བོ་ཉིད་ཀྱི་མཚན་ཉིད་དམ། བྱེ་བྲག་གི་མཚན་ཉིད་དུ་མིང་དང་བརྡར་རྣམ་པར་གཞག་པ་དང་། གཟུགས་ཀྱི་ཕུང་པོ་སྐྱེ་འོ་ཞེའམ། འགག་གོ་ཞེའམ། གཟུགས་ཀྱི་ཕུང་པོ་སྤང་བ་དང་། ཡོངས་སུ་ཤེས་པ་ཞེས་ངོ་བོ་ཉིད་ཀྱི་མཚན་ཉིད་དམ། བྱེ་བྲག་གི་མཚན་ཉིད་དུ་མིང་དང་བརྡར་རྣམ་པར་གཞག་པ་གང་ལགས་པ་དེ་ནི་ཀུན་བཏགས་པའི་མཚན་ཉིད་ལགས་ཏེ། དེ་ལ་བརྟེན་ནས་བཅོམ་ལྡན་འདས་ཆོས་རྣམས་ཀྱི་མཚན་ཉིད་ངོ་བོ་ཉིད་མ་མཆིས་པ་ཉིད་འདོགས་པར་མཛད་ལགས་སོ། །རྣམ་པར་རྟོག་པའི་སྤྱོད་ཡུལ་ཀུན་བཏགས་པའི་མཚན་ཉིད་ཀྱི་གནས་འདུ་བྱེད་ཀྱི་མཚན་མ་གང་ལགས་པ་དེ་ནི་གཞན་གྱི་དབང་གི་མཚན་ཉིད་ལགས་ཏེ། དེ་ལ་བརྟེན་ནས་བཅོམ་ལྡན་འདས་ཆོས་རྣམས་ཀྱི་སྐྱེ་བ་ངོ་བོ་ཉིད་མ་མཆིས་པ་ཉིད་དང་། དོན་དམ་པ་ངོ་བོ་ཉིད་མ་མཆིས་པ་དེ་ཉིད་ལས་གཅིག་ཀྱང་འདོགས་པར་མཛད་ལགས་སོ། །བཅོམ་ལྡན་འདས་བཅོམ་ལྡན་འདས་ཀྱིས་བཀའ་སྩལ་པའི་དོན་བདག་གིས་འདི་ལྟར་འཚལ་ཏེ། རྣམ་པར་རྟོག་པའི་སྤྱོད་ཡུལ་ཀུན་···· བཏགས་པའི་མཚན་ཉིད་ཀྱི་གནས་འདུ་བྱེད་ཀྱི་མཚན་མ་དེ་ཉིད་ཀུན་བཏགས་པའི་མཚན་ཉིད་དེར་ཡོངས་སུ་མ་གྲུབ་ཅིང་ངོ་བོ་ཉིད་མེད། དེ་ཁོ་ནས་ངོ་བོ་ཉིད་མ་མཆིས་པ་ཉིད་ཆོས་བདག་མ་མཆིས་པ་དེ་བཞིན་ཉིད་རྣམ་པར་དག་པའི་དམིགས་པ་གང་ལགས་པ་དེ་ནི་ཡོངས་སུ་གྲུབ་པའི་མཚན་ཉིད་ལགས་ཏེ། དེ་ལ་བརྟེན་ནས་བཅོམ་ལྡན་འདས་ཆོས་རྣམས་ཀྱི་དོན་དམ་པའི་ངོ་བོ་ཉིད་མ་མཆིས་པ་དེ་ཉིད་ལས་གཅིག་འདོགས་པར་མཛད་

"Just as this is applied to the form aggregate, so it should also be applied to the remaining aggregates. Just as this is applied to the aggregates, so it should also be applied to each of the sense spheres that comprise the twelve sense spheres. The same is true for each of the limbs of existence that comprise the twelve limbs of existence. The same is true for each of the sustenances that comprise the four sustenances. The same is true for each of the constituents that comprise the six constituents and the eighteen constituents.

"Bhagavan, I understand the meaning of the Bhagavan's teaching in this way: The imputational character consists of those things posited in terms of names and symbols–which are the objects of conceptual activity, the bases of the imputational character, and the signs of compounded phenomena–as the character of own-being and the character of attributes of the 'truth of suffering and understanding the truth of suffering'. In dependence upon that, the Bhagavan designated lack of own-being in terms of character of phenomena.

"Those things that are the objects of conceptual activity, the bases of the imputational character, and the signs of compounded phenomena are the other-dependent character. In dependence upon that, the Bhagavan additionally designated the lack of own-being in terms of production of phenomena and an ultimate lack of own-being.

"Bhagavan, I understand the meaning of the Bhagavan's teaching in this way: Those things that are the objects of

ཡུལ་ཀུན་བརྟགས་པའི་མཚན་ཉིད་ཀྱི་གནས་འདུ་བྱེད་ཀྱི་མཚན་མ་དེ་ཉིད་ཀུན་བརྟགས་
པའི་མཚན་ཉིད་དེར་ཡོངས་སུ་མ་གྲུབ་ཅིང་ངོ་བོ་ཉིད་དེ་ཁོ་ནས་ངོ་བོ་ཉིད་མ་མཆིས་པ་ཉིད་
ཆོས་བདག་མ་མཆིས་པ་དེ་བཞིན་ཉིད་རྣམ་པར་དག་པའི་དམིགས་པ་གང་ལགས་པ་དེ་ནི་
ཡོངས་སུ་གྲུབ་པའི་མཚན་ཉིད་ལགས་ཏེ། དེ་ལ་བརྟེན་ནས་བཅོམ་ལྡན་འདས་ཆོས་
རྣམས་ཀྱི་དོན་དམ་པ་ངོ་བོ་ཉིད་མ་མཆིས་པ་ཉིད་དེ་ལས་གཅིག་འདོགས་པར་མཛད་
ལགས་སོ། །སྡུག་བསྔལ་འཕགས་པའི་བདེན་པ་ལ་ཇི་ལྟ་བ་དེ་བཞིན་དུ་བདེན་པ་ལྷག་མ
རྣམས་ལ་ཡང་དེ་བཞིན་དུ་སྦྱར་བར་བགྱི་ལགས་སོ། །བདེན་པ་རྣམས་ལ་ཇི་ལྟ་བ་བཞིན
དུ་དྲན་པ་ཉེ་བར་གཞག་པ་རྣམས་དང་། ཡང་དག་པར་སྤོང་བ་རྣམས་དང་། རྫུ་འཕྲུལ
གྱི་རྐང་པ་རྣམས་དང་། དབང་པོ་རྣམས་དང་། སྟོབས་རྣམས་དང་། བྱང་ཆུབ་ཀྱི་ཡན
ལག་རྣམས་དང་། ལམ་གྱི་ཡན་ལག་རྣམས་ཀྱི་ཡན་ལག་རེ་རེ་ལ་ཡང་དེ་བཞིན་དུ་སྦྱར
བར་བགྱི་ལགས་སོ། །བཅོམ་ལྡན་འདས་བཅོམ་ལྡན་འདས་ཀྱིས་བཀའ་སྩལ་པའི་དོན
བདག་གིས་འདི་ལྟར་འཚལ་ཏེ། རྣམ་པར་རྟོག་པའི་སྤྱོད་ཡུལ་ཀུན་བརྟགས་པའི་མཚན
ཉིད་ཀྱི་གནས་འདུ་བྱེད་ཀྱི་མཚན་མ་ལ་ཡང་དག་པའི་ཏིང་ངེ་འཛིན་ཞེའམ། ཏིང་ངེ་འཛིན
གྱི་མི་འཐུན་པའི་ཕྱོགས་དང་གཉེན་པོ་ཞེའམ། ཏིང་ངེ་འཛིན་བསྒོམ་པ་ཞེའམ། མ་སྐྱེས
པ་སྐྱེ་བ་ཞེའམ། སྐྱེས་པ་གནས་པ་དང་། མི་བརྗེད་པ་དང་། སླར་ཞིང་འབྱུང་བ་དང་།
འཕེལ་ཞིང་རྒྱས་པ་ཉིད་ཅེས་ངོ་བོ་ཉིད་ཀྱི་མཚན་ཉིད་དམ། བྱེ་བྲག་གི་མཚན་ཉིད་དུ
མིང་དང་བརྡར་རྣམ་པར་བཞག་པ་གང་ལགས་པ་དེ་ནི་ཀུན་བརྟགས་པའི་མཚན་ཉིད་

conceptual activity, the bases of the imputational character, and the signs of compounded phenomena are not established as being the imputational character. And because of just that own-being, the lack of own-being, the selflessness of phenomena, suchness, and the object of observation for purification are the thoroughly established character. In dependence upon that, the Bhagavan additionally designated an ultimate lack of own-being of phenomena.

"Just as this is applied to the noble truth of suffering, so it should be applied to the remaining truths. Just as this is applied to the truths, so it should be applied to the mindful establishments, the correct abandonings, the bases of magical abilities, the powers, the forces, the branches of enlightenment, and each of the branches of the path of the Āryas.

"Bhagavan, I understand the meaning of the Bhagavan's teaching in this way: The imputational character consists of those things posited in terms of names and symbols—which are objects of conceptual activity, the bases of the imputational character, and the signs of compounded phenomena—as the character of own-being or the character of attributes of 'pure samādhi' or the 'discordances and antidotes of samādhis', or the 'production of those which have not been produced', or the 'abiding of those which have been produced, and their non-forgetting, their further arising, and their increasing and extending'. In dependence upon that, the

ལགས་ཏེ། དེ་ལ་བརྟེན་ནས་བཅོམ་ལྡན་འདས་ཆོས་རྣམས་ཀྱི་མཚན་ཉིད་ངོ་བོ་ཉིད་མ་མཆིས་པ་ཉིད་འདོགས་པར་མཛད་ལགས་སོ། །རྣམ་པར་རྟོག་པའི་སྤྱོད་ཡུལ་ཀུན་བརྟགས་པའི་མཚན་ཉིད་ཀྱི་གནས་འདུ་བྱེད་ཀྱི་མཚན་མ་གང་ལགས་པ་དེ་ནི་གཞན་གྱི་དབང་གི་མཚན་ཉིད་ལགས་ཏེ། དེ་ལ་བརྟེན་ནས་བཅོམ་ལྡན་འདས་ཆོས་རྣམས་ཀྱི་སྐྱེ་བ་ངོ་བོ་ཉིད་མ་མཆིས་པ་ཉིད་དང་། དོན་དམ་པ་ངོ་བོ་ཉིད་མ་མཆིས་པ་དེ་ལས་གཅིག་ཀྱང་འདོགས་པར་མཛད་ལགས་སོ། །བཅོམ་ལྡན་འདས་བཅོམ་ལྡན་འདས་ཀྱིས་བཀའ་སྩལ་པའི་དོན་བདག་གིས་འདི་ལྟར་འཚལ་ཏེ། རྣམ་པར་རྟོག་པའི་སྤྱོད་ཡུལ་ཀུན་བརྟགས་པའི་མཚན་ཉིད་ཀྱི་གནས་འདུ་བྱེད་ཀྱི་མཚན་མ་དེ་ཉིད་ཀུན་བརྟགས་པའི་མཚན་ཉིད་དེར་ཡོངས་སུ་མ་གྲུབ་ཅིང་ངོ་བོ་ཉིད་དེ་ཁོ་ནས་ངོ་བོ་ཉིད་མ་མཆིས་པ་ཉིད་ཆོས་བདག་མ་མཆིས་པ་དེ་བཞིན་ཉིད་རྣམ་པར་དག་པའི་དམིགས་པ་གང་ལགས་པ་དེ་ནི་ཡོངས་སུ་གྲུབ་པའི་མཚན་ཉིད་ལགས་ཏེ། དེ་ལ་བརྟེན་ནས་བཅོམ་ལྡན་འདས་ཆོས་རྣམས་ཀྱི་དོན་དམ་པ་ངོ་བོ་ཉིད་མ་མཆིས་པ་དེ་ལས་གཅིག་འདོགས་པར་མཛད་ལགས་སོ། །བཅོམ་ལྡན་འདས་འདི་ལྟ་སྟེ། དཔེར་བགྱི་ན་བཙའ་སྨན་ནི་ཕྱེ་མའི་སྨན་སྦྱོར་བ་དང་། བཅུད་ཀྱིས་ལེན་སྦྱོར་བ་ཐམས་ཅད་དུ་སྩལ་བར་བགྱི་བ་ལགས་སོ། །དེ་བཞིན་དུ་ཆོས་རྣམས་ཀྱི་ངོ་བོ་ཉིད་མ་མཆིས་པ་ཉིད་ལས་བརྩམས། སྐྱེ་བ་མ་མཆིས་པ་དང་། འགག་པ་མ་མཆིས་པ་དང་། གཟོད་མ་ནས་ཞི་བ་དང་། རང་བཞིན་གྱིས་ཡོངས་སུ་མྱ་ངན་ལས་འདས་པ་ཉིད་ལས་བརྩམས་ནས། བཅོམ་ལྡན་འདས་ངེས་པའི་དོན་བསྟན་པ་འདི་ཡང་དྲང་བའི་དོན་གྱི་མདོ་

Bhagavan designated the lack of own-being in terms of character of phenomena.

"Those things which are the objects of conceptual activity, the bases of the imputational character, and the signs of compounded phenomena are the other-dependent character. In dependence upon that, the Bhagavan additionally designated the lack of own-being in terms of production of phenomena and an ultimate lack of own-being.

"Bhagavan, I understand the meaning of the Bhagavan's teaching in this way: Those things which are the objects of conceptual activity, the bases of the imputational character, and the signs of compounded phenomena are not established as being the imputational character. And because of just that own-being, the lack of own-being, the selflessness of phenomena, suchness, and the object of observation for purification are the thoroughly established character. In dependence upon that, the Bhagavan additionally designated an ultimate lack of own-being of phenomena.

"Bhagavan, for example, dried ginger is added to all medicinal powders and elixirs. Similarly, beginning with the lack of own-being of phenomena, and beginning with [the teachings that phenomena are] unproduced, unceasing, quiescent from the start, and naturally in a state of nirvāṇa, the Bhagavan

སྡེ་ཐམས་ཅད་དུ་སྐུལ་བར་བགྱི་བ་ལགས་སོ། །བཅོམ་ལྡན་འདས་འདི་ལྟ་སྟེ་དཔེར་བགྱི་ན་རི་མོ་བྲི་བའི་གཞི་ནི་སྔོན་པོ་འམ། སེར་པོ་འམ། དམར་པོ་འམ། དཀར་པོ་འམ། རི་མོར་བགྱི་བ་ཐམས་ཅད་ལ་རོ་གཅིག་པ་ལགས་ཤིང་རི་མོར་བྲིས་པ་དེ་ཡང་ཤིན་ཏུ་གསལ་བར་བགྱིད་པ་ལགས་སོ། །དེ་བཞིན་དུ་ཆོས་རྣམས་ཀྱི་ངོ་བོ་ཉིད་མ་མཆིས་པ་ཉིད་དང་། རང་བཞིན་གྱིས་ཡོངས་སུ་མྱ་ངན་ལས་འདས་པ་ཉིད་ཀྱི་བར་ལས་བརྩམས་ནས་བཅོམ་ལྡན་འདས་ཀྱི་ངེས་པའི་དོན་བསྟན་པ་འདི་ཡང་དྲང་བའི་དོན་གྱི་མདོ་སྡེ་ཐམས་ཅད་ལ་རོ་གཅིག་པ་དང་དྲང་བའི་དོན་དེ་དག་ཤིན་ཏུ་གསལ་བར་བགྱིད་པ་ལགས་སོ། །བཅོམ་ལྡན་འདས་འདི་ལྟ་སྟེ་དཔེར་བགྱི་ན། ཆབ་མར་ནི་སྣོད་དུ་བསྲུལ་བ་དང་། ཤ་གཡོས་དང་། བག་ཆོས་ཀྱི་རྣམ་པ་ཐམས་ཅད་དུ་སྐུལ་ན་ཤིན་ཏུ་དགའ་བར་འགྱུར་ལགས་སོ། །དེ་བཞིན་དུ་ཆོས་རྣམས་ཀྱི་ངོ་བོ་ཉིད་མ་མཆིས་པ་ཉིད་དང་། རང་བཞིན་གྱིས་ཡོངས་སུ་མྱ་ངན་ལས་འདས་པ་ཉིད་ཀྱི་བར་ལས་བརྩམས་ནས་བཅོམ་ལྡན་འདས་ཀྱི་ངེས་པའི་དོན་བསྟན་པ་འདི་ཡང་དྲང་བའི་དོན་གྱི་མདོ་སྡེ་ཐམས་ཅད་དུ་སྐུལ་ན་དགའ་བ་དང་། མཆོག་ཏུ་དགའ་བ་ཆེན་པོར་འགྱུར་ལགས་སོ། །བཅོམ་ལྡན་འདས་འདི་ལྟ་སྟེ་དཔེར་བགྱི་ན། ནམ་མཁའ་ནི་ཐམས་ཅད་ལ་རོ་གཅིག་པ་དང་། བརྩམ་པ་ཐམས་ཅད་ལ་སྒྲིབ་པར་མི་འགྱུར་བ་ལགས་སོ། །དེ་བཞིན་དུ་ཆོས་རྣམས་ཀྱི་ངོ་བོ་ཉིད་མ་མཆིས་པ་ཉིད་དང་། རང་བཞིན་གྱིས་ཡོངས་སུ་མྱ་ངན་ལས་འདས་པ་ཉིད་ཀྱི་བར་ལས་བརྩམས་ནས་བཅོམ་ལྡན་འདས་ཀྱི་ངེས་པའི་དོན་བསྟན་པ་འདི་ཡང་དྲང་བའི་དོན་གྱི་མདོ་སྡེ་ཐམས་ཅད་ལ་རོ་གཅིག་པ་དང་།

also placed teachings of definitive meaning in all Sūtras of interpretable meaning.[15]

"Bhagavan, for example, the background of a painting, whether it is blue, yellow, red, or white, is of one taste throughout the entire painted work and also highlights the details of the painting. Similarly, the Bhagavan's teachings of definitive meaning, ranging from the lack of own-being of phenomena to their being naturally in a state of nirvāṇa, are all of one taste in all Sūtras of interpretable meaning and also highlight meanings that are interpretable.

"Bhagavan, for example, when one adds clarified butter to all types of dishes, for instance cooked grain or cooked meat, it is very satisfying. Similarly, when the Bhagavan's teachings of definitive meaning, ranging from the lack of own-being of phenomena to their being naturally in a state of nirvāṇa, are added to all Sūtras of interpretable meaning, it is satisfying, supremely satisfying!

"Bhagavan, for example, space is all of one taste and yet does not obstruct any undertakings. Similarly, the Bhagavan's teachings of definitive meaning, ranging from the lack of own-being of phenomena to their being naturally in a state of nirvāṇa, are also all of one taste in all Sūtras of interpretable meaning, and yet do not obstruct any undertaking concerned with either the Śrāvaka vehicle, or the Pratyekabuddha vehicle, or the Great Vehicle."[16]

ཉན་ཐོས་ཀྱི་ཐེག་པ་དང་། རང་སངས་རྒྱས་ཀྱི་ཐེག་པ་དང་། ཐེག་པ་ཆེན་པོར་བརྩམ་པ་
ཐམས་ཅད་ལ་སྒྲིབ་པར་མི་འགྱུར་བ་ལགས་སོ། །དེ་སྐད་ཅེས་གསོལ་པ་དང་། བཅོམ་
ལྡན་འདས་ཀྱིས་བྱང་ཆུབ་སེམས་དཔའ་དོན་དམ་ཡང་དག་འཕགས་ལ་ལེགས་སོ་ཞེས་བྱ་
བ་བྱིན་ཏེ། དོན་དམ་ཡང་དག་འཕགས་ལེགས་སོ་ལེགས་སོ། །དོན་དམ་ཡང་དག་
འཕགས་ཁྱོད་ཀྱིས་དེ་བཞིན་གཤེགས་པའི་དགོངས་ཏེ་བཤད་པ་ཤེས་ཏེ། དོན་དེ་ལ་འདི་
ལྟ་སྟེ། བཅའ་སྣ་དང་། རི་མོ་འདྲི་བའི་གཞི་དང་། མར་གྱིས་གདབ་པ་དང་། ནམ་
མཁའི་དཔེ་ལེགས་པར་བྱས་པ་དེ་ནི་དོན་དམ་ཡང་དག་འཕགས་དེ་བཞིན་ཏེ། གཞན་དུ་
མ་ཡིན་གྱིས་དེ་ནི་དེ་བཞིན་དུ་ཟུང་ཤིག །དེ་ནས་བཅོམ་ལྡན་འདས་ལ་བྱང་ཆུབ་སེམས་
དཔའ་དོན་དམ་ཡང་དག་འཕགས་ཀྱིས་ཡང་འདི་སྐད་ཅེས་གསོལ་ཏོ། །བཅོམ་ལྡན་
འདས་ཀྱིས་དང་པོར་ཡུལ་ཝཱ་རཱ་ཎ་སཱི་དྲང་སྲོང་སྨྲ་བ་རི་དགས་ཀྱི་ནགས་སུ་ཐེག་པ་ལ་ཡང་
དག་པར་ཞུགས་པ་རྣམས་ལ་འཕགས་པའི་བདེན་པ་བཞིའི་རྣམ་པར་བསྟན་པས་ཆོས་ཀྱི་
འཁོར་ལོ་ངོ་མཚར་རྨད་དུ་བྱུང་བ། སྔོན་ལྷར་གྱུར་པའམ། མིར་གྱུར་པ་སུས་ཀྱང་ཆོས་
དང་མཐུན་པར་འཇིག་རྟེན་དུ་མ་བསྐོར་བ་གཅིག་ཏུ་རབ་ཏུ་བསྐོར་ཏེ། བཅོམ་ལྡན་འདས་
ཀྱི་ཆོས་ཀྱི་འཁོར་ལོ་བསྐོར་བ་དེ་ཡང་བླ་ན་མཆིས་པ། སྐབས་མཆིས་པ། དྲང་བའི་དོན་
རྩོད་པའི་གཞིའི་གནས་སུ་གྱུར་པ་ལགས་ལ། བཅོམ་ལྡན་འདས་ཀྱིས་ཆོས་རྣམས་ཀྱི་ངོ་བོ་
ཉིད་མ་མཆིས་པ་ཉིད་ལས་བརྩམས། སྐྱེ་བ་མ་མཆིས་པ་དང་། འགག་པ་མ་མཆིས་པ་
དང་། གཟོད་མ་ནས་ཞི་བ་དང་། རང་བཞིན་གྱིས་ཡོངས་སུ་མྱ་ངན་ལས་འདས་པ་ཉིད་

"Excellent!" the Bhagavan replied to the Bodhisattva Paramārthasamudgata. "Paramārthasamudgata, that is good, good! Paramārthasamudgata, having the thought of the Tathāgata, you understand this explanation.

"Your good illustrations of the meaning, [analogies] such as dried ginger, the background of a painting, adding butter, and space, are accurate, Paramārthasamudgata. The [teaching] is not other than this. Therefore it should be apprehended in just this way."

Then the Bodhisattva Paramārthasamudgata said to the Bhagavan: "Initially, in the Vārānasī area, in the Deer Park called Sages' Teaching, the Bhagavan taught the aspects of the four truths of the Āryas for those who were genuinely engaged in the [Śrāvaka] vehicle. The wheel of doctrine you turned at first is wondrous. Similar doctrines had not been promulgated before in the world by gods or humans. However, this wheel of doctrine that the Bhagavan turned is surpassable, provides an opportunity [for refutation], is of interpretable meaning, and serves as a basis for dispute.[17]

"Then the Bhagavan turned a second wheel of doctrine which is more wondrous still for those who are genuinely engaged in the Great Vehicle, because of the aspect of teaching emptiness, beginning with the lack of own-being of phenomena, and beginning with their absence of production, absence of cessation, quiescence from the start, and being

ལས་བརྩམས་ནས་ཐེག་པ་ཆེན་པོ་ལ་ཡང་དག་པར་ཞུགས་པ་རྣམས་ལ་སྟོང་པ་ཉིད་སྟོན་
པའི་རྣམ་པས་ཆེས་ངོ་མཚར་རྨད་དུ་བྱུང་བའི་ཆོས་ཀྱི་འཁོར་ལོ་གཉིས་པ་བསྐོར་ཏེ།
བཅོམ་ལྡན་འདས་ཀྱི་ཆོས་ཀྱི་འཁོར་ལོ་བསྐོར་བ་དེ་ཡང་བླ་ན་མཆིས་པ། སྐབས་མཆིས
པ། དྲང་བའི་དོན་རྩོད་པའི་གཞིའི་གནས་སུ་གྱུར་པ་ལགས་ལ། བཅོམ་ལྡན་འདས་ཀྱིས
ཆོས་རྣམས་ཀྱི་ངོ་བོ་ཉིད་མ་མཆིས་པ་ཉིད་ལས་བརྩམས། སྐྱེ་བ་མ་མཆིས་པ་དང་།
འགག་པ་མ་མཆིས་པ་དང་། གཟོད་མ་ནས་ཞི་བ་དང་། རང་བཞིན་གྱིས་ཡོངས་སུ་མྱ
ངན་ལས་འདས་པ་ཉིད་ལས་བརྩམས་ནས། ཐེག་པ་ཐམས་ཅད་ལ་ཡང་དག་པར་ཞུགས
པ་རྣམས་ལ་ལེགས་པར་རྣམ་པར་ཕྱེ་བ་དང་ལྡན་པ། ཤིན་ཏུ་ངོ་མཚར་རྨད་དུ་བྱུང་བའི
ཆོས་ཀྱི་འཁོར་ལོ་གསུམ་པ་བསྐོར་ཏེ། བཅོམ་ལྡན་འདས་ཀྱི་ཆོས་ཀྱི་འཁོར་ལོ་བསྐོར་བ
འདི་ནི་བླ་ན་མ་མཆིས་པ། སྐབས་མ་མཆིས་པ། ངེས་པའི་དོན་ལགས་ཏེ། རྩོད་པའི
གཞིའི་གནས་སུ་གྱུར་པ་མ་ལགས་སོ། །བཅོམ་ལྡན་འདས་ཆོས་རྣམས་ཀྱི་ངོ་བོ་ཉིད་མ
མཆིས་པ་ཉིད་ལས་བརྩམས། རང་བཞིན་གྱིས་ཡོངས་སུ་མྱ་ངན་ལས་འདས་པ་ཉིད་ཀྱི
བར་ལས་བརྩམས་ནས། བཅོམ་ལྡན་འདས་ཀྱིས་ངེས་པའི་དོན་བསྟན་པ་འདི་རིགས་ཀྱི
བུ་འམ། རིགས་ཀྱི་བུ་མོ་གང་གིས་ཐོས་ནས་མོས་པར་བགྱིད་པ་དང་། ཡི་གེར་འབྲིར
སྐྱོལ་བ་དང་། ཡི་གེར་བྲིས་ནས་ཀྱང་འཆང་བ་དང་། ཀློག་པ་དང་། མཆོད་པ་དང་།
ཡང་དག་པར་འགྲེད་པ་དང་། ལུང་འདོན་པ་དང་། ཁ་ཏོན་བགྱིད་པ་དང་། སེམས་པ
དང་། བསྒོམ་པའི་རྣམ་པས་སྦྱོར་བར་བགྱིད་པ་དེ་བསོད་ནམས་ཇི་ཙམ་ཞིག་སྐྱེད་པར

naturally in a state of nirvāṇa. However, this wheel of doctrine that the Bhagavan turned is surpassable, provides an opportunity [for refutation], is of interpretable meaning, and serves as a basis for dispute.

"Then the Bhagavan turned a third wheel of doctrine, possessing good differentiations, and exceedingly wondrous, for those genuinely engaged in all vehicles, beginning with the lack of own-being of phenomena, and beginning with their absence of production, absence of cessation, quiescence from the start, and being naturally in a state of nirvāṇa. Moreover, that wheel of doctrine turned by the Bhagavan is unsurpassable, does not provide an opportunity [for refutation], is of definitive meaning, and does not serve as a basis for dispute.

"Bhagavan, when sons or daughters of good lineage hear the Bhagavan's teachings of definitive meaning, from [the teachings] of the lack of own-being of phenomena up to [the teachings] of [phenomena] being naturally in a state of nirvāṇa, they develop conviction in them and write them down. Having transcribed them, they also memorize them, read them, venerate them, propagate them, receive their oral transmission, recite them to others, and reflect and apply themselves to the types of meditative cultivation. How much merit will they generate?"

The Bhagavan replied to the Bodhisattva Paramārthasamudgata: "Paramārthasamudgata, those sons or daughters

འགྱུར་བ་ལགས། དེ་སྐད་ཅེས་གསོལ་པ་དང་། བཅོམ་ལྡན་འདས་ཀྱིས་བྱང་ཆུབ་སེམས་དཔའ་དོན་དམ་ཡང་དག་འཕགས་ལ་འདི་སྐད་ཅེས་བཀའ་སྩལ་ཏོ། །དོན་དམ་ཡང་དག་འཕགས་རིགས་ཀྱི་བུ་འམ། རིགས་ཀྱི་བུ་མོ་དེ་ནི་བསོད་ནམས་དཔག་ཏུ་མེད་གྲངས་མེད་པ་བསྐྱེད་དེ། དེའི་དཔེ་བྱ་བར་སླ་བམ་ཡིན་མོད་ཀྱི། འོན་ཀྱང་མདོར་བསྡུས་ཏེ་ཁྱོད་ལ་བཤད་པར་བྱའོ། །དོན་དམ་ཡང་དག་འཕགས་འདི་ལྟ་སྟེ་དཔེར་ན་སེན་མོའི་རྩེ་མོ་ལ་གནས་པའི་སའི་རྡུལ་གང་དག་ཡིན་པ་དེ་ནི། ས་ལ་གནས་པའི་རྡུལ་རྣམས་དང་བསྒྲུན་ན་བརྒྱའི་ཆར་ཡང་ཉེ་བར་མི་འགྲོ་ཞིང་སྟོང་གི་ཆ་དང་། འབུམ་གྱི་ཆ་དང་། གྲངས་དང་། ཆ་དང་། བགྲང་བ་དང་། དཔེ་དང་། རྒྱུར་ཡང་ཉེ་བར་མི་འགྲོའོ། །བལང་གི་རྗེས་ཀྱི་ཆུ་ནི་མཚོ་ཆེན་པོ་བཞིའི་ཆུ་དང་བསྒྲུན་ན་བརྒྱའི་ཆར་ཡང་ཉེ་བར་མི་འགྲོ་བ་ནས་རྒྱུའི་བར་དུ་ཡང་ཉེ་བར་མི་འགྲོའོ། །དོན་དམ་ཡང་དག་འཕགས་དེ་བཞིན་དུ་ངས་དྲང་བའི་དོན་གྱི་མདོ་སྡེ་ལ་སོགས་པ་ནས་བསྒོམ་པའི་རྣམ་པར་སྦྱོར་བར་བྱེད་པའི་བར་གྱི་བསོད་ནམས་གང་བཤད་པ་དེ་ནི་ངེས་པའི་དོན་བསྟན་པ་ལ་སོགས་པ་ལས་ཡང་དག་པར་གྲུབ་པ་ནས། བསྒོམ་པའི་རྣམ་པས་སྦྱོར་བ་ལས་ཡང་དག་པར་གྲུབ་པའི་བར་གྱི་བསོད་ནམས་དང་བསྒྲུན་ན་བརྒྱའི་ཆར་ཡང་ཉེ་བར་མི་འགྲོ་བ་ནས་རྒྱུའི་བར་དུ་ཡང་ཉེ་བར་མི་འགྲོའོ། །དེ་སྐད་ཅེས་བཀའ་སྩལ་པ་དང་། བཅོམ་ལྡན་འདས་ལ་བྱང་ཆུབ་སེམས་དཔའ་དོན་དམ་ཡང་དག་འཕགས་ཀྱིས་འདི་སྐད་ཅེས་གསོལ་ཏོ། །བཅོམ་ལྡན་འདས་དགོངས་པ་ངེས་པར་འགྲེལ་པའི་ཆོས་ཀྱི་རྣམ་གྲངས་འདིར་བསྟན་པ་འདིའི་མིང་ཅི་ལགས།

of good lineage will generate immeasurable, incalculable merit. It is not easy to give examples of that [merit], but I will explain it to you briefly.

"Paramārthasamudgata, for example, if one compares the particles of earth on the tip of a fingernail to all the particles of earth in the earth, they do not approach even a hundredth part. They do not approach even a thousandth part, [or] even a one-hundred-thousandth part. They do not approach any number, any part, any approximation, any comparison. If one compares the water in a cow's hoofprint to the water of the four great oceans, it does not approach even a hundredth part. It does not approach any comparison.

"Paramārthasamudgata, similarly, I have described the merit [generated] by people who develop conviction in Sūtras of interpretable meaning up to those who apply themselves to the types of meditative cultivation. If one compares this merit to the merit [generated] by people who are established in teachings of definitive meaning through conviction up to those who are established [in them] through applying themselves to the types of meditative cultivation, that merit does not approach even a hundredth part. It does not approach any comparison."

The Bodhisattva Paramārthasamudgata asked the Bhagavan: "Bhagavan, what is the name of this form of Dharma discourse that explains your thought? How should it be apprehended?"

འདི་ཇི་ལྟར་གཟུང་བར་བགྱི། བཅོམ་ལྡན་འདས་ཀྱིས་དེ་ལ་བཀའ་སྩལ་པ། དོན་དམ་ཡང་དག་འཕགས་འདི་ནི་དོན་དམ་པའི་ངེས་པའི་དོན་བསྟན་པ་ཡིན་ཏེ། འདི་དོན་དམ་པ་ངེས་པའི་དོན་བསྟན་པ་ཞེས་བྱ་བར་ཟུང་ཤིག །དོན་དམ་པ་ངེས་པའི་དོན་བསྟན་པ་འདི་བཤད་པ་ན་སྲོག་ཆགས་དྲུག་འབུམ་ནི་བླ་ན་མེད་པ་ཡང་དག་པར་རྫོགས་པའི་བྱང་ཆུབ་ཏུ་སེམས་སྐྱེས་སོ། །ཉན་ཐོས་སུམ་འབུམ་ནི་ཆོས་རྣམས་ལ་ཆོས་ཀྱི་མིག་རྡུལ་མེད་ཅིང་དྲི་མ་དང་བྲལ་བ་རྣམ་པར་དག་གོ། །ཉན་ཐོས་འབུམ་ལྔ་ཁྲི་ནི་ལེན་པ་མེད་པར་ཟག་པ་རྣམས་ལས་སེམས་རྣམ་པར་གྲོལ་ལོ། །བྱང་ཆུབ་སེམས་དཔའ་བདུན་ཁྲི་ལྔ་སྟོང་གིས་ནི་མི་སྐྱེ་བའི་ཆོས་ལ་བཟོད་པ་ཐོབ་པར་གྱུར་ཏོ། །དོན་དམ་ཡང་དག···འཕགས་ཀྱི་ལེའུ་སྟེ་བདུན་པའོ།། ༎

The Bhagavan replied: "Paramārthasamudgata, this is the teaching of the ultimate, the definitive meaning. Apprehend it as 'the teaching of the ultimate, the definitive meaning'."

When this teaching of the ultimate, the definitive meaning, was explained, six hundred thousand beings generated the aspiration toward unsurpassed, complete, and perfect enlightenment. Three hundred Śrāvakas purified the Dharma eye that is free from dust and stainless with respect to the Dharma. One hundred and fifty thousand Śrāvakas liberated their minds from contamination, becoming free from attachment. Seventy-five thousand Bodhisattvas attained the forbearance of the doctrine of non-production.

This completes the seventh chapter of the Bodhisattva Paramārthasamudgata.

Homage to the Mahābodhisattva Maitreya

།བྱམས་པའི་ལེའུ་སྟེ་བརྒྱད་པ།
The Questions of
Maitreya
Chapter Eight

༄༅། །དེ་ནས་བཅོམ་ལྡན་འདས་ལ་བྱང་ཆུབ་སེམས་དཔའ་བྱམས་པས་ཞུ་བ་ཞུས་པ། བཅོམ་ལྡན་འདས་བྱང་ཆུབ་སེམས་དཔའ་ཅི་ལ་གནས། ཅི་ལ་བརྟེན་ཏེ་ཐེག་པ་ཆེན་པོ་ལ་ཞི་གནས་དང་ལྷག་མཐོང་སྒོམ་པར་བགྱིད་ལགས། བཅོམ་ལྡན་འདས་ཀྱིས་བཀའ་སྩལ་པ། བྱམས་པ་ཆོས་གདགས་པ་རྣམ་པར་གཞག་པ་དང་། བླ་ན་མེད་པ་ཡང་དག་པར་རྫོགས་པའི་བྱང་ཆུབ་ཏུ་སྨོན་ལམ་མི་གཏོང་བ་ལ་གནས་ཤིང་རྟེན་ཅིང་བརྟེན་ནས་སོ། །བཅོམ་ལྡན་འདས་ཀྱིས་ཞི་གནས་དང་ལྷག་མཐོང་གི་དམིགས་པའི་དངོས་པོ་བཞི་པོ་འདི་ལྟ་སྟེ། རྣམ་པར་རྟོག་པ་དང་བཅས་པའི་གཟུགས་བརྙན་དང་། རྣམ་པར་མི་རྟོག་པའི་གཟུགས་བརྙན་དང་། དངོས་པོའི་མཐའ་དང་། དགོས་པ་ཡོངས་སུ་གྲུབ་པའོ་ཞེས་གང་དག་བསྟན་པ་དེ་ལ། བཅོམ་ལྡན་འདས་དུ་ཞིག་ཞི་གནས་ཀྱི་དམིགས་པ་ལགས། བཀའ་སྩལ་པ། གཅིག་སྟེ་འདི་ལྟ་སྟེ། རྣམ་པར་མི་རྟོག་པའི་གཟུགས་བརྙན་ནོ། །དུ་ཞིག་ལྷག་མཐོང་གི་དམིགས་པ་ལགས། བཀའ་སྩལ་པ། གཅིག་ཁོ་ན་སྟེ། རྣམ་པར་རྟོག་པ་དང་བཅས་པའི་གཟུགས་བརྙན་ནོ། །དུ་ཞིག་དེ་གཉི་གའི་དམིགས་པ་ལགས། བཀའ་སྩལ་པ། གཉིས་ཏེ། འདི་ལྟ་སྟེ། དངོས་པོའི་མཐའ་དང་། དགོས་པ་ཡོངས་སུ་གྲུབ་པའོ། །བཅོམ་ལྡན་འདས་བྱང་ཆུབ་སེམས་དཔའ་ཞི་གནས་དང་ལྷག་མཐོང་གི་དམིགས་པའི་དངོས་པོ་བཞི་པོ་དེ་དག་ལ་བརྟེན་ཅིང་གནས་ནས་ཇི་ལྟར་ཞི་གནས་ཡོངས་སུ་ཚོལ་བར་བགྱིད་པ་དང་། ལྷག་མཐོང་ལ་མཁས་པ་ལགས། བཀའ་སྩལ་པ། བྱམས་པ་ངས་ཆོས་གདགས་པ་རྣམ་པར་གཞག་པ་འདི་ལྟ་སྟེ། མདོའི

Then the Bodhisattva Maitreya[1] asked the Bhagavan: "Bhagavan, abiding in what and depending upon what do Bodhisattvas in the Great Vehicle cultivate śamatha and vipaśyanā?"[2]

The Bhagavan replied: "Maitreya, abiding in and depending upon an unwavering resolution to expound doctrinal teachings and to become unsurpassably, perfectly enlightened, [Bodhisattvas cultivate śamatha and vipaśyanā]."[3]

"The Bhagavan has taught that four things are objects of observation of śamatha and vipaśyanā:[4] conceptual images, non-conceptual images, the limits of phenomena, and accomplishment of the purpose.[5] Bhagavan, how many of these are objects of observation of śamatha ?"

[The Bhagavan] replied: "One: non-conceptual images."

"How many are objects of observation of vipaśyanā ?"

[The Bhagavan] replied: "Only one: conceptual images."

"How many are objects of observation of both?"

[The Bhagavan] replied: "There are two: the limits of phenomena and accomplishment of the purpose."

"Bhagavan, abiding in and depending upon these four objects of observation of śamatha and vipaśyanā, how do Bodhisattvas seek śamatha and become skilled in vipaśyanā?"

སྒོ་དང་། དབྱངས་ཀྱིས་བསྙད་པའི་སྒོ་དང་། ལུང་དུ་བསྟན་པའི་སྒོ་དང་། ཚིགས་སུ་བཅད་པའི་སྒོ་དང་། ཆེད་དུ་བརྗོད་པའི་སྒོ་དང་། གླེང་གཞིའི་སྒོ་དང་། རྟོགས་པ་བརྗོད་པའི་སྒོ་དང་། དེ་ལྟ་བུ་བྱུང་བའི་སྒོ་དང་། སྐྱེས་པའི་རབས་ཀྱི་སྒོ་དང་། ཤིན་ཏུ་རྒྱས་པའི་སྒོ་དང་། རྨད་དུ་བྱུང་བའི་ཆོས་ཀྱི་སྒོ་དང་། གཏན་ལ་ཕབ་པར་བསྟན་པའི་སྒོ་གང་དག་བྱང་ཆུབ་སེམས་དཔའ་རྣམས་ལ་བཤད་པ་དེ་དག་བྱང་ཆུབ་སེམས་དཔས་ལེགས་པར་ཐོས། ལེགས་པར་བཟུང་། ཁ་ཏོན་བྱང་བར་བྱས། ཡིད་ཀྱིས་ལེགས་པར་བརྟགས། མཐོང་བས་ཤིན་ཏུ་རྟོགས་པར་བྱས་ནས་དེ་གཅིག་པུ་དབེན་པར་འདུག་སྟེ། ནང་དུ་ཡང་དག་བཞག་ནས་ཇི་ལྟར་ལེགས་པར་བསམས་པའི་ཆོས་དེ་དག་ཡིད་ལ་བྱེད་ཅིང་། སེམས་གང་གིས་ཡིད་ལ་བྱེད་པའི་སེམས་དེ་ནང་དུ་རྒྱུན་ཆགས་སུ་ཡིད་ལ་བྱེད་པས་ཡིད་ལ་བྱེད་དོ། །དེ་ལྟར་ཞུགས་ཤིང་དེ་ལ་ལན་མང་དུ་གནས་པ་དེ་ལ་ལུས་ཤིན་ཏུ་སྦྱངས་པ་དང་སེམས་ཤིན་ཏུ་སྦྱངས་པ་འབྱུང་བ་གང་ཡིན་པ་དེ་ནི་ཞི་གནས་ཞེས་བྱ་སྟེ། དེ་ལྟར་ན་བྱང་ཆུབ་སེམས་དཔའ་ཞི་གནས་ཡོངས་སུ་ཚོལ་བར་བྱེད་པ་ཡིན་ནོ། །དེ་ལུས་ཤིན་ཏུ་སྦྱངས་པ་དང་། སེམས་ཤིན་ཏུ་སྦྱངས་པ་དེ་ཐོབ་ནས་དེ་ཉིད་ལ་གནས་ཏེ། སེམས་ཀྱི་རྣམ་པ་སྤངས་ནས་ཇི་ལྟར་བསམས་པའི་ཆོས་དེ་དག་ཉིད་ནང་དུ་ཏིང་ངེ་འཛིན་གྱི་སྤྱོད་ཡུལ་གཟུགས་བརྙན་དུ་སོ་སོར་རྟོག་པར་བྱེད་མོས་པར་བྱེད་དོ། །དེ་ལྟར་ཏིང་ངེ་འཛིན་གྱི་སྤྱོད་ཡུལ་གཟུགས་བརྙན་དེ་དག་ལ་ཤེས་བྱའི་དོན་དེ་རྣམ་པར་འབྱེད་པ་དང་། རབ་ཏུ་རྣམ་པར་འབྱེད་པ་དང་། ཡོངས་སུ་རྟོག་པ་དང་། ཡོངས་སུ་དཔྱོད་པ་དང་། བཟོད་པ་

"Maitreya, I have set forth these [twelve forms of] doctrinal teachings to Bodhisattvas: Sūtras, discourses in prose and verse, prophetic discourses, verses, purposeful statements, specific teachings, narratives, historical discourses, stories of [the Buddha's] former lives, extensive discourses, discourses on miraculous phenomena, and discourses that delineate [topics of specific knowledge]. Bodhisattvas hear well, apprehend well, repeat well, analyze well with their minds, and through insight, fully realize these [teachings].

"Then, remaining in seclusion, having genuinely settled [their minds] inwardly, they mentally attend to those doctrines just as they have contemplated them.[6] With continuous inner attention, they mentally attend to that mind which is mentally contemplated by any mind. The physical and mental pliancy that arises through engaging [in this practice] in this way and continuing in this [practice] is 'śamatha'. This is how Bodhisattvas seek śamatha.

"Having obtained physical and mental pliancy,[7] they abide in only that. Having abandoned [certain] aspects of the mind,[8] they analyze and inwardly consider those very doctrines in the way they have been contemplated as images that are the focus of samādhi. The differentiation, thorough differentiation, thorough investigation, thorough analysis, forbearance, interest, discrimination, view, and investigation of the objects that are known with respect to images that are the focus of

དང། འདོད་པ་དང། བྱེ་བྲག་འབྱེད་པ་དང། ལྟ་བ་དང། རྟོག་པ་གང་ཡིན་པ་དེ་
ནི་ལྷག་མཐོང་ཞེས་བྱ་སྟེ། དེ་ལྟར་ན་བྱང་ཆུབ་སེམས་དཔའ་ལྷག་མཐོང་ལ་མཁས་པ་ཡིན་
ནོ། །བཅོམ་ལྡན་འདས་བྱང་ཆུབ་སེམས་དཔའ་དེ་ལ་སེམས་ལ་དམིགས་པའི་སེམས་
ནང་དུ་ཡིད་ལ་བྱེད་པ་ན། ཇི་སྲིད་དུ་ལུས་ཤིན་ཏུ་སྦྱངས་པ་དང། སེམས་ཤིན་ཏུ་
སྦྱངས་པ་མ་ཐོབ་པ་དེའི་བར་དུ་ཡིད་ལ་བྱེད་པ་དེ་ལ་ཅི་ཞེས་བགྱི། བྱམས་པ་ཞི་གནས་
ནི་མ་ཡིན་ཏེ། ཞི་གནས་ཀྱི་རྗེས་སུ་འཐུན་པའི་མོས་པ་དང་མཚུངས་པར་ལྡན་པ་ཡིན་པར་
བརྗོད་པར་བྱའོ། །བཅོམ་ལྡན་འདས་བྱང་ཆུབ་སེམས་དཔའ་དེ་ཇི་སྲིད་དུ་ལུས་དང་
སེམས་ཤིན་ཏུ་སྦྱངས་པ་མ་ཐོབ་པ་དེའི་བར་དུ་ཇི་ལྟར་ལེགས་པར་བསམས་པའི་ཆོས་དེ་དག
ནང་དུ་ཏིང་ངེ་འཛིན་གྱི་སྤྱོད་ཡུལ་གཟུགས་བརྙན་དུ་ཡིད་ལ་བྱེད་པའི་ཡིད་ལ་བྱེད་པ་
དེ་ལ་ཅི་ཞེས་བགྱི། བྱམས་པ་ལྷག་མཐོང་ནི་མ་ཡིན་ཏེ། ལྷག་མཐོང་གི་རྗེས་སུ་འཐུན་
པའི་མོས་པ་དང་མཚུངས་ པར་ལྡན་པ་ཡིན་པར་བརྗོད་པར་བྱའོ། །བཅོམ་ལྡན་འདས་ཞི་
གནས་ཀྱི་ལམ་དང། ལྷག་མཐོང་གི་ལམ་ཐ་དད་ཅེས་བགྱིའམ། ཐ་དད་པ་མ་ལགས་
ཞེས་བགྱི། བཀའ་སྩལ་པ། བྱམས་པ་ཐ་དད་པ་ཡང་མ་ཡིན། ཐ་དད་པ་མ་ཡིན་པ་
ཡང་མ་ཡིན་ཞེས་བྱའོ། །ཅིའི་ཕྱིར་ཐ་དད་པ་མ་ཡིན་ཞེ་ན། ལྷག་མཐོང་གི་དམིགས་པའི་
སེམས་ལ་དམིགས་པའི་ཕྱིར་རོ། །ཅིའི་ཕྱིར་ཐ་དད་པ་མ་ཡིན་ཞེ་ན། རྣམ་པར་རྟོག་པ་
དང་བཅས་པའི་གཟུགས་བརྙན་ལ་དམིགས་པའི་ཕྱིར་རོ། །བཅོམ་ལྡན་འདས་རྣམ་པར་
ལྟ་བར་བྱེད་པའི་ཏིང་ངེ་འཛིན་གྱི་སྤྱོད་ཡུལ་གཟུགས་བརྙན་གང་ལགས་པ་དེ་ཅི་ལགས།

such samādhi is 'vipaśyanā'.[9] This is how Bodhisattvas become skilled in vipaśyanā."

"Bhagavan, prior to attaining physical and mental pliancy, when a Bodhisattva inwardly attends to the mind observing the mind, what is this mental activity called?"

"Maitreya, this is not śamatha. Know that it resembles intensified interest concordant with śamatha."

"Bhagavan, prior to attaining physical and mental pliancy, when a Bodhisattva inwardly attends to those doctrines just as they have been contemplated as images that are the focus of samādhi, what is this mental activity called?"

"Maitreya, this is not vipaśyanā. Know that it resembles intensified interest concordant with vipaśyanā."

"Bhagavan, are the path of śamatha and the path of vipaśyanā 'different' or 'not different'?"

The Bhagavan replied: "Maitreya, although they are not different, they are also not the same. Why are they not different? Because [śamatha] observes the mind, which is [also] the object of observation of vipaśyanā. Why are they not the same? Because [vipaśyanā] observes a conceptual image."

"Bhagavan, what is the image, the focus of samādhi which perceives [an image]?[10] Is it 'different from the mind' or is it 'not different'?"

སེམས་དེ་དང་ཐ་དད་པ་ཞེས་བགྱིའམ། ཐ་དད་པ་མ་ལགས་ཞེས་བགྱི། བྱམས་པ་ཐ་དད་པ་མ་ཡིན་ཞེས་བྱའོ། །ཅིའི་ཕྱིར་ཐ་དད་པ་མིན་ཞེ་ན། གཟུགས་བརྙན་དེ་རྣམ་པར་རིག་པ་ཙམ་དུ་ཟད་པའི་ཕྱིར་ཏེ། བྱམས་པ་རྣམ་པར་ཤེས་པ་ནི་དམིགས་པ་རྣམ་པར་རིག་པ་ཙམ་གྱིས་རབ་ཏུ་ཕྱེ་བ་ཡིན་ནོ། །ཞེས་ངས་བཤད་དོ། །བཅོམ་ལྡན་འདས་ཏིང་ངེ་འཛིན་གྱི་སྤྱོད་ཡུལ་གཟུགས་བརྙན་དེ་གལ་ཏེ་གཟུགས་སེམས་དེ་ལས་ཐ་དད་པ་མ་··· ལགས་ན། སེམས་དེ་ཉིད་ཀྱིས་སེམས་དེ་ཉིད་ལ་ཇི་ལྟར་རྟོག་པར་བགྱིད་ལགས། བཀའ་སྩལ་པ། བྱམས་པ་དེ་ལ་ཆོས་གང་ཡང་ཆོས་གང་ལ་ཡང་རྟོག་པར་མི་བྱེད་མོད་ཀྱི། འོན་ཀྱང་དེ་ལྟར་སྐྱེས་པའི་སེམས་གང་ཡིན་པ་དེ་དེ་ལྟར་སྣང་ངོ། །བྱམས་པ་འདི་ལྟ་སྟེ་དཔེར་ན། གཟུགས་ལ་བརྟེན་ནས་མེ་ལོང་གི་དཀྱིལ་འཁོར་ཤིན་ཏུ་ཡོངས་སུ་དག་པ་ལ་གཟུགས་ཉིད་མཐོང་ཡང་གཟུགས་བརྙན་མཐོང་ངོ་སྙམ་དུ་སེམས་ཏེ། དེ་ལ་གཟུགས་དེ་དང༌། གཟུགས་བརྙན་སྣང་བ་དེ་དོན་ཐ་དད་པར་སྣང་ངོ། །དེ་བཞིན་དུ་དེ་ལྟར་སྐྱེས་པའི་སེམས་དེ་དང༌། ཏིང་ངེ་འཛིན་གྱི་སྤྱོད་ཡུལ་གཟུགས་བརྙན་ཞེས་བྱ་བ་གང་ཡིན་པ་དེ་ཡང་དེ་ལས་དོན་གཞན་ཡིན་པ་ལྟ་བུར་སྣང་ངོ། །བཅོམ་ལྡན་འདས་སེམས་ཅན་རྣམས་ཀྱི་གཟུགས་ལ་སོགས་པར་སྣང་བ་སེམས་ཀྱི་གཟུགས་བརྙན་རང་བཞིན་དུ་གནས་པ་གང་ལགས་པ་དེ་ཡང་སེམས་དེ་དང་ཐ་དད་པ་མ་ལགས་ཞེས་བགྱིའམ། བཀའ་སྩལ་པ། བྱམས་པ་ཐ་དད་པ་མ་ཡིན་ཞེས་བྱ་སྟེ། བྱིས་པ་ཕྱིན་ཅི་ལོག་གི་བློ་ཅན་རྣམས་ནི་གཟུགས་བརྙན་དེ་དག་ལ་རྣམ་པར་རིག་པ་ཙམ་དེ་ཉིད་ཡང་དག་པ་ཇི་ལྟ་བ་བཞིན་མི་ཤེས་པས་ཕྱིན

"Maitreya, it is 'not different'. Why is it not different? Because that image is simply cognition-only.[11] Maitreya, I have explained that consciousness is fully distinguished by [the fact that its] object of observation is cognition-only."

"Bhagavan, if that image, the focus of samādhi, is not different from the physical mind, how does the mind itself investigate the mind itself?"[12]

The Bhagavan replied: "Maitreya, although no phenomenon apprehends any other phenomenon, nevertheless, the mind that is generated in that way appears in that way. Maitreya, for instance, based on form, form itself is seen in a perfectly clear round mirror, but one thinks, 'I see an image'. The form and the appearance of the image appear as different factualities. Likewise, the mind that is generated in that way and the focus of samādhi known as the 'image' also appear to be separate factualities."

"Bhagavan, are the appearances of the forms of sentient beings and so forth, which abide in the nature of images of the mind, 'not different' from the mind?"

The Bhagavan replied: "Maitreya, they are 'not different'. However, because childish beings with distorted understanding do not recognize these images as cognition-only, just as they are in reality, they misconstrue them."[13]

"Bhagavan, at what point do those Bodhisattvas solely cultivate [the practice of] vipaśyanā?"

ཅི་ཡོག་ཏུ་སེམས་སོ། །བཅོམ་ལྡན་འདས་བྱང་ཆུབ་སེམས་དཔའ་ཇི་ཙམ་གྱིས་ན། གཅིག་ཏུ་ལྷག་མཐོང་སྒོམ་པ་ལགས། བཀའ་སྩལ་པ། གང་གི་ཚེ་རྒྱུན་ཆགས་སུ་ཡིད་ལ་བྱེད་པས་སེམས་ཀྱི་མཚན་ཉིད་ལ་བྱེད་པའོ། །ཇི་ཙམ་གྱིས་ན་གཅིག་ཏུ་ཞི་གནས་སྒོམ་པ་ལགས། བཀའ་སྩལ་པ། གང་གི་ཚེ་རྒྱུན་ཆགས་སུ་ཡིད་ལ་བྱེད་པས་བར་ཆད་མེད་པའི་སེམས་ཡིད་ལ་བྱེད་པའོ། །ཇི་ཙམ་གྱིས་ན་ཞི་གནས་དང་ལྷག་མཐོང་གཉིས་འདྲེས་པར་འགྱུར་ཏེ་མཉམ་པར་ཟུང་དུ་འཇུག་པ་ལགས། བཀའ་སྩལ་པ། གང་གི་ཚེ་སེམས་རྩེ་གཅིག་པ་ཉིད་ཡིད་ལ་བྱེད་པའོ། །བཅོམ་ལྡན་འདས་སེམས་ཀྱི་མཚན་མ་གང་ལགས། བྱམས་པ་ལྷག་མཐོང་གི་དམིགས་པ་ཏིང་ངེ་འཛིན་གྱི་སྤྱོད་ཡུལ་རྣམ་པར་རྟོག་པ་དང་བཅས་པའི་གཟུགས་བརྙན་གང་ཡིན་པའོ། །བར་ཆད་མ་མཆིས་པའི་སེམས་གང་ལགས། བྱམས་པ་ཞི་གནས་ཀྱི་དམིགས་པ་གཟུགས་བརྙན་ལ་དམིགས་པའི་སེམས་གང་ཡིན་པའོ། །སེམས་རྩེ་གཅིག་པ་ཉིད་གང་ལགས། ཏིང་ངེ་འཛིན་གྱི་སྤྱོད་ཡུལ་གཟུགས་བརྙན་དེ་ལ་འདི་ནི་རྣམ་པར་རིག་པ་ཙམ་ཡིན་ནོ། །ཞེས་བྱ་བར་རྟོགས་ཏེ། དེ་རྟོགས་ནས་དེ་བཞིན་ཉིད་དུ་ཡིད་ལ་བྱེད་པ་གང་ཡིན་པའོ། །བཅོམ་ལྡན་འདས་ལྷག་མཐོང་ལ་རྣམ་པ་དུ་མཆིས། བྱམས་པ་རྣམ་པ་གསུམ་སྟེ། མཚན་མ་ལས་བྱུང་བ་དང་། ཡོངས་སུ་ཚོལ་བ་ལས་བྱུང་བ་དང་། སོ་སོར་རྟོག་པ་ལས་བྱུང་བའོ། །མཚན་མ་ལས་བྱུང་བ་གང་ཞེ་ན། ཏིང་ངེ་འཛིན་གྱི་སྤྱོད་ཡུལ་རྣམ་པར་རྟོག་པ་དང་བཅས་པའི་གཟུགས་བརྙན་འབའ་ཞིག་ཡིད་ལ་བྱེད་པའི་ལྷག་མཐོང་གང་ཡིན་པའོ། །ཡོངས་སུ་ཚོལ་བ་ལས་བྱུང་བ

The Bhagavan replied: "When they attend to mental signs with continuous mental attention."

"At what point do they solely cultivate śamatha?"

The Bhagavan replied: "When they attend to the uninterrupted mind with continuous mental attention."

"At what point, having combined the two, śamatha and vipaśyanā, do they unite them?"

The Bhagavan replied: "When they mentally attend to the one-pointed mind."

"Bhagavan, what are mental signs?"

"Maitreya, they are the conceptual images that are the focus of samādhi, the objects of observation of vipaśyanā."

"What is an uninterrupted mind?"

"Maitreya, it is a mind that observes the image, the object of observation of śamatha."

"What is the one-pointed mind?"

"It is the realization that: 'This image which is the focus of samādhi is cognition-only.' Having realized that, it is mental attention to suchness."[14]

"Bhagavan, how many kinds of vipaśyanā are there?"

"Maitreya, there are three kinds: that arisen from signs, that arisen from examination, and that arisen from individual investigation. What is [vipaśyanā] arisen from signs? It is vipaśyanā that mentally attends to just a conceptual image, the

གང་ཞེ་ན། དེ་དང་དེར་ཤེས་རབ་ཀྱིས་ཤིན་ཏུ་ལེགས་པར་མ་རྟོགས་པའི་ཆོས་དེ་དག་ཉིད་ཤིན་ཏུ་ལེགས་པར་རྟོགས་པར་བྱ་བའི་ཕྱིར་ཡིད་ལ་བྱེད་པའི་ལྷག་མཐོང་གང་ཡིན་པའོ། །སོ་སོར་རྟོག་པ་ལས་བྱུང་བ་གང་ཞེ་ན། དེ་དང་དེར་ཤེས་རབ་ཀྱིས་ཤིན་ཏུ་ལེགས་པར་རྟོགས་པའི་ཆོས་རྣམས་ལ་རྣམ་པར་གྲོལ་བས་ཤིན་ཏུ་ལེགས་པར་བདེ་བ་ལ་རེག་པར་བྱ་བའི་ཕྱིར་ཡིད་ལ་བྱེད་པའི་ལྷག་མཐོང་གང་ཡིན་པའོ། །ཞི་གནས་ལ་རྣམ་པ་དུ་མཆིས། བཀའ་སྩལ་པ། བར་ཆད་མེད་པའི་སེམས་དེའི་རྗེས་སུ་འབྲང་བས་དེ་ཡང་རྣམ་པ་གསུམ་དུ་བརྗོད་པར་བྱའོ། །བྱམས་པ་ཡང་ཞི་གནས་ནི་རྣམ་པ་བརྒྱད་དེ་བསམ་གཏན་དང་པོ་པ་དང་། གཉིས་པ་དང་། གསུམ་པ་དང་། བསམ་གཏན་བཞི་པ་དང་། ནམ་མཁའ་མཐའ་ཡས་སྐྱེ་མཆེད་དང་། རྣམ་ཤེས་མཐའ་ཡས་སྐྱེ་མཆེད་དང་། ཅི་ཡང་མེད་པའི་སྐྱེ་མཆེད་དང་། འདུ་ཤེས་མེད་འདུ་ཤེས་མེད་མིན་སྐྱེ་མཆེད་པའོ། །ཡང་རྣམ་པ་བཞི་སྟེ། བྱམས་པ་ཚད་མེད་པ་དང་། སྙིང་རྗེ་དང་། དགའ་བ་དང་། བཏང་སྙོམས་ཚད་མེད་པའོ༑ ༑བཅོམ་ལྡན་འདས་ཞི་གནས་དང་། ལྷག་མཐོང་ནི་ཆོས་ལ་གནས་པ་ཞེས་ཀྱང་བགྱི༑ ཆོས་ལ་མི་གནས་པ་ཞེས་ཀྱང་བགྱི་ན། ཆོས་ལ་གནས་པ་ནི་གང་ལགས། ཆོས་ལ་མི་གནས་པ་ནི་གང་ལགས། བྱམས་པ་ཇི་ལྟར་བཟུང་བ་དང་། བསམས་པའི་ཆོས་ཀྱི་མཚན་མའི་རྗེས་སུ་འབྲང་བས་དོན་ལ་ཞི་གནས་དང་ལྷག་མཐོང་གང་ཡིན་པ་དེ་ནི་ཆོས་ལ་གནས་པ་ཡིན་ནོ། །བཟུང་བ་དང་བསམས་པའི་ཆོས་ལ་མི་ལྟོས་པར་གཞན་གྱི་གདམས་ངག་དང་། རྗེས་སུ་བསྟན་པ་ལ་བརྟེན་ནས་དོན་ལ་ཞི་གནས་དང་། ལྷག་མཐོང་

focus of samādhi. What is that arisen from examination? It is vipaśyanā that mentally attends [to its object] in order to understand well through wisdom just those phenomena that were not well understood with respect to this or that [image]. What is that arisen from individual investigation? It is vipaśyanā that mentally attends [to its object] in order to contact great happiness through liberation regarding phenomena that have been understood well through wisdom with respect to this or that [image]."

"How many kinds of śamatha are there?"

The Bhagavan replied: "Since [śamatha] engages an uninterrupted mind, it is also said to be of three kinds.[15] Alternately, Maitreya, śamatha is of eight kinds: the first concentration, the second, third, and fourth concentrations, the sphere of limitless space, the sphere of limitless consciousness, the sphere of nothingness, and the sphere without [coarse] discriminations but not without [subtle] discriminations. Alternately, there are four kinds: immeasurable love, immeasurable compassion, immeasurable joy, and immeasurable equanimity."

"Bhagavan, if 'śamatha and vipaśyanā dwell on doctrines' and also 'do not dwell on doctrines', what is dwelling on doctrines? What is not dwelling on doctrines?"

"Maitreya, śamatha and vipaśyanā that relate to meaning—through engagement with the signs of the doctrine[16] in accord with how they have been apprehended and contemplated—dwell on doctrines.

འདི་ལྟ་སྟེ། རྣམ་པར་སྤྲོས་པའམ། རྣམ་པར་རྟགས་པའམ། དེ་ལྟ་བུ་དང་འཐུན་པ
རྣམས་སམ། འདུ་བྱེད་ཐམས་ཅད་མི་རྟག་པ་ཞེས་བྱ་བའམ། སྡུག་བསྔལ་བ་ཞེས་བྱ
བའམ། ཆོས་ཐམས་ཅད་བདག་མེད་པ་ཞེས་བྱ་བའམ། མྱ་ངན་ལས་འདས་པ་ཞི་བ
ཞེས་བྱ་བ་དང་། དེ་ལྟ་བུ་དང་འཐུན་པའི་ཞི་གནས་དང་ལྷག་མཐོང་དེ་ནི་ཆོས་ལ་མི་གནས
པ་ཡིན་པར་རིག་པར་བྱའོ། །བྱམས་པ་དེ་ལ་ང་ནི་ཆོས་ལ་གནས་པའི་ཞི་གནས་དང་ལྷག
མཐོང་ལ་བརྟེན་ནས་བྱང་ཆུབ་སེམས་དཔའ་ཆོས་ཀྱི་རྗེས་སུ་འབྲང་བ་དབང་པོ་རྣོན་པོར
འདོགས་སོ། །ཆོས་ལ་མི་གནས་པ་ལ་བརྟེན་ནས་དད་པས་རྗེས་སུ་འབྲང་བ་དབང་པོ
རྟུལ་པོར་འདོགས་སོ། །བཅོམ་ལྡན་འདས་ཞི་གནས་དང་ལྷག་མཐོང་ནི་མ་འདྲེས་པའི་ཆོས
ལ་དམིགས་པ་ཞེས་ཀྱང་བགྱི། འདྲེས་པའི་ཆོས་ལ་དམིགས་པ་ཞེས་ཀྱང་བགྱི་ན། མ
འདྲེས་པའི་ཆོས་ལ་དམིགས་པ་ནི་གང་ལགས། འདྲེས་པའི་ཆོས་ལ་དམིགས་པ་ནི་གང
ལགས། བྱམས་པ་གལ་ཏེ་བྱང་ཆུབ་སེམས་དཔའ་ཇི་ལྟར་བཟུང་བ་དང་བསམས་པའི
ཆོས་རྣམས་ལས་མདོའི་སྡེ་ལ་སོགས་པའི་ཆོས་སོ་སོ་ལ་དམིགས་པའི་ཞི་གནས་དང་།
ལྷག་མཐོང་སྒོམ་པར་བྱེད་པ་དེ་ནི་མ་འདྲེས་པའི་ཆོས་ལ་དམིགས་པའི་ཞི་གནས་དང་།
ལྷག་མཐོང་ཡིན་ནོ། །གལ་ཏེ་མདོ་སྡེ་ལ་སོགས་པའི་ཆོས་དེ་གཅིག་ཏུ་བཟླུམ་པ་དང་།
གཅིག་ཏུ་བསྡུ་བ་དང་། གཅིག་ཏུ་བརྟུལ་བ་དང་། ཕུང་པོ་གཅིག་ཏུ་བྱས་ཏེ། ཆོས
འདི་དག་ཐམས་ཅད་ནི་དེ་བཞིན་ཉིད་ལ་གཞོལ་བ། དེ་བཞིན་ཉིད་ལ་འབབ་པ། དེ
བཞིན་ཉིད་ལ་བབ་པ། བྱང་ཆུབ་ལ་གཞོལ་བ། བྱང་ཆུབ་ལ་འབབ་པ། བྱང་ཆུབ

"Śamatha and vipaśyanā that relate to meaning by relying on instructions and teachings from others, without attending to doctrines in accord with how they have been apprehended and contemplated—[focusing] on discolored or putrefying corpses or on what is concordant with that, or on the impermanence of compounded phenomena, or on suffering, or on the selflessness of all phenomena, or on the peace of nirvāṇa, or on what is concordant with that—are śamatha and vipaśyanā that do not dwell on doctrines.

"Maitreya, I designate Bodhisattvas who follow the teaching, depending upon śamatha and vipaśyanā that dwell on doctrines, as having sharp faculties. I designate those who follow with faith, depending upon [śamatha and vipaśyanā] that do not dwell on doctrines, as having dull faculties."

"Bhagavan, if 'śamatha and vipaśyanā observe unintegrated doctrines' and also 'observe integrated doctrines', what is observation of unintegrated doctrines? What is observation of integrated doctrines?"[17]

"Maitreya, if a Bodhisattva cultivates śamatha and vipaśyanā that observe particular doctrines of the Sūtras and so forth from among the doctrines, just as [those particular doctrines] have been apprehended and contemplated, this is the śamatha and vipaśyanā that observe unintegrated doctrines. But if [a Bodhisattva] gathers these doctrines from the Sūtras and so forth together, groups them comprehensively, draws them into an aggregated unit, and takes to mind the thought—

ལ་བབ་པ། རྒྱུ་དན་ལས་འདས་པ་ལ་གཞོལ་བ། རྒྱུ་དན་ལས་འདས་པ་ལ་འབབ་པ། རྒྱུ་དན་ལས་འདས་པ་ལ་བབ་པ། གནས་གྱུར་པ་ལ་གཞོལ་བ། གནས་གྱུར་པ་ལ་འབབ་པ། གནས་གྱུར་པ་ལ་བབ་པ་དག་སྟེ། ཆོས་འདི་དག་ཐམས་ཅད་ནི་དགེ་བའི་ཆོས་དཔག་ཏུ་མེད་པ། གྲངས་མེད་པ་དག་མངོན་པར་རྫོགས་པར་རྫོགས་པ་ཡིན་ནོ་སྙམ་དུ་ཡིད་ལ་བྱེད་པ་དེ་ནི། འདྲིས་པའི་ཆོས་ལ་དམིགས་པའི་ཞི་གནས་དང་ལྷག་མཐོང་ཡིན་ནོ། །བཅོམ་ལྡན་འདས་ཞི་གནས་དང་ལྷག་མཐོང་ནི་འདྲིས་པ་ཆུང་ངུའི་ཆོས་ལ་དམིགས་པ་ཞེས་ཀྱང་བགྱི། འདྲིས་པ་ཆེན་པོར་གྱུར་པའི་ཆོས་ལ་དམིགས་པ་ཞེས་ཀྱང་བགྱི། འདྲིས་པ་ཚད་མ་མཆིས་པའི་ཆོས་ལ་དམིགས་པ་ཞེས་ཀྱང་བགྱི་ན། འདྲིས་པ་ཆུང་ངུའི་ཆོས་ལ་དམིགས་པ་ནི་གང་ལགས། འདྲིས་པ་ཆེན་པོར་གྱུར་པའི་ཆོས་ལ་དམིགས་པ་ནི་གང་ལགས། འདྲིས་པ་ཚད་མ་མཆིས་པའི་ཆོས་ལ་དམིགས་པ་ནི་གང་ལགས། བྱམས་པ་མདོའི་སྡེ་ནས་ཤིན་ཏུ་རྒྱས་པའི་སྡེ་དང་། རྨད་དུ་བྱུང་བའི་ཆོས་ཀྱི་སྡེ་དང་། གཏན་ལ་ཕབ་པར་བསྟན་པའི་སྡེའི་བར་དག་སོ་སོར་གཅིག་ཏུ་བཟླུམས་ཏེ། ཡིད་ལ་བྱེད་པའི་ཞི་གནས་དང་ལྷག་མཐོང་ནི་འདྲིས་པ་ཆུང་ངུའི་ཆོས་ལ་དམིགས་པ་ཡིན་པར་རིག་པར་བྱའོ། །མདོའི་སྡེ་ལ་སོགས་པ་དེ་དག་ཉིད་ཇི་སྙེད་བཟུང་བ་དང་། བསམས་པ་སོ་སོར་གཅིག་ཏུ་བཟླུམས་ཏེ་ཡིད་ལ་བྱེད་པ་ནི་འདྲིས་པ་ཆེན་པོར་གྱུར་པའི་ཆོས་ལ་དམིགས་པ་ཡིན་པར་རིག་པར་བྱའོ། །དེ་བཞིན་གཤེགས་པ་རྣམས་ཀྱི་ཆོས་བསྟན་པ་ཚད་མེད་པ་རྣམས་དང་། ཆོས་ཀྱི་ཚིག་དང་། ཡི་གེ་ཚད་མེད་པ་རྣམས་དང་། གོང་ནས་གོང་དུ

'All these doctrines flow into suchness, descend into suchness, have descended into suchness; flow into enlightenment, descend into enlightenment, have descended into enlightenment; flow into nirvāṇa, descend into nirvāṇa, have descended into nirvāṇa; flow into transformation of the basis, descend into transformation of the basis, have descended into transformation of the basis.[18] All these doctrines have been expressed through the manifest expression of innumerable and measureless virtuous doctrines'—this is śamatha and vipaśyanā that observe integrated doctrines."

"Bhagavan, if 'śamatha and vipaśyanā observe somewhat integrated doctrines', and also 'observe highly integrated doctrines', and also 'observe immeasurably integrated doctrines': What is observation of somewhat integrated doctrines? What is observation of highly integrated doctrines? What is observation of immeasurably integrated doctrines?"[19]

"Maitreya, know that śamatha and vipaśyanā mentally attending to [doctrines]—from the Sūtra section up to the extensive discourses, the discourses on miraculous phenomena, and the discourses that delineate—as one unit are the observation of somewhat integrated doctrines. Know that [śamatha and vipaśyanā] mentally attending to the Sūtras and so forth, as many as have been collectively apprehended and contemplated, are the observation of highly integrated doctrines. Understand that [śamatha and vipaśyanā] mentally attending comprehensively to all the immeasurable Dharma teachings

ཤེས་རབ་དང་། སྤྲོབས་པ་ཚད་མེད་པ་རྣམས་གཅིག་ཏུ་བསྡུམས་ཏེ་ཡིད་ལ་བྱེད་པའི་ནི་འདྲིས་པ་ཚད་མེད་པའི་ཆོས་ལ་དམིགས་པ་ཡིན་པར་རིག་པར་བྱའོ། །བཅོམ་ལྡན་འདས་བྱང་ཆུབ་སེམས་དཔའ་ཇི་ཙམ་གྱིས་ན་འདྲིས་པའི་ཆོས་ལ་དམིགས་པའི་ཞི་གནས་དང་ལྷག་མཐོང་ཐོབ་པར་འགྱུར་ལགས། བྱམས་པ་དེ་ནི་རྒྱུ་ལྔས་ཐོབ་པར་འགྱུར་བར་རིག་པར་བྱ་སྟེ། འདི་ལྟ་སྟེ་ཡིད་ལ་བྱེད་པའི་ཚེ་སྐད་ཅིག་སྐད་ཅིག་ལ་གནས་ངན་ལེན་གྱི་རྟེན་ཐམས་ཅད་འཇིག་པར་བྱེད་པ་དང་། འདུ་བྱེད་སྣ་ཚོགས་རྣམ་པར་སྤངས་ཏེ། ཆོས་ཀྱི་ཀུན་དགའ་ལ་དགའ་བ་འཐོབ་པ་དང་། ཆོས་སྣང་བ་ཕྱོགས་བཅུར་ཚད་མེད་ཅིང་རྣམ་པ་ཡོངས་སུ་མ་ཆད་པ་ཡང་དག་པར་ཤེས་པ་དང་། དགོས་པ་ཡོངས་སུ་གྲུབ་པ་དང་ལྡན་པ་རྣམ་པར་དག་པའི་ཆ་དང་འཐུན་པའི་མཚན་མ་རྣམ་པར་མ་བརྟགས་པ་རྣམས་དེ་ལ་ཀུན་འབྱུང་བ་དང་། ཆོས་ཀྱི་སྐུ་འཐོབ་པ་དང་། ཡོངས་སུ་རྫོགས་པ་དང་ཡོངས་སུ་འགྲུབ་པར་བྱ་བའི་ཕྱིར་རྒྱུ་གོང་མ་བས་ཆེས་གོང་མ། བཟང་པོ་བས་ཆེས་བཟང་པོ་ཡང་དག་པར་ཡོངས་སུ་འཛིན་པར་བྱེད་པའོ། །བཅོམ་ལྡན་འདས་འདྲིས་པའི་ཆོས་ལ་དམིགས་པའི་ཞི་གནས་དང་ལྷག་མཐོང་དེ་གང་ལ་རྟོགས་ཤིང་གང་ལ་འཐོབ་པར་འཚལ་བར་བགྱི་ལགས། བཀའ་སྩལ་པ། བྱམས་པས་དང་པོ་རབ་ཏུ་དགའ་བ་ལ་ནི་རྟོགས་པ་ཡིན་ལ། ས་གསུམ་པ་འོད་བྱེད་པ་ལ་ནི་ཐོབ་པར་རིག་པར་བྱ་སྟེ། བྱམས་པ་དེ་ལྟ་མོད་ཀྱི། བྱང་ཆུབ་སེམས་དཔའ་ལས་དང་པོ་པས་ཀྱང་དེ་ལ་རྗེས་སུ་བསླབ་ཅིང་ཡིད་ལ་བྱ་བར་མི་གཏང་བར་བགྱིའོ། །བཅོམ་ལྡན་འདས་ཇི་ལྟར་ན་ཞི་གནས་དང་ལྷག་མཐོང་རྟོག་པ་དང་བཅས་ཤིང

of the Tathāgata, to [all] the immeasurable words and letters of the doctrine, and to immeasurable ever-increasing wisdom and inspiration are the observation of immeasurably integrated doctrines."

"Bhagavan, how is it that Bodhisattvas attain śamatha and vipaśyanā that observe integrated doctrines?"

"Maitreya, know that they attain them through five causes: In each moment of mental attention they destroy all of the bases of errant tendencies. Having abandoned various motivational factors, they attain joy in the joyousness of the Dharma. They correctly understand that the appearances of the Dharma are measureless in the ten directions and that their aspects are unlimited. They are endowed with accomplishment of the purpose, and the non-imaginary signs that are partially concordant with purification arise in them. In order to attain, perfect, and accomplish the Dharmakāya, they take hold of the causes of increasing goodness, the greatest auspiciousness."

"Bhagavan, on what [stage] are śamatha and vipaśyanā that observe integrated doctrines realized, and on what [stage] are they understood to be attained?"

The Bhagavan replied: "Maitreya, know that having been realized on the first stage, the Very Joyous, they are attained on the third stage, the Luminous. Nevertheless, Maitreya, even beginning Bodhisattvas should not neglect training in them and mentally attending to them."

དཔྱོད་པ་དང་བཅས་པའི་ཏིང་ངེ་འཛིན་དུ་འགྱུར་བ་ལགས། ཇི་ལྟར་རྟོག་པ་མ་མཆིས་ཤིང་དཔྱོད་པ་ཙམ་དུ་འགྱུར་བ་ལགས། ཇི་ལྟར་ན་རྟོག་པ་མ་མཆིས་པ་དང་དཔྱོད་པ་མ་མཆིས་པར་འགྱུར་བ་ལགས། བྱམས་པ་ཇི་ལྟར་བཟུང་ཞིང་བརྟགས་པ་དང་། དཔྱོད་པའི་ཆོས་རྣམས་ལ་དེ་དག་གི་མཚན་མ་གསལ་ཞིང་རགས་པ་མྱོང་བའི་རྗེས་སུ་དཔྱོད་པའི་ཞི་གནས་དང་ལྷག་མཐོང་གང་ཡིན་པ་དེ་ནི། རྟོག་པ་དང་བཅས་ཤིང་དཔྱོད་པ་དང་བཅས་པའི་ཏིང་ངེ་འཛིན་ཡིན་ནོ། །དེ་དག་ཉིད་ཀྱི་མཚན་མ་གསལ་ཞིང་རགས་པ་མྱོང་བའི་རྗེས་སུ་དཔྱོད་པ་མ་ཡིན་མོད་ཀྱི། འོན་ཀྱང་དེ་སྣང་བ་འོལ་ཕྱི་དྲན་པ་ཙམ་ཕྲ་མོ་མྱོང་བའི་རྗེས་སུ་དཔྱོད་པའི་ཞི་གནས་དང་། ལྷག་མཐོང་གང་ཡིན་པ་དེ་ནི་རྟོག་པ་མེད་ཅིང་དཔྱོད་པ་ཙམ་གྱི་ཏིང་ངེ་འཛིན་ཡིན་ནོ། །དེ་དག་གི་མཚན་མ་ལ་ཐམས་ཅད་ཀྱི་ཐམས་ཅད་དུ་ལྷུན་གྱིས་གྲུབ་པར་ཆོས་མྱོང་བ་ཡིད་ལ་བྱེད་པས་རྣམ་པར་དཔྱོད་པའི་ཞི་གནས་དང་ལྷག་མཐོང་གང་ཡིན་པ་དེ་ནི་རྟོག་པ་མེད་པ་དང་དཔྱོད་པ་མེད་པའི་ཏིང་ངེ་འཛིན་ཡིན་ནོ། །བྱམས་པ་ཡང་ཡོངས་སུ་ཚོལ་བ་ལས་བྱུང་བའི་ཞི་གནས་དང་ལྷག་མཐོང་གང་ཡིན་པ་དེ་ནི་རྟོག་པ་དང་བཅས་ཤིང་དཔྱོད་པ་དང་བཅས་པའི་ཏིང་ངེ་འཛིན་ཡིན་ནོ། །སོ་སོར་རྟོག་པ་ལས་བྱུང་བ་གང་ཡིན་པ་དེ་ནི། རྟོག་པ་མེད་ཅིང་དཔྱོད་པ་ཙམ་གྱི་ཏིང་ངེ་འཛིན་ཡིན་ནོ། །འདྲེས་པའི་ཆོས་ལ་དམིགས་པ་གང་ཡིན་པ་དེ་ནི་རྟོག་པ་མེད་པ་དང་། དཔྱོད་པ་མེད་པའི་ཏིང་ངེ་འཛིན་ཡིན་ནོ། །བཅོམ་ལྡན་འདས་ཞི་གནས་ཀྱི་རྒྱུ་མཚན་ནི་གང་ལགས། རབ་ཏུ་འཛིན་པའི་རྒྱུ་མཚན་ནི་གང་ལགས། བཏང་སྙོམས་ཀྱི་རྒྱུ་མཚན་ནི་གང་ལགས།

"Bhagavan, at what point are śamatha and vipaśyanā conceptual and analytical samādhi? At what point do they become non-conceptual and only analytical? At what point do they become non-conceptual and non-analytical?"[20]

"Maitreya, analytical śamatha and vipaśyanā that experience the clear and coarse signs of doctrines that are analyzed in just the way that they have been apprehended and investigated are samādhis that are conceptual and analytical.[21] The śamatha and vipaśyanā that are not analytical in experiencing the clear and coarse signs of these very [doctrines], but are analytical in experiencing a mere subtle mindfulness of their approximate appearances, are a non-conceptual and solely analytical samādhi. Śamatha and vipaśyanā that are completely analytical due to mentally attending to the experience of doctrines spontaneously and totally with respect to all their signs are a non-conceptual and non-analytical samādhi.

"Moreover, Maitreya, śamatha and vipaśyanā that arise from investigation are a conceptual and analytical samādhi. Śamatha and vipaśyanā that arise from individual realization are a non-conceptual and solely analytical samādhi. [Śamatha and vipaśyanā] that observe integrated doctrines are a non-conceptual, non-analytical samādhi."

"Bhagavan, what is the cause of śamatha? What is the cause of thorough stabilization? What is the cause of equanimity?"

བྱམས་པ་སེམས་རྒོད་པའམ། རྒོད་དུ་དོགས་པ་ན། ཀུན་ཏུ་སྐྱོ་བར་འགྱུར་བ་དང་འཐུན་པའི་ཆོས་རྣམས་དང་། བར་ཆད་མེད་པའི་སེམས་དེ་ཡིད་ལ་བྱེད་པ་གང་ཡིན་པ་དེ་ནི་གནས་ཀྱི་རྒྱུ་མཚན་ཞེས་བྱའོ། །བྱམས་པ་སེམས་བྱིང་ངམ། བྱིང་དུ་དོགས་པ་ན། མངོན་པར་དགའ་བར་འགྱུར་བ་དང་འཐུན་པའི་ཆོས་རྣམས་དང་། སེམས་ཀྱི་མཚན་མ་དེ་ཡིད་ལ་བྱེད་པ་གང་ཡིན་པ་དེ་ནི་རབ་ཏུ་འཛིན་པའི་རྒྱུ་མཚན་ཞེས་བྱའོ། །བྱམས་པ་ཞི་གནས་ལ་གཅིག་ཏུ་ངེས་པའམ། ལྷག་མཐོང་ལ་གཅིག་ཏུ་ངེས་པའམ། ཟུང་དུ་འབྲེལ་བའི་ལམ་ཡང་རུང་སྟེ། དེ་གཉིས་ཀའི་ཉེ་བའི་ཉོན་མོངས་པས་ཉེ་བར་ཉོན་མོངས་པ་མེད་པ་ལ་སེམས་རང་གི་ངང་གིས་འཇུག་པ་ན་ཡིད་ལ་བྱེད་པ་ལྷུན་གྱིས་གྲུབ་པ་གང་ཡིན་པ་དེ་ནི་བཏང་སྙོམས་ཀྱི་རྒྱུ་མཚན་ཞེས་བྱའོ། །བཅོམ་ལྡན་འདས་བྱང་ཆུབ་སེམས་དཔའ་ཞི་གནས་དང་ལྷག་མཐོང་བསྒོམ་པ། ཆོས་སོ་སོར་ཡང་དག་པར་རིག་པ་དང་། དོན་སོ་སོར་ཡང་དག་པར་རིག་པ་ལགས་ན། ཇི་ལྟར་ཆོས་སོ་སོར་ཡང་དག་པར་རིག་པ་ལགས། ཇི་ལྟར་དོན་སོ་སོར་ཡང་དག་པར་རིག་པ་ལགས། བྱམས་པ་རྣམ་པ་ལྔས་སོ་སོར་ཡང་དག་པར་རིག་པ་ཡིན་ཏེ། མིང་དང་ཚིག་དང་ཡི་གེ་དང་སོ་སོ་བ་དང་བསྡུས་པས་སོ། །མིང་གང་ཞེ་ན། ཀུན་ནས་ཉོན་མོངས་པ་དང་། རྣམ་པར་བྱང་བའི་ཆོས་རྣམས་ལ་ངོ་བོ་ཉིད་དང་། བྱེ་བྲག་གི་མིང་དུ་བྱ་བར་བཏགས་པ་གང་ཡིན་པའོ། །ཚིག་གང་ཞེ་ན། ཀུན་ནས་ཉོན་མོངས་པ་དང་། རྣམ་པར་བྱང་བ་པའི་དོན་རྗེས་སུ་ཐ་སྙད་གདགས་པའི་ཕྱིར་གནས་དང་རྟེན་མིང་དེ་དག་ཉིད་ཀྱི་ཚོགས་ལ་བརྟེན་པ་གང་ཡིན་པའོ། །ཡི་གེ་གང་ཞེ་ན།

"Maitreya, when the mind is excited, or when one fears that it will become excited, mental attention to sobering phenomena and to the uninterrupted mind is 'the cause of śamatha'.[22]

"Maitreya, when the mind becomes dull, or when one fears that it will become dull, mental attention to pleasant phenomena and to the characteristics of the mind is 'the cause of thorough stabilization'.

"Maitreya, when those following a path that is singly dedicated to śamatha, or that is singly dedicated to vipaśyanā, or that is a union of those two, naturally engage their minds in a [state] unafflicted by the two afflictions [of excitement and dullness], this spontaneous mental attention is 'the cause of equanimity'."

"Bhagavan, when Bodhisattvas cultivating śamatha and vipaśyanā comprehend doctrine and objects, how do they comprehend doctrine? How do they comprehend objects?"[23]

"Maitreya, they comprehend doctrine through five aspects: names, words, letters, individuality, and integration. What are names? They are what is attributed to afflicted or purified phenomena as the designation for entities or particulars. What are words? They are what depends upon collections of those very names which are associated through conventional designations of objects as being afflicted or pure. What are letters? They are the units that are the bases

དེ་གཉིས་གའི་གནས་ཀྱི་ཡིག་འབྲུ་གང་ཡིན་པའོ། །དེ་དག་སོ་སོ་ལས་སོ་སོ་ཡང་དག་པར་རིག་པ་གང་ཞེ་ན། མ་འདྲེས་པ་ལ་དམིགས་པའི་ཡིད་ལ་བྱེད་པས་སོ་སོ་ཡང་དག་པར་རིག་པ་གང་ཡིན་པའོ། །བསྡུས་པ་ལས་སོ་སོ་ཡང་དག་པར་རིག་པ་གང་ཞེ་ན། འདྲེས་པ་ལ་དམིགས་པའི་ཡིད་ལ་བྱེད་པས་སོ་སོར་ཡང་དག་པར་རིག་པ་གང་ཡིན་པའོ། །དེ་དག་ཐམས་ཅད་གཅིག་ཏུ་བསྡུ་ན་ཆོས་སོ་སོ་ཡང་དག་པར་རིག་པ་ཞེས་བྱ་སྟེ། དེ་ལྟར་ན་ཆོས་སོ་སོར་ཡང་དག་པར་རིག་པ་ཡིན་ནོ། །བྱང་ཆུབ་སེམས་དཔའ་རྣམ་པ་བཅུས་དོན་སོ་སོ་ཡང་དག་པར་རིག་པ་ཡིན་ཏེ། ཇི་སྙེད་ཡོད་པ་ཉིད་དང་། ཇི་ལྟ་བ་བཞིན་དུ་ཡོད་པ་ཉིད་དང་། འཛིན་པའི་དོན་དང་། གཟུང་བའི་དོན་དང་། གནས་པའི་དོན་དང་། ལོངས་སྤྱོད་ཀྱི་དོན་དང་། ཕྱིན་ཅི་ལོག་གི་དོན་དང་། ཕྱིན་ཅི་མ་ལོག་པའི་དོན་དང་། ཀུན་ནས་ཉོན་མོངས་པའི་དོན་དང་། རྣམ་པར་བྱང་བའི་དོན་གྱིས་སོ། །བྱམས་པ་དེ་ལ་ཀུན་ནས་ཉོན་མོངས་པ་དང་། རྣམ་པར་བྱང་བའི་ཆོས་རྣམས་ལ་རྣམ་པ་རབ་ཏུ་དབྱེ་བ་ཐམས་ཅད་ཀྱི་མཐར་ཐུག་པ་གང་ཡིན་པ་དེ་ནི་ཇི་སྙེད་ཡོད་པ་ཉིད་ཡིན་ཏེ། འདི་ལྟ་སྟེ། ཕུང་པོ་རྣམས་ཀྱི་ནི་གྲངས་ལྔས་སོ། །ནང་གི་སྐྱེ་མཆེད་རྣམས་ཀྱི་ནི་གྲངས་དྲུག་གིས་སོ། །ཕྱི་རོལ་གྱི་སྐྱེ་མཆེད་རྣམས་ཀྱི་ཡང་གྲངས་དྲུག་པོ་ནས་སོ་ཞེས་བྱ་བ་ལ་སོགས་པའོ། །བྱམས་པ་དེ་ལ་ཀུན་ནས་ཉོན་མོངས་པ་དང་། རྣམ་པར་བྱང་བ་བའི་ཆོས་དེ་དག་ཉིད་ཀྱི་དེ་བཞིན་ཉིད་གང་ཡིན་པ་དེ་ནི་ཇི་ལྟ་བ་བཞིན་དུ་ཡོད་པ་ཉིད་ཡིན་ཏེ། དེ་ཡང་རྣམ་པ་བདུན་ཏེ། འབྱུང་བའི་དེ་བཞིན་ཉིད་ནི་འདུ་བྱེད་རྣམས་ཀྱི་ཐོག་མ་དང་ཐ་མ་མེད་པ་ཉིད་གང

of these two. What is comprehended through their 'individuality'? It is comprehension due to mental attention that observes unintegrated [doctrines]. What is comprehended through their 'integration'? It is comprehension due to mental attention that observes integrated [doctrines]. All of these are collectively known as 'comprehension of doctrine'. That is how [Bodhisattvas] comprehend doctrine.

"Bodhisattvas comprehend objects through these ten aspects: through what exists relatively; through what exists in fact; through apprehending objects; through apprehended objects; through objects that are abodes; through objects that are resources; through mistaken objects; through non-mistaken objects; through afflicted objects; and through purified objects.

"Maitreya, the totality of all the types of divisions among afflicted or purified phenomena is 'that which exists relatively'. This [totality] includes the fivefold enumeration of the aggregates, the sixfold enumeration of the internal sense spheres, the sixfold enumeration of the external sense spheres, and so forth.

"Maitreya, the suchness of those same afflicted and purified phenomena is 'that which exists in fact'. Furthermore, [suchness] has seven aspects: the 'suchness of arising' is the beginninglessness and endlessness of compounded phenomena; the 'suchness of character' is the selflessness of persons

ཡིན་པའོ། །མཚན་ཉིད་ཀྱི་དེ་བཞིན་ཉིད་ནི་ཆོས་ཐམས་ཅད་ཀྱི་གང་ཟག་བདག་མེད་པ་
དང་། ཆོས་བདག་མེད་པ་གང་ཡིན་པའོ། །རྣམ་པར་རིག་པའི་དེ་བཞིན་ཉིད་ནི་འདུ་
བྱེད་རྣམས་རྣམ་པར་རིག་པ་ཉིད་གང་ཡིན་པའོ། །གནས་པའི་དེ་བཞིན་ཉིད་ནི་ངས་སྡུག་
བསྔལ་གྱི་བདེན་པ་བསྟན་པ་གང་ཡིན་པའོ། །ལོག་པར་སྒྲུབ་པའི་དེ་བཞིན་ཉིད་ནི་ངས་
ཀུན་འབྱུང་བའི་བདེན་པ་བསྟན་པ་གང་ཡིན་པའོ། །རྣམ་པར་དག་པའི་དེ་བཞིན་ཉིད་ནི་
ངས་འགོག་པའི་བདེན་པ་བསྟན་པ་གང་ཡིན་པའོ། །ཡང་དག་པར་སྒྲུབ་པའི་དེ་བཞིན་
ཉིད་ནི་ངས་ལམ་གྱི་བདེན་པ་བསྟན་པ་གང་ཡིན་པའོ། །བྱམས་པ་དེ་ལ་འབྱུང་བའི་དེ་
བཞིན་ཉིད་གང་ཡིན་པ་དེ་དང་། གནས་པའི་དེ་བཞིན་ཉིད་གང་ཡིན་པ་དེ་དང་། ལོག་
པར་སྒྲུབ་པའི་དེ་བཞིན་ཉིད་གང་ཡིན་པ་དེས་ནི་སེམས་ཅན་ཐམས་ཅད་མཚུངས་ཤིང་མཉམ་
མོ། །བྱམས་པ་དེ་ལ་མཚན་ཉིད་ཀྱི་དེ་བཞིན་ཉིད་གང་ཡིན་པ་དེ་དང་། རྣམ་པར་རིག་
པའི་དེ་བཞིན་ཉིད་གང་ཡིན་པ་དེས་ནི་ཆོས་ཐམས་ཅད་དང་མཚུངས་ཤིང་མཉམ་མོ། །
བྱམས་པ་རྣམ་པར་དག་པའི་དེ་བཞིན་ཉིད་གང་ཡིན་པ་དེས་ནི་ཉན་ཐོས་ཀྱི་བྱང་ཆུབ་གང་
ཡིན་པ་དང་། རང་སངས་རྒྱས་ཀྱི་བྱང་ཆུབ་གང་ཡིན་པ་དང་། བླ་ན་མེད་པ་ཡང་དག་
པར་རྫོགས་པའི་བྱང་ཆུབ་གང་ཡིན་པའི་བྱང་ཆུབ་ཐམས་ཅད་མཚུངས་ཤིང་མཉམ་མོ། །
བྱམས་པ་དེ་ལ་ཡང་དག་པར་སྒྲུབ་པའི་དེ་བཞིན་ཉིད་དེས་ནི་ཐོས་པ་ཐམས་ཅད་འདྲེས་པའི་
ཆོས་ལ་དམིགས་པའི་ཞི་གནས་དང་ལྷག་མཐོང་གི་བསྡུས་པའི་ཤེས་རབ་མཚུངས་ཤིང་
མཉམ་མོ། །བྱམས་པ་དེ་ལ་འཛིན་པའི་དོན་ནི་སྐྱེ་མཆེད་གཟུགས་ཅན་ལྔ་དང་། སེམས་

and the selflessness of phenomena in all phenomena; the 'suchness of cognition' [understands] that compounded phenomena are cognition-only; the 'suchness of abiding' is what I taught as the truth of suffering; the 'suchness of wrong establishment' is what I taught as the truth of the origin of suffering; the 'suchness of purification' is what I taught as the truth of the cessation of suffering; and the 'suchness of right establishment' is what I taught as the truth of the path.

"Maitreya, due to the suchness of arising, the suchness of abiding, and the suchness of wrong establishment, all sentient beings are similar and equal.

"Maitreya, due to the suchness of character and the suchness of cognition, all phenomena are similar and equal.

"Maitreya, due to the suchness of purification, all enlightenments—the enlightenment of Śrāvakas, the enlightenment of Pratyekabuddhas, and supreme, perfect enlightenment—are similar and equal.

"Maitreya, due to the suchness of right establishment, wisdom conjoined with śamatha and vipaśyanā, that observes all that one hears as integrated doctrine, is similar and equal.

"Maitreya, 'apprehending objects' are the phenomena of the five physical sense spheres, mind, thought, consciousness, and mental factors.

དང་ཡིད་དང་། རྣམ་པར་ཤེས་པ་དང་། སེམས་ལས་བྱུང་བའི་ཆོས་རྣམས་སོ། །བྱམས་པ་དེ་ལ་གཟུང་བའི་དོན་ནི་ཕྱི་རོལ་གྱི་སྐྱེ་མཆེད་དྲུག་པོ་དག་ཡིན་ནོ། །བྱམས་པ་ཡང་འཛིན་པའི་དོན་གང་ཡིན་པ་དེ་ནི་གཟུང་བའི་དོན་ཀྱང་ཡིན་ནོ། །བྱམས་པ་དེ་ལ་གནས་ཀྱི་དོན་ནི་འཇིག་རྟེན་གྱི་ཁམས་གང་ཡིན་པ་སྟེ། གང་ལ་གནས་ན་སེམས་ཅན་གྱི་ཁམས་སྣང་བའོ། །འདི་ལྟ་སྟེ། གྲོང་ཚིགས་དང་། གྲོང་ཚིགས་བརྒྱ་དང་། དེ་སྟོང་དང་། དེ་འབུམ་དང་། རྒྱ་མཚོ་ལ་ཐུག་པའིས་དང་། དེ་བརྒྱ་དང་དེ་འབུམ་དང་། འཛམ་བུའི་གླིང་དང་། དེ་བརྒྱ་དང་། དེ་སྟོང་དང་། དེ་འབུམ་དང་། གླིང་བཞི་པ་དང་། དེ་བརྒྱ་དང་། དེ་སྟོང་དང་། དེ་འབུམ་དང་། སྟོང་གི་འཇིག་རྟེན་གྱི་ཁམས་དང་། དེ་བརྒྱ་དང་། དེ་སྟོང་དང་། དེ་འབུམ་དང་། སྟོང་གཉིས་པ་བར་མའི་འཇིག་རྟེན་གྱི་ཁམས་དང་། དེ་བརྒྱ་དང་། དེ་སྟོང་དང་། དེ་འབུམ་དང་། སྟོང་གསུམ་གྱི་སྟོང་ཆེན་པོའི་འཇིག་རྟེན་གྱི་ཁམས་དེ་བརྒྱ་དང་། དེ་སྟོང་དང་། དེ་འབུམ་དང་། དེ་བྱེ་བ་དང་། དེ་བྱེ་བ་ཕྲག་བརྒྱ་དང་། དེ་བྱེ་བ་ཕྲག་སྟོང་དང་། དེ་བྱེ་བ་ཕྲག་འབུམ་དང་། དེ་གྲངས་མེད་པ་དང་། དེ་གྲངས་མེད་པ་ཕྲག་བརྒྱ་དང་། དེ་གྲངས་མེད་པ་ཕྲག་སྟོང་དང་། དེ་གྲངས་མེད་པ་ཕྲག་འབུམ་དང་། ཕྱོགས་བཅུ་དག་གི་འཇིག་རྟེན་གྱི་ཁམས་དཔག་ཏུ་མེད་གྲངས་མེད་པ་སྟོང་གསུམ་གྱི་སྟོང་ཆེན་པོའི་འཇིག་རྟེན་གྱི་ཁམས་གྲངས་མེད་པ་ཕྲག་འབུམ་གྱི་རྡུལ་ཕྲ་རབ་ཀྱི་རྡུལ་སྙེད་དག་གོ། །བྱམས་པ་དེ་ལ་ཡོངས་སྤྱོད་ཀྱི་དོན་ནི་ཡོངས་སུ་སྤྱོད་པར་བྱ་བའི་ཕྱིར་དེས་སེམས་ཅན་རྣམས་ཀྱི་ཡོངས་སུ་བཟུང་བ་དང་། ཡོ་

"Maitreya, 'apprehended objects' are the six external sense spheres. Moreover, Maitreya, apprehending objects are also apprehended objects.

"Maitreya, 'objects that are abodes' are the worldly realms: realms of sentient beings that appear in various places. These include: a village, one hundred villages, one thousand of these, or one hundred thousand of these; a region, one hundred of these, or one hundred thousand of these; a Jambudvīpa,[24] one hundred of these, one thousand of these, or one hundred thousand of these; the four great continents, one hundred of these, one thousand of these, or one hundred thousand of these; a universe of a thousand worlds, one hundred of these, one thousand of these, or one hundred thousand of these; a medium-sized universe of two thousand worlds, one hundred of these, one thousand of these, or one hundred thousand of these; a great universe of three thousand worlds, one hundred of these, one thousand of these, one hundred thousand of these, ten million of these, one hundred times ten million of these, one thousand times ten million of these, one hundred thousand times ten million of these, an incalculable number of these, one hundred times an incalculable number of these, one thousand times an incalculable number of these, one hundred thousand times an incalculable number of these, or a number equal to however many atomic particles there are in the dust motes in a hundred thousand times an incalculable number of the great trichiliocosms of the immeasurable, incalculable universes of the ten directions.

བྱང་བསྟན་པ་གང་དག་ཡིན་པ་རྣམས་སོ། །བྱམས་པ་དེ་ལ་ཕྱིན་ཅི་ལོག་གི་དོན་ནི་འཛིན་
པ་ལ་སོགས་པའི་དོན་དེ་དག་ཉིད་ལ་མི་རྟག་པ་ལ་རྟག་པར་འདུ་ཤེས་པ་ཕྱིན་ཅི་ལོག་དང་།
སེམས་ཕྱིན་ཅི་ལོག་དང་། ལྟ་བ་ཕྱིན་ཅི་ལོག་དང་། སྡུག་བསྔལ་བ་ལ་བདེ་བ་དང་། མི་
གཙང་བ་ལ་གཙང་བ་དང་། བདག་མེད་པ་ལ་བདག་ཏུ་འདུ་ཤེས་ཕྱིན་ཅི་ལོག་དང་།
སེམས་ཕྱིན་ཅི་ལོག་དང་། ལྟ་བ་ཕྱིན་ཅི་ལོག་གང་ཡིན་པའོ། །བྱམས་པ་དེ་ལ་ཕྱིན་ཅི་མ་
ལོག་པའི་དོན་ནི་དེ་ལས་བཟློག་པ་སྟེ། དེའི་གཉེན་པོ་ཡིན་པར་རིག་པར་བྱའོ། །བྱམས་
པ་དེ་ལ་ཀུན་ནས་ཉོན་མོངས་པའི་དོན་ནི་རྣམ་པ་གསུམ་སྟེ། ཁམས་གསུམ་པའི་ཉོན་
མོངས་པའི་ཀུན་ནས་ཉོན་མོངས་པ་དང་། ལས་ཀྱི་ཀུན་ནས་ཉོན་མོངས་པ་དང་། སྐྱེ་བའི་
ཀུན་ནས་ཉོན་མོངས་པའོ། །བྱམས་པ་དེ་ལ་རྣམ་པར་བྱང་བའི་དོན་ནི་ཀུན་ནས་ཉོན་མོངས་
པ་རྣམ་པ་གསུམ་པོ་དེ་དག་ཉིད་དང་བྲལ་བར་བྱ་བའི་ཕྱིར་བྱང་ཆུབ་ཀྱི་ཕྱོགས་དང་འཐུན་
པའི་ཆོས་གང་དག་ཡིན་པ་རྣམས་ཏེ། བྱམས་པ་རྣམ་པ་བཅུ་པོ་དེ་དག་གིས་དོན་ཐམས་
ཅད་བསྡུས་པར་རིག་པར་བྱའོ། །བྱམས་པ་ཡང་བྱང་ཆུབ་སེམས་དཔས་རྣམ་པ་ལྔས་
དོན་སོ་སོ་ཡང་དག་པར་རིག་པ་ཡིན་ཏེ། དོན་རྣམ་པ་ལྔ་གང་ཞེ་ན། ཡོངས་སུ་ཤེས་པར་
བྱ་བའི་དངོས་པོ་དང་། ཡོངས་སུ་ཤེས་པར་བྱ་བའི་དོན་དང་། ཡོངས་སུ་ཤེས་པ་དང་།
ཡོངས་སུ་ཤེས་པའི་འབྲས་བུ་ཐོབ་པ་དང་། དེ་རབ་ཏུ་རིག་པར་བྱེད་པའོ། །བྱམས་པ་དེ་
ལ་ཡོངས་སུ་ཤེས་པར་བྱ་བའི་དངོས་པོ་ནི་ཤེས་བྱ་ཐམས་ཅད་ཡིན་པར་བལྟ་བར་བྱ་སྟེ།
འདི་ལྟ་སྟེ། ཕུང་པོ་རྣམས་ཞེས་བྱ་བའམ། ནང་གི་སྐྱེ་མཆེད་རྣམས་ཞེས་བྱ་བའམ། ཕྱི་

"Maitreya, I have taught that 'objects that are resources' are the possessions and assets that sentient beings enjoy.[25]

"Maitreya, 'mistaken objects' are mistaken discriminations, mistaken thoughts, and mistaken views, such as [conceiving] the impermanent as being permanent with respect to those objects that are apprehenders and so forth; mistaken discriminations, mistaken thoughts, and mistaken views, such as [conceiving] suffering as bliss, the impure as pure, or the selfless as having a self.

"Maitreya, know that 'non-mistaken objects' are the opposite of those and that they are antidotes to them.

"Maitreya, there are three kinds of 'afflicted objects': afflictions that are the afflictions of the three realms, afflictions of actions, and afflictions of birth.

"Maitreya, 'purified objects' are whatever phenomena are in harmony with enlightenment due to separating one from those three types of affliction.

"Maitreya, know that all objects are encompassed by these ten aspects.

"Maitreya, Bodhisattvas also comprehend objects through five aspects. What are these five aspects of objects? They are: knowable things, knowable meanings, knowledge, obtaining the fruit of knowledge, and full awareness of that.

"Maitreya, you should view 'knowable things' as being all objects of knowledge. This includes what is known as 'the

རོལ་གྱི་སྐྱེ་མཆེད་རྣམས་ཞེས་བྱ་བའམ། དེ་ལྟ་བུ་ལ་སོགས་པ་དག་གོ། །བྱམས་པ་དེ་ལ་ཡོངས་སུ་ཤེས་པར་བྱ་བའི་དོན་ནི་རྣམ་པ་ཇི་སྙེད་ཀྱིས་ཤེས་བྱ་དེ་ཇི་ལྟ་བ་བཞིན་ཤེས་པར་བྱ་བ་སྟེ། འདི་ལྟ་སྟེ། ཀུན་རྫོབ་དང་། དོན་དམ་པ་དང་། སྐྱོན་དང་། ཡོན་ཏན་དང༏ རྐྱེན་དང་། དུས་དང་། སྐྱེ་བ་དང་། གནས་པ་དང་། འཇིག་པའི་མཚན་ཉིད་དང༏ ནད་ལ་སོགས་པ་དང་། སྡུག་བསྔལ་དང་། ཀུན་འབྱུང་བ་ལ་སོགས་པ་དང་། དེ་བཞིན་ཉིད་དང་། ཡང་དག་པའི་མཐའ་དང་། ཆོས་ཀྱི་དབྱིངས་དང་། བསྡུ་བ་དང་། དབྱེ་བ་དང་། མགོ་གཅིག་ཏུ་ལན་གདབ་པ་དང་། རྣམ་པར་དབྱེ་བ་དང་། དྲིས་ཏེ་ལན་གདབ་པ་དང་། གཞག་པ་དང་། གསང་བ་དང་། བསྒྲགས་པ་དང་། དེ་ལྟ་བུ་དང་ལྡན་པ་ནི་ཡོངས་སུ་ཤེས་པར་བྱ་བའི་དོན་ཡིན་པར་རིག་པར་བྱའོ། །བྱམས་པ་དེ་ལ་ཡོངས་སུ་ཤེས་པ་ནི་དེ་གཉིག་འཛིན་པར་བྱེད་པ། བྱང་ཆུབ་ཀྱི་ཕྱོགས་དང་ལྡན་པའི་ཆོས་གང་ཡིན་པ་དག་སྟེ། འདི་ལྟ་སྟེ། དྲན་པ་ཉེ་བར་གཞག་པ་རྣམས་དང་། ཡང་དག་པར་སྤོང་བ་རྣམས་དང་། དེ་ལ་སོགས་པའོ། །བྱམས་པ་དེ་ལ་ཡོངས་སུ་ཤེས་པའི་འབྲས་བུ་འཐོབ་པ་ནི་འདི་ལྟ་སྟེ། འདོད་ཆགས་དང་། ཞེ་སྡང་དང་། གཏི་མུག་འདུལ་བ་དང་། འདོད་ཆགས་དང་། ཞེ་སྡང་དང་། གཏི་མུག་མ་ལུས་པར་སྤོང་བ་དང་། དགེ་སྦྱོང་ཉིད་ཀྱི་འབྲས་བུ་རྣམས་དང་། ཉན་ཐོས་དང་། དེ་བཞིན་གཤེགས་པའི་ཡོན་ཏན་འཇིག་རྟེན་པ་དང་། འཇིག་རྟེན་པ་ལས་འདས་པ་ཐུན་མོང་དང་ཐུན་མོང་མ་ཡིན་པ་གང་དག་བསྟན་པ་དེ་དག་མངོན་དུ་བྱ་བ་གང་ཡིན་པའོ། །བྱམས་པ་དེ་ལ་རབ་ཏུ་རིག

aggregates', 'the internal sense spheres', 'the external sense spheres', and the like.

"Maitreya, 'knowable meanings' are correctly known by way of their various aspects. They include: the conventional and the ultimate, faults and good qualities, conditions, time, the characteristics of production, abiding, and disintegration, sickness and so forth; suffering and the source of suffering and so forth; suchness, the reality limit,[26] the Dharmadhātu, condensed [discourses], extensive [discourses], certain prophecies, differentiation, scriptural questions and answers, pronouncements, secrets, and [scriptural] teachings. Know that things concordant with these are knowable meanings.[27]

"Maitreya, 'knowledge' refers to phenomena that are in harmony with enlightenment, including both [the ultimate and the conventional]. These [phenomena in harmony with enlightenment] include: the mindful establishments, the correct abandonings, and so forth.

"Maitreya, 'obtaining the fruit of knowledge' is: disciplining desire, anger, and bewilderment; entirely abandoning desire, anger, and bewilderment; [attaining] the fruits of virtuous application; and those common and uncommon, mundane and supramundane qualities of Śrāvakas and Tathāgatas that I have taught and that should be actualized.

"Maitreya, 'full awareness' is knowledge liberated from those very things that have been actualized, and extensively

པར་བྱེད་པ་ནི་མངོན་སུམ་དུ་བྱས་པའི་ཆོས་དེ་དག་ཉིད་ལས་རྣམ་པར་གྲོལ་བར་ཞེས་པ་དང་། གཞན་དག་ལ་ཡང་རྒྱ་ཆེར་སྟོན་པ་དང་། ཡང་དག་པར་སྟོན་པ་གང་ཡིན་པ་སྟེ། བྱམས་པ་དོན་ལྔ་པོ་དེ་དག་གིས་ཀྱང་དོན་ཐམས་ཅད་བསྡུས་པར་རིག་པར་བྱའོ། །བྱམས་པ་ཡང་བྱང་ཆུབ་སེམས་དཔས་རྣམ་པ་བཞིས་དོན་སོ་སོ་ཡང་དག་པར་རིག་པ་ཡིན་ཏེ། དོན་རྣམ་པ་བཞི་གང་ཞེ་ན། སེམས་ཀྱི་ལེན་པའི་དོན་དང་། མྱོང་བའི་དོན་དང་། རྣམ་པར་རིག་པའི་དོན་དང་། ཀུན་ནས་ཉོན་མོངས་པ་དང་། རྣམ་པར་བྱང་བའི་དོན་གྱིས་ཏེ། བྱམས་པ་དོན་རྣམ་པ་བཞི་པོ་དེ་དག་གིས་ཀྱང་དོན་ཐམས་ཅད་བསྡུ་བར་རིག་པར་བྱའོ། །བྱམས་པ་ཡང་བྱང་ཆུབ་སེམས་དཔའི་རྣམ་པ་གསུམ་གྱིས་དོན་སོ་སོ་ཡང་དག་པར་རིག་པ་ཡིན་ཏེ། དོན་རྣམ་པ་གསུམ་གང་ཞེ་ན། ཚིག་འབྲུའི་དོན་དང་། དོན་གྱི་དོན་དང་། ཁམས་ཀྱི་དོན་གྱིས་སོ། །བྱམས་པ་དེ་ལ་ཚིག་འབྲུའི་དོན་ནི་མིང་གི་ཚོགས་ལ་སོགས་པ་ཡིན་པར་བལྟ་བར་བྱའོ། །བྱམས་པ་དེ་ལ་དོན་གྱི་དོན་ནི་རྣམ་པ་བཅུར་རིག་པར་བྱ་སྟེ། དེ་ཁོ་ནའི་མཚན་ཉིད་དང་། ཡོངས་སུ་ཤེས་པའི་མཚན་ཉིད་དང་། སྤང་བའི་མཚན་ཉིད་དང་། མངོན་དུ་བྱ་བའི་མཚན་ཉིད་དང་། བསྒོམ་པའི་མཚན་ཉིད་དང་། དེ་ཁོ་ནའི་མཚན་ཉིད་ལ་སོགས་པ་དེ་དག་ཉིད་ཀྱི་རྣམ་པ་རབ་ཏུ་དབྱེ་བའི་མཚན་ཉིད་དང་། གནས་དང་གནས་པར་འབྲེལ་བའི་མཚན་ཉིད་དང་། ཡོངས་སུ་ཤེས་པ་ལ་སོགས་པའི་བར་དུ་གཅོད་པའི་ཆོས་ཀྱི་མཚན་ཉིད་དང་། རྗེས་སུ་འཐུན་པའི་ཆོས་ཀྱི་མཚན་ཉིད་དང་། ཡོངས་སུ་མི་ཤེས་པ་ལ་སོགས་པ་དང་། ཡོངས་སུ་ཤེས་པ་ལ་སོགས་པའི་ཉེས་དམིགས

and consummately teaching other beings. Maitreya, know that all objects are encompassed by these five objects.

"Maitreya, Bodhisattvas also comprehend objects through four aspects. What are the four aspects of objects? They are: appropriated objects of mind, objects of experience, objects of cognition, and objects of affliction and purification. Know, Maitreya, that all objects are also encompassed by these four aspects of objects.

"Maitreya, Bodhisattvas also comprehend objects through three aspects. What are the three aspects of objects? They are: objects that are words, objects that are meanings, and objects that are realms.

"Maitreya, 'objects that are words' should be viewed as being collections of names and so forth.

"Maitreya, know that 'objects that are meanings' have ten aspects: the character of reality; the character of knowledge; the character of abandonment; the character of actualization; the character of cultivation; the character which differentiates the aspects of those very characters of reality and so forth; the character of basis and what relates to a basis; the character of phenomena that interrupt knowledge and so forth; the character of concordant phenomena; and the character of the harmfulness of ignorance and the like and the benefits of knowledge and the like.

དང་། ཕན་ཡོན་གྱི་མཚན་ཉིད་དོ། །བྱམས་པ་དེ་ལ་ཁམས་ཀྱི་དོན་ནི་ཁམས་ལྔ་སྟེ།
འཇིག་རྟེན་གྱི་ཁམས་དང་། སེམས་ཅན་གྱི་ཁམས་དང་། ཆོས་ཀྱི་ཁམས་དང་། འདུལ
བའི་ཁམས་དང་། འདུལ་བའི་ཐབས་ཀྱི་ཁམས་ཏེ། བྱམས་པ་དོན་རྣམ་པ་གསུམ་པོ་དེ
དག་གིས་ཀུན་དོན་ཐམས་ཅད་བསྡུས་པར་རིག་པར་བྱའོ། །བཅོམ་ལྡན་འདས་ཐོས་པ
ལས་བྱུང་བའི་ཤེས་རབ་ཀྱིས་དོན་སོ་སོ་ཡང་དག་པར་རིག་པ་གང་ལགས་པ་དང་།
བསམས་པ་ལས་བྱུང་བའི་ཤེས་རབ་ཀྱིས་དོན་སོ་སོ་ཡང་དག་པར་རིག་པ་གང་ལགས་པ
དང་། བཅོམ་ལྡན་འདས་ཞི་གནས་དང་ལྷག་མཐོང་བསྒོམས་པ་ལས་བྱུང་བའི་ཤེས་རབ
ཀྱིས་དོན་སོ་སོ་ཡང་དག་པར་རིག་པ་གང་ལགས་པ་དེ་དག་ལ་ཐ་དད་དུ་བགྱི་བཅི་མཆིས
ལགས། བཀའ་སྩལ་པ། བྱམས་པ་བྱང་ཆུབ་སེམས་དཔས་ཐོས་པ་ལས་བྱུང་བའི
ཤེས་རབ་ཀྱིས་ནི་ཚིག་འབྲུ་ལ་གནས་པ། སྒྲ་ཇི་བཞིན་པ། དགོངས་པ་མེད་པ།
མངོན་དུ་མ་གྱུར་པ། རྣམ་པར་ཐར་པའི་རྗེས་སུ་འཐུན་པ། རྣམ་པར་ཐར་པར་བྱེད་པམ
ཡིན་པའི་དོན་སོ་སོ་ཡང་དག་པར་རིག་པར་བྱེད་དོ། །བྱམས་པ་བསམས་པ་ལས་བྱུང
བའི་ཤེས་རབ་ཀྱིས་ནི་ཚིག་འབྲུ་ལ་གནས་པ་ཁོ་ན་ཡིན་ལ། སྒྲ་ཇི་བཞིན་མ་ཡིན་པ།
དགོངས་པ་ཅན། མངོན་དུ་གྱུར་པ། རྣམ་པར་ཐར་པའི་རྗེས་སུ་ཆེས་འཐུན་པ། རྣམ
པར་ཐར་པར་བྱེད་པམ་ཡིན་པའི་དོན་སོ་སོ་ཡང་དག་པར་རིག་པར་བྱེད་དོ། །བྱམས་པ
བྱང་ཆུབ་སེམས་དཔས་བསྒོམས་པ་ལས་བྱུང་བའི་ཤེས་རབ་ཀྱིས་ནི་ཚིག་འབྲུ་ལ་གནས་པ
དང་། ཚིག་འབྲུ་ལ་གནས་པམ་ཡིན་པ་དང་། སྒྲ་ཇི་བཞིན་པ་དང་། དགོངས་པ་ཅན

"Maitreya, 'objects that are realms' are the five realms: worldly realms, the realm of sentient beings, the realm of qualities, the realm of discipline, and the realm of methods of discipline.[28]

"Maitreya, know that all objects are also encompassed by these three aspects."

"Bhagavan, what are the differences between comprehending objects through wisdom arisen from listening, comprehending objects through wisdom arisen from reflection, and, Bhagavan, comprehending objects through wisdom arisen from cultivating śamatha and vipaśyanā?"

The Bhagavan replied: "Maitreya, through wisdom arisen from listening, Bodhisattvas abide in words; they take them literally, do not grasp their intent, and do not actualize them. They are concordant with liberation and they comprehend objects that are not liberative.[29]

"Maitreya, through wisdom arisen from reflection, they still adhere to words, but they do not take them literally; they grasp their intent and actualize them. They are very concordant with liberation and they comprehend objects that are not liberative.

"Maitreya, through wisdom that arises from meditation, Bodhisattvas adhere to words and do not adhere to words; they take them literally and grasp their intent; they actualize

དང༌། ཤེས་བྱའི་དངོས་པོ་དང་ཆ་འཐུན་པའི་ཏིང་ངེ་འཛིན་གྱི་སྤྱོད་ཡུལ་གྱི་གཟུགས་བརྙན་གྱིས་མངོན་དུ་གྱུར་པ། རྣམ་པར་ཐར་པའི་རྗེས་སུ་ཆེས་ཤིན་ཏུ་འཐུན་པ། རྣམ་པར་ཐར་པར་བྱེད་པའི་དོན་ཀུན་སོ་སོར་ཡང་དག་པར་རིག་པར་བྱེད་དོ། །བྱམས་པ་དེ་དག་གི་ཕ་དང་དུ་བྱ་བ་ནི་དེ་ཡིན་ནོ་ཞེས་བཅོམ་ལྡན་འདས་ཀྱིས་བཀའ་སྩལ་ཏོ། །བཅོམ་ལྡན་འདས་བྱང་ཆུབ་སེམས་དཔའི་གནས་དང༌། ལྷག་མཐོང་སྒོམ་པ་ཆོས་སོ་སོར་ཡང་དག་པར་རིག་པ་དང༌། དོན་སོ་སོ་ཡང་དག་པར་རིག་པའི་ཤེས་པ་ནི་གང་ལགས། མཐོང་བ་ནི་གང་ལགས། བྱམས་པ་ང་ནི་ཤེས་པ་དང༌། མཐོང་བ་རྣམ་གྲངས་དུ་མས་སྟོན་པར་བྱེད་མོད་ཀྱི། འོན་ཀྱང་མདོར་བསྡུས་ཏེ་བཤད་པར་བྱའོ། །འདྲེས་པའི་ཆོས་ལ་དམིགས་པའི་ཞི་གནས་དང༌། ལྷག་མཐོང་གི་ཤེས་རབ་གང་ཡིན་པ་དེ་ནི་ཤེས་པ་ཡིན་ནོ། །མ་འདྲེས་པའི་ཆོས་ལ་དམིགས་པའི་ཞི་གནས་དང༌། ལྷག་མཐོང་གི་ཤེས་རབ་གང་ཡིན་པ་དེ་ནི་མཐོང་བ་ཡིན་ནོ། །བཅོམ་ལྡན་འདས་བྱང་ཆུབ་སེམས་དཔའི་གནས་དང༌། ལྷག་མཐོང་སྒོམ་པས་ཡིད་ལ་བགྱིད་པ་གང་གིས་མཚན་མ་གང་ཇི་ལྟར་རྣམ་པར་སེལ་བར་བགྱིད་ལགས། བྱམས་པ་དེ་བཞིན་ཉིད་ཡིད་ལ་བྱེད་པས་ཆོས་ཀྱི་མཚན་མ་དང༌། དོན་གྱི་མཚན་མ་རྣམ་པར་སེལ་བར་བྱེད་ལ། མིང་ལ་མིང་གི་ངོ་བོ་ཉིད་མི་དམིགས་ཤིང་དེའི་གནས་མཚན་མ་ཡང་དག་པར་རྗེས་སུ་མི་མཐོང་བས་རྣམ་པར་སེལ་ལོ། །མིང་ལ་ཇི་ལྟ་བ་བཞིན་དུ་ཚིག་དང༌། ཡི་གེ་དང༌། དོན་ཐམས་ཅད་ལ་ཡང་དེ་བཞིན་དུ་རིག་པར་བྱའོ། །བྱམས་པ་ཁམས་ཀྱི་བར་ལ་ཁམས་ཀྱི་ངོ་བོ་ཉིད་མི་དམིགས་ཤིང༌། དེའི་གནས་ཀྱི་མཚན

them through the images that are the focus of samādhi that accord with knowable things. They are completely concordant with liberation and they also comprehend objects that are liberative. Maitreya, these are the differences among them."

"Bhagavan, what is the knowledge of Bodhisattvas cultivating śamatha and vipaśyanā that comprehends doctrine and that comprehends objects? What is [their] insight?"

"Maitreya, although I teach knowledge and insight in many ways, I will explain them concisely: The wisdom of śamatha and vipaśyanā that observes integrated doctrines is knowledge. The wisdom of śamatha and vipaśyanā that observes unintegrated doctrines is insight."

"Bhagavan, through cultivating śamatha and vipaśyanā, how do Bodhisattvas remove which signs with what [kind of] mental attention?"

"Maitreya, through mental attention to suchness they remove the signs of doctrines and the signs of objects. With respect to names, by not observing the nature of names, and also by not perceiving as real the signs of their abiding, they eliminate [signs].

"Just as it is with respect to names, so it is also with respect to all words, letters, and meanings. Maitreya, with respect to [everything] up through realms: By not observing the nature

མ་ཡང་ཡང་དག་པར་རྗེས་སུ་མི་མཐོང་བས་རྣམ་པར་སེལ་ལོ། །བཅོམ་ལྡན་འདས་ཅི་ལགས་དེ་བཞིན་ཉིད་ཀྱི་དོན་སོ་སོར་ཡང་དག་པར་རིག་པའི་མཚན་མ་གང་ལགས་པ་དེ་ཡང་རྣམ་པར་སེལ་བར་བགྱིད་ལགས་སམ། བྱམས་པ་དེ་བཞིན་ཉིད་ཀྱི་དོན་སོ་སོ་ཡང་དག་པར་རིག་པ་ལ་ནི་མཚན་མ་མེད་དེ་མི་དམིགས་ན། དེ་ལ་ཅི་ཞིག་རྣམ་པར་སེལ་བར་འགྱུར་ཏེ། བྱམས་པ་དེ་བཞིན་ཉིད་ཀྱི་དོན་སོ་སོ་ཡང་དག་པར་རིག་པས་ནི་ཆོས་དང་དོན་གྱི་མཚན་མ་ཐམས་ཅད་ཟིལ་གྱིས་གནོན་གྱི་དེ་ནི་གང་གིས་ཀྱང་ཟིལ་གྱིས་མནན་པར་བྱ་བ་ཡིན་པར་ང་མི་སྨྲའོ། །བཅོམ་ལྡན་འདས་བཅོམ་ལྡན་འདས་ཀྱིས་ཆབ་རྙོག་པ་ཅན་མཆིས་པའི་སྣོད་ཀྱི་དཔེ་དང་། མེ་ལོང་ཡོངས་སུ་མ་དག་པའི་དཔེ་དང་། མཚེའུ་འཁྲུགས་པའི་དཔེས་ཇི་ལྟར་རང་བཞིན་གྱི་མཚན་མ་བརྟག་པར་མི་ནུས་པ་དེ་ལས་བཟློག་པར་ནི་ནུས་པ་དེ་བཞིན་དུ་མ་བསྒོམས་པའི་སེམས་ཀྱིས་ཡང་དག་པ་ཇི་ལྟ་བ་བཞིན་ཤེས་པར་མི་ནུས་ཀྱི། བསྒོམས་པས་ནི་ནུས་སོ་ཞེས་བཀའ་སྩལ་པ་གང་ལགས་པ་དེ་ལ་སེམས་ཀྱིས་སོ་སོར་བརྟག་པ་ནི་གང་ལགས། དེ་བཞིན་ཉིད་ནི་གང་ལས་དགོངས་ཏེ་བཀའ་སྩལ་པ་ནི་གང་ལགས། བཀའ་སྩལ་པ། བྱམས་པ་སེམས་ཀྱིས་སོ་སོར་བརྟག་པ་རྣམ་པ་གསུམ་གྱི་ཕྱིར་ཏེ། ཐོས་པ་ལས་བྱུང་བའི་སེམས་ཀྱིས་སོ་སོར་བརྟག་པ་དང་། བསམས་པ་ལས་བྱུང་བའི་སེམས་ཀྱིས་སོ་སོར་བརྟག་པ་དང་། བསྒོམས་པ་ལས་བྱུང་བའི་སེམས་ཀྱིས་སོ་སོར་བརྟག་པའོ། །རྣམ་པར་རིག་པའི་དེ་བཞིན་ཉིད་ལས་དགོངས་ཏེ་ཡོངས་སུ་བསྟན་པ་ཡིན་ནོ། །བཅོམ་ལྡན་འདས་བྱང་ཆུབ་སེམས་དཔའ་དེ་ལྟར་ཆོས་དང་དོན་སོ་སོར་ཡང་

of realms, and also by not perceiving as real the signs of their abiding, they eliminate [signs]."

"Bhagavan, are the signs of comprehending the object of suchness also eliminated?"

"Maitreya, with respect to comprehending the object of suchness, since one does not observe what is without signs, what is there to eliminate? Maitreya, comprehending the object of suchness overwhelms all signs of doctrines and objects. I do not assert that it is overwhelmed by anything."

"Bhagavan, the Bhagavan has said, 'One cannot examine the signs of one's own face with, for example, a pot of filthy water, a dirty mirror, or an agitated pond; one can with their opposites. Similarly, minds that do not meditate cannot know reality just as it is, whereas those that have meditated can do so.' In this context, what is mental analysis? Of what kind of suchness were you thinking?"

The Bhagavan replied: "Maitreya, [in this context] there are three kinds of mental analysis: mental analysis arisen from listening, mental analysis arisen from reflection, and mental analysis arisen from meditating. I taught this, thinking of the suchness of cognition."

"Bhagavan, how many kinds of signs do you speak of for Bodhisattvas who comprehend doctrines and comprehend objects and are engaged in eliminating signs? By what are these signs eliminated?"

དག་པར་རིག་པ་དང་། མཚན་མ་རྣམ་པར་སེལ་བ་ལ་ཞུགས་པའི་མཚན་མ་དྲུག་ནི་
བཀའ་སྩལ་པ་ལགས་ལ། གང་གིས་ནི་དེ་དག་རྣམ་པར་སེལ་ལགས། བྱམས་པ་བཅུ་
སྟེ། དེ་དག་ནི་སྟོང་པ་ཉིད་ཀྱིས་རྣམ་པར་སེལ་ལོ། །བཅུ་གང་ཞེ་ན། ཆོས་ཀྱི་དོན་སོ་
སོར་ཡང་དག་པར་རིག་པར་བྱེད་པའི་ཚིག་དང་། ཡི་གེའི་མཚན་མ་སྣ་ཚོགས་གང་ཡིན་
པ་དེ་ནི་ཆོས་ཐམས་ཅད་སྟོང་པ་ཉིད་ཀྱིས་རྣམ་པར་སེལ་ལོ། །གནས་པའི་དེ་བཞིན་ཉིད་
ཀྱིས་དོན་སོ་སོར་ཡང་དག་པར་རིག་པར་བྱེད་པའི་སྐྱེ་བ་དང་། འཇིག་པ་དང་། གནས་
པ་དང་། གཞན་དུ་འགྱུར་བ་ཉིད་ཀྱི་རྒྱུན་གྱི་རྗེས་སུ་འཇུག་པའི་མཚན་མ་གང་ཡིན་པ་དེ་
ནི་མཚན་ཉིད་སྟོང་པ་ཉིད་དང་། ཐོག་མ་དང་ཐ་མ་མེད་པ་སྟོང་པ་ཉིད་ཀྱིས་རྣམ་པར་སེལ་
ལོ། །འཛིན་པའི་དོན་སོ་སོར་ཡང་དག་པར་རིག་པར་བྱེད་པའི་འཇིག་ཚོགས་ལ་ལྟ་བའི་
མཚན་མ་དང་། ངའོ་སྙམ་པའི་མཚན་མ་གང་ཡིན་པ་དེ་ནི་ནང་སྟོང་པ་ཉིད་དང་། མི་
དམིགས་པ་སྟོང་པ་ཉིད་ཀྱིས་རྣམ་པར་སེལ་ལོ། །གཟུང་བའི་དོན་སོ་སོར་ཡང་དག་པར་
རིག་པར་བྱེད་པའི་ལོངས་སྤྱོད་ལ་ལྟ་བའི་མཚན་མ་གང་ཡིན་པ་དེ་ནི་ཕྱི་སྟོང་པ་ཉིད་ཀྱིས་
རྣམ་པར་སེལ་ལོ། །ལོངས་སུ་ལོངས་སྤྱོད་པའི་དོན་དུ་སྐྱེས་པ་དང་། བུད་མེད་ཀྱི་བསྙེན་
བཀུར་དང་ཡོ་བྱད་དང་ལྡན་པ་སོ་སོར་ཡང་དག་པར་རིག་པར་བྱེད་པའི་ནང་གི་བདེ་བའི་
མཚན་མ་དང་། ཕྱི་རོལ་གྱི་སྡུག་པའི་མཚན་མ་གང་ཡིན་པ་དེ་ནི་ཕྱི་སྟོང་པ་ཉིད་དང་།
རང་བཞིན་སྟོང་པ་ཉིད་ཀྱིས་རྣམ་པར་སེལ་ལོ། །གནས་ཀྱི་དོན་སོ་སོར་ཡང་དག་པར་རིག་
པར་བྱེད་པའི་ཚད་མེད་པའི་མཚན་མ་གང་ཡིན་པ་དེ་ནི་ཆེན་པོ་སྟོང་པ་ཉིད་ཀྱིས་རྣམ་པར་

"Maitreya, there are ten kinds, and they are eliminated by emptiness. What are these ten? They are:

"The various signs of syllables and words through which the meaning of doctrine is comprehended. These are eliminated by the emptiness of all phenomena.

"The signs that are a continuum of production, destruction, abiding, and transformation through which the meaning of the suchness of abiding is comprehended are eliminated by the emptiness of character and the emptiness of what is beginningless and endless.

"The signs of discerning true personhood and the signs of thinking 'I am' through which one comprehends the apprehending object are eliminated by the emptiness of the internal and the emptiness of the unobservable.

"The signs of discerning enjoyment through which one comprehends the apprehended object are eliminated by the emptiness of the external.

"The signs of inner happiness and the signs of external allure through which one comprehends the objects that are resources, [such as] the services of men and women and possessions, are eliminated by the emptiness of the external and by the emptiness of self-nature.

"The signs of the immeasurable through which one comprehends the objects that are abodes are eliminated by the emptiness of the great.

སེལ་ལོ། །གཟུགས་མེད་པ་ལ་བརྟེན་ཏེ། ནང་གི་ཞི་བའི་རྣམ་པར་ཐར་པའི་མཚན་མ་གང་ཡིན་པ་དེ་ནི་འདུས་བྱས་སྟོང་པ་ཉིད་ཀྱིས་རྣམ་པར་སེལ་ལོ། །མཚན་ཉིད་ཀྱི་དེ་བཞིན་ཉིད་ཀྱི་དོན་སོ་སོར་ཡང་དག་པར་རིག་པར་བྱེད་པའི་གང་ཟག་བདག་མེད་པའི་མཚན་མ་དང་། ཆོས་བདག་མེད་པའི་མཚན་མ་དང་། རྣམ་པར་རིག་པ་ཙམ་གྱི་མཚན་མ་དང་། དོན་དམ་པའི་མཚན་མ་གང་ཡིན་པ་དེ་ནི་མཐའ་ལས་འདས་པ་སྟོང་པ་ཉིད་དང་། དངོས་པོ་མེད་པ་སྟོང་པ་ཉིད་དང་། དངོས་པོ་མེད་པའི་ངོ་བོ་ཉིད་སྟོང་པ་ཉིད་དང་། དོན་དམ་པ་སྟོང་པ་ཉིད་ཀྱིས་རྣམ་པར་སེལ་ལོ། །རྣམ་པར་དག་པའི་དེ་བཞིན་ཉིད་ཀྱི་དོན་སོ་སོ་ཡང་དག་པར་རིག་པར་བྱེད་པའི་འདུས་མ་བྱས་ཀྱི་མཚན་མ་དང་། འགྱུར་བ་མེད་པའི་མཚན་མ་གང་ཡིན་པ་དེ་ནི་འདུས་མ་བྱས་སྟོང་པ་ཉིད་དང་། དོར་བ་མེད་པ་སྟོང་པ་ཉིད་ཀྱིས་རྣམ་པར་སེལ་ལོ། །མཚན་མ་དེའི་གཉེན་པོ་སྟོང་པ་ཉིད་དེ་ཉིད་ཡིད་ལ་བྱེད་པའི་སྟོང་པ་ཉིད་ཀྱི་མཚན་མ་གང་ཡིན་པ་དེ་ནི་སྟོང་པ་ཉིད་སྟོང་པ་ཉིད་ཀྱིས་རྣམ་པར་སེལ་ལོ། །བཅོམ་ལྡན་འདས་མཚན་མ་རྣམ་བཅུ་རྣམ་པར་སེལ་བར་བགྱིད་ན། མཚན་མ་གང་རྣམ་པར་སེལ་བར་བགྱིད་ཅིང་འཆིང་བའི་མཚན་མ་གང་ལས་ཡོངས་སུ་གྲོལ་བར་འགྱུར་ལགས། བྱམས་པ་ཏིང་ངེ་འཛིན་གྱི་སྤྱོད་ཡུལ་གཟུགས་བརྙན་གྱི་མཚན་མ་རྣམ་པར་སེལ་བར་བྱེད་ཅིང་ཀུན་ནས་ཉོན་མོངས་པའི་མཚན་མའི་མཚན་མ་ལས་ཡོངས་སུ་གྲོལ་བར་འགྱུར་བ་དེ་ཡང་རྣམ་པར་སེལ་ལོ། །བྱམས་པ་སྟོང་པ་ཉིད་དེ་དག་ནི་དངོས་སུ་ན་མཚན་མ་དེ་དག་གི་གཉེན་པོར་གྱུར་པ་ཡིན་པར་རིག་པར་བྱའོ། །རེ་རེ་ཡང་མཚན་མ་ཐམས་ཅད་

"The internal signs of peaceful liberation dependent upon [comprehending] formlessness are eliminated by the emptiness of compounded phenomena.

"The signs of the selflessness of persons, the signs of the selflessness of phenomena, the signs of cognition-only, and the signs of the ultimate through which one comprehends the object of the suchness of character are eliminated by the emptiness of what has passed beyond the extremes, by the emptiness of non-things, by the emptiness of the own-being of non-things, and by the emptiness of the ultimate.

"The signs of the uncompounded and the signs of the immutable through which one comprehends the object of pure suchness are eliminated by the emptiness of uncompounded phenomena and the emptiness of inclusiveness.

"The signs of emptiness through which one takes to mind the very emptiness that is an antidote to these signs are eliminated by the emptiness of emptiness."[30]

"Bhagavan, when [Bodhisattvas] eliminate the ten kinds of signs, what are the signs that they eliminate? From what signs of bondage are they liberated?"

"Maitreya, eliminating the sign of the image, the focus of samādhi, one is liberated from the signs that are the signs of the afflictions; these [signs] are also eliminated.[31] Maitreya, know that the emptinesses are, in actuality, antidotes to the signs. Each [emptiness] is also an antidote to any of the signs.

ཀྱི་གཉེན་པོར་མི་འགྱུར་བ་ནི་མ་ཡིན་ནོ། །བྱམས་པ་འདི་ལྟ་སྟེ་དཔེར་ན། མ་རིག་པ་ནི་ཤ
ཤིའི་བར་གྱི་ཀུན་ནས་ཉོན་མོངས་པ་སྒྲུབ་པར་མི་བྱེད་པ་ཡིན་མོད་ཀྱི། ཉེ་བ་དང་ཤིན་ཏུ་ཉེ
བའི་རྐྱེན་ཉིད་ཡིན་པའི་ཕྱིར། དངོས་སུ་ན་འདུ་བྱེད་འགྲུབ་པར་བྱེད་པ་ཡིན་པར་བསྟན་པ
བཞིན་དུ་འདི་ལ་ཡང་ཚུལ་དེ་བཞིན་དུ་བལྟ་བར་བྱའོ། །བཅོམ་ལྡན་འདས་ཐེག་པ་ཆེན
པོ་ལ་བྱང་ཆུབ་སེམས་དཔའ་རྣམས་ཀྱིས་གང་རྟོགས་ན་སྟོང་པ་ཉིད་ཀྱི་མཚན་ཉིད་ལ
མངོན་པའི་ང་རྒྱལ་མ་མཆིས་པས་རབ་ཏུ་ཉམས་པར་མི་འགྱུར་བའི་སྟོང་པ་ཉིད་ཀྱི་མཚན
ཉིད་བསྡུས་པ་གང་ལགས། དེ་ནས་བཅོམ་ལྡན་འདས་ཀྱིས་བྱང་ཆུབ་སེམས་དཔའ
བྱམས་པ་ལ་ལེགས་སོ་ཞེས་བྱ་བ་བྱིན་ཏེ། བྱམས་པ་ཁྱོད་དེ་ལྟར་བྱང་ཆུབ་སེམས་དཔའ
རྣམས་སྟོང་པ་ཉིད་ལས་རབ་ཏུ་ཉམས་པར་མི་འགྱུར་བར་བྱ་བའི་ཕྱིར། དེ་བཞིན
གཤེགས་པ་ལ་ཁྱོད་དོན་འདི་ཉིད་འདྲི་བ་ལེགས་སོ་ལེགས་སོ། །དེ་ཅིའི་ཕྱིར་ཞེ་ན།
བྱམས་པ་བྱང་ཆུབ་སེམས་དཔའ་སྟོང་པ་ཉིད་ལས་རབ་ཏུ་ཉམས་པ་ནི་ཐེག་པ་ཆེན་པོ
མཐའ་དག་ལས་ཀྱང་རབ་ཏུ་ཉམས་པར་འགྱུར་བའི་ཕྱིར་རོ། །བྱམས་པ་དེའི་ཕྱིར་ཉོན
ཅིག་དང་། སྟོང་པ་ཉིད་ཀྱི་མཚན་ཉིད་བསྡུས་པ་ཁྱོད་ལ་བཤད་པར་བྱའོ། །བྱམས་པ
གཞན་གྱི་དབང་གི་མཚན་ཉིད་དང་། ཡོངས་སུ་གྲུབ་པའི་མཚན་ཉིད་རྣམ་པ་ཐམས་ཅད
དུ་ཀུན་ནས་ཉོན་མོངས་པ་དང་། རྣམ་པར་བྱང་བའི་ཀུན་བརྟགས་པའི་མཚན་ཉིད་དང་།
ཤིན་ཏུ་རྣམ་པར་བྲལ་བའི་མཚན་ཉིད་དང་། དེ་ལ་དེ་དམིགས་པ་གང་ཡིན་པ་དེ་ནི་ཐེག
པ་ཆེན་པོ་ལ་སྟོང་པ་ཉིད་ཀྱི་མཚན་ཉིད་བསྟན་པ་ཞེས་བྱའོ། །བཅོམ་ལྡན་འདས་ཞི་གནས

"Maitreya, for example, although the afflictions are not established, due to proximity or close proximity with conditions, from ignorance up to old age and death, in actuality, compounded phenomena are described as being established. You should also discern [these emptinesses] in just this way."

"Bhagavan, what do Bodhisattvas realize in the Mahāyāna that merges the signs of unchanging emptiness without degenerating into arrogance about the character of emptiness?"

Then the Bhagavan replied to the Bodhisattva Maitreya: "Excellent! Maitreya, you ask the Tathāgata about this issue so that Bodhisattvas will not fall away from emptiness. This is very good! Why? Maitreya, Bodhisattvas who do not fall away from emptiness also do not fall away from all of the Mahāyāna. Therefore, Maitreya, listen well and I will concisely explain to you the character of emptiness.

"Maitreya, the other-dependent character and the thoroughly established character are observed in all aspects to be a character free from the imputational character which is either afflicted or purified. This [character] is 'that which has been taught in the Mahāyāna as the character of emptiness'."

"Bhagavan, how many kinds of samādhis of śamatha and vipaśyanā are included [in this teaching]?"

The Bhagavan replied: "Know that all of the many kinds of samādhis of Śrāvakas, Bodhisattvas, and Tathāgatas that I have taught are included."

དང་ལྷག་མཐོང་དག་གི་ཏིང་ངེ་འཛིན་དུ་ཞིག་བསྡུས་ལགས། བཀའ་སྩལ་པ། བྱམས་པ་ངས་ཉན་ཐོས་རྣམས་དང་། བྱང་ཆུབ་སེམས་དཔའ་རྣམས་དང་། དེ་བཞིན་གཤེགས་པ་རྣམས་ཀྱི་ཏིང་ངེ་འཛིན་རྣམ་པ་དུ་མ་བསྟན་པ་གང་ཡིན་པ་དེ་དག་ཐམས་ཅད་བསྡུས་པར་རིག་པར་བྱའོ། །བཅོམ་ལྡན་འདས་ཞི་གནས་དང་། ལྷག་མཐོང་རྒྱུ་གང་ལས་བྱུང་བ་ལགས། བྱམས་པ་ཚུལ་ཁྲིམས་རྣམ་པར་དག་པའི་རྒྱུ་ལས་བྱུང་བ་དང་། ཐོས་པ་དང་བསམས་པ་ལས་བྱུང་བའི་ལྟ་བ་རྣམ་པར་དག་པའི་རྒྱུ་ལས་བྱུང་བ་ཡིན་ནོ། །བཅོམ་ལྡན་འདས་དེ་དག་གི་འབྲས་བུ་གང་ལགས་པར་བརྗོད་པར་བགྱི། བྱམས་པ་སེམས་རྣམ་པར་དག་པ་ནི་འབྲས་བུ་ཡིན། ཤེས་རབ་རྣམ་པར་དག་པ་ནི་འབྲས་བུ་ཡིན་ནོ། །བྱམས་པ་ཡང་ཉན་ཐོས་རྣམས་ཀྱི་འམ། བྱང་ཆུབ་སེམས་དཔའ་རྣམས་ཀྱི་འམ། དེ་བཞིན་གཤེགས་པ་རྣམས་ཀྱི་དགེ་བའི་ཆོས་འཇིག་རྟེན་པ་དང་། འཇིག་རྟེན་ལས་འདས་པ་ཐམས་ཅད་ཀྱང་ཞི་གནས་དང་ལྷག་མཐོང་གི་འབྲས་བུ་ཡིན་པར་རིག་པར་བྱའོ། །བཅོམ་ལྡན་འདས་ཞི་གནས་དང་ལྷག་མཐོང་གི་ལས་ཅི་ལགས། བྱམས་པ་འཆིང་བ་རྣམ་པ་གཉིས་པོ་མཚན་མའི་འཆིང་བ་དང་། གནས་ངན་ལེན་གྱི་འཆིང་བ་ལས་རྣམ་པར་ཐར་པར་བྱེད་པ་ཡིན་ནོ། །བཅོམ་ལྡན་འདས་བཅོམ་ལྡན་འདས་ཀྱིས་གེགས་རྣམ་པ་ལྔ་གསུངས་པ་གང་དག་ལགས་པ་དེ་དག་ལས་དུ་ནི་ཞི་གནས་ཀྱི་གེགས་དག་ལགས། དུ་ནི་ལྷག་མཐོང་གི་གེགས་དག་ལགས། དུ་ནི་གཉིས་ཀའི་གེགས་དག་ལགས། བྱམས་པ་ལུས་དང་ལོངས་སྤྱོད་ལ་ལྟ་བ་ནི་ཞི་གནས་ཀྱི་གེགས་ཡིན་ནོ། །འཕགས་པའི་གཏམ

"Bhagavan, from what causes do śamatha and vipaśyanā arise?"

"Maitreya, they arise from the cause of pure moral practice, and they arise from the cause of the pure view which comes from listening and reflecting."

"Bhagavan, will you explain the results of these?"

"Maitreya, pure mind is the result. Pure wisdom is the result. Moreover, Maitreya, know that all mundane and supramundane virtuous qualities of Śrāvakas, or of Bodhisattvas, or of Tathāgatas are the result of śamatha and vipaśyanā."

"Bhagavan, what are the functions of śamatha and vipaśyanā?"

"Maitreya, they liberate from the two bonds, the bonds of signs and the bonds of errant tendencies."

"Bhagavan, from among the five kinds of obstacles spoken of by the Bhagavan, which are obstacles to śamatha? Which are obstacles to vipaśyanā? Which are obstacles to both?"

"Maitreya, know that views [that overvalue] the body and resources are obstacles to śamatha.[32] Not obtaining the instructions of the Āryas in accordance with one's wishes is an obstacle to vipaśyanā. Abiding in turmoil and being satisfied

འདོད་པ་བཞིན་མཐོང་བ་ནི་ལྷག་མཐོང་གི་གེགས་ཡིན་ནོ། །འདྲེས་པར་གནས་པ་དང་། ཉུང་ཟད་ཙམ་གྱིས་ཆོག་པར་འཛིན་པ་ནི་དེ་གཉིས་ཀའི་གེགས་ཡིན་ཏེ། དེ་ལ་ཡང་གཅིག་གིས་ཀྱང་སྦྱོར་བར་མི་བྱེད་དོ། །ཅིག་ཤོས་ཀྱིས་ནི་སྦྱོར་བ་མཐར་ཕྱུག་པར་མི་འགྱུར་རོ། ། བཅོམ་ལྡན་འདས་སྒྲིབ་པ་ལྔ་པོ་གང་དག་ལགས་པ་དེ་དག་ལས་དུ་ནི་ཞི་གནས་ཀྱི་སྒྲིབ་པ་དག་ལགས། དུ་ནི་ལྷག་མཐོང་གི་སྒྲིབ་པ་དག་ལགས། དུ་ནི་གཉིས་ཀའི་སྒྲིབ་པ་དག་ལགས། བྱམས་པ་རྒོད་པ་དང་འགྱོད་པ་ནི་ཞི་གནས་ཀྱི་སྒྲིབ་པ་ཡིན་ནོ། །རྨུགས་པ་དང་གཉིད་དང་། ཐེ་ཚོམ་ནི་ལྷག་མཐོང་གི་སྒྲིབ་པ་ཡིན་ནོ། །འདོད་པ་ལ་འདུན་པ་དང་གནོད་སེམས་ནི་གཉིས་ཀའི་སྒྲིབ་པ་ཡིན་ནོ། །བཅོམ་ལྡན་འདས་ཅི་ཙམ་གྱིས་ན་ཞི་གནས་ཀྱི་ལམ་ཡོངས་སུ་དག་པ་ལགས། བྱམས་པ་གང་གི་ཚེ་རྨུགས་པ་དང་གཉིད་ལེགས་པར་རབ་ཏུ་ཆོམས་པར་གྱུར་པའོ། །བཅོམ་ལྡན་འདས་ཇི་ཙམ་གྱིས་ན་ལྷག་མཐོང་གི་ལམ་ཡོངས་སུ་དག་པ་ལགས། བྱམས་པ་གང་གི་ཚེ་རྒོད་པ་དང་འགྱོད་པ་ལེགས་པར་རབ་ཏུ་ཆོམས་པར་གྱུར་པའོ། །བཅོམ་ལྡན་འདས་བྱང་ཆུབ་སེམས་དཔའ་ཞི་གནས་དང་ལྷག་མཐོང་ལ་ཞུགས་པས་རྣམ་པ་དུ་དག་གིས་སེམས་རྣམ་པར་གཡེང་བར་འཚལ་བར་བགྱི་ལགས། བཀའ་སྩལ་པ། བྱམས་པ་རྣམ་པ་ལྔས་ཏེ། ཡིད་ལ་བྱེད་པའི་རྣམ་པར་གཡེང་བ་དང་། ཕྱི་རོལ་ཏུ་སེམས་རྣམ་པར་གཡེང་བ་དང་། ནང་དུ་སེམས་རྣམ་པར་གཡེང་བ་དང་། མཚན་མའི་རྣམ་པར་གཡེང་བ་དང་། གནས་ངན་ལེན་གྱི་རྣམ་པར་གཡེང་བས་སོ། །བྱམས་པ་གལ་ཏེ་བྱང་ཆུབ་སེམས་དཔའ་ཐེག་པ་ཆེན་པོ་དང་ལྡན་པའི

with inferior [attainment] are obstacles to both.[33] Because of the first of these, one does not apply oneself; because of the second, one does not complete the training."

"Bhagavan, from among the five obstructions, which is an obstruction to śamatha? Which is an obstruction to vipaśyanā? Which is an obstruction to both of these?"

"Maitreya, excitement and contrition are obstructions to śamatha. Lethargy, sleep, and doubt are obstructions to vipaśyanā. Fixation on desirable experience and harmful intent are obstructions to both of these."

"Bhagavan, when is the path of śamatha wholly purified?"

"Maitreya, at the point when lethargy and sleep are completely conquered."

"Bhagavan, when is the path of vipaśyanā wholly purified?"

"At the point when excitement and contrition are completely conquered."

"Bhagavan, how many types of mental distractions do Bodhisattvas engaged in śamatha and vipaśyanā discover?"

The Bhagavan replied: "Maitreya, there are five types: the distraction of mental contemplation, external mental distraction, internal mental distraction, the distraction of signs, and the distraction of errant tendencies.

"Maitreya, if Bodhisattvas forsake the mental contemplations of the Mahāyāna and adopt the mental contemplations

ཡིད་ལ་བྱེད་པ་བཏང་སྟེ། ཉན་ཐོས་དང་། རང་སངས་རྒྱས་དང་ལྡན་པའི་ཡིད་ལ་བྱེད་པར་རབ་ཏུ་ལྷུང་ན་དེ་ནི་ཡིད་ལ་བྱེད་པའི་རྣམ་པར་གཡེང་བ་ཡིན་ནོ། །གལ་ཏེ་ཕྱི་རོལ་གྱི་འདོད་པའི་ཡོན་ཏན་ལྔ་པོ་དག་དང་། འདུ་འཛི་དང་། མཚན་མ་དང་། རྣམ་པར་རྟོག་པ་དང་། ཉོན་མོངས་པ་དང་། ཉེ་བའི་ཉོན་མོངས་པ་དང་། ཕྱི་རོལ་གྱི་དམིགས་པ་རྣམས་ལ་སེམས་རྣམ་པར་འཕྲོ་བར་གཏོང་ན་དེ་ནི་ཕྱི་རོལ་ཏུ་སེམས་རྣམ་པར་གཡེང་བ་ཡིན་ནོ། །གལ་ཏེ་རྨུགས་པ་དང་གཉིད་ཀྱིས་བྱིང་བའམ། སྙོམས་པར་འཇུག་པའི་རོ་མྱང་བའམ། སྙོམས་པར་འཇུག་པའི་ཉེ་བའི་ཉོན་མོངས་པ་གང་ཡང་རུང་བས་ཉོན་མོངས་པར་གྱུར་ན། དེ་ནི་ནང་དུ་སེམས་རྣམ་པར་གཡེང་བ་ཡིན་ནོ། །གལ་ཏེ་ཕྱི་རོལ་གྱི་མཚན་མ་ལ་བརྟེན་ནས་ནང་གི་ཏིང་ངེ་འཛིན་གྱི་སྤྱོད་ཡུལ་གྱི་མཚན་མ་ཡིད་ལ་བྱེད་ན་དེ་ནི་མཚན་མའི་རྣམ་པར་གཡེང་བ་ཡིན་ནོ། །གལ་ཏེ་ནང་གི་ཡིད་ལ་བྱེད་པ་ལ་བརྟེན་ནས་བྱུང་བའི་ཚོར་བ་ལ་གནས་ངན་ལེན་གྱི་ལུས་ཀྱིས་ངའོ་སྙམ་དུ་རློམ་སེམས་སུ་བྱེད་ན་དེ་ནི་གནས་ངན་ལེན་གྱི་རྣམ་པར་གཡེང་བ་ཡིན་ནོ། །བཅོམ་ལྡན་འདས་ཞི་གནས་དང་ལྷག་མཐོང་དག་བྱང་ཆུབ་སེམས་དཔའི་ས་དང་པོ་ནས་བཟུང་སྟེ། དེ་བཞིན་གཤེགས་པའི་སའི་བར་ལ་གང་གི་གཉེན་པོ་ལགས། བྱམས་པ་ཞི་གནས་དང་ལྷག་མཐོང་ས་དང་པོ་ལ་ནི་ངན་སོང་བའི་ཉོན་མོངས་པ་དང་། ལས་དང་སྐྱེ་བའི་ཀུན་ནས་ཉོན་མོངས་པའི་གཉེན་པོ་ཡིན་ནོ། །གཉིས་པ་ལ་ནི་ལྟུང་བ་ཕྲ་མོའི་འཁྲུལ་པ་ཀུན་ཏུ་འབྱུང་བ་རྣམས་ཀྱིའོ། ། གསུམ་པ་ལ་ནི་འདོད་པའི་འདོད་ཆགས་ཀྱིའོ། །བཞི་པ་ལ་ནི་སྙོམས་པར་འཇུག་པ་ལ་

of Śrāvakas and Pratyekabuddhas, this is a distraction of mental contemplation.[34]

"If they let their minds scatter to the five external desirable qualities, or to diversions, signs, conceptuality, afflictions, secondary afflictions, and external objects of observation, this is external mental distraction.[35]

"If they become afflicted either by laxity due to lethargy, sleep, or relishing the taste of meditative absorption, or by any of the secondary afflictions associated with meditative absorption, this is internal mental distraction.[36]

"If, depending on external signs, they mentally attend to signs that are the focus of internal samādhis, this is the distraction of signs.

"If, depending on internal mental engagement, they attribute the concept 'I am' to arising feelings due to collective errant tendencies, this is the distraction of errant tendencies."

"Bhagavan, what do śamatha and vipaśyanā counteract, from the first Bodhisattva stage up to the stage of the Tathāgata?"

"Maitreya, on the first stage, śamatha and vipaśyanā counteract the afflictions of bad transmigrations and the afflictions of actions and of birth. On the second stage, they counteract the arising of errors that are very subtle infractions. On the third stage, they counteract attachment to desirable experiences. On the fourth stage, they counteract craving for

སྲིད་པ་དང་། ཆོས་ལ་སྲིད་པའིའོ། །ལྔ་པ་ལ་ནི་འཁོར་བ་དང་། མྱ་ངན་ལས་འདས་པ
དག་ལ་གཅིག་ཏུ་མི་ཕྱོགས་པ་ཉིད་དང་། མངོན་དུ་ཕྱོགས་པ་ཉིད་ཀྱིའོ། །དྲུག་པ་ལ་ནི
མཚན་མ་མང་པོ་ཀུན་ཏུ་འབྱུང་བའིའོ། །བདུན་པ་ལ་ནི་མཚན་མ་ཕྲ་མོ་ཀུན་ཏུ་འབྱུང
བའིའོ༑ ༑བརྒྱད་པ་ལ་ནི་མཚན་མ་མེད་པ་ལ་རྩོལ་བ་དང་། མཚན་མ་ལ་དབང་དུ་མ
གྱུར་པའིའོ། །དགུ་པ་ལ་ནི་རྣམ་པ་ཐམས་ཅད་དུ་ཆོས་སྟོན་པ་ལ་དབང་དུ་མ་གྱུར་པའིའོ། །
བཅུ་པ་ལ་ནི་ཆོས་ཀྱི་སྐུ་ཡོངས་སུ་རྫོགས་པ་སོ་སོ་ཡང་དག་པར་རིག་པ་མི་འཐོབ་པའིའོ། །
བྱམས་པ་ཞི་གནས་དང་ལྷག་མཐོང་དེ་བཞིན་གཤེགས་པའི་ས་ལ་ནི་ཉོན་མོངས་པ་དང་ཤེས
བྱའི་སྒྲིབ་པ་ཤིན་ཏུ་ཕྲ་བ་མཆོག་ཏུ་ཆེས་ཤིན་ཏུ་ཕྲ་བའི་གཉེན་པོ་ཡིན་ཏེ། དེ་ལེགས་པར
བཅོམ་པས་ཐམས་ཅད་ལ་ཆགས་པ་མེད་པ་དང་། ཐོགས་པ་མེད་པའི་ཤེས་པ་དང་།
མཐོང་བ་ཐོབ་ཅིང་དགོས་པ་ཡོངས་སུ་གྲུབ་པའི་དམིགས་པ་ལ་ཆོས་ཀྱི་སྐུ་ཤིན་ཏུ་རྣམ་པར
དག་པ་ལ་གནས་པ་ཡིན་ནོ༎ །བཅོམ་ལྡན་འདས་བྱང་ཆུབ་སེམས་དཔའ་ཞི་གནས་དང
ལྷག་མཐོང་ལ་ཇི་ལྟར་སྒྲུབ་ན་བླ་ན་མེད་པ་ཡང་དག་པར་རྫོགས་པའི་བྱང་ཆུབ་མངོན་པར
རྫོགས་པར་འཚང་རྒྱ་བར་འགྱུར་ལགས། བཅོམ་ལྡན་འདས་ཀྱིས་བཀའ་སྩལ་པ།
བྱམས་པ་འདི་ལ་བྱང་ཆུབ་སེམས་དཔའ་ཞི་གནས་དང་ལྷག་མཐོང་ཐོབ་ནས་དེ་བཞིན་ཉིད
རྣམ་པ་བདུན་ལས་བརྩམས་ཏེ། ཇི་ལྟར་ཐོས་པ་དང་བསམས་པའི་ཆོས་རྣམས་མཉམ་པར
བཞག་པའི་སེམས་ཀྱིས་བཟུང་བ་དང་། ལེགས་པར་བསམས་པ་དང་། ལེགས་པར
མཉམ་པར་བཞག་པའི་དེ་བཞིན་ཉིད་ནང་དུ་ཡིད་ལ་བྱེད་དེ། དེ་ལྟར་དེ་བཞིན་ཉིད་ཡིད

meditative absorption and craving for phenomena. On the fifth stage, they counteract exclusively turning away from or moving toward either saṁsāra or nirvāṇa. On the sixth stage, they counteract the arising of manifold signs. On the seventh stage, they counteract the arising of subtle signs. On the eighth stage, they counteract the search for signlessness and not having mastery over signs. On the ninth stage they counteract not having mastery over teaching the doctrine in all its aspects. On the tenth stage, they counteract not attaining perfect comprehension of the Dharmakāya.

"Maitreya, on the stage of the Tathāgata, śamatha and vipaśyanā counteract afflictive obstructions and obstructions to omniscience that are supremely subtle. Through fully conquering those [obstructions], [Tathāgatas] obtain vision and knowledge that is unattached and unobstructed with respect to everything. They abide in the object of observation which is the accomplishment of purpose, the very pure Dharmakāya."

"Bhagavan, after Bodhisattvas have achieved śamatha and vipaśyanā, how do they completely and perfectly realize unsurpassed enlightenment?"

The Bhagavan replied: "Maitreya, Bodhisattvas, having obtained śamatha and vipaśyanā, begin with the seven types of suchness. With minds absorbed in doctrines in accordance with how they have been heard and contemplated, they inwardly attend to the suchness that is apprehended, well

ལ་བྱེད་པ་ན་མཚན་མ་ཕྲ་མོ་ཀུན་ཏུ་འབྱུང་བ་ཐམས་ཅད་ལ་ཡང་རེ་ཞིག་སེམས་ལྷག་པར་བཏང་སྙོམས་སུ་འཇོག་ན་རགས་པ་དག་ལ་ལྟ་སྨོས་ཀྱང་ཅི་དགོས། བྱམས་པ་དེ་ལ་མཚན་མ་ཕྲ་མོ་ནི་འདི་དག་ཡིན་ཏེ། སེམས་ཀྱི་ལེན་པའི་མཚན་མའམ། སྤྱོད་པའི་མཚན་མའམ། རྣམ་པར་རིག་པའི་མཚན་མའམ། ཀུན་ནས་ཉོན་མོངས་པ་དང་རྣམ་པར་བྱང་བའི་མཚན་མའམ། ནང་གི་མཚན་མའམ། ཕྱི་རོལ་གྱི་མཚན་མའམ། དེ་གཉི་གའི་མཚན་མའམ། སེམས་ཅན་ཐམས་ཅད་ཀྱི་དོན་ལ་སྦྱར་བར་བྱའོ་སྙམ་པའི་མཚན་མའམ། ཤེས་པའི་མཚན་མའམ། དེ་བཞིན་ཉིད་དང་། སྡུག་བསྔལ་བ་དང་། ཀུན་འབྱུང་བ་དང་། འགོག་པ་དང་། ལམ་གྱི་མཚན་མའམ། འདུས་བྱས་ཀྱི་མཚན་མའམ། འདུས་མ་བྱས་ཀྱི་མཚན་མའམ། རྟག་པའི་མཚན་མའམ། མི་རྟག་པའི་མཚན་མའམ། སྡུག་བསྔལ་བ་དང་འགྱུར་བ་དང་བཅས་པའི་རང་བཞིན་གྱི་མཚན་མའམ། དེ་མི་འགྱུར་བའི་རང་བཞིན་གྱི་མཚན་མའམ། འདུ་བྱས་ཀྱི་མཚན་ཉིད་མི་འདྲ་བའི་མཚན་མའམ། དེ་རང་གི་མཚན་ཉིད་ཀྱི་མཚན་མའམ། ཐམས་ཅད་ཐམས་ཅད་ཅེས་བྱ་བར་རིག་ནས་ཐམས་ཅད་ཀྱི་མཚན་མའམ། གང་ཟག་བདག་མེད་པའི་མཚན་མའམ། ཆོས་བདག་མེད་པའི་མཚན་མ་གང་དག་ཡིན་པ་སྟེ། དེ་དག་ཀུན་ཏུ་འབྱུང་བ་ལ་སེམས་ལྷག་པར་བཏང་སྙོམས་སུ་འཇུག་གོ། །དེ་ལྟར་ཞུགས་ཤིང་དེ་ལ་མང་དུ་གནས་པ་དུས་དུས་སུ་གེགས་དང་། སྒྲིབ་པ་དང་། རྣམ་པར་གཡེང་བ་དག་ལས་སེམས་རྣམ་པར་སྦྱོང་བར་བྱེད་པ་དེ་ལ་ནང་གི་སོ་སོའི་བདག་ཉིད་ལ་སོ་སོར་རང་རིག་པ་དེ་བཞིན་ཉིད་

considered, and well attained. Since they mentally attend to suchness in this way, the mind soon enters great equipoise with regard to any arising of even the most subtle signs. What need be said about the coarse [signs]?

"Maitreya, the very subtle signs are these: signs of mental appropriation; signs of experience; signs of cognition; signs of affliction and purification; internal signs; external signs; signs of both; signs involved in thinking, 'I must work for the sake of all sentient beings'; signs of knowledge; signs of suchness, the [truth] of suffering, [the truth] of the source [of suffering], [the truth] of the cessation [of suffering], and [the truth] of the path; signs of compounded phenomena; signs of uncompounded phenomena; signs of permanence; signs of impermanence; signs that have a nature associated with suffering and change; signs having a nature that is unchangeable; signs unlike the characteristics of compounded phenomena; signs of their own characteristics; signs of universality, as in the context of knowing everything as 'everything'; signs of the selflessness of persons; and signs of the selflessness of phenomena.[37] In relationship to their arising, the mind enters into great equipoise.

"Entering into [suchness] in this way and abiding there often, they completely cleanse their minds of occasional obstacles, obstructions, and distractions, producing the seven aspects of knowledge which individually realize the seven

རྣམ་པ་བདུན་སོ་སོར་རྟོག་པའི་ཤེས་པ་རྣམ་པ་བདུན་སྐྱེ་བར་འགྱུར་ཏེ། དེ་ནི་དེའི་མཐོང་བའི་ལམ་ཡིན་ནོ། །དེ་ཐོབ་པས་བྱང་ཆུབ་སེམས་དཔའ་ཡང་དག་པ་ཉིད་སྐྱོན་མེད་པ་ལ་ཞུགས་པ་ཡིན། དེ་བཞིན་གཤེགས་པའི་རིགས་སུ་སྐྱེས་པ་ཡིན། ས་དང་པོ་ཐོབ་པ་དང་། ས་དེའི་ཕན་ཡོན་ཡང་ཉམས་སུ་མྱོང་བ་ཡིན་ནོ། །དེས་སྔར་ཞི་གནས་དང་། ལྷག་མཐོང་ཐོབ་པས་ནི་རྣམ་པར་རྟོག་པ་དང་བཅས་པའི་གཟུགས་བརྙན་དང་། རྣམ་པར་མི་རྟོག་པའི་གཟུགས་བརྙན་གྱི་དམིགས་པ་རྣམ་པ་གཉིས་ཐོབ་པ་ཡིན་ནོ། །དེ་ལྟར་ན་མཐོང་བའི་ལམ་ཐོབ་པས་དངོས་པོའི་མཐའི་དམིགས་པ་ཐོབ་པ་ཡིན་ཏེ། དེ་ས་གོང་མ་གོང་མ་རྣམས་སུ་བསྒོམ་པའི་ལམ་ལ་ཞུགས་ཤིང་། དམིགས་པ་རྣམ་པ་གསུམ་པོ་དེ་དག་ཉིད་ཡིད་ལ་བྱེད་པ་ན། འདི་ལྟ་སྟེ་དཔེར་ན། ལ་ལ་ཞིག་ཕྱིའུ་ཚེས་ཕྲ་མོས་ཕྱིའུ་ཚེས་སྦོམ་པོ་འབྱིན་པར་བྱེད་པ་དེ་བཞིན་དུ་དེ་ཡང་ཕྱིའུས་ཕྱིའུ་དབྱུང་བའི་ཚུལ་དུ་ནང་གི་མཚན་མ་རྣམ་པར་སེལ་བ་ཉིད་ཀྱིས་ཀུན་ནས་ཉོན་མོངས་པའི་ཆ་དང་འཐུན་པའི་མཚན་མ་ཐམས་ཅད་རྣམ་པར་སེལ་བར་བྱེད་དེ། མཚན་མ་རྣམས་རྣམ་པར་སེལ་བ་ན་གནས་ངན་ལེན་རྣམས་ཀྱང་རྣམ་པར་སེལ་བར་བྱེད་དོ། །མཚན་མ་དང་གནས་ངན་ལེན་ཐམས་ཅད་ལེགས་པར་བཅོམ་པས་རིམ་གྱིས་ས་གོང་མ་གོང་མ་རྣམས་སུ་གསེར་ལྟ་བུར་སེམས་རྣམ་པར་སྦྱོང་ལ། བླ་ན་མེད་པ་ཡང་དག་པར་རྫོགས་པའི་བྱང་ཆུབ་ཀྱི་བར་དུ་མངོན་པར་རྫོགས་པར་འཚང་རྒྱ་ཞིང་དགོས་པ་ཡོངས་སུ་གྲུབ་པའི་དམིགས་པ་ཡང་འཐོབ་སྟེ། བྱམས་པ་བྱང་ཆུབ་སེམས་དཔའ་ཞི་གནས་དང་ལྷག་མཐོང་ལ་དེ་ལྟར་སློབ་ན་བླ་ན་མེད་པ

aspects of suchness that are known by oneself individually and internally.[38] Such is the [Bodhisattva] path of seeing.

"By attaining this, Bodhisattvas enter into faultless reality. They are born into the lineage of the Tathāgata. They attain the first stage and also experience the benefits of that stage. Because they have previously attained śamatha and vipaśyanā, they attain the [first] two types of objects of observation: conceptual images and non-conceptual images. By attaining the path of seeing in such a way, they attain the [stage of] observing the limits of phenomena.

"Entering the path of meditation, they progress to higher stages. When they mentally attend to the three types of objects of observation, it is like removing a large nail with a small nail.[39] In the same way that a nail draws out a nail, by eliminating internal signs they eliminate all the signs concordant with the afflictions. When they eliminate the signs, they also eliminate the errant tendencies.

"By subduing signs and errant tendencies, [Bodhisattvas] gradually proceed higher and higher on the stages, purifying the mind like gold. They completely and perfectly realize unsurpassed enlightenment and obtain the object of observation which is the accomplishment of the purpose.

"Maitreya, when Bodhisattvas attain śamatha and vipaśyanā in that way, they completely and perfectly realize unsurpassed enlightenment."

ཡང་དག་པར་རྫོགས་པའི་བྱང་ཆུབ་མངོན་པར་རྫོགས་པར་འཚང་རྒྱ་བར་འགྱུར་རོ། །
བྱང་ཆུབ་སེམས་དཔའ་ཇི་ལྟར་སྒྲུབ་པར་བགྱིད་ན། བྱང་ཆུབ་སེམས་དཔའི་མཐུ་ཆེན་པོ
མངོན་པར་སྒྲུབ་པ་ལགས། བྱམས་པ་བྱང་ཆུབ་སེམས་དཔའ་གནས་དྲུག་ལ་མཁས་པ
ནི་བྱང་ཆུབ་སེམས་དཔའི་མཐུ་ཆེན་པོ་མངོན་པར་སྒྲུབ་པ་ཡིན་ཏེ། སེམས་ཀྱི་སྐྱེ་བ་ལ
མཁས་པ་དང་། གནས་པ་ལ་མཁས་པ་དང་། བསླང་བ་ལ་མཁས་པ་དང་། འཕེལ
བ་ལ་མཁས་པ་དང་། འགྲིབ་པ་ལ་མཁས་པ་དང་། ཐབས་ལ་མཁས་པའོ། །ཇི་ལྟར
ན་སེམས་ཀྱི་སྐྱེ་བ་ལ་མཁས་པ་ཡིན་ཞེ་ན། སེམས་ཀྱི་སྐྱེ་བ་རྣམ་པ་བཅུ་དྲུག་ཤེས་ན
སེམས་ཀྱི་སྐྱེ་བ་ལ་ཡང་དག་པ་ཇི་ལྟ་བ་བཞིན་དུ་མཁས་པ་ཡིན་ཏེ། དེ་ལ་སེམས་ཀྱི་སྐྱེ་བ
རྣམ་པ་བཅུ་དྲུག་ནི་བརྟན་པ་དང་སྣོད་རྣམ་པར་རིག་པའི་ནི་འདི་ལྟ་སྟེ། ལེན་པའི་རྣམ་པར
ཤེས་པའོ། །དམིགས་པའི་རྣམ་པ་སྣ་ཚོགས་རྣམ་པར་རིག་པའི་ནི་འདི་ལྟ་སྟེ། རྣམ
པར་རྟོག་པའི་ཡིད་ཀྱི་རྣམ་པར་ཤེས་པ་གཟུགས་ལ་སོགས་པ་ཡུལ་ཅིག་ཅར་འཛིན་པ་ཕྱི
རོལ་དང་། ནང་གི་ཡུལ་ཅིག་ཅར་འཛིན་པ། སྐད་ཅིག་དང་ཐང་ཅིག་དང་ཡུད་ཙམ་ཅིག
ལ་ཅིག་ཅར་ཏིང་ངེ་འཛིན་མང་པོ་ལ་སྙོམས་པར་འཇུག་པ། སངས་རྒྱས་ཀྱི་ཞིང་མང་པོ
མཐོང་བ། དེ་བཞིན་གཤེགས་པ་མང་པོ་མཐོང་བ། རྣམ་པར་རྟོག་པའི་ཡིད་ཀྱི་རྣམ་པར
ཤེས་པ་ཁོ་ནའོ། །དམིགས་པའི་མཚན་མ་ཆུང་ངུ་རྣམ་པར་རིག་པའི་ནི་འདི་ལྟ་སྟེ།
འདོད་པ་དང་ལྡན་པའོ། །དམིགས་པའི་མཚན་མ་ཆེན་པོར་གྱུར་པ་རྣམ་པར་རིག་པའི་ནི
འདི་ལྟ་སྟེ། གཟུགས་དང་ལྡན་པའོ། །དམིགས་པའི་མཚན་མ་ཚད་མེད་པ་རྣམ་པར

"How should a Bodhisattva practice in order to manifestly achieve the Bodhisattva's great powers?"[40]

"Maitreya, Bodhisattvas who are skillful[41] with respect to six topics manifestly achieve the Bodhisattva's great powers. These [powers] include skill with respect to the arising of mind, the abiding of mind, the emergence of mind, the increasing of mind, the diminishing of mind, and skill in means.

"At what point do [Bodhisattvas] become skillful with respect to the arising of mind? They are skillful with respect to the arising of mind as it really is when they know the sixteen aspects of the arising of mind. The sixteen aspects of the arising of mind are:

"Cognition that is a foundation and a receptacle, that is the appropriating consciousness.[42]

"Cognition that has various objects of observation, a conceptual mental consciousness that simultaneously apprehends objects such as form and the like; that simultaneously apprehends [both] the outer and inner object; that in a moment, an instant, or in a short time is simultaneously absorbed in many samādhis; that sees many Buddha fields and many Tathāgatas. [This cognition] is solely a conceptual mental consciousness.[43]

"Cognition of small observable signs related to the desire realm.

"Cognition of vast observable signs related to the form realm.

"Cognition of limitless observable signs related to the spheres of limitless space and limitless consciousness.

རིག་པའི་ནི་འདི་ལྟ་སྟེ། ནམ་མཁའ་མཐའ་ཡས་དང་། རྣམ་ཤེས་མཐའ་ཡས་སྐྱེ་མཆེད་ཀྱི་
དང་ལྡན་པའོ། །དམིགས་པའི་མཚན་མ་ཕྲ་མོ་རྣམ་པར་རིག་པའི་ནི་འདི་ལྟ་སྟེ། ཅི་
ཡང་མེད་པའི་སྐྱེ་མཆེད་དང་ལྡན་པའོ། །དམིགས་པའི་མཚན་མ་མཐར་ཐུག་པ་རྣམ་
པར་རིག་པའི་ནི་འདི་ལྟ་སྟེ། འདུ་ཤེས་མེད་འདུ་ཤེས་མེད་མིན་སྐྱེ་མཆེད་དང་ལྡན་པའོ། །
མཚན་མ་མེད་པ་རྣམ་པར་རིག་པའི་ནི་འདི་ལྟ་སྟེ། འཇིག་རྟེན་ལས་འདས་པ་དང་འགོག་པ
ལ་དམིགས་པའོ། །སྡུག་བསྔལ་དང་ལྡན་པའི་ནི་འདི་ལྟ་སྟེ། སེམས་ཅན་དམྱལ་
བའོ། །ཚོར་བ་འདྲེན་མ་དང་ལྡན་པའི་ནི་འདི་ལྟ་སྟེ། འདོད་པ་ན་སྤྱོད་པའོ། །
དགའ་བ་དང་ལྡན་པའི་ནི་འདི་ལྟ་སྟེ། བསམ་གཏན་དང་པོ་དང་། བསམ་གཏན་གཉིས
པ་པའོ། །བདེ་བ་དང་ལྡན་པའི་ནི་འདི་ལྟ་སྟེ། བསམ་གཏན་གསུམ་པ་པའོ། །
སྡུག་བསྔལ་ཡང་མ་ཡིན་བདེ་བ་ཡང་མ་ཡིན་པ་དང་ལྡན་པའི་ནི་འདི་ལྟ་སྟེ། བསམ་གཏན
བཞི་པ་པ་དང་། འདུ་ཤེས་མེད་འདུ་ཤེས་མེད་མིན་སྐྱེ་མཆེད་པའི་བར་གྱིའོ། །ཉོན་མོངས
པ་ཅན་དང་ལྡན་པའི་ནི་འདི་ལྟ་སྟེ། ཉོན་མོངས་པ་དང་ཉེ་བའི་ཉོན་མོངས་པ་དང་ལྡན་
པའོ། །དགེ་བ་དང་ལྡན་པའི་ནི་འདི་ལྟ་སྟེ། དད་པ་ལ་སོགས་པ་དང་ལྡན་པའོ། །
ལུང་དུ་མ་བསྟན་པ་དང་ལྡན་པའི་ནི་འདི་ལྟ་སྟེ། དེ་གཉིས་ཀའི་དང་མི་ལྡན་པའོ། །ཇི་ལྟར
ན་གནས་པ་ལ་མཁས་པ་ཡིན་ཞེ་ན། གལ་ཏེ་རྣམ་པར་རིག་པའི་དེ་བཞིན་ཉིད་ཡང་དག་
པ་ཇི་ལྟ་བ་བཞིན་རབ་ཏུ་ཤེས་པའོ། །ཇི་ལྟར་ན་བསླང་བ་ལ་མཁས་པ་ཡིན་ཞེ་ན། གལ
ཏེ་འཆིང་བ་རྣམ་པ་གཉིས་པོ་མཚན་མའི་འཆིང་བ་དང་། གནས་ངན་ལེན་གྱི་འཆིང་བ

"Cognition of subtle observable signs related to the sphere of nothingness.

"Cognition of final observable signs related to the sphere of neither discrimination nor non-discrimination.

"Cognition of signlessness, which observes the supramundane and cessation.

"That which is involved with suffering is the state of hell beings.

"That which is involved with diverse feelings is enacted in the desire realm.

"That involved with joy is the first and second concentrations.

"That which is involved with bliss is the third concentration.

"That which is involved with neither suffering nor non-suffering, neither bliss nor non-bliss is that which is involved with the fourth concentration up to the sphere of neither discrimination nor non-discrimination.[44]

"That which is involved with affliction is involvement with the afflictions and the secondary afflictions.

"That which is involved with virtue is involvement with faith and so forth.[45]

"That which is involved with the neutral is not involved with either [afflictions or virtues].

"At what point do [Bodhisattvas] become skilled with respect to the [mind's] abiding? This occurs when they know the suchness of cognition just as it is.

"At what point do [Bodhisattvas] become skilled with respect to the [mind's] emergence? This occurs when they

ཡང་དག་པ་ཇི་ལྟ་བ་བཞིན་རབ་ཏུ་ཤེས་ཏེ། དེ་རབ་ཏུ་ཤེས་ནས་དེ་ལས་སེམས་འདི་བསྲུང
བར་བྱའོ་ཞེས་བྱ་བ་ལ་མཁས་པ་ཡིན་ནོ། །ཇི་ལྟར་ན་འཕེལ་བ་ལ་མཁས་པ་ཡིན་ཞེ་ན།
གལ་ཏེ་མཚན་མ་དང་གནས་ངན་ལེན་གྱི་གཉེན་པོའི་སེམས་གང་ཡིན་པ་དེ་སྐྱེ་བ་དང
འཕེལ་བའི་ཚེ། སྐྱེ་བ་དང་འཕེལ་ལོ་ཞེས་འཕེལ་བ་ལ་མཁས་པ་ཡིན་ནོ། །ཇི་ལྟར་ན
འགྲིབ་པ་ལ་མཁས་པ་ཡིན་ཞེ་ན། གལ་ཏེ་དེ་དང་མི་འཐུན་པའི་ཕྱོགས་སུ་གྱུར་པ་མཚན
མ་གནས་ངན་ལེན་གྱི་ཀུན་ནས་ཉོན་མོངས་པ་ཅན་དུ་གྱུར་པའི་སེམས་དེ་འགྲིབ་ཅིང་འབྲི
བར་གྱུར་པ་ན་འགྲིབ་ཅིང་འབྲིའོ་ཞེས་འགྲིབ་པ་ལ་མཁས་པ་ཡིན་ནོ། །ཇི་ལྟར་ན་ཐབས
ལ་མཁས་པ་ཡིན་ཞེ་ན། གལ་ཏེ་རྣམ་པར་ཐར་པ་དང་། ཟིལ་གྱིས་གནོན་པའི་སྐྱེ་མཆེད
དག་དང་། ཟད་པར་གྱི་སྐྱེ་མཆེད་དག་སྒོམ་པར་བྱེད་པ་སྟེ། བྱམས་པ་དེ་ལྟར་ན་བྱང
ཆུབ་སེམས་དཔའ་རྣམས་བྱང་ཆུབ་སེམས་དཔའི་མཐུ་ཆེན་པོ་མངོན་པར་བསྒྲུབས་པ་དང་།
མངོན་པར་སྒྲུབ་པར་འགྱུར་བ་དང་། མངོན་པར་སྒྲུབ་པར་བྱེད་པ་ཡིན་ནོ། །བཅོམ་ལྡན
འདས་བཅོམ་ལྡན་འདས་ཀྱིས་ཕུང་པོའི་ལྷག་མ་མེད་པའི་མྱ་ངན་ལས་འདས་པའི་དབྱིངས
སུ་ཚོར་བ་ཐམས་ཅད་མ་ལུས་པར་འགག་གོ་ཞེས་གང་གསུངས་པ་ལ། བཅོམ་ལྡན་འདས
ཡང་དག་པའི་ཚོར་བ་དེ་དག་གང་ལགས། བྱམས་པ་མདོར་བསྡུས་ན་ཚོར་བ་རྣམ་པ
གཉིས་འགག་སྟེ། གནས་ཀྱི་གནས་ངན་ལེན་རིག་པ་དང་། དེའི་འབྲས་བུ་ཡུལ་རིག
པའོ། །དེ་ལ་གནས་ཀྱི་གནས་ངན་ལེན་རིག་པ་ནི་རྣམ་པ་བཞིར་རིག་སྟེ། གཟུགས་ཀྱི
གནས་ངན་ལེན་རིག་པ་དང་། གཟུགས་མེད་པའི་གནས་ངན་ལེན་རིག་པ་དང་། འབྲས

know, just as they are, the two types of bonds, the bonds of signs and the bonds of errant tendencies.[46] Having thoroughly come to know this, they are skilled in terms of [knowing]: 'This mind emerges from that.'

"At what point do [Bodhisattvas] become skilled with respect to [the mind's] increasing? When the mind that is an antidote to signs and errant tendencies is produced and increases, they are skilled with respect to increasing, [knowing]: 'This is produced and increases.'

"At what point do [Bodhisattvas] become skilled with respect to [the mind's] diminishing? When the mind that is afflicted with signs and errant tendencies discordant with that [skill] diminishes and decreases, they are skilled with respect to diminishing, [knowing]: 'It diminishes and decreases.'

"At what point do [Bodhisattvas] become skilled imeans?[47] This occurs when they meditate on the [eight] liberations, the [eight] spheres of surpassing, and the [ten] spheres of totality. Maitreya, in this way Bodhisattvas have manifestly achieved, will manifestly achieve, and are manifestly achieving the Bodhisattva's great powers."

"Bhagavan, the Bhagavan has said, 'In the sphere of nirvāṇa without a remainder of aggregates, all feelings completely cease.' Bhagavan, what are those valid feelings [that cease]?"

"Maitreya, in brief, two kinds of feelings cease: awareness of the errant tendencies that are abodes and awareness of objects that are the fruits of those [tendencies].[48] Awareness

བུ་གྲུབ་པའི་གནས་ངན་ལེན་རིག་པ་དང་། འབྲས་བུ་མ་གྲུབ་པའི་གནས་ངན་ལེན་རིག་པའོ། །དེ་ལ་འབྲས་བུ་གྲུབ་པ་ནི་ད་ལྟར་གྱི་གང་ཡིན་པའོ། །འབྲས་བུ་མ་གྲུབ་པ་ནི་མ་འོངས་པའི་རྒྱུར་གྱུར་པ་གང་ཡིན་པའོ། །ཡུལ་རིག་པ་ཡང་རྣམ་པ་བཞིར་རིག་པར་བྱ་སྟེ། གནས་རིག་པ་དང་། ཡོ་བྱད་རིག་པ་དང་། ལོངས་སྤྱོད་རིག་པ་དང་། ལྟོས་པ་རིག་པའོ། །དེ་ཡང་ཕུང་པོ་ལྷག་མ་དང་བཅས་པའི་མྱ་ངན་ལས་འདས་པའི་དབྱིངས་ནའོ། །འབྲས་བུ་མ་གྲུབ་པ་རིག་པའི་འདུས་ཏེ་རིག་པ་ལས་བྱུང་བའི་ཚོར་བ་སྨྱོང་བ་དེའི་མི་འཐུན་པའི་ཕྱོགས་ཐམས་ཅད་ཀྱི་ཐམས་ཅད་དུ་འགག་པ་མ་ཡིན་ཏེ། འདྲེན་མར་སྨྱོང་ངོ་། །འབྲས་བུ་གྲུབ་པ་སྨྱོང་བའི་ནི་ཚོར་བ་རྣམ་པ་དེ་གཉིས་ཀ་ཐམས་ཅད་ཀྱི་ཐམས་ཅད་དུ་འགགས་ཏེ། རིག་པའི་འདུས་ཏེ་རིག་པ་ལས་བྱུང་བའི་ཚོར་བ་འབའ་ཞིག་སྨྱོང་ངོ༎

ཕུང་པོའི་ལྷག་མ་མེད་པའི་མྱ་ངན་ལས་འདས་པའི་དབྱིངས་སུ་ཡོངས་སུ་མྱ་ངན་ལས་འདའ་བ་ན་དེ་ཡང་འགག་པར་འགྱུར་ཏེ། དེའི་ཕྱིར་ཕུང་པོ་ལྷག་མ་མེད་པའི་མྱ་ངན་ལས་འདས་པའི་དབྱིངས་སུ་ཚོར་བ་ཐམས་ཅད་འགག་ཅེས་བྱའོ། །དེ་སྐད་ཅེས་བཀའ་སྩལ་ནས། བཅོམ་ལྡན་འདས་ཀྱིས་བྱང་ཆུབ་སེམས་དཔའ་བྱམས་པ་ལ་བཀའ་སྩལ་པ། བྱམས་པ་ཁྱོད་ཀྱིས་རྣལ་འབྱོར་གྱི་ལམ་ཡོངས་སུ་རྫོགས་པ་དང་། ཤིན་ཏུ་ཡོངས་སུ་དག་པ་ལས་བརྩམས་ནས། འདི་ལྟ་སྟེ། རྣལ་འབྱོར་ལ་ཤིན་ཏུ་རྣམ་པར་ངེས་ཤིང་མཁས་པས་དེ་བཞིན་གཤེགས་པ་ལ་དྲི་བ་དྲིས་པ་ལེགས་སོ་ལེགས་སོ། །ངས་ཀྱང་རྣལ་འབྱོར་གྱི་ལམ་དེ་ཡོངས་སུ་རྫོགས་པ་དང་། ཡོངས་སུ་དག་པར་བསྟན་ཏེ། འདས་པ་དང་མ་འོངས་པའི

of the errant tendencies that are abodes should be known as being of four kinds: awareness of errant tendencies of the form realm, awareness of errant tendencies of the formless realm, awareness of errant tendencies that have come to fruition, and awareness of errant tendencies that have not come to fruition.[49] Those that have come to fruition are whatever now exists; those that have not come to fruition are whatever will serve as causes in the future.

"Know that awareness of objects is also of four kinds: awareness of abodes, awareness of property, awareness of resources, and awareness of reliances. Moreover, [awareness of objects] occurs in the sphere of nirvāṇa that has a remainder of the aggregates. Although this [category of awareness of objects] includes awareness of what has not come to fruition, that which is discordant with the experiences of feelings that arise from contact has not completely ceased. Thus one experiences affiliated [feelings]. With the awareness of that which has come to fruition, the two kinds of feelings completely cease: Although this includes awareness, one experiences just those feelings that arise from contact. When one passes beyond sorrow altogether in the sphere of nirvāṇa that is without a remainder of the aggregates, even that ceases. Therefore, it is said that, 'All feelings cease in the sphere of nirvāṇa that is without a remainder of the aggregates.'"[50]

Having said this, the Bhagavan said to Bodhisattva Maitreya, "Maitreya, you question the Tathāgata about yoga with skill and good ascertainment beginning with the most complete

ཡང་དག་པར་རྫོགས་པའི་སངས་རྒྱས་གང་དག་ཡིན་པ་དེ་དག་ཐམས་ཅད་ཀྱིས་ཀྱང་དེ་ལྟར་
བསྟན་ཅིང་སྟོན་པར་འགྱུར་རོ། །རིགས་ཀྱི་བུ་རྣམས་དང་། རིགས་ཀྱི་བུ་མོ་དག་གིས་
འདི་ལ་ཤིན་ཏུ་བརྩོན་པར་བྱ་བའི་རིགས་སོ། །དེ་ནས་བཅོམ་ལྡན་འདས་ཀྱིས་དེའི་ཚེ་
ཚིགས་སུ་བཅད་པ་འདི་དག་བཀའ་སྩལ་ཏོ། །ཆོས་རྣམས་གདགས་པ་རྣམ་གཞག་
གང་ཡིན་པ། །དེ་ནི་རྣལ་འབྱོར་བག་ཡོད་དོན་ཆེན་ཡིན། །གང་དག་ཆོས་དེར་བརྟེན་
ནས་རྣལ་འབྱོར་འདིར། །ཡང་དག་བརྩོན་པ་དེ་དག་བྱང་ཆུབ་འཐོབ། །གང་དག་
གླགས་ལྟ་དེ་སྐད་རྒོལ་བ་ལས། །ཕར་པར་ལྟ་བ་ཆོས་ཀུན་ཆུབ་བྱེད་པ། །བྱམས་པ་
དེ་དག་རྣལ་འབྱོར་འདི་ལས་ནི། །ཐག་རིང་གནམ་ས་རིང་བ་ཇི་བཞིན་ནོ། །བློ་ལྡན་
སེམས་ཅན་དོན་ཞིས་དེ་དག་ལས། །ཕན་བྱེད་རིག་ནས་སེམས་ཅན་དོན་བརྩོན་མིན། །
ཕན་དེ་རྟོག་ན་ཀུན་གྱི་དམ་པ་དང་། །ཟང་ཟིང་མེད་པའི་དགའ་བ་འཐོབ་མི་འགྱུར། །
གང་དག་འདོད་ཕྱིར་ཆོས་ཀྱི་ལུང་འབོགས་པ། །དེ་དག་འདོད་པ་སྤངས་པ་ཕྱིར་ལེན་
ཏེ། །རྨོངས་པ་དེ་དག་ཆོས་ཀྱི་རིན་པོ་ཆེ། །རིན་ཐང་མེད་པ་རྙེད་ཀྱང་སྤྱོང་ཞིང་རྒྱུ། །
དེ་ཕྱིར་རྩོད་དང་འདུ་འཛི་སྤྲོས་ལྡན་པ། །རྣམ་པར་སྤོངས་ཏེ་བརྩོན་འགྲུས་མཆོག་བྱོས་
ཏེ། །ལྷ་བཅས་འཇིག་རྟེན་བསྒྲལ་བར་བྱ་བའི་ཕྱིར། །རྣལ་འབྱོར་འདི་ལ་རབ་ཏུ་
བརྩོན་པར་གྱིས། །དེ་ནས་བཅོམ་ལྡན་འདས་ལ་བྱང་ཆུབ་སེམས་དཔའ་བྱམས་པས་
འདི་སྐད་ཅེས་གསོལ་ཏོ། །བཅོམ་ལྡན་འདས་དགོངས་པ་ངེས་པར་འགྲེལ་པའི་ཆོས་ཀྱི་
རྣམ་གྲངས་འདིར་བསྟན་པ་འདིའི་མིང་ཅི་ལགས། འདི་ཇི་ལྟར་གཟུང་བར་བགྱི།

and pure path of yoga. This is excellent and good! I also teach this path of yoga completely and flawlessly. All those who have become perfect Buddhas in the past or will become Buddhas in the future have also taught or will teach in this way. It is fitting that sons and daughters of good lineage strive for this."

Then the Bhagavan spoke these verses:

"Whatever doctrines are designated and posited
are for the great purpose of diligence in yoga.
Those who rely on these doctrines and
work at this yoga will attain enlightenment.

"Those who, seeking flaws, dispute these words
and study all doctrines seeking liberation
are, Maitreya, as far from this yoga
as the sky is distant from the earth.

"Those wise ones who benefit sentient beings
do not seek rewards when striving to aid beings.
Those who hope for a reward will not attain
supreme joy free from materialistic concerns.

"Those who, with desire, give Dharma instructions,
have renounced desire, but still cling to it.
These deluded ones obtain the precious, priceless Dharma,
but wander in destitution.

"Therefore, vigorously abandon disputation,
worldly commotion, and conceptual elaboration.
In order to liberate worldly beings, including gods,
make great effort in this yoga."

བཅོམ་ལྡན་འདས་ཀྱིས་དེ་ལ་བཀའ་སྩལ་པ། བྱམས་པ་འདི་ནི་རྣལ་འབྱོར་ངེས་པའི་དོན་བསྟན་པ་ཡིན་ཏེ། རྣལ་འབྱོར་ངེས་པའི་དོན་བསྟན་པ་ཞེས་བྱ་བར་ཟུང་ཤིག །རྣལ་འབྱོར་ངེས་པའི་དོན་བསྟན་པ་འདི་བཤད་པ་ན་སྲོག་ཆགས་དྲུག་འབུམ་ནི་བླ་ན་མེད་པ་ཡང་དག་པར་རྫོགས་པའི་བྱང་ཆུབ་ཏུ་སེམས་སྐྱེས་སོ། །ཉན་ཐོས་སུམ་འབུམ་ནི་ཆོས་རྣམས་ལ་ཆོས་ཀྱི་མིག་རྡུལ་མེད་ཅིང་དྲི་མ་དང་བྲལ་བ་རྣམ་པར་དག་གོ། །ཉན་ཐོས་འབུམ་ལྔ་ཁྲི་ནི་ལེན་པ་མེད་པར་ཟག་པ་རྣམས་ལས་སེམས་རྣམ་པར་གྲོལ་ལོ། །བྱང་ཆུབ་སེམས་དཔའ་བདུན་ཁྲི་ལྔ་སྟོང་གིས་ནི་རྣལ་འབྱོར་ཆེན་པོའི་ཡིད་ལ་བྱེད་པ་ཐོབ་པར་གྱུར་ཏོ། །བྱམས་པའི་ལེའུ་སྟེ་བརྒྱད་པའོ།། །།

Then the Bodhisattva Maitreya asked the Bhagavan: "Bhagavan, what is the name of this form of Dharma discourse that explains your thought? How should it be apprehended?"

The Bhagavan replied: "Maitreya, this is the teaching of the definitive meaning of yoga. Apprehend it as 'the teaching of the definitive meaning of yoga'."

When this teaching of the definitive meaning of yoga was explained, six hundred thousand living beings generated the aspiration toward completely perfect and unsurpassed enlightenment. Three hundred thousand Śrāvakas purified the Dharma eye that is free from dust and stainless with respect to the Dharma. One hundred and fifty thousand Śrāvakas liberated their minds from contamination such that they would not take rebirth. Seventy-five thousand Bodhisattvas attained the mental contemplation of the great yoga.

This completes the eighth chapter of Maitreya.

Homage to the Mahābodhisattva Avalokiteśvara

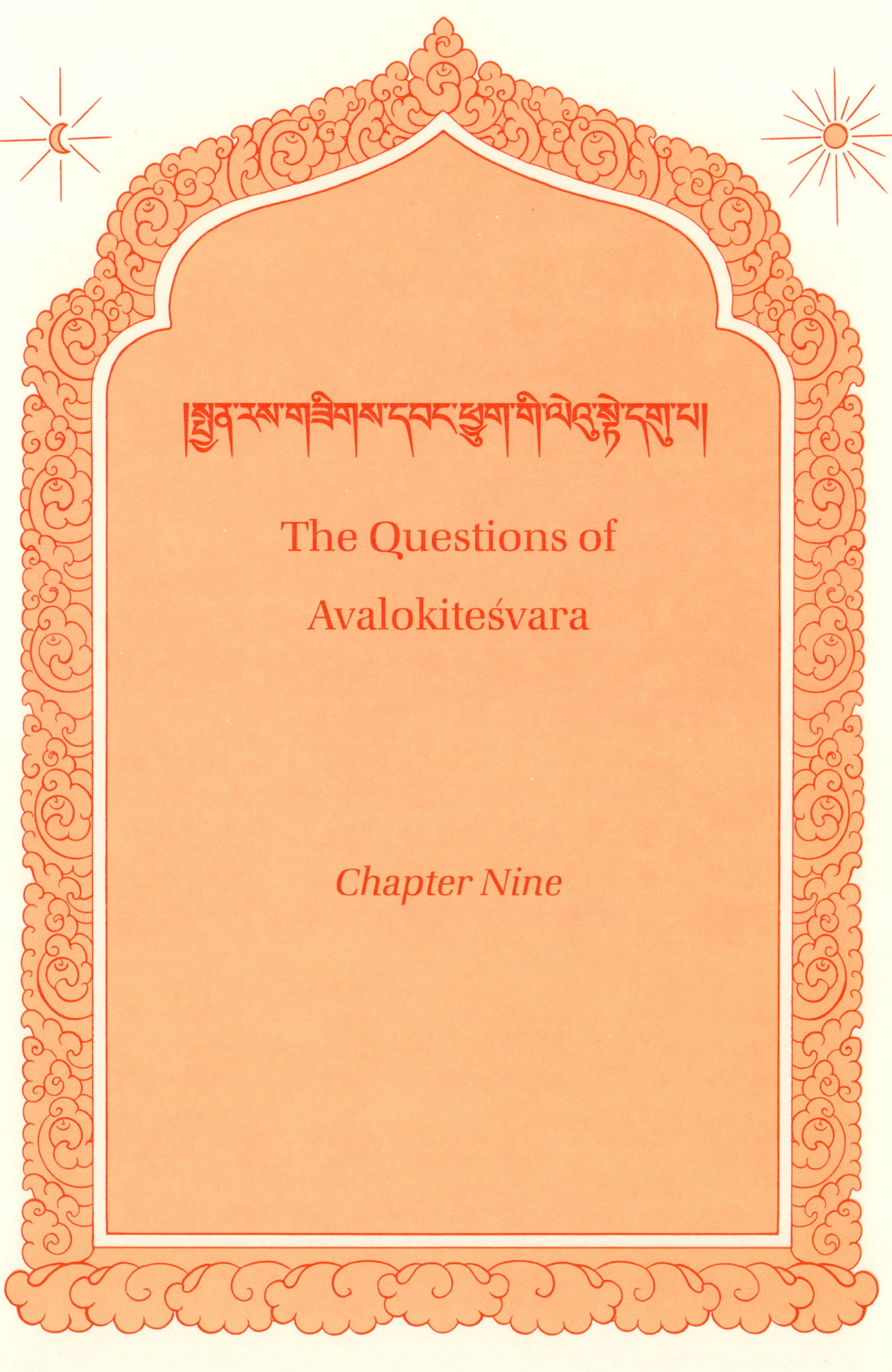
།སྤྱན་རས་གཟིགས་དབང་ཕྱུག་གི་ལེའུ་སྟེ་དགུ་པ།
The Questions of
Avalokiteśvara
Chapter Nine

༄༅། །དེ་ནས་བཅོམ་ལྡན་འདས་ལ་བྱང་ཆུབ་སེམས་དཔའ་སྤྱན་རས་གཟིགས་ཀྱི་དབང་ཕྱུག་གིས་ཞུ་བ་ཞུས་པ། བཅོམ་ལྡན་འདས་བྱང་ཆུབ་སེམས་དཔའ་རྣམས་ཀྱིས་བཅུ་གང་ལགས་པ་དེ་དག་ནི་འདི་ལྟ་སྟེ། བྱང་ཆུབ་སེམས་དཔའི་ས་རབ་ཏུ་དགའ་བ་ཞེས་བགྱི་བ་དང་། དྲི་མ་མེད་པ་དང་། འོད་བྱེད་པ་དང་། འོད་འཕྲོ་བ་ཅན་དང་། ཤིན་ཏུ་སྦྱང་དཀའ་དང་། མངོན་དུ་གྱུར་པ་དང་། རིང་དུ་སོང་བ་དང་། མི་གཡོ་བ་དང་། ལེགས་པའི་བློ་གྲོས་དང་། ཆོས་ཀྱི་སྤྲིན་ལགས། སངས་རྒྱས་ཀྱི་ས་ནི་བཅུ་གཅིག་པ་ལགས་ན། ས་དེ་དག་རྣམ་པར་དག་པ་དུ་དག་དང་། ཡན་ལག་དུ་དག་གིས་བསྡུས་ལགས། བཅོམ་ལྡན་འདས་ཀྱིས་བཀའ་སྩལ་པ། སྤྱན་རས་གཟིགས་དབང་ཕྱུག་དེ་དག་ནི་རྣམ་པར་དག་པ་བཞི་དང་། ཡན་ལག་བཅུ་གཅིག་གིས་བསྡུས་པར་རིག་པར་བྱའོ། །སྤྱན་རས་གཟིགས་དབང་ཕྱུག་དེ་ལ་ས་དང་པོ་ནི་བསམ་པ་རྣམ་པར་དག་པས་བསྡུས་སོ། །ས་གཉིས་པ་ནི་ལྷག་པའི་ཚུལ་ཁྲིམས་རྣམ་པར་དག་པས་སོ། །ས་གསུམ་པ་ནི་ལྷག་པའི་སེམས་རྣམ་པར་དག་པས་སོ། །ས་བཞི་པ་ནས་བཟུང་སྟེ་སངས་རྒྱས་ཀྱི་སའི་བར་ནི་ལྷག་པའི་ཤེས་རབ་རྣམ་པར་དག་པ་གོང་ནས་གོང་དུ་བྲུ་ནོམ་པ་བས་ཀྱང་ཆེས་བྲུ་ནོམ་པས་བསྡུས་པར་རིག་པར་བྱ་སྟེ། ས་དེ་དག་ནི་རྣམ་པར་དག་པ་བཞི་པོ་དག་གིས་བསྡུས་པ་ཡིན་ནོ། །ཡན་ལག་བཅུ་གཅིག་གང་ཞེ་ན། སྤྱན་རས་གཟིགས་དབང་ཕྱུག་མོས་པས་སྤྱོད་པའི་ས་ལ་བྱང་ཆུབ་སེམས་དཔའ་ཆོས་སྤྱོད་པ་རྣམ་པ་བཅུ་པོ་དག་ལ་མོས་པ་ཤིན་ཏུ་བསྒོམས་པའི་ཕྱིར་བཟོད་པས་ས་དེ་ལས་ཡང་དག་པར་འདས་ནས་བྱང་ཆུབ་

Then Bodhisattva Avalokiteśvara[1] asked the Bhagavan: "Bhagavan, since there are ten Bodhisattva stages—the Very Joyous, the Stainless, the Luminous, the Radiant, the Unconquerable, the Manifest, the Gone Afar, the Immovable, the Good Intelligence, and the Cloud of Dharma, and the eleventh stage of a Buddha—of how many purities and how many limbs are these stages comprised?"

The Bhagavan replied: "Avalokiteśvara, know that these [stages] are comprised of four purities and eleven limbs. Avalokiteśvara, know that pure thought comprises the first stage; pure surpassing ethics comprises the second stage; pure surpassing intention comprises the third stage; and pure surpassing wisdom comprises the progressively higher [stages] ranging from the fourth stage up to the Buddha stage. These four purities comprise these [stages].[2]

"What are the eleven limbs?[3] Avalokiteśvara, by acting patiently to finely cultivate conviction in the ten aspects of doctrinal practices,[4] Bodhisattvas on the stage of engagement through conviction pass completely beyond that stage and enter the faultless reality of the Bodhisattva.[5]

"Although the [first stage] is achieved by this [first] limb, due to inability to employ introspection into the source of the errors that are subtle infractions, the [second stage] is not achieved by the [first] limb. Through striving to achieve the [second] limb, the [second stage] will also be attained.[6]

སེམས་དཔའི་ཡང་དག་པ་ཉིད་སྐྱོན་མེད་པ་ལ་འཇུག་གོ། །དེ་ཡན་ལག་དེས་ཡོངས་སུ་རྫོགས་པ་ཡིན་ཡང་ལྟུང་བ་ཕྲ་མོའི་འཁྲུལ་པ་ཀུན་ཏུ་འབྱུང་བ་དག་ལ་ཤེས་བཞིན་དུ་སྤྱོད་པར་མི་ནུས་པས་དེ་ཡན་ལག་དེས་ཡོངས་སུ་མ་རྫོགས་པ་ཡིན་ཏེ། དེ་ཡན་ལག་དེ་ཡོངས་སུ་རྫོགས་པར་བྱ་བའི་ཕྱིར་འབད་པས་དེ་ཡང་འཐོབ་བོ། །དེ་ཡན་ལག་དེས་ཡོངས་སུ་རྫོགས་པ་ཡིན་ཡང་འཇིག་རྟེན་པའི་ཏིང་ངེ་འཛིན་ཡོངས་སུ་རྫོགས་པ་ལ་སྙོམས་པར་འཇུག་པ་དང་། ཐོས་པའི་གཟུངས་ཡོངས་སུ་རྫོགས་པ་ཐོབ་པར་མི་ནུས་པས་དེ་ཡན་ལག་དེས་ཡོངས་སུ་མ་རྫོགས་པ་ཡིན་ཏེ། དེ་ཡན་ལག་དེ་ཡོངས་སུ་རྫོགས་པར་བྱ་བའི་ཕྱིར་འབད་པས་ཡན་ལག་དེས་ཡོངས་སུ་རྫོགས་པ་ཡིན་ཡང་བྱང་ཆུབ་ཀྱི་ཕྱོགས་དང་འཐུན་པའི་ཆོས་ཇི་ལྟར་ཐོབ་པ་དག་གིས་དེ་ལ་མང་དུ་གནས་པར་བྱ་བ་དང་། སྙོམས་པར་འཇུག་པ་ལ་སྲིད་པ་དང་། ཆོས་ལ་སྲིད་པ་ལས་སེམས་ལྷག་པར་བཏང་སྙོམས་སུ་འཇུག་མི་ནུས་པས་དེ་ཡན་ལག་དེས་ཡོངས་སུ་མ་རྫོགས་པ་ཡིན་ཏེ། དེ་ཡན་ལག་དེ་ཡོངས་སུ་རྫོགས་པར་བྱ་བའི་ཕྱིར་འབད་པས་དེ་ཡང་འཐོབ་བོ། །དེ་ཡན་ལག་དེས་ཡོངས་སུ་རྫོགས་པ་ཡིན་ཡང་བདེན་པ་རྣམས་རྣམ་པར་དཔྱད་པ་དང་། འཁོར་བ་དང་མྱ་ངན་ལས་འདས་པ་དག་ལ་གཅིག་ཏུ་མི་ཕྱོགས་པ་ཉིད་དང་། མངོན་དུ་ཕྱོགས་པའི་ཡིད་ལ་བྱེད་པ་ལྷག་པར་བཏང་སྙོམས་སུ་བཞག་སྟེ། ཐབས་ཀྱིས་ཡོངས་སུ་ཟིན་པའི་བྱང་ཆུབ་ཀྱི་ཕྱོགས་དང་འཐུན་པའི་ཆོས་རྣམས་བསྒོམ་པར་མི་ནུས་པས་དེ་ཡན་ལག་དེས་ཡོངས་སུ་མ་རྫོགས་པ་ཡིན་ཏེ། དེ་ཡན་ལག་དེ་ཡོངས་སུ་རྫོགས་པར་བྱ་བའི་ཕྱིར་འབད་པས་དེ་ཡང་འཐོབ་བོ། །དེ་ཡན

"Although the [second stage] is achieved by the [second] limb, due to inability to enter fully into absorption in worldly samādhis, or to retain fully what is heard, the [third stage] is not achieved by the [second] limb.[7] Through striving to achieve the [third] limb, the [third stage] will also be attained.

"Although the [third stage] is achieved by the [third] limb, due to inability to always abide in doctrines concordant with enlightenment just as they have been attained, and inability to make the mind dispassionate with respect to craving for meditative absorption and for phenomena, the [fourth stage] is not achieved by the [third] limb. Through striving to achieve the [fourth] limb, the [fourth stage] will also be attained.[8]

"Although the [fourth stage] is achieved by the [fourth] limb, and [those Bodhisattvas] have analyzed the truths and have completely dispassionate mental attention which neither exclusively turns away from nor moves toward saṁsāra or nirvāṇa, because they are not able to cultivate doctrines that are concordant with enlightenment which are fully conjoined with method, the [fifth stage] is not achieved by the [fourth] limb. Through striving to achieve the [fifth] limb, the [fifth stage] will also be attained.[9]

"Although the [fifth stage] is achieved by the [fifth] limb, and [those Bodhisattvas] have realized as they really are the workings of the compounded, due to inability to always abide in mental attention to renunciation and signlessness, the [sixth

ལག་དེས་ཡོངས་སུ་རྫོགས་པ་ཡིན་ཡང་འདུ་བྱེད་ཀྱི་འཇུག་པ་ཇི་ལྟ་བ་བཞིན་མངོན་སུམ་དུ་
བྱས་ནས་དེ་ལ་སྐྱོ་བ་མང་བ་དང་། མཚན་མ་མེད་པ་ཡིད་ལ་བྱེད་པས་མང་དུ་གནས་པར་
མི་ནུས་པས་དེ་ཡོངས་སུ་མ་རྫོགས་པ་ཡིན་ཏེ། དེ་ཡན་ལག་དེ་ཡོངས་སུ་རྫོགས་པར་བྱ་
བའི་ཕྱིར་འབད་པས་དེ་ཡང་འཐོབ་བོ། །དེ་ཡན་ལག་དེས་ཡོངས་སུ་རྫོགས་པ་ཡིན་ཡང་
བར་ཆད་མེད་པ་དང་། རྒྱུན་མི་འཆད་པར་མཚན་མ་མེད་པའི་ཡིད་ལ་བྱེད་པས་མང་དུ་
གནས་པར་མི་ནུས་པས། དེ་ཡན་ལག་དེས་ཡོངས་སུ་མ་རྫོགས་པ་ཡིན་ཏེ། དེ་ཡན་ལག་
དེས་ཡོངས་སུ་རྫོགས་པར་བྱ་བའི་ཕྱིར་འབད་པས་དེ་ཡང་ཐོབ་བོ། །དེ་ཡན་ལག་དེས་
ཡོངས་སུ་རྫོགས་པ་ཡིན་ཡང་མཚན་མ་མེད་པར་གནས་པ་དེ་ལ་རྩོལ་བ་ལྷག་པར་བཏང་
སྙོམས་སུ་བཞག་པ་དང་། མཚན་མ་ལ་དབང་ཐོབ་པར་མི་ནུས་པས་དེ་ཡན་ལག་དེས་
ཡོངས་སུ་མ་རྫོགས་པ་ཡིན་ཏེ། དེ་ཡན་ལག་དེ་ཡོངས་སུ་རྫོགས་པར་བྱ་བའི་ཕྱིར་འབད་
པས་དེ་ཡང་འཐོབ་བོ། །དེ་ཡན་ལག་དེས་ཡོངས་སུ་རྫོགས་པ་ཡིན་ཡང་རྣམ་གྲངས་དང་།
མཚན་ཉིད་དང་། ངེས་པའི་ཚིག་དང་། རབ་ཏུ་དབྱེ་བས་རྣམ་པ་ཐམས་ཅད་དུ་ཆོས་སྟོན་
པ་ལའང་དབང་ཐོབ་པར་མི་ནུས་པས་དེ་ཡན་ལག་དེས་ཡོངས་སུ་མ་རྫོགས་པ་ཡིན་ཏེ། དེ་
ཡན་ལག་དེ་ཡོངས་སུ་རྫོགས་པར་བྱ་བའི་ཕྱིར་འབད་པས་དེ་ཡང་འཐོབ་བོ། །དེ་ཡན་
ལག་དེས་ཡོངས་སུ་རྫོགས་པ་ཡིན་ཡང་ཆོས་ཀྱི་སྐུ་ཡོངས་སུ་རྫོགས་པ་སོ་སོར་ཡང་དག་
པར་རིག་པ་འཐོབ་པར་མི་ནུས་པས་དེ་ཡན་ལག་དེས་ཡོངས་སུ་མ་རྫོགས་པ་ཡིན་ཏེ། དེ་
ཡན་ལག་དེ་ཡོངས་སུ་རྫོགས་པར་བྱ་བའི་ཕྱིར་འབད་པས་དེ་ཡང་འཐོབ་བོ། །དེ་ཡན་

stage] is not achieved by the [fifth] limb. Through striving to achieve the [sixth] limb, the [sixth stage] will also be attained.[10]

"Although the [sixth stage] is achieved by the [sixth] limb, due to inability to abide in mental attention to signlessness continuously and uninterruptedly, the [seventh stage] is not achieved by the [sixth] limb. Through striving to achieve the [seventh] limb, the [seventh stage] will also be attained.[11]

"Although the [seventh stage] is achieved by the [seventh] limb, due to inability to make dispassionate efforts to abide in signlessness and inability to attain mastery over signs, the [eighth stage] is not achieved by the [seventh] limb. Through striving to achieve the [eighth] limb, the [eighth stage] will also be attained.[12]

"Although the [eighth stage] is achieved by the [eighth] limb, due to inability to also attain mastery in teaching the doctrine in all its aspects by means of enumerations, characteristics, etymologies, and divisions, the [ninth stage] is not achieved by the [eighth] limb. Through striving to achieve the [ninth] limb, the [ninth stage] will also be attained.[13]

"Although the [ninth stage] is achieved by the [ninth] limb, because of inability to attain comprehension of the perfect Dharmakāya, the [tenth stage] is not achieved by the [ninth] limb. Through striving to complete the [tenth] limb, the [tenth stage] will also be attained.[14]

ལག་དེ་ཡོངས་སུ་རྫོགས་པ་ཡིན་ཡང་ཤེས་བྱ་ཐམས་ཅད་ལ་ཆགས་པ་མེད་པ་དང་། ཐོགས་པ་མེད་པའི་ཤེས་པ་དང་། མཐོང་བ་ཐོབ་པར་མི་ནུས་པས་དེ་ཡན་ལག་དེས་ཡོངས་སུ་མ་རྫོགས་པ་ཡིན་ཏེ། དེ་ཡན་ལག་དེ་ཡོངས་སུ་རྫོགས་པར་བྱ་བའི་ཕྱིར་འབད་པས་དེ་ཡང་འཐོབ་སྟེ། དེ་ཡན་ལག་དེ་ཡོངས་སུ་རྫོགས་པ་ཡིན་ནོ། །དེ་ཡན་ལག་དེས་ཡོངས་སུ་རྫོགས་པའི་ཕྱིར་ཡན་ལག་ཐམས་ཅད་ཡོངས་སུ་རྫོགས་པ་ཡིན་ཏེ། སྤྱན་རས་གཟིགས་དབང་ཕྱུག་དེ་དག་ནི་ཡན་ལག་བཅུ་གཅིག་པོ་དེ་དག་གིས་བསྡུས་པར་རིག་པར་བྱའོ། །

བཅོམ་ལྡན་འདས་ཅིའི་སླད་དུ་ས་དང་པོ་ལ་རབ་ཏུ་དགའ་བ་ཞེས་བགྱི། ཅིའི་སླད་དུ་སངས་རྒྱས་ཀྱི་སའི་བར་ལ་སངས་རྒྱས་ཀྱི་ས་ཞེས་བགྱི་ལགས། ས་དང་པོ་ནི་དོན་ཆེ་བ་འདྲིས་པ་མ་ཡིན་པ་འཇིག་རྟེན་ལས་འདས་པའི་སེམས་ཐོབ་པས་དགའ་བ་དང་། མཆོག་ཏུ་དགའ་བ་རྒྱ་ཆེ་བའི་ཕྱིར་རབ་ཏུ་དགའ་བ་ཞེས་བྱའོ། །ས་གཉིས་པ་ནི་ལྟུང་བ་ཕྲ་མོ་དང་འཆལ་བའི་ཚུལ་ཁྲིམས་ཀྱི་དྲི་མ་ཐམས་ཅད་དང་བྲལ་བ་ཉིད་ཀྱི་ཕྱིར་དྲི་མ་མེད་པ་ཞེས་བྱའོ། །ས་གསུམ་པ་ནི་ཏིང་ངེ་འཛིན་དེ་དང་ཐོས་པའི་གཟུངས་དེ་ཤེས་པའི་སྣང་བ་ཚད་མེད་པའི་གནས་ཉིད་ཡིན་པའི་ཕྱིར་འོད་བྱེད་པ་ཞེས་བྱའོ། །ས་བཞི་པ་ནི་ཉོན་མོངས་པའི་ཤིང་བསྲེག་པའི་ཕྱིར་བྱང་ཆུབ་ཀྱི་ཕྱོགས་དང་འཐུན་པའི་ཆོས་སྒོམ་པ་དེ་ཡེ་ཤེས་ཀྱི་མེའི་འོད་འཕྲོ་བར་གྱུར་པའི་ཕྱིར་འོད་འཕྲོ་ཅན་ཞེས་བྱའོ། །ས་ལྔ་པ་ནི་བྱང་ཆུབ་ཀྱི་ཕྱོགས་དང་འཐུན་པའི་ཆོས་དེ་དག་ཉིད་ཐབས་ཀྱིས་སྒོམ་པ་དེ་ལ་དབང་བྱ་བར་དཀའ་བ་ཉིད་ཀྱི་ཕྱིར་ཤིན་ཏུ་སྦྱང་དཀའ་ཞེས་བྱའོ། །ས་དྲུག་པ་ནི་འདུ་བྱེད་ཀྱི་འཇུག་པ་མངོན་སུམ་དུ་གྱུར་པ

"Although the [tenth stage] is achieved by the [tenth] limb, due to inability to attain knowledge and insight that is unattached and unimpeded with respect to all objects of knowledge, the [Buddha stage] is not achieved by the [tenth] limb. Through striving to achieve the [eleventh] limb, the [Buddha stage] will also be attained. The [Buddha stage] is achieved by the [eleventh] limb.[15] Through achieving the [Buddha stage] by the [eleventh] limb, all limbs are achieved. Avalokiteśvara, know that the [eleven stages] are comprised of these eleven limbs."

"Bhagavan, why is the first stage called the 'Very Joyous'? Why are the stages up to the Buddha stage given names [such as] the 'Buddha stage'?"

"The first stage is called the 'Very Joyous' because, through attaining a mind that is of supreme worth, that is exceptional, and that transcends the world, one becomes supremely joyous and extensively joyous. The second stage is called the 'Stainless' because one is free from all stains that are subtle infractions or faulty ethics. The third stage is called the 'Luminous' because it is a state of limitless illuminating knowledge of samādhi and the retention of what is heard. The fourth stage is called the 'Radiant' because one who cultivates qualities concordant with enlightenment in order to burn the fuel of the afflictions radiates the fire of wisdom.

"The fifth stage is called the 'Unconquerable' because one who skillfully cultivates those same qualities concordant with enlightenment is difficult to overcome. The sixth stage is

ཉིད་དང་། མཚན་མ་མེད་པ་མང་དུ་ཡོད་ལ་བྱེད་པ་མངོན་སུམ་དུ་གྱུར་པའི་ཕྱིར་མངོན་དུ
གྱུར་ཅེས་བྱའོ། །ས་བདུན་པ་ནི་མཚན་མ་མེད་པ་ཡོད་ལ་བྱེད་པ་བར་ཆད་མེད་ཅིང་རྒྱུན
མི་འཆད་པ་རིང་དུ་རྗེས་སུ་ཞུགས་པ་དང་། རྣམ་པར་དག་པའི་ས་དང་རྗེས་སུ་འབྲེལ་པ
ཉིད་ཀྱི་ཕྱིར་རིང་དུ་སོང་བ་ཞེས་བྱའོ། །ས་བརྒྱད་པ་ནི་མཚན་མ་མེད་པ་ལ་ལྷུན་གྱིས་གྲུབ
པ་ཉིད་དང་། མཚན་མའི་ཉོན་མོངས་པ་ཀུན་ཏུ་བྱུང་བས་མི་བསྐྱོད་པ་ཉིད་ཀྱི་ཕྱིར་མི་གཡོ
བ་ཞེས་བྱའོ། །ས་དགུ་པ་ནི་རྣམ་པ་ཐམས་ཅད་དུ་ཆོས་སྟོན་པའི་དབང་ལ་ཁ་ན་མ་ཐོ་བ
མེད་པའི་བློ་གྲོས་ཤིན་ཏུ་ཡངས་པ་ཐོབ་པ་ཉིད་ཀྱི་ཕྱིར་ལེགས་པའི་བློ་གྲོས་ཞེས་བྱའོ། །ས
བཅུ་པ་ནི་གནས་ངན་ལེན་གྱི་ལུས་ནམ་མཁའ་ལྟ་བུ་ལ་ཆོས་ཀྱི་ཚོགས་སྤྲིན་ཆེན་ལྟ་བུས
ཁྱབ་ཅིང་ཁེབས་པའི་ཕྱིར་ཆོས་ཀྱི་སྤྲིན་ཞེས་བྱའོ། །ས་བཅུ་གཅིག་པ་ནི་ཉོན་མོངས་པ་དང
ཤེས་བྱའི་སྒྲིབ་པ་ཤིན་ཏུ་ཕྲ་མོ་སྤངས་པས་ཆགས་པ་མེད་ཅིང་ཐོགས་པ་མེད་པར་ཤེས་བྱའི
རྣམ་པ་ཐམས་ཅད་མངོན་པར་རྫོགས་པར་བྱང་ཆུབ་པ་ཉིད་ཀྱི་ཕྱིར་སངས་རྒྱས་ཀྱི་ས་ཞེས
བྱའོ། །བཅོམ་ལྡན་འདས་ས་དེ་དག་ལ་ཀུན་ཏུ་རྨོངས་པ་ནི་དུ་མཆིས། གནས་ངན་ལེན
མི་འཐུན་པའི་ཕྱོགས་ནི་དུ་མཆིས་ལགས། བཅོམ་ལྡན་འདས་ཀྱིས་བཀའ་སྩལ་པ། སྤྱན
རས་གཟིགས་དབང་ཕྱུག་ཀུན་ཏུ་རྨོངས་པ་ཉི་ཤུ་རྩ་གཉིས་དང་། གནས་ངན་ལེན་མི་འཐུན
པའི་ཕྱོགས་བཅུ་གཅིག་སྟེ། ས་དང་པོ་ལ་ནི་གང་ཟག་དང་ཆོས་ལ་མངོན་པར་ཞེན་པ
ཀུན་ཏུ་རྨོངས་པ་དང་། ངན་སོང་བའི་ཉོན་མོངས་པས་ཀུན་ཏུ་ཉོན་མོངས་པ་དང་། དེའི
གནས་ངན་ལེན་མི་འཐུན་པའི་ཕྱོགས་སོ། །གཉིས་པ་ལ་ནི་ལྟུང་བ་ཕྲ་མོའི་འཁྲུལ་པ་ཀུན

called the 'Manifest' because one manifestly realizes the operation of compounded phenomena and manifestly realizes regular mental attention to signlessness.

"The seventh stage is called the 'Gone Afar' because one enters into uninterrupted, continuous mental attention to signlessness for a long time and is subsequently connected to a completely pure stage. The eighth stage is called the 'Immovable' because one spontaneously accomplishes signlessness and is unshaken by the arising of the afflictions of signs.

"The ninth stage is called the 'Good Intelligence' because one attains comprehensive intelligence, faultless in its mastery of teaching the doctrine in all its aspects. The tenth stage is called the 'Cloud of Dharma' because the great cloudlike gathering of Dharma pervades and covers the skylike body of errant tendencies. The eleventh stage is called the 'Buddha stage' because, through having abandoned the most subtle afflictive obstructions and obstructions to omniscience, unattached and unimpeded, one is manifestly, perfectly enlightened with respect to all aspects of objects of knowledge."[16]

"Bhagavan, how many obscurations are there to these stages? How many discordant classes of errant tendencies?"

The Bhagavan replied, "Avalokiteśvara, there are twenty-two obscurations and eleven discordant classes of errant tendencies.[17] On the first stage, there are: the obscuration of exaggerated adherence to persons and phenomena; [the obscuration]

ཏུ་རྨོངས་པ་དང་། ལས་ཀྱི་རྣམ་པར་སྨིན་པ་རྣམ་པ་སྣ་ཚོགས་ལ་ཀུན་ཏུ་རྨོངས་པ་དང་། དེའི་གནས་ངན་ལེན་མི་འཐུན་པའི་ཕྱོགས་སོ། །གསུམ་པ་ལ་ནི་འདོད་པའི་འདོད་ཆགས་ཀྱི་ཀུན་ཏུ་རྨོངས་པ་དང་། ཐོས་པའི་གཟུངས་ཡོངས་སུ་རྫོགས་པ་ལ་ཀུན་ཏུ་རྨོངས་པ་དང་། དེའི་གནས་ངན་ལེན་མི་འཐུན་པའི་ཕྱོགས་སོ། །བཞི་པ་ལ་ནི་སྙོམས་པར་འཇུག་པ་ལ་སྲེད་པ་ཀུན་ཏུ་རྨོངས་པ་དང་། ཆོས་ལ་སྲེད་པ་ཀུན་ཏུ་རྨོངས་པ་དང་། དེའི་གནས་ངན་ལེན་མི་འཐུན་པའི་ཕྱོགས་སོ། །ལྔ་པ་ལ་ནི་འཁོར་བ་ལ་གཅིག་ཏུ་མི་ཕྱོགས་པ་ཉིད་དང་། མངོན་དུ་ཕྱོགས་པ་ཉིད་ཡིད་ལ་བྱེད་པ་ཀུན་ཏུ་རྨོངས་པ་དང་། མྱ་ངན་ལས་འདས་པ་ལ་གཅིག་ཏུ་མི་ཕྱོགས་པ་ཉིད་དང་། མངོན་དུ་ཕྱོགས་པ་ཉིད་ཡིད་ལ་བྱེད་པ་ཀུན་ཏུ་རྨོངས་པ་དང་། དེའི་གནས་ངན་ལེན་མི་འཐུན་པའི་ཕྱོགས་སོ། །དྲུག་པ་ལ་ནི་འདུ་བྱེད་ཀྱི་འཇུག་པ་མངོན་སུམ་དུ་བྲ་བ་ཉིད་ལ་ཀུན་ཏུ་རྨོངས་པ་དང་། མཚན་མ་མང་པོ་ཀུན་ཏུ་འབྱུང་བ་ཀུན་ཏུ་རྨོངས་པ་དང་། དེའི་གནས་ངན་ལེན་མི་འཐུན་པའི་ཕྱོགས་སོ། །བདུན་པ་ལ་ནི་མཚན་མ་ཕྲ་མོ་ཀུན་ཏུ་འབྱུང་བ་ཀུན་ཏུ་རྨོངས་པ་དང་། མཚན་མ་མེད་པ་གཅིག་ཏུ་ཡིད་ལ་བྱེད་པས་ཐབས་ལ་ཀུན་ཏུ་རྨོངས་པ་དང་། དེའི་གནས་ངན་ལེན་མི་འཐུན་པའི་ཕྱོགས་སོ། །བརྒྱད་པ་ལ་ནི་མཚན་མ་མེད་པ་ལ་རྩོལ་བ་ཀུན་ཏུ་རྨོངས་པ་དང་། མཚན་མ་རྣམས་ལ་མི་དབང་བ་ཀུན་ཏུ་རྨོངས་པ་དང་། དེའི་གནས་ངན་ལེན་མི་འཐུན་པའི་ཕྱོགས་སོ། །དགུ་པ་ལ་ནི་ཆོས་བསྟན་པ་དཔག་ཏུ་མེད་པ་དང་། ཆོས་ཀྱི་ཚིག་དང་ཡི་གེ་དཔག་ཏུ་མེད་པ་དང་། གོང་ནས་གོང་དུ་ཤེས་རབ་དང་སྤོབས་པ་ལ་གཟུངས་ཀྱི་དབང་ལ

of the afflictions due to the afflictions of bad transmigrations; and the discordant class of their errant tendencies.

"On the second [stage], there are: the obscuration of errors that are subtle infractions, the obscuration of the diverse aspects of the fruition of actions, and the discordant class of their errant tendencies. On the third [stage], there are: the obscuration of attachment to desirable experiences, the obscuration to full retention of what is heard, and the discordant class of their errant tendencies.

"On the fourth [stage],[18] there are: the obscuration of craving for meditative absorption, the obscuration of craving for phenomena, and the discordant class of their errant tendencies. On the fifth [stage], there are: the obscuration of mental attention that exclusively turns away from or moves toward saṁsāra; the obscuration of mental attention that exclusively turns away from or moves toward nirvāṇa; and the discordant class of their errant tendencies.[19]

"On the sixth [stage], there are: the obscuration to manifestly realizing the operation of compounded phenomena; the obscuration of the arising of many signs; and the discordant class of their errant tendencies.[20]

"On the seventh [stage], there are: the obscuration of the arising of subtle signs; obscuration with respect to the method of mentally attending just to signlessness; and the discordant class of their errant tendencies.[21] On the eighth [stage], there are: the obscuration of exertion towards signlessness; the

ཀུན་ཏུ་ཉོན་མོངས་པ་དང་། སྤོབས་པའི་དབང་ལ་ཀུན་ཏུ་ཉོན་མོངས་པ་དང་། དེའི་གནས་ངན་
ལེན་མི་འཐུན་པའི་ཕྱོགས་སོ། །བཅུ་པ་ལ་ནི་མངོན་པར་ཤེས་པ་ཆེན་པོ་ལ་ཀུན་ཏུ་ཉོན་མོངས་
པ་དང་། གསང་བ་དང་ཕྲ་བ་ལ་འཇུག་པ་ལ་ཀུན་ཏུ་ཉོན་མོངས་པ་དང་། དེའི་གནས་ངན་
ལེན་མི་འཐུན་པའི་ཕྱོགས་སོ། །སངས་རྒྱས་ཀྱི་ས་ལ་ནི་ཤེས་བྱ་ཐམས་ཅད་ལ་ཆགས་པ་
ཤིན་ཏུ་ཕྲ་མོ་ཀུན་ཏུ་ཉོན་མོངས་པ་དང་། ཐོགས་པ་ཀུན་ཏུ་ཉོན་མོངས་པ་དང་། དེའི་གནས་ངན་
ལེན་མི་འཐུན་པའི་ཕྱོགས་སོ། །སྤྱན་རས་གཟིགས་དབང་ཕྱུག་དེ་དག་ནི། ཀུན་ཏུ་
ཉོན་མོངས་པ་ཉི་ཤུ་རྩ་གཉིས་དང་། གནས་ངན་ལེན་བཅུ་གཅིག་པོ་དེ་དག་གིས་རྣམ་པར་
བཞག་སྟེ། བླ་ན་མེད་པ་ཡང་དག་པར་རྫོགས་པའི་བྱང་ཆུབ་ནི། མི་ལྡན་པ་ཡིན་ནོ། །
བཅོམ་ལྡན་འདས་གང་ལ་དེ་ལྟར། བྱང་ཆུབ་སེམས་དཔའ་རྣམས་དེ་ལྟར་ཀུན་ཏུ་ཉོན་མོངས་
པའི་དྲ་བ་ཆེན་པོ་རབ་ཏུ་དྲལ་ཞིང་དེའི་གནས་ངན་ལེན་ཐིབས་པོ་ཆེན་པོ་ལས་ཡང་དག་པར་
འདས་ཏེ། བླ་ན་མེད་པ་ཡང་དག་པར་རྫོགས་པའི་བྱང་ཆུབ་མངོན་པར་རྫོགས་པར་
འཚང་རྒྱ་བའི་བླ་ན་མེད་པ་ཡང་དག་པར་རྫོགས་པའི་བྱང་ཆུབ་ཇི་ཙམ་དུ་ཕན་ཡོན་ཆེ་ཞིང་
འབྲས་བུ་ཆེ་བ་ནི་ངོ་མཚར་ལགས་སོ། །བཅོམ་ལྡན་འདས་དེ་དག་རྣམ་པར་དག་པ་དུ
དག་གིས་རྣམ་པར་བཞག་པ་ལགས། སྤྱན་རས་གཟིགས་དབང་ཕྱུག་བརྒྱད་ཀྱིས་ཏེ།
ལྷག་པའི་བསམ་པ་རྣམ་པར་དག་པ་དང་། སེམས་རྣམ་པར་དག་པ་དང་། སྙིང་རྗེ་རྣམ་
པར་དག་པ་དང་། ཕ་རོལ་ཏུ་ཕྱིན་པ་རྣམ་པར་དག་པ་དང་། སངས་རྒྱས་མཐོང་ཞིང་
བསྙེན་བཀུར་བྱེད་པ་རྣམ་པར་དག་པ་དང་། སེམས་ཅན་ཡོངས་སུ་སྨིན་པར་བྱེད་པ་རྣམ་

obscuration of not having mastery over signs; and the discordant class of their errant tendencies.[22]

"On the ninth [stage], there are: the obscuration to mastery of the retention of the immeasurable doctrinal teachings, doctrinal words, doctrinal letters, and increasing wisdom and fearless inspiration; the obscuration to mastery of fearless inspiration; and the discordant class of their errant tendencies.[23] On the tenth [stage], there are: the obscuration to the great clairvoyances; obscuration to entering into the secret and subtle; and the discordant class of their errant tendencies.

"On the Buddha stage, there are: the obscuration of very subtle attachment to all that is knowable; the obscuration of [very subtle] obstacles; and the discordant class of their errant tendencies.[24] Avalokiteśvara, these [eleven stages] are distinguished by these twenty-two obscurations and these eleven errant tendencies. [Due to them] one does not possess unsurpassed, perfect, complete enlightenment."

"Bhagavan, since Bodhisattvas rend the great net of the obscurations and completely transcend the great jungle of errant tendencies and become awakened—completely, manifestly and perfectly enlightened—the great benefits and great fruits are marvelous! Bhagavan, by how many purities are these [stages] distinguished?"

"Avalokiteśvara, [they are distinguished] by eight [purities]: purity of surpassing thought, purity of mind, purity of compassion, purity of the perfections, purity of perception of and

པར་དག་པ་དང་། སྐྱེ་བ་རྣམ་པར་དག་པ་དང་། མཐུ་རྣམ་པར་དག་པས་སོ། །སྤྱན་རས་གཟིགས་དབང་ཕྱུག་ས་དང་པོ་ལ་ལྷག་པའི་བསམ་པ་རྣམ་པར་དག་པ་ནས་མཐུ་རྣམ་པར་དག་པའི་བར་གང་ཡིན་པ་དང་། ས་གོང་མ་གོང་མ་རྣམས་དང་། སངས་རྒྱས་ཀྱི་སའི་བར་ལ་ལྷག་པའི་བསམ་པ་རྣམ་པར་དག་པ་ནས་མཐུ་རྣམ་པར་དག་པའི་བར་གང་ཡིན་པ་དེ་ནི་ཆེས་རྣམ་པར་དག་པ་དང་། ཆེས་ཤིན་ཏུ་རྣམ་པར་དག་པ་ཡིན་པར་རིག་པར་བྱའོ། །དེ་ལ་སངས་རྒྱས་ཀྱི་ས་ལ་སྐྱེ་བ་རྣམ་པར་དག་པ་མ་གཏོགས་པ་ས་དང་པོའི་ཡོན་ཏན་གང་ཡིན་པ་དེ་དག་གིས་དེའི་གོང་མའི་ས་རྣམས་དེའི་ཡོན་ཏན་དང་ཡང་མཉམ་ལ། རང་གི་སའི་ཡོན་ཏན་གྱིས་ཁྱད་པར་དུ་འཕགས་པ་ཡང་ཡིན་པར་རིག་པར་བྱའོ། །བྱང་ཆུབ་སེམས་དཔའི་ས་བཅུ་པོ་ཐམས་ཅད་ནི་ཡོན་ཏན་བླ་ན་ཡོད་པ་དག་ཡིན་ལ། སངས་རྒྱས་ཀྱི་ས་ནི་ཡོན་ཏན་བླ་ན་མེད་པར་ཡང་དག་པར་རིག་པར་བྱའོ། །བཅོམ་ལྡན་འདས་ཅིའི་སླད་དུ་སྲིད་པར་སྐྱེ་བ་ཐམས་ཅད་ཀྱི་ནང་ན་བྱང་ཆུབ་སེམས་དཔའི་སྐྱེ་བ་རབ་ཏུ་མཆོག་ཅེས་བགྱི་ལགས། སྤྱན་རས་གཟིགས་དབང་ཕྱུག་རྣམ་པ་བཞིའི་ཕྱིར་ཏེ། དགེ་བའི་རྩ་བ་ཤིན་ཏུ་རྣམ་པར་དག་པ་འགྲུབ་པ་ཉིད་ཀྱི་ཕྱིར་དང་། སོ་སོར་བརྟགས་ཏེ་ལེན་པ་ཉིད་ཀྱི་ཕྱིར་དང་། འགྲོ་བ་ཐམས་ཅད་ཡོངས་སུ་བསྐྱབ་པའི་སྙིང་རྗེ་དང་ལྡན་པ་ཉིད་ཀྱི་ཕྱིར་དང་། བདག་ཉིད་ཀུན་ནས་ཉོན་མོངས་པ་ཅན་མ་ཡིན་པ་ཉིད་དང་། གཞན་གྱི་ཀུན་ནས་ཉོན་མོངས་པ་རྣམ་པར་ཟློག་པར་བྱེད་པ་ཉིད་ཀྱི་ཕྱིར་རོ། །བཅོམ་ལྡན་འདས་ཅིའི་སླད་དུ་བྱང་ཆུབ་སེམས་དཔའ་རྣམས་སྨོན་ལམ་རྒྱ་ཆེན་པོས་མཆིབ་དང་། སྨོན་ལམ་གྲུ་ནོམ་པ་དང་

reverence for the Buddhas, purity of fully ripening sentient beings, purity of birth, and purity of power.

"Avalokiteśvara, know that those purities on the first stage, ranging from the purity of surpassing thought to purity of power, and those purities on progressively higher stages up to the Buddha stage, ranging from the purity of surpassing thought up to the purity of power, are great purities and supreme purities.

"Know that, except for the purity of birth on the Buddha stage, the qualities of the first stage match the qualities of the stages above them, but the qualities particular to each stage have distinct superiorities. Know that all ten Bodhisattva stages have surpassable qualities, but that the Buddha stage has unsurpassable qualities."

"Bhagavan, why is it that, among all births in cyclic existence, a Bodhisattva's birth is known as 'the most excellent'?"

"Avalokiteśvara, this is because of four aspects: [Bodhisattvas] establish exceedingly pure roots of virtue; after individually investigating, they appropriate [what is learned]; they have compassion that protects all beings; and not having afflictions themselves, they overcome others' afflictions."[25]

"Bhagavan, why is it that Bodhisattvas progress by way of extensive aspirations, have auspicious aspirations, and have the force of aspirations?"[26]

ལྡན་པ་དང༌། སྨོན་ལམ་གྱི་སྟོབས་ཅན་ལགས། སྤྱན་རས་གཟིགས་དབང་ཕྱུག་རྣམ་པ་བཞིའི་ཕྱིར་རོ། འདི་ལྟར་བྱང་ཆུབ་སེམས་དཔའ་རྣམས་ནི་མྱ་ངན་ལས་འདས་པའི་བདེ་བ་ལ་གནས་པ་ལ་མཁས་པ་དང༌། དེ་མྱུར་དུ་འཐོབ་པར་ནུས་པ་དང༌། མྱུར་དུ་ཐོབ་པ་དེ་དང་བདེ་བར་གནས་པ་དེ་ཡང་སྤངས་ཏེ། སེམས་ཅན་གྱི་དོན་རྒྱུ་བ་མེད་པ་དགོས་པ་མེད་པ་སྡུག་བསྔལ་མང་པོ་སྣ་ཚོགས་ཡུན་རིང་པོར་འབྱུང་བ་ལ་ཡིད་ཀྱིས་སྨོན་པར་བྱེད་པས་ཏེ། དེའི་ཕྱིར་སྨོན་ལམ་རྒྱ་ཆེན་པོས་འཁྲོ་བ་དང༌། སྨོན་ལམ་གྱུ་ནོམ་པ་དང་ལྡན་པ་དང༌། སྨོན་ལམ་གྱི་སྟོབས་ཅན་རྣམས་ཞེས་བྱའོ། །བཅོམ་ལྡན་འདས་བྱང་ཆུབ་སེམས་དཔའ་རྣམས་ཀྱི་བསླབ་པའི་གཞི་དུ་མཆིས་ལགས། སྤྱན་རས་གཟིགས་དབང་ཕྱུག་དྲུག་སྟེ། སྦྱིན་པ་དང༌། ཚུལ་ཁྲིམས་དང༌། བཟོད་པ་དང༌། བརྩོན་འགྲུས་དང༌། བསམ་གཏན་དང༌། ཤེས་རབ་བོ། །བཅོམ་ལྡན་འདས་གཞི་དྲུག་པོ་དེ་དག་ལས་དུ་ནི་ལྷག་པའི་ཚུལ་ཁྲིམས་ཀྱི་བསླབ་པ་ལགས། དུ་ནི་ལྷག་པའི་སེམས་ཀྱི་བསླབ་པ་ལགས། དུ་ནི་ལྷག་པའི་ཤེས་རབ་ཀྱི་བསླབ་པ་ལགས། སྤྱན་རས་གཟིགས་དབང་ཕྱུག་དང་པོ་གསུམ་ནི་ལྷག་པའི་ཚུལ་ཁྲིམས་ཀྱི་བསླབ་པ་ཡིན་པར་རིག་པར་བྱའོ། །བསམ་གཏན་ནི་ལྷག་པའི་སེམས་ཀྱི་བསླབ་པ་ཡིན་ནོ། །ཤེས་རབ་ནི་ལྷག་པའི་ཤེས་རབ་ཀྱི་བསླབ་པ་ཡིན་ནོ། །བརྩོན་འགྲུས་ནི་ཀུན་ཏུ་འགྲོ་བ་ཡིན་པར་ངས་སྨྲའོ། །བཅོམ་ལྡན་འདས་བསླབ་པའི་གཞི་དྲུག་པོ་དེ་དག་ལས་དུ་ནི་བསོད་ནམས་ཀྱི་ཚོགས་ལགས། དུ་ནི་ཡེ་ཤེས་ཀྱི་ཚོགས་ལགས། སྤྱན་རས་གཟིགས་དབང་ཕྱུག་ལྷག་པའི་ཚུལ་ཁྲིམས་ཀྱི་བསླབ་པ་གང་ཡིན་པ་དེ་ནི་བསོད་ནམས་

"Avalokiteśvara, it is because of four aspects: Bodhisattvas are skilled regarding the blissful state of nirvāṇa;[27] they are able to quickly attain it; having given up both that quick attainment and that peaceful state, for the benefit of sentient beings they wish to undergo, for a very long time, the manifold sufferings that arise without cause and without purpose.[28] Therefore, they are called: 'those who progress by way of extensive aspirations, those who have auspicious aspirations, and those with the force of aspirations'."

"Bhagavan, how many bases of training for Bodhisattvas are there?"

"Avalokiteśvara, there are six: generosity, ethics, patience, effort, concentration, and wisdom."[29]

"Bhagavan, how many of the six bases are trainings in surpassing ethics? How many are trainings in surpassing mind? How many are trainings in surpassing wisdom?"

"Avalokiteśvara, know that the first three are trainings in surpassing ethics. Concentration is a training in surpassing mind. Wisdom is a training in surpassing wisdom. I explain that effort is omnipresent."[30]

"Bhagavan, how many of these six bases of training belong to the accumulation of merit? How many belong to the accumulation of wisdom?"

"Avalokiteśvara, training in surpassing ethics belongs to the accumulation of merit. Training in surpassing wisdom

ཀྱི་ཚོགས་ཡིན་ནོ། །ལྷག་པའི་ཤེས་རབ་ཀྱི་བསླབ་པ་གང་ཡིན་པ་དེ་ནི་ཡེ་ཤེས་ཀྱི་ཚོགས་ཡིན་ནོ། །བརྩོན་འགྲུས་དང་བསམ་གཏན་ནི་ཀུན་ཏུ་འགྲོ་བ་ཡིན་པར་དགོངས་སོ། །བཅོམ་ལྡན་འདས་བསླབ་པའི་གཞི་དྲུག་པོ་དེ་དག་ལ་བྱང་ཆུབ་སེམས་དཔས་ཇི་ལྟར་བསླབ་པར་བགྱི་ལགས། སྤྱན་རས་གཟིགས་དབང་ཕྱུག་རྣམ་པ་ལྔས་ཏེ། ཕ་རོལ་ཏུ་ཕྱིན་པ་དང་ལྡན་པའི་དམ་པའི་ཆོས་བསྟན་པ། བྱང་ཆུབ་སེམས་དཔའི་སྡེ་སྣོད་ལ་ཐོག་མ་ཁོ་ནར་ཤིན་ཏུ་མོས་པ་དང་། དེའི་འོག་ཏུ་ཆོས་སྤྱོད་པ་བཅུ་པོ་དག་གིས་ཐོས་པ་དང་། བསམས་པ་དང་བསྒོམས་པ་ལས་བྱུང་བའི་ཤེས་རབ་བསྒྲུབ་པ་དང་། བྱང་ཆུབ་ཀྱི་སེམས་རྗེས་སུ་བསྲུང་བ་དང་། དགེ་བའི་བཤེས་གཉེན་ལ་བསྟེན་པ་དང་། རྒྱུན་མི་འཆད་པར་དགེ་བའི་ཕྱོགས་ལ་སྦྱོར་བས་བསླབ་པར་བྱའོ། །བཅོམ་ལྡན་འདས་ཅིའི་སླད་དུ་བསླབ་པའི་གཞི་དེ་དག་གྲངས་དྲུག་ཏུ་གདགས་པར་རིག་པར་བགྱི་ལགས། སྤྱན་རས་གཟིགས་དབང་ཕྱུག་རྣམ་པ་གཉིས་ཀྱི་ཕྱིར་ཏེ། སེམས་ཅན་ལ་ཕན་གདགས་པ་དང་། ཉོན་མོངས་པའི་གཉེན་པོ་ཉིད་ཀྱི་ཕྱིར་རོ། །དེ་ལ་གསུམ་ནི་སེམས་ཅན་ལ་ཕན་གདགས་པ་ཡིན་ལ། གསུམ་ནི་ཉོན་མོངས་པའི་གཉེན་པོ་ཡིན་པར་རིག་པར་བྱ་སྟེ། དེ་ལ་བྱང་ཆུབ་སེམས་དཔའ་སྦྱིན་པས་ནི་སེམས་ཅན་རྣམས་ལ་ཡོ་བྱད་ཉེ་བར་བསྒྲུབ་པའི་ཕན་འདོགས་པས་ཕན་འདོགས་སོ། །ཚུལ་ཁྲིམས་ཀྱིས་ནི་ཕོངས་པ་དང་གནོད་པ་དང་། རྣམ་པར་ཐོ་འཚམས་པ་ཉེ་བར་མི་སྒྲུབ་པའི་ཕན་འདོགས་པས་ཕན་འདོགས་སོ། །བཟོད་པས་ནི་ཕོངས་པ་དང་གནོད་པ་དང་རྣམ་པར་ཐོ་འཚམས་པ་ལ་ཅི་མི་སྙམ་པས་ཕན་འདོགས་ཏེ། དེ་གསུམ་གྱིས་ནི་སེམས་

belongs to the accumulation of wisdom. I explain that effort and concentration are omnipresent."

"Bhagavan, how do Bodhisattvas train in these six bases of training?"

"Avalokiteśvara, [Bodhisattvas] train through five aspects: Initially they have great conviction in the Bodhisattva canon that teaches the sacred doctrine including the perfections. Later, through the ten doctrinal practices, they achieve the wisdom arisen from listening, reflecting, and meditating; they safeguard the mind of enlightenment; they rely on spiritual guides; and they apply themselves ceaselessly to a virtuous course."[31]

"Bhagavan, why are these bases of training known as a six-fold classification?"

"Avalokiteśvara, there are two reasons. It is because they benefit sentient beings, and because they are antidotes to the afflictions. Know that three [perfections] benefit sentient beings, while three are antidotes to the afflictions.

"Because Bodhisattvas benefit sentient beings by giving them material goods, they benefit them through generosity. Because they benefit beings by not impoverishing them, not harming them, nor scorning them, they benefit them through ethics. Because they benefit beings by not even considering [their own] impoverishment, harm, or scorn, they benefit

ཅན་ལ་ཕན་འདོགས་སོ། །བརྩོན་འགྲུས་ཀྱིས་ནི་ཉོན་མོངས་པ་རྣམ་པར་བཅིལ་བ་དང་།
ཉོན་མོངས་པ་ཡང་དག་པར་བཅོམ་པའི་དགེ་བའི་ཕྱོགས་ལ་སྦྱོར་བར་བྱེད་དེ། དེ་ནི་ཉོན
མོངས་པས་དགེ་བའི་ཕྱོགས་ལ་སྦྱོར་བ་ལས་བཟློག་པར་མི་ནུས་སོ། །བསམ་གཏན་གྱིས
ནི་ཉོན་མོངས་པ་རྣམས་རྣམ་པར་གནོན་ཏོ། །ཤེས་རབ་ཀྱིས་ནི་བག་ལ་ཉལ་ལེགས་པར
འཇོམས་པར་བྱེད་དེ། དེ་གསུམ་ནི་ཉོན་མོངས་པའི་གཉེན་པོ་ཡིན་ནོ། །བཅོམ་ལྡན
འདས་ཅིའི་སླད་དུ་ཕ་རོལ་ཏུ་ཕྱིན་པ་གཞན་དག་གྲངས་བཞིར་གདགས་པར་རིག་པར་བགྱི
ལགས། སྤྱན་རས་གཟིགས་དབང་ཕྱུག་ཕ་རོལ་ཏུ་ཕྱིན་པ་དྲུག་པོ་དེ་དག་ཉིད་ཀྱི་གྲོགས
སུ་གྱུར་པ་ཉིད་ཡིན་པའི་ཕྱིར་ཏེ། དེ་ལ་ཕ་རོལ་ཏུ་ཕྱིན་པ་གསུམ་གྱིས་སེམས་ཅན་རྣམས
ལ་ཕན་བཏགས་ནས་བྱང་ཆུབ་སེམས་དཔས་བསྡུ་བའི་དངོས་པོས་ཟིན་པའི་ཐབས་ལ
མཁས་པས་དགེ་བ་ལ་འཇོག་པར་བྱེད་དེ། དེའི་ཕྱིར་ངས་ཐབས་མཁས་པའི་ཕ་རོལ་ཏུ
ཕྱིན་པ་ནི་གསུམ་པོ་དག་གི་གྲོགས་སུ་གྱུར་པ་ཡིན་པར་ཡོངས་སུ་བསྟན་ཏོ། །སྤྱན་རས
གཟིགས་དབང་ཕྱུག་གལ་ཏེ་བྱང་ཆུབ་སེམས་དཔའ་ཚེ་འདི་ལ་ཉོན་མོངས་པ་མང་བས
རྟག་ཏུ་སྒོམ་མི་ནུས་པ་དང་། ཁམས་དང་མོས་པ་དམའ་བའི་ཕྱིར་ལྷག་པའི་བསམ་པ
སྟོབས་ཆུང་བས་སེམས་ནང་དུ་འཇོག་མི་ནུས་པ་དང་། བྱང་ཆུབ་སེམས་དཔའི་སྡེ་སྣོད
ཐོས་པའི་དམིགས་པ་ལ་བསམ་གཏན་ཡོངས་སུ་མ་བསྒོམས་པས་འཇིག་རྟེན་ལས་འདས
པའི་ཤེས་རབ་མངོན་པར་སྒྲུབ་མི་ནུས་པ་ཡིན་ན། དེ་བསོད་ནམས་ཀྱི་ཚོགས་ཆུང་ངུ་ཡང
ཡང་དག་པར་བླངས་ཏེ་གནས་ཤིང་ཕྱི་མ་ལ་ཉོན་མོངས་པ་ཆུང་བ་ཉིད་དུ་ཡིད་ཀྱིས་སྨོན་པར

them through patience. Thus they benefit sentient beings through these three [perfections].

"Through effort they apply themselves to a virtuous course that overcomes and completely conquers the afflictions. Thus, the afflictions are unable to sway them from implementing a virtuous course. Through concentration, they suppress the afflictions. Through wisdom, they completely destroy the predispositions [toward afflictions]. These three [perfections] are antidotes to the afflictions."

"Bhagavan, why are the other perfections known to be classified into four types?"[32]

"Avalokiteśvara, it is because they assist the six perfections. Having benefitted sentient beings by means of three of the perfections, Bodhisattvas engage in virtue through skillful means conjoined with the [four] means of gathering disciples.[33] Therefore, I teach that the perfection of skillful means assists those [first] three [perfections].

"Avalokiteśvara, if, in this lifetime, due to many afflictions, Bodhisattvas are unable to meditate uninterruptedly; and if, due to inferior constituents and conviction, they have little capacity for surpassing thought and are thus unable to settle the mind internally; and if they have not fully cultivated concentration on the objects of observation that come from hearing the Bodhisattva canon, then they are unable to manifestly achieve the wisdom that transcends the world. Since they have taken up the accumulation of merit, even to a small

བྱེད་པ་དེ་ནི་དེའི་སྨོན་ལམ་གྱི་ཕ་རོལ་ཏུ་ཕྱིན་པ་ཡིན་ཏེ། དེས་ཉོན་མོངས་པ་ཆུང་བ་དང་།
བརྩོན་འགྲུས་རྩོམ་ནུས་པར་འགྱུར་བས། དེའི་ཕྱིར་སྨོན་ལམ་གྱི་ཕ་རོལ་ཏུ་ཕྱིན་པ་ནི
བརྩོན་འགྲུས་ཀྱི་ཕ་རོལ་ཏུ་ཕྱིན་པའི་གྲོགས་སུ་འགྱུར་བ་ཡིན་ནོ། །དེས་སྐྱེས་བུ་དམ་པ་ཡང
དག་པར་བསྟེན་པ་དང་དམ་པའི་ཆོས་མཉན་པ་ལ་བརྟེན་ནས་ཚུལ་བཞིན་ཡིད་ལ་བྱེད་པ
ཐོབ་ཅིང་ལྷག་པའི་བསམ་པ་སྟོབས་ཆུང་བ་ཉིད་རྣམ་པར་བཟློག་ནས་ཁམས་གྱི་ནོམ་པ
ལས་བསམ་པའི་སྟོབས་ཐོབ་པར་འགྱུར་བ་དེ་ནི་དེའི་སྟོབས་ཀྱི་ཕ་རོལ་ཏུ་ཕྱིན་པ་ཡིན་ཏེ།
དེས་སེམས་ནང་དུ་འཇོག་ནུས་པས་དེའི་ཕྱིར་སྟོབས་ཀྱི་ཕ་རོལ་ཏུ་ཕྱིན་པའི་བསམ་གཏན་གྱི
ཕ་རོལ་ཏུ་ཕྱིན་པའི་གྲོགས་སུ་འགྱུར་བ་ཡིན་ནོ། །དེ་ལ་བྱང་ཆུབ་སེམས་དཔའི་སྡེ་སྣོད་ཐོས
པའི་དམིགས་པ་ཡོངས་སུ་བསྒོམས་པ་ལ་བསམ་གཏན་བྱེད་དེ། དེ་ནི་དེའི་ཕྱིར་ཤེས་རབ
ཀྱི་ཕ་རོལ་ཏུ་ཕྱིན་པ་ཡིན་ཏེ། དེས་འཇིག་རྟེན་ལས་འདས་པའི་ཤེས་རབ་མངོན་པར་སྒྲུབ
ནུས་པར་འགྱུར་བས་དེའི་ཕྱིར་ངས་ཡེ་ཤེས་ཀྱི་ཕ་རོལ་ཏུ་ཕྱིན་པ་ནི་ཤེས་རབ་ཀྱི་ཕ་རོལ་ཏུ
ཕྱིན་པའི་གྲོགས་སུ་འགྱུར་བ་ཡིན་པར་ཡོངས་སུ་བསྟན་ཏོ། །བཅོམ་ལྡན་འདས་ཅིའི་སླད་དུ
ཕ་རོལ་ཏུ་ཕྱིན་པ་དྲུག་པོ་དེ་དག་གི་གོ་རིམས་དེ་ལྟར་བསྟན་པར་རིག་པར་བགྱི་ལགས།
སྤྱན་རས་གཟིགས་དབང་ཕྱུག་དེ་དག་གོང་ནས་གོང་དུ་འགྲུབ་པའི་རྟེན་ཉིད་ཡིན་པའི་ཕྱིར
ཏེ། བྱང་ཆུབ་སེམས་དཔའ་ལུས་དང་ལོངས་སྤྱོད་ལ་མི་ལྟ་ན་ཚུལ་ཁྲིམས་ཡང་དག་པར
ལེན་པར་བྱེད་དོ། །ཚུལ་ཁྲིམས་རྗེས་སུ་སྲུང་ན་བཟོད་པ་དང་ལྡན་པར་འགྱུར་རོ། །
བཟོད་པ་དང་ལྡན་ན་བརྩོན་འགྲུས་རྩོམ་པར་འགྱུར་རོ། །བརྩོན་འགྲུས་བརྩམས་ན་བསམ

extent, the wish that their afflictions decrease in the present and future constitutes the perfection of aspiration. Through this, they are able to lessen afflictions and to initiate effort. Therefore, [I teach that] the perfection of aspiration assists the perfection of effort.

"Then, having relied on holy beings and depended on hearing the holy Dharma, they obtain correct mental contemplation and reverse their limited capacity for surpassing thought. Achieving the power of reflection over the excellent constituents is the perfection of power. Through this, they are able to settle the mind internally. In this way, the perfection of power assists the perfection of concentration.

"They concentrate on full cultivation of the object of observation: the hearing of the Bodhisattva canon. Through this, there [arises] the perfection of exalted wisdom. Because they become able to manifestly achieve the wisdom that transcends the world, I teach that the perfection of exalted wisdom assists the perfection of wisdom."

"Bhagavan, how does one know that the order of the teaching of these six perfections is like this?"

"Avalokiteśvara, it is because [the six perfections] serve as bases for progressively higher achievements. Bodhisattvas who do not focus on their bodies and physical resources attain ethics. Those who guard their moral practice become patient. Those who have patience initiate effort. Those who initiate

གཏན་སྒྲུབ་པར་འགྱུར་རོ། །བསམ་གཏན་གྲུབ་ན་འཇིག་རྟེན་ལས་འདས་པའི་ཤེས་རབ་འཐོབ་བོ། །བཅོམ་ལྡན་འདས་ཕ་རོལ་ཏུ་ཕྱིན་པ་དེ་དག་རྣམ་པ་དུ་རུ་རབ་ཏུ་དབྱེ་ལགས། སྤྱན་རས་གཟིགས་དབང་ཕྱུག་རྣམ་པ་གསུམ་དུ་སྟེ། སྦྱིན་པ་རྣམ་པ་གསུམ་ནི་ཆོས་སྦྱིན་པ་དང་། ཟང་ཟིང་སྦྱིན་པ་དང་། མི་འཇིགས་པ་སྦྱིན་པའོ། །ཚུལ་ཁྲིམས་རྣམ་པ་གསུམ་ནི་མི་དགེ་བ་ལས་ལྡོག་པའི་ཚུལ་ཁྲིམས་དང་། དགེ་བ་ལ་འཇུག་པའི་ཚུལ་ཁྲིམས་དང་། སེམས་ཅན་གྱི་དོན་ལ་འཇུག་པའི་ཚུལ་ཁྲིམས་སོ། །བཟོད་པ་རྣམ་པ་གསུམ་ནི་གནོད་པ་བྱེད་པ་ལ་མི་མཇེད་པའི་བཟོད་པ་དང་། སྡུག་བསྔལ་ལ་ཅི་མི་སྙམ་པའི་བཟོད་པ་དང་། ཆོས་ལ་ངེས་པར་རྟོག་པའི་བཟོད་པའོ། །བརྩོན་འགྲུས་རྣམ་པ་གསུམ་ནི་གོ་ཆའི་བརྩོན་འགྲུས་དང་། དགེ་བ་ལ་སྦྱོར་བའི་བརྩོན་འགྲུས་དང་། སེམས་ཅན་གྱི་དོན་ལ་སྦྱོར་བའི་བརྩོན་འགྲུས་སོ། །བསམ་གཏན་རྣམ་པ་གསུམ་ནི་རྣམ་པར་མི་རྟོག་ཅིང་ཞི་ལ་རབ་ཏུ་ཞི་བས་ཉོན་མོངས་པ་དང་། སྡུག་བསྔལ་གྱི་གཉེན་པོ་བདེ་བར་གནས་པའི་བསམ་གཏན་དང་། ཡོན་ཏན་མངོན་པར་སྒྲུབ་པའི་བསམ་གཏན་དང་། སེམས་ཅན་གྱི་དོན་མངོན་པར་སྒྲུབ་པའི་བསམ་གཏན་ནོ། །ཤེས་རབ་རྣམ་པ་གསུམ་ནི་ཀུན་རྫོབ་ཀྱི་བདེན་པ་ལ་དམིགས་པ་དང་། དོན་དམ་པའི་བདེན་པ་ལ་དམིགས་པ་དང་། སེམས་ཅན་གྱི་དོན་ལ་དམིགས་པའོ། །བཅོམ་ལྡན་འདས་ཅིའི་སླད་དུ་ཕ་རོལ་ཏུ་ཕྱིན་པ་དེ་དག་ཕ་རོལ་ཏུ་ཕྱིན་པ་རྣམས་ཞེས་བགྱི་ལགས། སྤྱན་རས་གཟིགས་དབང་ཕྱུག་ལྔའི་ཕྱིར་ཏེ། ཆགས་པ་མེད་པ་ཉིད་དང་། མི་ལྟ་བ་ཉིད་དང་། ཁ་ན་མ་ཐོ་བ་མེད་པ་ཉིད་དང་། རྣམ་པར་མི་རྟོག་པ་

effort achieve concentration. Those who achieve concentration attain wisdom that transcends the world."

"Bhagavan, into how many aspects are the perfections divided?"

"Avalokiteśvara, the aspects are threefold. Generosity has three aspects: giving the Dharma, giving material things, and granting fearlessness.[34]

"Ethics has three aspects: ethics that overcomes non-virtue, ethics that engages in virtue, and ethics that engages in the welfare of sentient beings.

"Patience has three aspects: patience that endures injury, patience that does not consider one's own suffering at all, and patience in discerning the Dharma.[35]

"Effort has three aspects: effort that is armor, effort applied to virtue, and effort applied for the welfare of sentient beings.[36]

"Concentration has three aspects: samādhi of blissful abiding that is an antidote to suffering and the afflictions because it is non-conceptual and peaceful; samādhi that manifestly achieves good qualities; and samādhi that manifestly achieves the welfare of sentient beings.[37]

"Wisdom has three aspects: focusing on conventional truth, focusing on ultimate truth, and focusing on the welfare of sentient beings."[38]

"Bhagavan, why are the perfections called 'perfections'?"

ཉིད་དང༌། ཡོངས་སུ་བསྔོ་བ་ཉིད་ཀྱི་ཕྱིར་རོ། །དེ་ལ་ཆགས་པ་མེད་པ་ཉིད་ནི་ཕ་རོལ་ཏུ
ཕྱིན་པ་དང་མི་འཐུན་པའི་དངོས་པོ་ལ་ལྷག་པར་ཆགས་པ་མེད་པ་གང་ཡིན་པའོ། །དེ་ལ
མི་ལྟ་བ་ཉིད་ནི་ཕ་རོལ་ཏུ་ཕྱིན་པའི་འབྲས་བུ་རྣམ་པར་སྨིན་པ་དང༌། ལན་དུ་ཕན་འདོགས
པ་དང་འབྲེལ་བའི་སེམས་མེད་པ་གང་ཡིན་པའོ། །དེ་ལ་ཁ་ན་མ་ཐོ་བ་མེད་པ་ཉིད་ནི་ཕ
རོལ་ཏུ་ཕྱིན་པ་དེ་དག་ཀུན་ནས་ཉོན་མོངས་པ་ཅན་གྱི་ཆོས་དང་མ་འདྲེས་ཤིང་ཐབས་མ་ཡིན
པ་རྣམ་པར་སྤངས་པ་གང་ཡིན་པའོ། །དེ་ལ་རྣམ་པར་མི་རྟོག་པ་ཉིད་ནི་ཕ་རོལ་ཏུ་ཕྱིན་པ
དེ་དག་གི་རང་གི་མཚན་ཉིད་ལ་སྒྲ་ཇི་བཞིན་དུ་མངོན་པར་ཞེན་པ་མེད་པ་གང་ཡིན་པའོ། །
དེ་ལ་ཡོངས་སུ་བསྔོ་བ་ཉིད་ནི་ཕ་རོལ་ཏུ་ཕྱིན་པ་དེ་དག་ཉིད་བྱས་ཤིང་བསགས་པ་བྱང
ཆུབ་སེམས་དཔའི་འབྲས་བུར་སློན་པ་གང་ཡིན་པའོ། །བཅོམ་ལྡན་འདས་ཕ་རོལ་ཏུ་ཕྱིན
པ་དང་མི་འཐུན་པའི་དངོས་པོ་གང་ལགས། སྤྱན་རས་གཟིགས་དབང་ཕྱུག་དེ་དག་ནི
དངོས་པོ་དྲུག་ཏུ་རིག་པར་བྱ་སྟེ། འདོད་པའི་དགའ་བ་དང་ལོངས་སྤྱོད་དང་དབང་ཕྱུག
དང་བདག་ཉིད་ཀྱི་བསོད་ནམས་ལ་ཡོན་ཏན་གྱི་ཕན་ཡོན་དུ་ལྟ་བ་དང༌། ལུས་དང་ངག
དང་ཡིད་ཀྱི་འདོད་དགུར་ཀུན་ཏུ་སྤྱོད་པ་དང༌། བརྙས་པ་མི་བཟོད་པ་དང་མི་བརྩོན་པས
བསོད་ནམས་དང་འདུ་འཛི་དང༌། འཇིག་རྟེན་གྱི་ལས་སྣ་ཚོགས་དང་རྣམ་པར་གཡེང་བ་ལ
འདུག་པ་དང༌། མཐོང་བ་དང་ཐོས་པ་དང༌། བྱེ་བྲག་ཕྱེད་པ་དང༌། རྣམ་པར་ཤེས་པའི
ཐ་སྙད་ཀྱི་སྤྲོས་པ་དག་ལ་ཡོན་ཏན་གྱི་ཕན་ཡོན་དུ་ལྟ་བའོ། །བཅོམ་ལྡན་འདས་ཕ་རོལ་ཏུ
ཕྱིན་པ་དེ་དག་གི་རྣམ་པར་སྨིན་པའི་འབྲས་བུ་གང་ལགས། སྤྱན་རས་གཟིགས་དབང

"Avalokiteśvara, this is due to five [reasons]: non-attachment, non-anticipation [of a reward], non-corruption, non-conceptuality, and complete dedication. Non-attachment is the absence of excessive attachment to things that are contrary to the perfections. Non-anticipation [of a reward] is the absence of mental attachment to the fruitional results or to the beneficial rewards of the perfections. Non-corruption is not adulterating the perfections with afflicted phenomena and abandoning whatever is not skillful. Non-conceptuality is not grasping the characteristics of the perfections literally. Complete dedication is wishing for the fruit of a Bodhisattva, having practiced and accumulated the perfections."

"Bhagavan, what things are contrary to the perfections?"

"Avalokiteśvara, know that there are six things: viewing the pleasure of desirable things, material resources, power, and one's own merit as advantageous qualities; making use of body, speech, and mind according to desire; not enduring scorn; overindulgence through lack of effort; engaging in distractions, diverse worldly activities, and entertainments; and viewing the conventional elaborations of seeing, hearing, distinguishing, and discerning as advantageous qualities."

"Bhagavan, what results from maturing the perfections?"

"Avalokiteśvara, know that [the results] also have six aspects: great resources; going to happy transmigrations; non-enmity,

ཕྱུག་དེ་ཡང་རྣམ་པ་དྲུག་ཏུ་རིག་པར་བྱ་སྟེ། ཡོངས་སྤྱོད་ཆེན་པོ་ཉིད་དང་། བདེ་འགྲོར་འགྲོ་བ་དང་། ཁོན་མེད་ཅིང་དབྱེན་མེད་ལ་བདེ་བ་དང་། ཡིད་བདེ་བ་མང་བ་དང་། སེམས་ཅན་གྱི་བདག་པོ་དང་། ལུས་ལ་གནོད་པ་མེད་པ་དང་། དབང་ཆེ་བར་གྲགས་པའོ༑ ༑བཅོམ་ལྡན་འདས་ཕ་རོལ་ཏུ་ཕྱིན་པ་དེ་དག་ལ་ཀུན་ནས་ཉོན་མོངས་པ་ཅན་གྱི་ཆོས་དང་འདྲེས་པ་གང་ལགས། སྤྱན་རས་གཟིགས་དབང་ཕྱུག་དེ་ནི་སྦྱོར་བ་བཞིས་རིག་པར་བྱ་སྟེ། སྙིང་རྗེ་མེད་པའི་སྦྱོར་བ་དང་། ཚུལ་བཞིན་མ་ཡིན་པའི་སྦྱོར་བ་དང་། རྟག་ཏུ་མི་བྱེད་པའི་སྦྱོར་བ་དང་། གུས་པར་མི་བྱེད་པའི་སྦྱོར་བས་སོ། །དེ་ལ་ཚུལ་བཞིན་མ་ཡིན་པའི་སྦྱོར་བ་ནི་འདི་ཡིན་ཏེ། དེ་ལས་གཞན་པའི་ཕ་རོལ་ཏུ་ཕྱིན་པ་དག་ལ་དེ་ལས་གཞན་པའི་ཕ་རོལ་ཏུ་ཕྱིན་པའི་སྨོན་པ་ཉམས་པ་གང་ཡིན་པའོ། །བཅོམ་ལྡན་འདས་ཐབས་མ་ལགས་པ་གང་ལགས། སྤྱན་རས་གཟིགས་དབང་ཕྱུག་བྱང་ཆུབ་སེམས་དཔའ་ཕ་རོལ་ཏུ་ཕྱིན་པ་དེ་དག་གིས་སེམས་ཅན་རྣམས་ལ་ཕན་འདོགས་པ་ན། གལ་ཏེ་ཟང་ཟིང་གིས་ཕན་འདོགས་པ་ཉེ་བར་སྒྲུབ་པ་ཙམ་གྱིས་ཆོག་པར་འཛིན་ཅིང་མི་དགེ་བའི་གནས་ལས་བསླང་སྟེ། དགེ་བའི་གནས་སུ་འཛོག་པར་མི་བྱེད་ན། དེ་ནི་ཐབས་མ་ཡིན་པ་ཡིན་ནོ། ། དེ་ཅིའི་ཕྱིར་ཞེ་ན། སྤྱན་རས་གཟིགས་དབང་ཕྱུག་དེ་ཙམ་གྱིས་སེམས་ཅན་ལ་ཕན···གདགས་པ་མ་ཡིན་པའི་ཕྱིར་ཏེ། འདི་ལྟ་སྟེ་དཔེར་ན། མི་གཙང་བ་ནི་ཆེ་ཡང་རུང་ཆུང་ཡང་རུང་སྟེ། རྣམ་གྲངས་གང་གིས་ཀྱང་དྲི་ཞིམ་པོར་བྱ་བར་མི་ནུས་སོ། །དེ་བཞིན་དུ་འདུ་བྱེད་ཀྱི་སྡུག་བསྔལ་ཉིད་ཀྱི་རང་བཞིན་གྱིས་སྡུག་བསྔལ་བར་གྱུར་པའི་སེམས་ཅན་རྣམས

non-dissension, happiness, and great pleasure; sovereignty over sentient beings; freedom from physical injury; and being renowned as powerful."

"Bhagavan, what are the things that adulterate the perfections with the afflictions?"

"Avalokiteśvara, know that [the perfections are adulterated] through four types of association: non-compassionate association, incorrect association, inconstant association, and disrespectful association.

"An incorrect association is when, with respect to the other perfections, one lessens one's cultivation of the perfections other than the one [presently being cultivated]."

"Bhagavan, what is not skillful?"

"Avalokiteśvara, when Bodhisattvas benefit sentient beings by means of the perfections, if they are satisfied merely by providing benefits to beings through [giving] material goods and do not establish them in virtuous states after having raised them up from non-virtuous states, this is not skillful.

"Why is this? Avalokiteśvara, sentient beings are not benefitted by [material goods] alone. For example, no matter whether filth is great or small, one cannot by any means make it sweet-smelling. Similarly, sentient beings who suffer due to

ཀྱང་ཟང་ཟིང་གིས་ཕན་གདགས་པ་ཉེ་བར་སྒྲུབ་པ་ཙམ་གྱི་རྣམ་གྲངས་ཀྱིས་ཀྱང་བདེ་བར་བྱར་མི་ནུས་ཀྱི། དགེ་བ་ལ་འཛོག་པ་གང་ཡིན་པ་དེ་ནི་དེ་དག་ལ་ཕན་འདོགས་པའི་མཆོག་ཁོ་ན་ཡིན་ནོ། །བཅོམ་ལྡན་འདས་ཕ་རོལ་ཏུ་ཕྱིན་པ་དེ་དག་གི་རྣམ་པར་དག་པ་དུ་མཆིས་ལགས། སྤྱན་རས་གཟིགས་དབང་ཕྱུག་ང་ནི་རྣམ་པ་ལྔ་པོ་དེ་དག་མ་གཏོགས་པར་ཕ་རོལ་ཏུ་ཕྱིན་པ་རྣམས་ཀྱི་རྣམ་པར་དག་པ་གཞན་ཡོད་པར་མི་སྨྲ་མོད་ཀྱི། འོན་ཀྱང་དེ་དག་ཉིད་ལ་བརྟེན་ནས་ཕ་རོལ་ཏུ་ཕྱིན་པ་རྣམས་ཀྱི་རྣམ་པར་དག་པ་བསྡུས་པ་དང་། སོ་སོ་བཀྲོད་ལ་བཤད་པར་བྱའོ། །དེ་ལ་ཕ་རོལ་ཏུ་ཕྱིན་པ་ཐམས་ཅད་ཀྱི་རྣམ་པར་དག་པ་བསྡུས་པ་ནི་རྣམ་པ་བདུན་གྱིས་རིག་པར་བྱ་སྟེ། བདུན་གང་ཞེ་ན། འདི་ལྟ་སྟེ། བྱང་ཆུབ་སེམས་དཔའི་ཆོས་དེ་དག་གིས་གཞན་ལས་ཞེས་ཀྱི་ཁེ་ཡོངས་སུ་མི་འཚོལ་བ་དང་། ཆོས་དེ་དག་ལ་ལྟ་བས་མངོན་པར་ཞེན་པར་མི་བྱེད་པ་དང་། ཆོས་འདི་དག་བྱང་ཆུབ་ཏུ་ངེས་པར་འགྱུར་བ་ཡིན་ནམ་མ་ཡིན་སྙམ་དུ་ཡིད་གཉིས་དང་ཐེ་ཚོམ་སྐྱེད་པར་མི་བྱེད་པ་དང་། བདག་ལ་མི་སྟོད་གཞན་ལ་མི་སྨོད་ཅིང་བརྙས་པར་མི་བྱེད་པ་དང་། དྲེགས་པར་མི་བྱེད་ཅིང་བག་མེད་པར་མི་བྱེད་པ་དང་། ཅུང་ཟད་ཙམ་དང་ངན་ངོན་ཙམ་གྱིས་ཆོག་པར་མི་འཛིན་པ་དང་། ཆོས་དེ་དག་གིས་སེར་སྣ་མི་བྱེད་ཅིང་གཞན་དག་ལ་ཕྲག་དོག་མི་བྱེད་པ་ཡིན་ནོ། །ཕ་རོལ་ཏུ་ཕྱིན་པའི་རྣམ་པར་དག་པ་སོ་སོ་ཐ་དད་པ་དེ་ཡང་རྣམ་པ་བདུན་པོ་ནར་རིག་པར་བྱ་སྟེ། ཐ་དད་པའི་རྣམ་པ་བདུན་གང་ཞེ་ན། འདི་ལྟ་སྟེ་སྦྱིན་པ་རྣམ་པར་དག་པ་རྣམ་པ་བདུན་པོ་སྦྱིན་པར་བྱ་བའི་དངོས་པོ་རྣམ་པར་དག་པས་སྦྱིན་པ་རྣམ

the nature of the suffering of conditioned [existence] cannot be made happy by any means that benefits them through material goods alone. However, whatever establishes [sentient beings] in virtue is of supreme benefit to them."

"Bhagavan, how many kinds of purities are there of the perfections?"

"Avalokiteśvara, I do not state that there are purities of these perfections aside from those five kinds [of purity mentioned previously]. However, in dependence upon just those, I will explain to you—collectively and particularly—the purities of the perfections.

"Know that the collective purities of all the perfections are sevenfold. What are these seven? They are: [Bodhisattvas] do not seek to profit from others through the Bodhisattva teachings; they do not produce obsessive attachment because of viewing these teachings; they do not produce doubt or indecision, thinking 'Do these teachings lead to enlightenment or not?'; they do not praise themselves, nor do they deprecate or despise others; they are not proud and do not act non-conscientiously; they are not content simply with small and inferior [attainments]; and they are not miserly with the teachings, or jealous of others.[39]

"Know that the specific purities of the perfections are also sevenfold. What are these seven distinctions? They include the seven kinds of pure generosity that I have taught: giving

པར་དག་པ་སྦྱིན་པར་བྱེད་པ་དང་། ཚུལ་ཁྲིམས་རྣམ་པར་དག་པ་དང་། ལྟ་བ་རྣམ་པར
དག་པ་དང་། སེམས་རྣམ་པར་དག་པ་དང་། དགེ་རྣམ་པར་དག་པ་དང་། ཤེས་པ་རྣམ
པར་དག་པ་དང་། དྲི་མ་རྣམ་པར་དག་པས་སྦྱིན་པ་རྣམ་པར་དག་པ་སྦྱིན་པར་བྱེད་དོ་ཞེས
ངེས་བསྟན་པ་གང་ཡིན་པ་དེ་དག་བྱང་ཆུབ་སེམས་དཔས་ཡང་དག་པར་བླངས་ཏེ་གནས
པ་དེ་ནི་སྦྱིན་པ་རྣམ་པར་དག་པ་བདུན་ཡིན་ནོ། །འདི་ལྟ་སྟེ། བྱང་ཆུབ་སེམས་དཔའ
སྡོམ་པ་བཅས་པ་ལ་བསླབ་པའི་གཞི་རྣམ་པ་ཐམས་ཅད་ལ་མཁས་པ་དང་། ལྟུང་བ་ལས
བསླང་བ་ལ་མཁས་པ་དང་། དེ་ལ་ངེས་པའི་ཚུལ་ཁྲིམས་ཅན་དང་། བརྟན་པའི་ཚུལ
ཁྲིམས་ཅན་དང་། རྟག་ཏུ་བྱེད་པ་དང་། རྟག་ཏུ་འཇུག་པ་དང་། བསླབ་པའི་གཞི
རྣམས་ཡང་དག་པར་བླངས་ཏེ་སློབ་པར་བྱེད་པ་དེ་ནི་ཚུལ་ཁྲིམས་རྣམ་པར་དག་པ་རྣམ་པ
བདུན་ཡིན་ནོ། །འདི་ལྟ་སྟེ། ཐམས་ཅད་ལས་གནོད་པ་ཐམས་ཅད་ཉེ་བར་གནས་པ་ན།
བདག་ཉིད་ཀྱི་ལས་ཀྱི་རྣམ་པར་སྨིན་པ་ལ་རྟོན་པས་མི་འཁྲུག་པ་དང་། ལན་བྱ་བའི་ཕྱིར
སྨྲར་སྒྲོ་བ་དང་། ག་ཤེ་བ་དང་། བརྡེག་པ་དང་། བསྡིགས་པ་དང་། མཚང་འབྲུ་བའི
གནོད་པ་དག་གིས་སྒྱུར་བར་མི་བྱེད་པ་དང་། ཁོན་གྱི་བསམ་པ་མི་འཛིན་པ་དང་། ཤད
ཀྱིས་འཆགས་པ་ན་ཡོངས་སུ་ཉོན་མོངས་པར་མི་བྱེད་པ་དང་། ཤད་ཀྱིས་འཆགས་པ་ལ
མི་སྡོད་པ་དང་། འཇིགས་པ་དང་ཟང་ཟིང་གི་སེམས་ཀྱིས་བཟོད་པར་བྱེད་པ་མ་ཡིན་པ
དང་། ཕན་གདགས་པར་བྱ་བ་ལ་ཡལ་བར་མི་འདོར་བ་དེ་ནི་བཟོད་པ་རྣམ་པར་དག་པ
རྣམ་པ་བདུན་ནོ། །འདི་ལྟ་སྟེ། བརྩོན་འགྲུས་ཀྱི་མཉམ་པ་ཉིད་རབ་ཏུ་ཤེས་པ་དང་།

as pure gifts pure things that are suitable gifts; and giving pure gifts with: purity of ethics, purity of view, purity of mind, purity of speech, purity of knowledge, and purity from defilements.[40] Bodhisattvas correctly taking up and abiding in these constitute the seven purities of generosity.

"Bodhisattvas are skilled in all aspects of the bases of training with respect to vows; they are skilled in rising above infractions; they have ethics that are certain with respect to that; they have ethics that are firm; they continually practice [ethics]; they continually engage in [ethics]; and they correctly take up the bases of training. These trainings are the seven purities of ethics.

"[Bodhisattvas] do not get angry in situations in which harm comes from all directions, because they are confident in the ripening of their own karma. They do not engage in blaming, reviling, striking, threatening, or harming [others] for the sake of retaliation. They do not cling to resentment. When confessing [their faults], they do not produce afflictions. They do not postpone their confession.[41] They do not practice patience with a mind that is fearful or acquisitive. They do not neglect benefitting others. These are the seven aspects of purity of patience.

"[Bodhisattvas] understand consistent effort. They do not praise themselves or deprecate others because of initiating effort. They are endowed with strength. They are endowed

བརྩོན་འགྲུས་བརྩམ་པ་དེས་བདག་ལ་མི་སྟོད་ཅིང་གཞན་ལ་མི་སྨོད་པ་དང་། མཐུ་དང
ལྡན་པ་དང་། བརྩོན་འགྲུས་དང་ལྡན་པ་དང་། སྤྲོ་བ་དང་ལྡན་པ་དང་། རྟུལ་བ་བརྟན་པ
དང་། དགེ་བའི་ཆོས་རྣམས་ལ་བརྩོན་པ་མ་གཏང་བ་དེ་ནི་བརྩོན་འགྲུས་རྣམ་པར་དག་པ
བདུན་ཡིན་ནོ། །འདི་ལྟ་སྟེ། མཚན་མ་ལེགས་པར་རྟོགས་པའི་ཏིང་ངེ་འཛིན་ལ་བསམ
གཏན་པ་དང་། ཡོངས་སུ་རྫོགས་པའི་ཏིང་ངེ་འཛིན་ལ་བསམ་གཏན་པ་དང་། གཉི་གའི
ཆའི་ཏིང་ངེ་འཛིན་ལ་བསམ་གཏན་པ་དང་། ཤུགས་ཀྱིས་འབྱུང་བའི་ཏིང་ངེ་འཛིན་ལ
བསམ་གཏན་པ་དང་། མི་གནས་པའི་ཏིང་ངེ་འཛིན་ལ་བསམ་གཏན་པ་དང་། ཤིན་ཏུ
སྦྱང་བ་བྱས་པའི་ཏིང་ངེ་འཛིན་ལ་བསམ་གཏན་པ་དང་། བྱང་ཆུབ་སེམས་དཔའི་སྡེ་སྣོད
ཀྱི་དམིགས་པ་ཡོངས་སུ་བསྒོམས་པ་དཔག་ཏུ་མེད་པའི་ཏིང་ངེ་འཛིན་ལ་བསམ་གཏན་པ
དེ་ནི་བསམ་གཏན་རྣམ་པར་དག་པ་རྣམ་པ་བདུན་ཡིན་ནོ། །འདི་ལྟ་སྟེ། དེའི་ཤེས་རབ་དེ
སྒྲོ་འདོགས་པའི་མཐའ་དང་སྐུར་བ་འདེབས་པའི་མཐའ་རྣམ་པར་སྤངས་ཏེ་དབུ་མའི་ལམ
གྱིས་ངེས་པར་འབྱུང་བ་དང་། ཤེས་རབ་དེས་སྟོང་པ་ཉིད་དང་། སྨོན་པ་མེད་པ་དང་།
མཚན་མ་མེད་པའི་རྣམ་པར་ཐར་པའི་སྒོ་གསུམ་པོ་དག་ལ་རྣམ་པར་ཐར་པའི་སྒོའི་དོན་ཀྱང
ཡང་དག་པ་ཇི་ལྟ་བ་བཞིན་དུ་རབ་ཏུ་ཤེས་པ་དང་། ཀུན་བརྟགས་པ་དང་། གཞན་གྱི
དབང་དང་། ཡོངས་སུ་གྲུབ་པའི་ངོ་བོ་ཉིད་གསུམ་པོ་དག་ལ་ངོ་བོ་ཉིད་ཀྱི་དོན་ཡང་དག
པ་ཇི་ལྟ་བ་བཞིན་དུ་རབ་ཏུ་ཤེས་པ་དང་། མཚན་ཉིད་དང་། སྐྱེ་བ་དང་། དོན་དམ་པ་ངོ
བོ་ཉིད་མེད་པ་གསུམ་པོ་དག་ལ་ངོ་བོ་ཉིད་མེད་པའི་དོན་ཀྱང་ཡང་དག་པ་ཇི་ལྟ་བ་བཞིན་དུ

with effort, enthusiasm, and firm discipline. They never give up striving for virtuous things. These are the seven aspects of purity of effort.

"[Bodhisattvas] concentrate on samādhi that thoroughly understands signs. They concentrate on perfect samādhi. They concentrate on samādhi that includes some of both [the above aspects].[42] They concentrate on samādhi that arises powerfully. They concentrate on non-abiding samādhi. They concentrate on pliant samādhi. They concentrate on an immeasurable samādhi that fully cultivates the objects of observation of the Bodhisattva canon. These are the seven aspects of purity of concentration.

"[Bodhisattvas] renounce cyclic existence by means of the middle way, having abandoned in their wisdom the extreme of exaggeration and the extreme of deprecation.[43] Through wisdom, they also correctly know, just as it is, the meaning of the doors of liberation, the three doors of emptiness, of wishlessness, and of signlessness.

"[Bodhisattvas] also correctly know, just as it is, the meaning of own-being with respect to the three own-beings: the imputational, the other-dependent, and the thoroughly established.

"[Bodhisattvas] also correctly know, just as it is, the meaning of the lack of own-being with respect to the three absences of own-being: of character, of production, and of the ultimate.

རབ་ཏུ་ཤེས་པ་དང་། རིག་པའི་གནས་ལྔ་པོ་དག་ལ་ཀུན་རྫོབ་ཀྱི་བདེན་པའི་དོན་ཀྱང་ཡང་དག་པ་ཇི་ལྟ་བ་བཞིན་དུ་རབ་ཏུ་ཤེས་པ་དང་། དེ་བཞིན་ཉིད་རྣམ་པ་བདུན་ལ་དོན་དམ་པའི་བདེན་པའི་དོན་ཀྱང་ཡང་དག་པ་ཇི་ལྟ་བ་བཞིན་དུ་རབ་ཏུ་ཤེས་པ་དང་། རྣམ་པར་མི་རྟོག་ཅིང་སྤྲོས་པ་མེད་ལ་ཚུལ་གཅིག་ཏུ་དེ་ལ་མང་དུ་གནས་པ་དང་། འདྲིས་པ་ཚད་མེད་པའི་ཆོས་ལ་དམིགས་པའི་ལྷག་མཐོང་གིས་ཆོས་ཀྱི་རྗེས་སུ་འཐུན་པའི་ཆོས་སྒྲུབ་པ་ཡང་དག་པར་སྒྲུབ་པར་བྱེད་པ་དེ་ནི་ཤེས་རབ་རྣམ་པར་དག་པ་རྣམ་པ་བདུན་ཡིན་པར་རིག་པར་བྱའོ། །བཅོམ་ལྡན་འདས་རྣམ་པ་ལྔ་པོ་དེ་དག་གི་སོ་སོའི་ལས་གང་ལགས། སྤྱན་རས་གཟིགས་དབང་ཕྱུག་དེ་དག་གི་ལས་ཀྱང་རྣམ་པ་ལྔར་རིག་པར་བྱ་སྟེ། ཆགས་པ་མེད་པ་ཉིད་ཀྱིས་ནི་བྱང་ཆུབ་སེམས་དཔའ་ཚེ་འདི་ལ་ཕ་རོལ་ཏུ་ཕྱིན་པ་རྣམས་ལ་རྟག་ཏུ་བྱེད་པ་དང་། གུས་པར་བྱེད་པའི་སྦྱོར་བས་བག་ཡོད་པར་བྱེད་དོ། །མི་ལྟ་བ་ཉིད་ཀྱིས་ནི་ཕྱི་མར་དེ་དག་ལ་བག་ཡོད་པའི་རྒྱུ་ཡོངས་སུ་འཛིན་པར་བྱེད་དོ། །ཁ་ན་མ་ཐོ་བ་མེད་པ་ཉིད་ཀྱིས་ནི་ཕ་རོལ་ཏུ་ཕྱིན་པ་ཤིན་ཏུ་ཡོངས་སུ་རྫོགས་པ་དང་། ཡོངས་སུ་དག་པ་དང་། ཡོངས་སུ་བྱང་བ་དག་སྒོམ་པར་བྱེད་དོ། །རྣམ་པར་མི་རྟོག་པ་ཉིད་ཀྱིས་ནི་ཐབས་ལ་མཁས་པ་དེས་མྱུར་དུ་ཕ་རོལ་ཏུ་ཕྱིན་པ་ཡོངས་སུ་རྫོགས་པར་བྱེད་དོ། །ཡོངས་སུ་བསྔོ་བ་ཉིད་ཀྱིས་ནི་བླ་ན་མེད་པ་ཡང་དག་པར་རྫོགས་པའི་བྱང་ཆུབ་ཀྱི་བར་དུ་ཚེ་རབས་ཐམས་ཅད་དུ་རྣམ་པར་སྨིན་པའི་འབྲས་བུ་འདོད་པ་དང་བཅས་པའི་ཕ་རོལ་ཏུ་ཕྱིན་པ་མི་ཟད་པ་ཉིད་འཕེལ་བར་བྱེད་དོ། །བཅོམ་ལྡན་འདས་ཕ་རོལ་ཏུ་ཕྱིན་པ་དེ་དག་གི་རྒྱ་ཆེ་བ་ཉིད་གང

"[Bodhisattvas] also correctly know, just as it is, the meaning of conventional truths with respect to the five topics of knowledge.[44]

"[Bodhisattvas] also correctly know, just as it is, the meaning of ultimate truths with respect to the seven aspects of suchness. And, through abiding often in the single mode that is non-conceptual and free from elaboration, and through vipaśyana which observes doctrines that are immeasurably integrated, they correctly accomplish the attainment of the teachings that are concordant with doctrine. Know that these are the seven forms of purity of wisdom."

"Bhagavan, what are the individual capabilities of the five aspects?"[45]

"Avalokiteśvara, know that there are also five kinds of capabilities: Because they are free from attachment, Bodhisattvas act conscientiously in this lifetime, applying themselves to the perfections with uninterrupted and devoted application. Because they do not anticipate [rewards], they sustain the cause of future conscientiousness. Because they are without corruption, they cultivate the perfections completely, purely, and proficiently. Because they are free from conceptuality, they quickly complete the perfections through skillful means. Because they dedicate [themselves] completely [for others], in all their lifetimes—up to the time of unsurpassed, complete, perfect enlightenment—they obtain inexhaustible perfections that have the fruitional results that they wish for."

ལགས། སྤྱན་རས་གཟིགས་དབང་ཕྱུག་ཆགས་པ་མེད་པ་ཉིད་དང་། མི་ལྟ་བ་ཉིད་དང་།
ཡོངས་སུ་བསྔོ་བ་ཉིད་གང་ཡིན་པའོ། །ཀུན་ནས་ཉོན་མོངས་པ་མ་མཆིས་པ་གང་ལགས།
ཁ་ན་མ་ཐོ་བ་མེད་པ་ཉིད་དང་། རྣམ་པར་མི་རྟོག་པ་ཉིད་གང་ཡིན་པའོ། །སྦྱངས་པ་ཉིད
གང་ལགས། སོ་སོར་བརྟག་ཅིང་བྱ་བ་ཉིད་གང་ཡིན་པའོ། །མི་གཡོ་བ་ཉིད་གང་
ལགས། སར་ཚུད་པ་རྣམས་ཀྱི་ཡོངས་སུ་མི་ཉམས་པའི་ཆོས་ཉིད་གང་ཡིན་པའོ། །ཤིན
ཏུ་རྣམ་པར་དག་པ་ཉིད་གང་ལགས། སྤྱན་རས་གཟིགས་དབང་ཕྱུག་ས་བཅུ་པར་
གཏོགས་པ་ཉིད་དང་། སངས་རྒྱས་ཀྱི་སར་གཏོགས་པ་ཉིད་གང་ཡིན་པའོ། །བཅོམ
ལྡན་འདས་ཅིའི་སླད་དུ་བྱང་ཆུབ་སེམས་དཔའ་རྟག་ཏུ་ཕ་རོལ་ཏུ་ཕྱིན་པའི་རྣམ་པར་སྨིན་པའི
འབྲས་བུ་འདོད་པ་བས་མ་འཚལ་བ་དང་། ཕ་རོལ་ཏུ་ཕྱིན་པ་བས་མ་འཚལ་བ་དང་ལྡན
པ་ལགས། སྤྱན་རས་གཟིགས་དབང་ཕྱུག་གཅིག་ལ་གཅིག་བརྟེན་ན་སར་གྲུབ་པ་
བསྒོམ་པ་ཉིད་ཀྱི་ཕྱིར་རོ། །བཅོམ་ལྡན་འདས་ཅིའི་སླད་དུ་བྱང་ཆུབ་སེམས་དཔའ་རྣམས
ཕ་རོལ་ཏུ་ཕྱིན་པ་རྣམས་ལ་ཇི་ལྟར་དེ་ལྟར་ཕ་རོལ་ཏུ་ཕྱིན་པའི་རྣམ་པར་སྨིན་པའི་འབྲས་བུ
འདོད་པ་ལ་དང་པས་གནས་པ་མ་ལགས། སྤྱན་རས་གཟིགས་དབང་ཕྱུག་རྒྱུ་ལྔའི་ཕྱིར་ཏེ།
ཕ་རོལ་ཏུ་ཕྱིན་པ་རྣམས་ནི་ཆེས་ལྷག་པར་བདེ་བ་དང་། ཡིད་བདེ་བའི་རྒྱུ་ཡིན་པའི་ཕྱིར
དང་། བདག་དང་གཞན་ལ་ཕན་འདོགས་པའི་རྒྱུ་ཡིན་པའི་ཕྱིར་དང་། ཕྱི་མ་ལ་དེའི་རྣམ
པར་སྨིན་པའི་འབྲས་བུ་འདོད་པའི་རྒྱུ་ཡིན་པའི་ཕྱིར་དང་། ཀུན་ནས་ཉོན་མོངས་པ་མེད
པའི་གཞི་ཡིན་པའི་ཕྱིར་དང་། མི་འགྱུར་བའི་ཆོས་ཉིད་ཡིན་པའི་ཕྱིར་རོ། །བཅོམ་ལྡན

"Bhagavan, what are the vastnesses of these perfections?"

"Avalokiteśvara, these are: non-attachment, non-anticipation [of reward], and complete dedication."

"What is the absence of the afflictions?"

"It is non-corruption and non-conceptuality."

"What is purification?"

"It is individual investigation and action."

"What is non-fluctuation?"

"It is the non-degenerating reality of those who have entered the [Bodhisattva] stages."

"What is exceptional purity?"

"Avalokiteśvara, it is what belongs to the tenth stage and what belongs to the Buddha stage."

"Bhagavan, why are Bodhisattvas always endowed with the inexhaustible desirable fruitional results of the perfections and the inexhaustible perfections?"

"Avalokiteśvara, it is because they cultivate the progressive attainment of each [perfection] in dependence on the others."

"Bhagavan, why is it that Bodhisattvas do not abide through faith in the desirable fruitional results of the perfections in the same way that they abide in the perfections?"

"Avalokiteśvara, this is due to five causes: The perfections are causes of surpassingly great happiness and pleasure; they are causes of benefit for oneself and others; they bring about

འདས་པ་ཕ་རོལ་ཏུ་ཕྱིན་པ་དེ་དག་གི་སོ་སོའི་མཐུ་གང་ལགས། སྤྱན་རས་གཟིགས་དབང་
ཕྱུག་དེ་དག་གི་སོ་སོའི་མཐུ་ནི་རྣམ་པ་བཞིར་རིག་པར་བྱ་སྟེ། ཕ་རོལ་ཏུ་ཕྱིན་པ་བསྒོམ་པ
ན་མི་འཕྲུན་པའི་ཕྱོགས་སེར་སྣ་དང་། འཆལ་བའི་ཚུལ་ཁྲིམས་དང་། སེམས་འཁྲུག་པ
དང་། ལེ་ལོ་དང་། རྣམ་པར་གཡེང་བ་དང་། ལྟ་བའི་རྣམ་པ་རབ་ཏུ་སྤོང་བ་དང་། བླ
ན་མེད་པ་ཡང་དག་པར་རྫོགས་པའི་བྱང་ཆུབ་ཏུ་འགྱུར་བ་དང་། ཚེ་འདི་ལ་བདག་དང
སེམས་ཅན་རྣམས་ལ་ཕན་འདོགས་པར་འགྱུར་བ་དང་། ཕྱི་མ་ལ་རྣམ་པར་སྨིན་པའི
འབྲས་བུ་འདོད་པ་རྒྱ་ཆེན་པོ་ཟད་མི་ཤེས་པ་འཐོབ་པར་འགྱུར་བའོ། །བཅོམ་ལྡན་འདས
ཕ་རོལ་ཏུ་ཕྱིན་པ་དེ་དག་རྒྱུ་གང་ལས་བྱུང་བ་དང་། འབྲས་བུ་གང་དང་ལྡན་པ་དང་།
དོན་གང་དང་ལྡན་པ་ལགས། བཅོམ་ལྡན་འདས་ཀྱིས་བཀའ་སྩལ་པ། སྤྱན་རས་
གཟིགས་དབང་ཕྱུག་ཕ་རོལ་ཏུ་ཕྱིན་པ་རྣམས་ནི་སྙིང་རྗེའི་རྒྱུ་ལས་བྱུང་བ་དང་། རྣམ་པར
སྨིན་པའི་འབྲས་བུ་འདོད་པ་དང་། སེམས་ཅན་ལ་ཕན་འདོགས་པའི་འབྲས་བུ་དང་ལྡན་པ
དང་། བྱང་ཆུབ་ཆེན་པོ་ཡོངས་སུ་རྫོགས་པར་བྱེད་པའི་དོན་ཆེན་པོ་དང་ལྡན་པ་ཡིན་ནོ། །
བཅོམ་ལྡན་འདས་གལ་ཏེ་བྱང་ཆུབ་སེམས་དཔའ་རྣམས་ལོངས་སྤྱོད་པས་མ་འཚལ་པ་དང
ལྡན་པ་དང་། སྙིང་རྗེ་ཅན་ལགས་ན་ཅིའི་སླད་དུ་འཇིག་རྟེན་ན་དབུལ་པོ་གདའ་ལགས།
སྤྱན་རས་གཟིགས་དབང་ཕྱུག་དེ་ནི་སེམས་ཅན་རྣམས་ཀྱི་རང་གི་ལས་ཀྱི་ཉེས་པ་བོ་ན་ཡིན
ནོ། །དེ་ལྟ་མ་ཡིན་ཏེ་སེམས་ཅན་རྣམས་ཀྱི་རང་གི་ཉེས་བྱས་དེའི་གགས་སུ་གྱུར་པ་མ་ཡིན
དུ་ཟིན་ན། དེ་དག་ལ་རྟག་ཏུ་བྱ་བ་ཉིད་ལ་ཞུགས་པ་དང་། ལོངས་སྤྱོད་མི་ཟད་པ་ཉིད

desirable fruitional results in the future; they are the bases of non-affliction; and they are unchangeable reality."

"Bhagavan, what are the distinct powers of the perfections?"

"Avalokiteśvara, know that they have four distinct kinds of power. When [Bodhisattvas] cultivate the perfections, they abandon the discordances of greed, faulty ethics, mental agitation, laziness, distraction, and [wrong] views. They become unsurpassably, completely, and perfectly enlightened. In this lifetime, they benefit themselves and others. In the future, they obtain desirable results that are extensive and inexhaustible."

"Bhagavan, from what cause do the perfections arise? What are their results? What is their significance?"

The Bhagavan replied: "Avalokiteśvara, the perfections arise from the cause of compassion. Their results are desirable fruits and benefits for sentient beings. Their great significance is the completion of great enlightenment."

"Bhagavan, if the resources of Bodhisattvas are inexhaustible and if they have compassion, why are there poor people in the world?"

"Avalokiteśvara, that is solely the fault of the actions of those sentient beings themselves. If this were not so, if sentient beings' own faults did not become obstacles, then beings could always engage in actions, and they would have inexhaustible resources; in which case how could any suffering appear in the world?

ཡོད་བཞིན་དུ་འཇིག་རྟེན་སྡུག་བསྔལ་བ་ལྟ་སྣང་བར་ག་ལ་འགྱུར། སྤྱན་རས་གཟིགས་
དབང་ཕྱུག་འདི་ལྟ་སྟེ་དཔེར་ན། ཡི་དྭགས་ལུས་སྐྲོམ་པས་གདུངས་པ་རྣམས་ཀྱིས་རྒྱ་
མཚོའི་ཆུ་སྐམས་པར་མཐོང་བ་དེ་ནི་རྒྱ་མཚོ་དག་གིས་ཉེས་པ་མ་ཡིན་གྱི། ཡི་དྭགས་དེ
དག་ཉིད་ཀྱི་རང་གི་ལས་ཀྱི་འབྲས་བུའི་ཉེས་པ་ཡིན་ནོ། །དེ་བཞིན་དུ་འབྲས་བུ་མེད་པར
གྱུར་པ་གང་ཡིན་པ་དེ་ནི་བྱང་ཆུབ་སེམས་དཔའི་སྦྱིན་པ་དག་གིས་རྒྱ་མཚོ་ལྟ་བུར་གྱུར་པ་
རྣམས་ཀྱི་ཉེས་པ་མ་ཡིན་གྱི་སེམས་ཅན་རང་གི་ཉེས་པ་བྱས་པ་ཡི་དྭགས་ལྟ་བུ་རྣམས་ཀྱི་རང་
གི་ལས་ཀྱི་ཉེས་པ་ཡིན་ནོ། །བཅོམ་ལྡན་འདས་བྱང་ཆུབ་སེམས་དཔའ་ཆོས་རྣམས་ཀྱི་ངོ་
བོ་ཉིད་མ་མཆིས་པ་ཉིད་ཕ་རོལ་ཏུ་ཕྱིན་པ་གང་གིས་འཛིན་ལགས། སྤྱན་རས་གཟིགས་
དབང་ཕྱུག་ཤེས་རབ་ཀྱི་ཕ་རོལ་ཏུ་ཕྱིན་པས་འཛིན་ནོ། །བཅོམ་ལྡན་འདས་གལ་ཏེ་ཤེས་
རབ་ཀྱི་ཕ་རོལ་ཏུ་ཕྱིན་པས་ངོ་བོ་ཉིད་མ་མཆིས་པ་ཉིད་འཛིན་ན། ངོ་བོ་ཉིད་དང་བཅས་པ་
ཉིད་ཀྱང་ཅིའི་སླད་དུ་མི་འཛིན་ལགས། སྤྱན་རས་གཟིགས་དབང་ཕྱུག་ང་ནི་ངོ་བོ་ཉིད་ཀྱིས་
ངོ་བོ་ཉིད་མེད་པ་ཉིད་འཛིན་པར་མི་སྨྲ་མོད་ཀྱི། འོན་ཀྱང་ཡི་གེས་བསྟན་པ་མེད་པར་ངོ་བོ་
ཉིད་མེད་པ་ཡི་གེ་མེད་པ་སོ་སོ་རང་རིག་པ་དེ་བསྟན་པར་མི་ནུས་པས་དེའི་ཕྱིར་ངོ་བོ་ཉིད་
མེད་པ་ཉིད་འཛིན་ནོ་ཞེས་དེ་སྐད་བརྗོད་དོ། །བཅོམ་ལྡན་འདས་ཕ་རོལ་ཏུ་ཕྱིན་པ་ཞེས་
ཀྱང་བགྱི། ཉེ་བའི་ཕ་རོལ་ཏུ་ཕྱིན་པ་ཞེས་ཀྱང་བགྱི། ཕ་རོལ་ཏུ་ཕྱིན་པ་ཆེན་པོ་ཞེས་ཀྱང་
བགྱི་ལགས་ན། བཅོམ་ལྡན་འདས་ཕ་རོལ་ཏུ་ཕྱིན་པ་གང་ལགས། ཉེ་བའི་ཕ་རོལ་ཏུ་
ཕྱིན་པ་ནི་གང་ལགས། ཕ་རོལ་ཏུ་ཕྱིན་པ་ཆེན་པོ་ནི་གང་ལགས། སྤྱན་རས་གཟིགས་

"Avalokiteśvara, for example, the fact that hungry ghosts, whose bodies are pained by thirst, perceive the watery ocean as dry is not the ocean's failing. It is a fault resulting from those hungry ghosts' own actions.

"Similarly, the absence of good results is not a failing of the ocean-like generosity of Bodhisattvas. The faulty actions of those sentient beings who are like hungry ghosts are their own fault."[46]

"Bhagavan, with what perfection do Bodhisattvas apprehend the lack of own-being of phenomena?"

"Avalokiteśvara, they apprehend this with the perfection of wisdom."

"Bhagavan, if they apprehend lack of own-being with the perfection of wisdom, why do they also not apprehend it with own-being?"

"Avalokiteśvara, I do not say that own-being apprehends what is without own-being. Yet, since lack of own-being is individually known without words, without being taught by words, I have spoken of 'apprehension of lack of own-being'."

"Bhagavan, when you say, 'perfection', 'further perfection', and 'great perfection', Bhagavan, what is perfection? What is further perfection? What is great perfection?"

"Avalokiteśvara, there are Bodhisattvas endowed with virtuous qualities, generosity and the like, which they cultivate through immeasurable time. Still, afflictions arise in them and

དབང་ཕྱུག་འདི་ལ་བྱང་ཆུབ་སེམས་དཔའ་དུས་དཔག་ཏུ་མེད་པ་ནས་ཡོངས་སུ་བསྒོམས་པའི་སྦྱིན་པ་ལ་སོགས་པ་དགེ་བའི་ཆོས་རྣམས་དང་ལྡན་པ་ཡང་ཡིན་ལ། དེ་ལ་ཉོན་མོངས་པ་ཡང་ཀུན་འབྱུང་ཞིང་དེ་ཟིལ་གྱིས་གནོན་པར་ནི་མི་ནུས་ཀྱི། དེས་ཟིལ་གྱིས་གནོན་པར་འགྱུར་བ་འདི་ལྟ་སྟེ། མོས་པས་སྤྱོད་པའི་ས་ལ་མོས་པ་ཆུང་ངུ་དང་འབྲིང་ལ་ཞུགས་པ་དེ་ནི་ཕ་རོལ་ཏུ་ཕྱིན་པ་ཞེས་བྱའོ། །ཡང་དུས་དཔག་ཏུ་མེད་པ་ནས་ཆེས་ཡོངས་སུ་བསྒོམས་པའི་དགེ་བའི་ཆོས་དེ་དག་ཉིད་དང་ལྡན་ཞིང་དེ་ལ་ཉོན་མོངས་པ་ཡང་ཀུན་ཏུ་འབྱུང་ལ། དེ་ཟིལ་གྱིས་གནོན་ཅིང་དེས་ཟིལ་གྱིས་གནོན་པར་མི་འགྱུར་བ་འདི་ལྟ་སྟེ། ས་དང་པོ་ནས་བཟུང་བ་དེ་ནི་ཉེ་བའི་ཕ་རོལ་ཏུ་ཕྱིན་པ་ཞེས་བྱའོ། །ཡང་དུས་དཔག་ཏུ་མེད་པ་ནས་ཆེས་ཤིན་ཏུ་ཡོངས་སུ་བསྒོམས་པའི་དགེ་བའི་ཆོས་དེ་དག་ཉིད་དང་ལྡན་ཞིང་དེ་ལ་ཐམས་ཅད་ཀྱི་ཐམས་ཅད་དུ་ཉོན་མོངས་པ་ཀུན་ཏུ་མི་འབྱུང་བའི་ཆོས་ཅན་དུ་གྱུར་པ་འདི་ལྟ་སྟེ། ས་བརྒྱད་པ་ནས་བཟུང་བ་དེ་ནི་ཕ་རོལ་ཏུ་ཕྱིན་པ་ཆེན་པོ་ཞེས་བྱའོ། །བཅོམ་ལྡན་འདས་ས་དེ་དག་ལ་ཉོན་མོངས་པའི་བག་ལ་ཉལ་རྣམ་པ་དུ་མཆིས་ལགས། སྤྱན་རས་གཟིགས་དབང་ཕྱུག་རྣམ་པ་གསུམ་སྟེ། སྤྱན་རས་གཟིགས་དབང་ཕྱུག་གྲོགས་ཡང་དག་པར་བཅོམ་པ་ནི་འདི་ལྟ་སྟེ། ས་ལྔ་པོ་དག་ན་ཉོན་མོངས་པ་ལྷན་ཅིག་སྐྱེས་པ། ཀུན་ཏུ་འབྱུང་བའི་གྲོགས་ཉོན་མོངས་པ་ལྷན་ཅིག་སྐྱེས་པ་མ་ཡིན་པ་ཀུན་ཏུ་འབྱུང་བ་དེ་དེའི་ཚེ་དེ་ལ་མེད་པས་དེའི་ཕྱིར་གྲོགས་ཡང་དག་པར་བཅོམ་པ་ཞེས་བྱའོ། །བག་ལ་ཉལ་སྟོབས་ཆུང་བ་ནི་འདི་ལྟ་སྟེ། ས་དྲུག་པ་དང་བདུན་པ་ལ་ཕྲ་མོ་ཀུན་ཏུ་འབྱུང་བ་ཉིད་དང་། བསྒོམས་པས་མནན་པས

they are unable to overcome them. Instead, they are overcome by them. Involvement in small or middling conviction on the stage of engagement through conviction is called 'perfection'.

"There are also those endowed with virtuous qualities which they greatly and thoroughly cultivate through immeasurable time. Although afflictions arise in them, they overcome them and are not overcome by them. Those [states] beginning with the first [Bodhisattva] stage are called 'further perfections'.

"There are, further, those endowed with virtuous qualities which they greatly and very thoroughly cultivate through immeasurable time. They are distinguished by the fact that the afflictions never arise in them at all. Those [states] beginning with the eighth [Bodhisattva] stage are called 'great perfections'."

"Bhagavan, how many kinds of predispositions toward afflictions are there on those stages?"

"Avalokiteśvara, there are three kinds. Avalokiteśvara, there are 'the assistors that are completely destroyed'. On the first five stages the production of non-innate afflictions that assist in the production of innate afflictions does not occur; this is called 'the assistors that are completely destroyed'.[47]

"There are also the predispositions that are of little power: On the sixth and seventh stages, there are extremely subtle arisings and arisings that are suppressed by meditation.

ཀུན་ཏུ་འབྱུང་བ་ཉིད་ཀྱི་ཕྱིར་རོ། །བག་ལ་ཉལ་བྲོ་མོ་ནི་འདི་ལྟ་སྟེ། ས་བརྒྱད་པ་དང་དེའི་
གོང་མ་རྣམས་ལ་ཉོན་མོངས་པ་ཐམས་ཅད་ཀྱི་ཐམས་ཅད་དུ་ཀུན་ཏུ་མི་འབྱུང་བ་དང་།
ཤེས་བྱའི་སྒྲིབ་པ་ཙམ་ལ་གནས་པ་ཉིད་ཀྱི་ཕྱིར་རོ། །བཅོམ་ལྡན་འདས་བག་ལ་ཉལ་དེ་
དག་གནས་ངན་ལེན་སྤྲངས་པ་རྣམ་པ་དུས་རབ་ཏུ་ཕྱེ་བ་ལགས། སྤྱན་རས་གཟིགས་དབང་
ཕྱུག་རྣམ་པ་གསུམ་གྱིས་ཏེ། གནས་ངན་ལེན་ལྤགས་ཤུན་ལ་ཡོད་པ་ལྟ་བུ་སྤྲངས་པས་ནི
དང་པོ་དང་གཉིས་པ་རབ་ཏུ་ཕྱེ་བ་ཡིན་ནོ། །ཁྲི་ལ་ཡོད་པ་ལྟ་བུ་སྤྲངས་པ་ནི་གསུམ་པའོ། །
གནས་ངན་ལེན་སྙིང་པོ་ལ་ཡོད་པ་ལྟ་བུ་སྤྲངས་པ་གང་ཡིན་པ་དེ་ནི་ཐམས་ཅད་ཀྱི་ཐམས་
ཅད་དུ་བག་ལ་ཉལ་མེད་པའི་གནས་སྐབས་ཡིན་ཏེ། སངས་རྒྱས་ཀྱི་ས་ཡིན་པར་ངས་
ཡོངས་སུ་བསྟན་ཏོ། །བཅོམ་ལྡན་འདས་གནས་ངན་ལེན་དེ་དག་བསྐལ་པ་གྲངས་མ་
མཆིས་པ་དུ་དག་གིས་སྤོང་བར་འགྱུར་ལགས། སྤྱན་རས་གཟིགས་དབང་ཕྱུག་གྲངས་
མེད་པ་གསུམ་གྱིས་སམ། དུས་ཚིགས་དང་། ཟླ་བ་དང་། ཟླ་བ་ཕྱེད་དང་། ཞག་དང་།
ཉིམ་དང་། ཐུན་དང་། ཐུན་ཕྱེད་དང་། སྐད་ཅིག་དང་། ཐང་ཅིག་དང་། ཡུད་ཙམ
དང་། བསྐལ་པ་དཔག་ཏུ་མེད་པ་དག་གིས་སྤོང་ངོ་། །བཅོམ་ལྡན་འདས་ས་དེ་དག་ལ་
བྱང་ཆུབ་སེམས་དཔའ་རྣམས་ཀྱི་ཉོན་མོངས་པ་སྐྱེ་བའི་མཚན་ཉིད་ནི་གང་ལགས། སྐྱོན་
ནི་གང་ལགས། ཡོན་ཏན་ནི་གང་ལགས་པར་རིག་པར་བགྱི། སྤྱན་རས་གཟིགས་དབང་
ཕྱུག་བྱང་ཆུབ་སེམས་དཔའ་རྣམས་ཀྱི་ཉོན་མོངས་པ་སྐྱེ་བ་ནི་ཀུན་ནས་ཉོན་མོངས་པ་མེད་
པའི་མཚན་ཉིད་ཡིན་ནོ། །དེ་ཅིའི་ཕྱིར་ཞེ་ན། བྱང་ཆུབ་སེམས་དཔའས་དང་པོ་ལ་སོ་

"There are the extremely subtle predispositions: On the eighth stage and those [stages] above it, the afflictions do not arise at all and thus abide only as obstructions to omniscience."

"Bhagavan, into how many kinds of abandonment of errant tendencies are these predispositions divided?"

"Avalokiteśvara, [they are divided] into three kinds. The first and second are the abandoning of errant tendencies that are like something existing on the outer layer of the skin; the third is the abandoning [of errant tendencies] that are like something existing in subcutaneous skin. As for those who have abandoned errant tendencies that are like something existing in the marrow, in which state predispositions do not exist at all, I have taught that they are on the Buddha stage."[48]

"Bhagavan, for how many incalculable eons does one abandon these errant tendencies?"

"Avalokiteśvara, [one abandons them] for three incalculable eons. One abandons them for incalculable eons of: seasons, months, half-months, days and nights, days, three-hour periods, one-and-one-half-hour periods, moments, instants, and microseconds."[49]

"Bhagavan, what are the characteristics of the arising of a Bodhisattva's afflictions on those stages? What are the faults? What are the good qualities that should be known?"

"Avalokiteśvara, the arising of a Bodhisattva's afflictions is characterized by an absence of affliction. Why is this so? One realizes the entire Dharmadhātu with certainty on the first

སོར་ངེས་པ་ཁོ་ནར་ཆོས་ཀྱི་དབྱིངས་ཐམས་ཅད་རབ་ཏུ་རྟོགས་པའི་ཕྱིར་རོ། དེས་ན་བྱང་ཆུབ་སེམས་དཔའི་ཉོན་མོངས་པ་ནི་ཤེས་བཞིན་ཁོ་ནར་སྐྱེ་བ་ཡིན་གྱི། མི་ཤེས་པར་མ་ཡིན་པས་དེའི་ཕྱིར་ཀུན་ནས་ཉོན་མོངས་པ་མེད་པའི་མཚན་ཉིད་ཡིན་ནོ། །རང་གི་རྒྱུད་ལ་སྡུག་བསྔལ་སྐྱེད་པར་མི་ནུས་པ་ཉིད་ཀྱི་ཕྱིར་སྐྱོན་མེད་པ་ཡིན་ནོ། །སེམས་ཅན་གྱི་ཁམས་ཀྱི་སྡུག་བསྔལ་རྣམ་པར་བཟློག་པའི་རྒྱུ་ཉིད་ཡིན་པའི་ཕྱིར་ཡོན་ཏན་དཔག་ཏུ་མེད་པ་ཡིན་ནོ། །

བཅོམ་ལྡན་འདས་གང་ལ་དཔེར་བྱང་ཆུབ་སེམས་དཔའ་རྣམས་ཀྱི་ཉོན་མོངས་སྐྱེ་བ་དག་གིས་ཀྱང་སེམས་ཅན་དང་། ཉན་ཐོས་དང་། རང་སངས་རྒྱས་ཐམས་ཅད་ཀྱི་དགེ་བའི་རྩ་བ་རྣམས་དེ་ཙམ་དུ་ཟིལ་གྱིས་གནོན་པར་བགྱིད་ན། དེ་ལས་གཞན་པའི་ཡོན་ཏན་རྣམས་ཀྱིས་ལྟ་སྨོས་ཀྱང་ཅི་འཚལ་ཏེ། བྱང་ཆུབ་ཇི་ཙམ་དུ་དོན་ཆེ་བ་ནི་ངོ་མཚར་ལགས་སོ། །

བཅོམ་ལྡན་འདས་བཅོམ་ལྡན་འདས་ཀྱིས་ཉན་ཐོས་ཀྱི་ཐེག་པ་གང་ཡིན་པ་དང་། ཐེག་པ་ཆེན་པོ་གང་ཡིན་པ་དེ་ནི་ཐེག་པ་གཅིག་གོ་ཞེས་བཀའ་སྩལ་པ་དེ་ལ་དགོངས་པ་གང་ལགས། སྤྱན་རས་གཟིགས་དབང་ཕྱུག་ངས་ཉན་ཐོས་ཀྱི་ཐེག་པར་ཆོས་སྣ་ཚོགས་ཀྱི་ངོ་བོ་ཉིད་འདི་ལྟ་སྟེ། ཕུང་པོ་ལྔ་དང་། ནང་གི་སྐྱེ་མཆེད་དྲུག་དང་། ཕྱི་རོལ་གྱི་སྐྱེ་མཆེད་དྲུག་དང་། དེ་དག་ལ་སོགས་པ་གང་དག་བསྟན་པ་དེ་དག་ཉིད་ངས་ཐེག་པ་ཆེན་པོར་ཆོས་ཀྱི་དབྱིངས་ཚུལ་གཅིག་པར་བསྟན་པས་བཤད་དེ། དེའི་ཕྱིར་ང་ནི་ཐེག་པ་ཐ་དད་པར་མི་སྨྲའོ། །དེ་ལ་གང་དག་དོན་ལ་སྒྲ་ཇི་བཞིན་ཁོ་ནར་རྣམ་པར་རྟོག་པ་ཁ་ཅིག་ནི་སྒྲོ་འདོགས་པར་བྱེད། ཁ་ཅིག་ནི་སྐུར་བ་འདེབས་པར་བྱེད་ཅིང་ཐེག་པ་ཐ་དད་པ་ཉིད་དུ་རྣམ

Bodhisattva stage. Thereafter, the afflictions of Bodhisattvas arise only consciously, and never unconsciously. Thus [Bodhisattvas] are characterized by an absence of affliction.[50]

"Because suffering cannot arise in their continuums, [Bodhisattvas] are faultless. Because they are causes of overcoming suffering in the realms of sentient beings, [a Bodhisattva's afflictions] are immeasurably good qualities."[51]

"Bhagavan, if in that way even the arising of the Bodhisattvas' afflictions outshines all the roots of virtue of sentient beings, [including] Śrāvakas and Pratyekabuddhas, what need is there to mention that their other good qualities [do so also]? The great significance of their enlightenment is marvelous!

"Bhagavan, the Bhagavan has said: 'The Śrāvaka vehicle and the Great Vehicle are one vehicle.' What was your thought when [you said] that?"

"Avalokiteśvara, those very things that I have taught in the Śrāvaka vehicle as the own-being of diverse things—such as the five aggregates, the six internal sense spheres, the six external sense spheres, and the like—I have also taught in the Mahāyāna as being of one mode in terms of the Dharmadhātu. Therefore, I do not speak of there being different vehicles.

"Some who understand [my teachings] according to the literal meaning engage in exaggeration and some in deprecation, thinking that there are various vehicles. [When I spoke] my thought was of those two who were thinking discordantly and disputing with one another."

པར་རྟོག་པར་ཡང་བྱེད་དེ། དེ་གཉིས་ནི་མི་འཐུན་པར་སེམས་ཤིང་ཕན་ཚུན་རྩོད་པར་ཟད
དེ༑ དེ་ལས་དགོངས་པ་ནི་དེ་ཡིན་ནོ། །དེ་ནས་བཅོམ་ལྡན་འདས་ཀྱིས་དེའི་ཚེ་ཚིགས་སུ
བཅད་པ་འདི་དག་བཀའ་སྩལ་ཏོ། །ཐེག་པ་ཆེ་དང་ཐེག་པ་དམན་པ་ལ། །རང་བཞིན་སྣ
ཚོགས་ཆོས་རྣམས་གང་བསྟན་པ། །དེ་དག་ཉིད་ནི་ཚུལ་གཅིག་ཡང་བསྟན་ཏེ། །དེ་ཕྱིར
ཐེག་པ་ཐ་དད་དང་མི་སྨྲ། །དོན་ལ་སྒྲ་བཞིན་རྣམ་པར་རྟོག་བྱེད་པ། །སྒྲོ་བཏགས་བྱས་ཤིང
སྐུར་བ་བཏབ་བྱས་ནས། །དེ་དག་འགལ་བ་སྐམ་དུ་སེམས་པ་ན། །རྣམ་པར་རྨོངས་ནས
ཕྲ་ཕྲོས་སྣ་ཚོགས་འགྱུར། །ས་རྣམས་བསྡུས་དང་མིང་དང་མི་འཐུན་ཕྱོགས། །ཁྱད་པར
སྐྱེ་དང་སྨོན་དང་བསྒྲུབ་པ་རྣམས། །དེ་ནི་སངས་རྒྱས་རྣམས་ཀྱིས་ཐེག་ཆེན་བཤད། །འདི
ལ་གང་བརྩོན་དེ་དག་སངས་རྒྱས་འགྱུར། །དེ་ནས་བཅོམ་ལྡན་འདས་ལ་བྱང་ཆུབ་སེམས
དཔའ་སྤྱན་རས་གཟིགས་དབང་ཕྱུག་གིས་འདི་སྐད་ཅེས་གསོལ་ཏོ། །བཅོམ་ལྡན་འདས
དགོངས་པ་ངེས་པར་འགྲེལ་པའི་ཆོས་ཀྱི་རྣམ་གྲངས་འདིར་བསྟན་པ་འདིའི་མིང་ཅི་ལགས།
འདི་ཇི་ལྟར་གཟུང་བར་བགྱི། བཅོམ་ལྡན་འདས་ཀྱིས་དེ་ལ་བཀའ་སྩལ་པ། སྤྱན་རས
གཟིགས་དབང་ཕྱུག་འདི་ནི་ས་དང་ཕ་རོལ་ཏུ་ཕྱིན་པའི་ངེས་པའི་དོན་བསྟན་པ་ཡིན་ཏེ།
འདི་ས་དང་ཕ་རོལ་ཏུ་ཕྱིན་པའི་ངེས་པའི་དོན་བསྟན་པ་ཞེས་བྱ་བར་ཟུང་ཤིག །ས་དང་ཕ
རོལ་ཏུ་ཕྱིན་པའི་ངེས་པའི་དོན་བསྟན་པ་འདི་བཤད་པ་ན། བྱང་ཆུབ་སེམས་དཔའ་བདུན
ཁྲི་ལྔ་སྟོང་གིས་བྱང་ཆུབ་སེམས་དཔའི་ཏིང་ངེ་འཛིན་ཐེག་པ་ཆེན་པོ་སྣང་བ་ཐོབ་པར་གྱུར
ཏོ༑ །སྤྱན་རས་གཟིགས་དབང་ཕྱུག་གི་ལེའུ་སྟེ་དགུ་པའོ།། །།

Then the Bhagavan spoke these verses:

"Phenomena that I described as having
various natures in Mahāyāna and Hīnayāna
I taught again as having one mode.
Thus, I do not propound different vehicles.

"Thinking in terms of the literal meaning
creates exaggerations and deprecations.
If one thinks that they are contradictory,
in confusion, one forms various ideas.

"The collective stages and their names, discordances,
distinctive arisings, aspirations, and trainings
are the Buddha's explanation of the Great Vehicle.[52]
Those who make effort at these become Buddhas."

Then the Bodhisattva Avalokiteśvara asked the Bhagavan: "Bhagavan, what is the name of this form of Dharma discourse that explains your thought? How should it be apprehended?"

The Bhagavan replied, "Avalokiteśvara, this is the teaching of the definitive meaning of the stages and the perfections. Apprehend it as 'the teaching of the definitive meaning of the stages and the perfections'."

When this teaching of the definitive meaning of the stages and the perfections was explained, seventy-five thousand Bodhisattvas attained the Bodhisattva's samādhi that illuminates the Mahāyāna.

This completes the ninth chapter of Avalokiteśvara.

Homage to the Mahābodhisattva Mañjuśrī

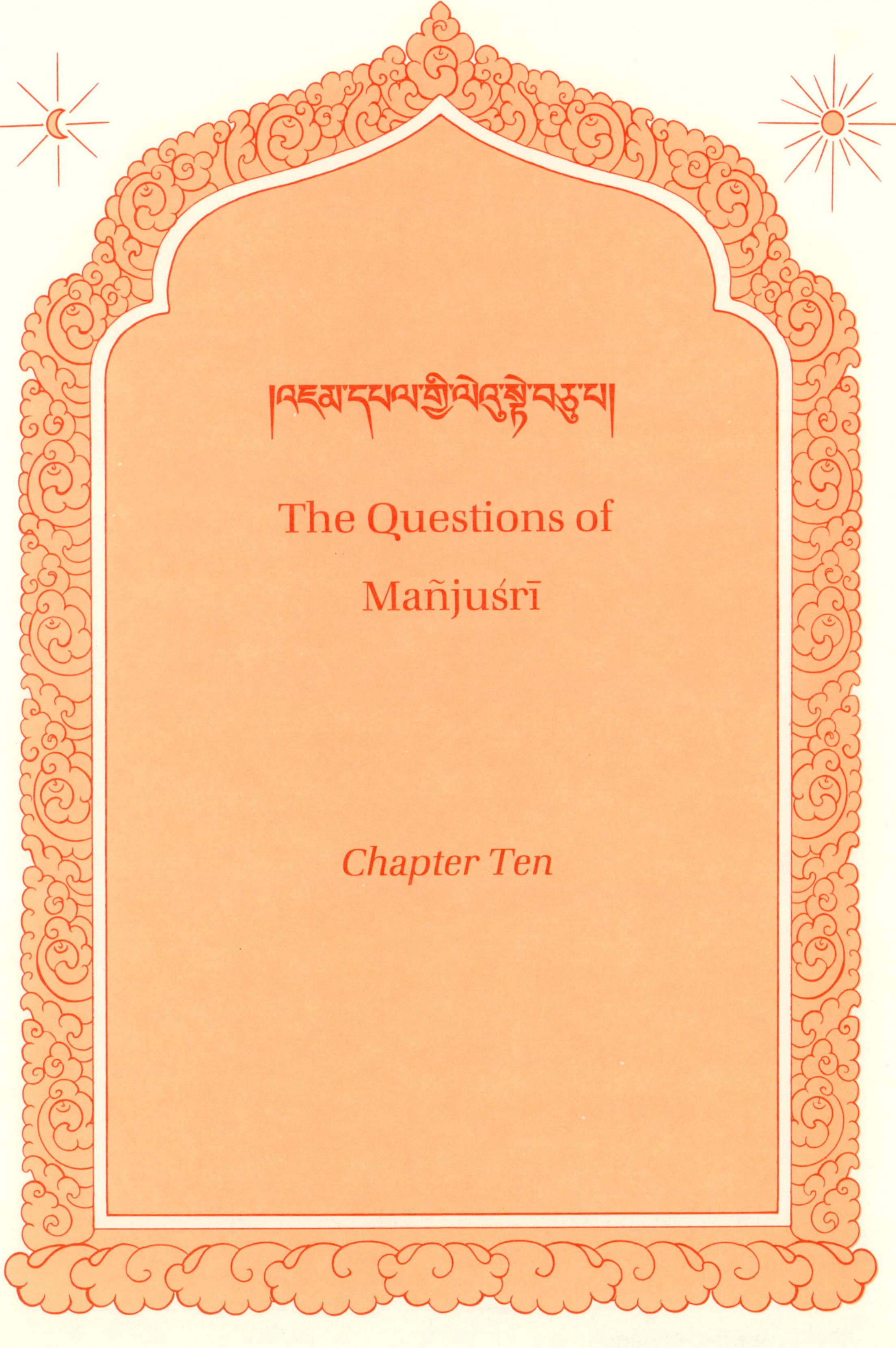
།འཇམ་དཔལ་གྱི་ལེའུ་སྟེ་བཅུ་པ།
The Questions of
Mañjuśrī
Chapter Ten

༄༅། །དེ་ནས་བཅོམ་ལྡན་འདས་ལ་བྱང་ཆུབ་སེམས་དཔའ་འཇམ་དཔལ་གྱིས་ཞུ་བ་ཞུས་པ། བཅོམ་ལྡན་འདས་དེ་བཞིན་གཤེགས་པ་རྣམས་ཀྱི་ཆོས་སྐུ་ཞེས་བགྱི་ན། བཅོམ་ལྡན་འདས་དེ་བཞིན་གཤེགས་པ་རྣམས་ཀྱི་ཆོས་ཀྱི་སྐུའི་མཚན་ཉིད་ཇི་ལྟ་བུ་ལགས། བཅོམ་ལྡན་འདས་ཀྱིས་བཀའ་སྩལ་པ། འཇམ་དཔལ་དེ་བཞིན་གཤེགས་པ་རྣམས་ཀྱི་ཆོས་ཀྱི་སྐུའི་མཚན་ཉིད་ནི་ས་དང་ཕ་རོལ་ཏུ་ཕྱིན་པ་ཤིན་ཏུ་བསྒོམས་པའི་ངེས་པར་འབྱུང་བའི་གནས་གྱུར་པ་ཡང་དག་པར་གྲུབ་པ་ཡིན་ནོ། །དེ་ཡང་རྒྱུ་གཉིས་ཀྱིས་བསམ་གྱིས་མི་ཁྱབ་པའི་མཚན་ཉིད་དུ་རིག་པར་བྱ་སྟེ། དེ་ནི་སྤྲོས་པ་མེད་ཅིང་མངོན་པར་འདུ་བྱ་བ་མེད་པ་ཉིད་ཀྱི་ཕྱིར་དང་། སེམས་ཅན་རྣམས་ནི་སྤྲོས་པ་དང་མངོན་པར་འདུ་བྱ་བ་ལ་མངོན་པར་ཞེན་པ་ཉིད་ཀྱི་ཕྱིར་རོ། །བཅོམ་ལྡན་འདས་ཅི་ལགས། ཉན་ཐོས་དང་། རང་སངས་རྒྱས་རྣམས་ཀྱི་གནས་གྱུར་པ་གང་ལགས་པ་དེ་ཡང་ཆོས་ཀྱི་སྐུ་ལེགས་པར་བརྗོད་པར་བགྱིའམ། འཇམ་དཔལ་བརྗོད་པར་མི་བྱའོ། །བཅོམ་ལྡན་འདས་འོ་ན་ཅི་ལགས་པར་བརྗོད་པར་བགྱི། འཇམ་དཔལ་རྣམ་པར་གྲོལ་བའི་ལུས་ཡིན་ཏེ། འཇམ་དཔལ་རྣམ་པར་གྲོལ་བའི་ལུས་ཀྱིས་ནི་དེ་བཞིན་གཤེགས་པ་རྣམས་དང་། ཉན་ཐོས་དང་། རང་སངས་རྒྱས་རྣམས་ཀྱང་མཚུངས་ཤིང་མཉམ་མོ། །ཆོས་ཀྱི་སྐུས་ནི་ཁྱད་པར་དུ་འཕགས་ཏེ། ཆོས་ཀྱི་སྐུ་ཁྱད་པར་དུ་འཕགས་ན་ཡོན་ཏན་གྱི་ཁྱད་པར་དཔག་ཏུ་མེད་པས་ཀྱང་ཁྱད་པར་འཕགས་པ་ཡིན་ཏེ། དེ་ལ་ནི་དཔེ་བྱ་བར་ཡང་སླ་བ་མ་ཡིན་ནོ། །བཅོམ་ལྡན་འདས་དེ་བཞིན་གཤེགས་པ་རྣམས་ཀྱི་སྐྱེ་བ་འབྱུང་བའི་མཚན་ཉིད་ཇི་ལྟ་བུར་རིག་པར་བགྱི་ལགས།

Then the Bodhisattva Mañjuśrī[1] asked the Bhagavan: "Bhagavan, when you speak of 'the Dharmakāya of the Tathāgatas', Bhagavan, what are the characteristics of the Dharmakāya of the Tathāgatas?"

The Bhagavan replied: "Mañjuśrī, the characteristics of the Dharmakāya of the Tathāgatas are the well-established transformation of the basis through renunciation, the complete cultivation of the [ten] stages and the [six] perfections.[2] Moreover, know that this [Dharmakāya] has an inconceivable characteristic for two reasons: because it is free from elaborations and free from manifest activity; and because sentient beings very strongly adhere to elaborations and manifest activity."[3]

"Bhagavan, is the transformation of the basis of Śrāvakas and Pratyekabuddhas also suitably referred to as 'Dharmakāya'?"

"Mañjuśrī, they are not spoken of [in this way]."

"Bhagavan, in that case, what should they be called?"

"Mañjuśrī, they are liberation bodies. Mañjuśrī, in terms of liberation bodies, Tathāgatas, Śrāvakas, and Pratyekabuddhas are similar and equal. In terms of the Dharmakāya, [Tathāgatas] are superior. Since the Dharmakāya is superior, [Tathāgatas] are also superior in terms of immeasurably good qualities. It is not easy to provide examples of that."[4]

"Bhagavan, how should one know the characteristics of a Tathāgata's genesis?"

འཇམ་དཔལ་སྤྲུལ་པའི་སྐུའི་མཚན་ཉིད་འཇིག་རྟེན་གྱི་ཁམས་འབྱུང་བ་དང་འདྲའོ། །སྤྲུལ་པའི་སྐུའི་མཚན་ཉིད་འབྱུང་བའི་དེ་བཞིན་གཤེགས་པའི་ཡོན་ཏན་བཀོད་པའི་རྒྱན་གྱི་རྣམ་པ་ཐམས་ཅད་ཀྱིས་བྱིན་གྱིས་བརླབས་པའི་མཚན་ཉིད་དུ་བལྟ་བར་བྱའོ། །ཆོས་ཀྱི་སྐུ་ལ་ནི་སྐྱེ་བ་འབྱུང་བ་མེད་དོ། །བཅོམ་ལྡན་འདས་སྤྲུལ་པའི་སྐུ་སྟོན་པའི་ཐབས་མཁས་པ་གང་ལགས་པར་བལྟ་བར་བགྱི་ལགས། འཇམ་དཔལ། སྤྲུལ་པའི་སྐུ་]སྟོན་པའི་ཐབས་ལ་མཁས་པ་ནི་སྟོང་གསུམ་གྱི་སྟོང་ཆེན་པོའི་སངས་རྒྱས་ཀྱི་ཞིང་ཐམས་ཅད་དུ་བདག་པོར་གྲགས་པའམ། སྦྱིན་གནས་སུ་གྲགས་པའི་ཁྱིམ་དུ་མངལ་དུ་འཇུག་པ་དང་། བཙས་པ་དང་། སྐྱེ་བ་དང་། འདོད་པ་ལ་ལོངས་སྤྱོད་པ་དང་། མངོན་པར་འབྱུང་བ་དང་། དཀའ་བ་སྤྱད་པ་ཅིག་ཅར་ཀུན་ཏུ་སྟོན་པ་དང་། དེ་གཏོང་བ་དང་། མངོན་པར་རྫོགས་པར་བྱང་ཆུབ་པའི་རིམ་པ་ཀུན་ཏུ་སྟོན་པ་ཡིན་པར་བལྟ་བར་བྱའོ། །བཅོམ་ལྡན་འདས་དེ་བཞིན་གཤེགས་པ་དེ་བཞིན་གཤེགས་པའི་བྱིན་གྱིས་བརླབས་ཀྱི་སྐུས་གསུང་གང་དག་བརྗོད་པས་འདུལ་བའི་ཁམས་ཡོངས་སུ་མ་སྨིན་པ་ནི་ཡོངས་སུ་སྨིན་པར་མཛད་ལ། ཡོངས་སུ་སྨིན་པ་ནི་དམིགས་པ་དེ་ཉིད་ཀྱིས་རྣམ་པར་གྲོལ་བར་མཛད་པའི་གསུང་བརྗོད་པ་དུ་ཞིག་རྗོད་པར་མཛད་ལགས། འཇམ་དཔལ་དེ་བཞིན་གཤེགས་པའི་གསུང་བརྗོད་པ་ནི་གསུམ་པོ་འདི་དག་ཡིན་ཏེ། མདོ་སྡེ་རྗོད་པ་དང་། འདུལ་བ་རྗོད་པ་དང་། མ་མོ་རྗོད་པའོ། །བཅོམ་ལྡན་འདས་མདོ་སྡེ་ནི་གང་ལགས། འདུལ་བ་ནི་གང་ལགས། མ་མོ་ནི་གང་ལགས། འཇམ་དཔལ་འདི་ལྟ་སྟེ། དངོས་པོ་བཞིའམ། དགུའམ། ཉི་ཤུ་རྩ་དགུའི

"Mañjuśrī, the characteristics of the Nirmāṇakāya are like the arising of worldly realms. You should see the characteristics of the Nirmāṇakāya as characteristics that are empowered by all the types of adornments displaying the qualities of the Tathāgatas which arise.[5] The Dharmakāya has no genesis."

"Bhagavan, how should one view the skillful method that displays the Nirmāṇakāya?"

"Mañjuśrī, view the skillful method[6] that displays the Nirmāṇakāya as everywhere displaying the stages: entering the womb in a household of one renowned as a sovereign in all the Buddha fields of the trichiliocosm or of one renowned as being worthy of gifts; taking birth; growing up; enjoying worldly pleasures; leaving home; fully demonstrating the practice of austerities all at once; renouncing them; and displaying the stages of complete, perfect enlightenment."

"Bhagavan, through the Tathāgatas' empowerment-body, Tathāgatas mature trainees' immature constituents by expressing their teachings, and they teach mature beings in a liberative way by these objects of observation. How many expressions [of the teachings] are there?"

"Mañjuśrī, the teachings of the Tathāgatas are threefold: Sūtra, Vinaya, and Mātṛkā."

"Bhagavan, what are the Sūtra teachings? What are Vinaya? What are Mātṛkā?"

དབང་དུ་བྱས་ནས་ཆོས་རྣམས་ཀྱི་དངོས་པོ་བསྡུས་པ་ཙམ་ངས་གང་དུ་བསྟན་པ་དེ་ནི་མདོ་སྡེ་ཡིན་ནོ། །དངོས་པོ་བཞི་གང་ཞེ་ན། འདི་ལྟ་སྟེ། ཐོས་པའི་དངོས་པོ་དང་། སྐྱབས་སུ་འགྲོ་བའི་དངོས་པོ་དང་། བསླབ་པའི་དངོས་པོ་དང་། བྱང་ཆུབ་ཀྱི་དངོས་པོའོ། །དངོས་པོ་དགུ་གང་ཞེ་ན། སེམས་ཅན་དུ་གདགས་པའི་དངོས་པོ་དང་། དེའི་ལོངས་སྤྱོད་ཀྱི་དངོས་པོ་དང་། དེ་འབྱུང་བའི་དངོས་པོ་དང་། དེ་འབྱུང་བ་གནས་པའི་དངོས་པོ་དང་། དེའི་ཀུན་ནས་ཉོན་མོངས་པ་དང་། རྣམ་པར་བྱང་བའི་དངོས་པོ་དང་། དེའི་སྣ་ཚོགས་ཀྱི་དངོས་པོ་དང་། སྟོན་པའི་དངོས་པོ་དང་། བསྟན་པར་བྱ་བའི་དངོས་པོ་དང་། འཁོར་གྱི་དངོས་པོའོ། །དངོས་པོ་ཉི་ཤུ་རྩ་དགུ་གང་ཞེ་ན། ཀུན་ནས་ཉོན་མོངས་པའི་ཕྱོགས་ལས་བརྩམས་ཏེ། འདུ་བྱེད་བསྡུ་བའི་དངོས་པོ་དང་། དེའི་གོ་རིམས་རྗེས་སུ་འཇུག་པའི་དངོས་པོ་དང་། དེ་དག་ཉིད་ལ་གང་ཟག་གི་མིང་དུ་བྱས་ནས་ཕྱི་མར་འབྱུང་བའི་རྒྱུའི་དངོས་པོ་དང་། ཆོས་ཀྱི་མིང་དུ་བྱས་ནས་ཕྱི་མར་འབྱུང་བའི་རྒྱུའི་དངོས་པོ་དང་། རྣམ་པར་བྱང་བའི་ཕྱོགས་ལས་བརྩམས་ཏེ། དམིགས་པ་ལ་ཉེ་བར་གཏོད་པའི་དངོས་པོ་དང་། དེ་ཉིད་ལ་རྩོལ་བའི་དངོས་པོ་དང་། སེམས་ཅན་གནས་པའི་དངོས་པོ་དང་། ཚེ་འདི་ལ་བདེ་བར་གནས་པའི་དངོས་པོ་དང་། སྡུག་བསྔལ་ཐམས་ཅད་ལས་ཡང་དག་པར་འདའ་བའི་ཐབས་ཀྱི་དམིགས་པའི་དངོས་པོ་དང་། དེ་ཡོངས་སུ་ཤེས་པའི་དངོས་པོ་ནི་ཕྱིན་ཅི་ལོག་གི་གནས་ཡོངས་སུ་ཤེས་པ་དང་། སེམས་ཅན་དུ་འདུ་ཤེས་པ་ལས་བརྩམས་ཏེ་ཕྱི་རོལ་གྱི་སེམས་ཅན་རྣམས་ལ་ལོག་པར་སྒྲུབ་པའི་གནས་ཡོངས་སུ་ཤེས་པ་དང་། ནང་ལ་མངོན་པའི་ང་རྒྱལ་

"Mañjuśrī, my teachings which gather together the categories of the Dharma, classifying them into four, nine, or twenty-nine subjects, are the Sūtras.

"What are the four categories? They are: listening, taking refuge, training, and enlightenment.[7]

"What are the nine categories? They are the categories of designating sentient beings, of their resources, their births, their states of being, their affliction and purification, their varieties, the teacher, the teaching, and associates.

"What are the twenty-nine categories? Those [categories] concerned with the class of afflicted phenomena are the following:[8] (1) collected compounded phenomena, (2) progressive engagement with them, (3) the cause of their future arising after having named persons with respect to them, and (4) the cause of their future arising after having named things.

"Those [categories] concerned with the class of purified phenomena are the following:[9] (5) designating objects of observation, (6) exertion with respect to just those, (7) the abodes of sentient beings, (8) abiding happily in this lifetime, (9) objects of observation that are means for completely transcending all suffering, and (10) thoroughly knowing those [objects of observation], which is threefold: thoroughly knowing the basis of error; thoroughly knowing the basis of the mistaken attainments of non-Buddhists, beginning with the conception of sentient beings [as existing in terms of a self]; and thoroughly knowing the basis of the absence of conceit among Buddhists.

མེད་པའི་གནས་ཡོངས་སུ་ཤེས་པས་དེ་ཡང་རྣམ་པ་གསུམ་དང་། བསྒོམ་པའི་གནས་ཀྱི་དངོས་པོ་དང་། མངོན་དུ་བྱ་བའི་དངོས་པོ་དང་། བསྒོམ་པའི་དངོས་པོ་དང་། དེ་སྙིང་པོར་བྱ་བའི་དངོས་པོ་དང་། དེའི་རྣམ་པའི་དངོས་པོ་དང་། དེའི་དམིགས་པའི་དངོས་པོ་དང་། སྤྲངས་པ་དང་། མ་སྤྲངས་པ་ལ་དཔྱོད་པ་ལ་མཁས་པའི་དངོས་པོ་དང་། དེ་ལས་རྣམ་པར་གཡེང་བའི་དངོས་པོ་དང་། དེ་ལས་རྣམ་པར་མི་གཡེང་བའི་དངོས་པོ་དང་། རྣམ་པར་མི་གཡེང་བ་གནས་ཀྱི་དངོས་པོ་དང་། བསྒོམ་པ་ལས་ཡོངས་སུ་སྦྱོབ་པའི་སྦྱོར་བ་གསལ་བའི་དངོས་པོ་དང་། བསྒོམ་པའི་ཕན་ཡོན་གྱི་དངོས་པོ་དང་། དེ་བརྟན་པའི་དངོས་པོ་དང་། འཕགས་པའི་དབང་ཕྱུག་བསྡུ་བའི་དངོས་པོ་དང་། འཕགས་པའི་ཕྱོགས་དང་འཁོར་བསྡུ་བའི་དངོས་པོ་དང་། དེ་ཁོ་ན་རབ་ཏུ་རྟོགས་པའི་དངོས་པོ་དང་། མྱ་ངན་ལས་འདས་པ་ཡང་དག་པར་འཐོབ་པའི་དངོས་པོ་དང་། ལེགས་པར་གསུངས་པའི་ཆོས་འདུལ་བ་ལ་འཇིག་རྟེན་པའི་ཡང་དག་པའི་ལྟ་བ་འདི་ལས་ཕྱི་རོལ་པ་ཐམས་ཅད་ཀྱི་ཡང་དག་པའི་ལྟ་བ་ལས་སྒྲི་བོར་གྱུར་པ་ཉིད་ཀྱི་དངོས་པོ་དང་། དེ་མི་བསྒོམ་པས་ཡོངས་སུ་ཉམས་པས་དངོས་པོ་སྟེ། འཇམ་དཔལ་འདི་ལྟར་ལེགས་པར་གསུངས་པའི་ཆོས་འདུལ་བ་ལ་ནི་མི་བསྒོམ་པས་ཡོངས་སུ་ཉམས་པར་འགྱུར་གྱི། ལྟ་བའི་ཉེས་པས་ནི་མ་ཡིན་ནོ། །འཇམ་དཔལ་ངས་གང་དུ་ཉན་ཐོས་རྣམས་དང་། བྱང་ཆུབ་སེམས་དཔའ་རྣམས་ཀྱི་སོ་སོར་ཐར་པའམ། སོ་སོར་ཐར་པ་དང་ལྡན་པ་ཡོངས་སུ་བསྟན་པ་གང་ཡིན་པ་དེ་ནི་འདུལ་བའི་དངོས་པོ་ཡིན་ནོ། །བཅོམ་ལྡན་འདས་བྱང་ཆུབ་སེམས་དཔའ་རྣམས་ཀྱི་སོ་སོར་ཐར་པ་རྣམ་

"[There are also] the categories of: (11) the basis of meditation, (12) actualization, (13) meditation, (14) doing [meditation] as an essential activity, (15) the aspects of [meditation], (16) its objects of observation, (17) skill concerning investigation into what has been abandoned and what has not yet been abandoned, (18) being distracted from that [meditation], (19) not being distracted from [meditation], (20) the basis of non-distraction, (21) clearing away aversion to meditation through meditating, (22) the benefits of meditation, (23) the stability of that [meditation], (24) the collection of the Āryas' sovereign traits, (25) the gathering of Āryas and their associates, (26) the realization of suchness, (27) the complete attainment of nirvāṇa, (28) the fact that the correct views held by worldlings with respect to the disciplinary doctrine that has been well explained are superior to the correct views held by all of those who are outside of this [doctrine].

"[Finally,] (29) the category of degeneration due to not cultivating that [disciplinary doctrine]. Mañjuśrī, with respect to the disciplinary doctrine that has been well explained, degeneration occurs due to non-cultivation, not due to faulty view.

"Mañjuśrī, this category [of the Vinaya] consists of my teachings of the prātimokṣa for Śrāvakas and Bodhisattvas and what is associated with prātimokṣa."

"Bhagavan, of how many aspects is the Bodhisattvas' prātimokṣa known to consist?"

པ་དུས་བསྡུས་པར་རིག་པར་བགྱི་ལགས། འཇམ་དཔལ་རྣམ་པ་བདུན་གྱིས་ཏེ། ཡང་
དག་པར་བླང་བའི་ཚིག་བསྟན་པ་དང་། ཐམ་པའི་གནས་ལྟ་བུའི་དངོས་པོ་བསྟན་པ་དང་།
ལྟུང་བའི་གནས་ལྟ་བུའི་དངོས་པོ་བསྟན་པ་དང་། ལྟུང་བའི་ངོ་བོ་ཉིད་བསྟན་པ་དང་། ལྟུང་
བམ་ཡིན་པའི་ངོ་བོ་ཉིད་བསྟན་པ་དང་། ལྟུང་བ་ལས་དབྱུང་བ་བསྟན་པ་དང་། སྡོམ་པ་
གཏོང་བ་བསྟན་པས་སོ། །འཇམ་དཔལ་ངས་གང་དུ་མཚན་ཉིད་རྣམ་པ་བཅུ་གཅིག
བཤད་པ་དང་། རྣམ་པར་ཕྱེ་བ་དང་། བསྟན་པ་གང་ཡིན་པ་དེ་ནི་མ་མོ་ཞེས་བྱའོ། །དེ་
ལ་མཚན་ཉིད་རྣམ་པ་བཅུ་གཅིག་གང་ཞེ་ན། ཀུན་རྫོབ་ཀྱི་མཚན་ཉིད་དང་། དོན་དམ་
པའི་མཚན་ཉིད་དང་། བྱང་ཆུབ་ཀྱི་ཕྱོགས་དང་མཐུན་པའི་ཆོས་རྣམས་ཀྱི་དམིགས་པའི་
མཚན་ཉིད་དང་། རྣམ་པའི་མཚན་ཉིད་དང་། ངོ་བོ་ཉིད་ཀྱི་མཚན་ཉིད་དང་། དེའི་
འབྲས་བུའི་མཚན་ཉིད་དང་། དེ་མྱོང་བ་རྣམ་པར་བསྙད་པའི་མཚན་ཉིད་དང་། དེའི་བར་
དུ་གཅོད་པའི་ཆོས་ཀྱི་མཚན་ཉིད་དང་། དེ་དང་རྗེས་སུ་མཐུན་པའི་ཆོས་ཀྱི་མཚན་ཉིད་
དང་། དེའི་ཉེས་དམིགས་ཀྱི་མཚན་ཉིད་དང་། དེའི་ཕན་ཡོན་གྱི་མཚན་ཉིད་དོ། །
འཇམ་དཔལ་དེ་ལ་ཀུན་རྫོབ་ཀྱི་མཚན་ཉིད་ནི་རྣམ་པ་གསུམ་སྟེ། གང་ཟག་བསྟན་པ་
དང་། ཀུན་བརྟགས་པའི་ངོ་བོ་ཉིད་བསྟན་པ་དང་། ཆོས་རྣམས་ཀྱི་བྱེད་པ་དང་། གཡོ་
བ་དང་། ལས་བྱེད་པ་བསྟན་པར་བལྟ་བར་བྱའོ། །དེ་ལ་དོན་དམ་པའི་མཚན་ཉིད་ནི་དེ་
བཞིན་ཉིད་རྣམ་པ་བདུན་བསྟན་པ་ཡིན་པར་བལྟ་བར་བྱའོ། །དམིགས་པའི་མཚན་ཉིད་ནི་
ཤེས་བྱའི་དངོས་པོ་རྣམ་པ་ཐམས་ཅད་བསྟན་པ་ཡིན་པར་བལྟ་བར་བྱའོ། །རྣམ་པའི་

"Mañjuśrī, it consists of seven aspects: teachings concerning properly performed rites, teachings of things such as the bases of defeat,[10] teachings of things such as the bases of infractions, teachings of the own-being of infractions, teachings of the own-being of non-infractions, teachings concerning emerging from infractions, and teachings concerning abandonment of vows.

"Mañjuśrī, 'Mātṛkās' are that which I have explained, differentiated, and taught in terms of eleven types of characters: the conventional character, the ultimate character, the character of the objects of observation of phenomena in harmony with enlightenment, the character of aspects, the character of own-being, the character of the fruition of that, the character of describing the experience of that, the character of phenomena which interrupt that, the character of phenomena concordant with that, the character of disadvantages to that, and the character of benefits to that.

"Mañjuśrī, view the conventional character as being of three types: the teaching of persons; the teaching of the own-being of the imputational nature; and the teaching of the activities, movements, and workings of phenomena.

"View the ultimate character in terms of the teaching of suchness in seven aspects. View the character of the objects of observation in terms of the teaching of all aspects of things that are objects of knowledge. View the character of aspects in terms of the teaching of the eight types of analytical reasoning.

མཚན་ཉིད་ནི་བརྟག་པ་རྣམ་པ་བརྒྱད་བསྟན་པ་ཡིན་པར་བལྟ་བར་བྱ་སྟེ། བརྟག་པ་རྣམ་པ་བརྒྱད་གང་ཞེ་ན། བདེན་པ་དང་། གནས་པ་དང་། སྐྱོན་དང་། ཡོན་ཏན་དང་། ཚུལ་དང་། འཇུག་པ་དང་། རིགས་པ་དང་། བསྡུས་པ་དང་རྒྱས་པས་སོ། །དེ་ལ་བདེན་པ་ནི་དེ་བཞིན་ཉིད་གང་ཡིན་པའོ། །གནས་པ་ནི་གང་ཟག་རྣམ་པར་གཞག་པའམ། ཀུན་བརྟགས་པའི་ངོ་བོ་ཉིད་རྣམ་པར་གཞག་པའམ། མགོ་གཅིག་དང་། རྣམ་པར་དབྱེ་བ་དང་། དྲིས་ཏེ་ལན་གདབ་པ་རྣམ་པར་གཞག་པའམ། གཞག་པ་རྣམ་པར་གཞག་པའམ། གསང་བ་དང་རྣམ་པར་དབྱེ་བ་ལ་ལན་གདབ་པ་རྣམ་པར་གཞག་པ་གང་ཡིན་པའོ། །སྐྱོན་རྣམས་ནི་ངས་ཀུན་ནས་ཉོན་མོངས་པའི་ཆོས་རྣམས་ཀྱི་ཉེས་དམིགས་རྣམ་གྲངས་དུ་མར་བསྟན་པ་གང་ཡིན་པ་དག་གོ། །ཡོན་ཏན་རྣམས་ནི་ངས་རྣམ་པར་བྱང་བའི་ཆོས་རྣམས་ཀྱི་ཕན་ཡོན་རྣམ་གྲངས་དུ་མར་བསྟན་པ་གང་ཡིན་པ་དག་གོ། །ཚུལ་ནི་རྣམ་པ་དྲུག་ཏུ་རིག་པར་བྱ་སྟེ། དེ་ཁོ་ནའི་དོན་གྱི་ཚུལ་དང་། འཐོབ་པའི་ཚུལ་དང་། བཤད་པའི་ཚུལ་དང་། མཐའ་གཉིས་རྣམ་པར་སྤངས་པའི་ཚུལ་དང་། བསམ་གྱིས་མི་ཁྱབ་པའི་ཚུལ་དང་། དགོངས་པའི་ཚུལ་ལོ། །འཇུག་པ་ནི་དུས་གསུམ་དང་འདུས་བྱས་ཀྱི་མཚན་ཉིད་གསུམ་དང་། རྐྱེན་བཞི་པོ་དག་གོ། །རིགས་པ་ནི་རྣམ་པ་བཞིར་རིག་པར་བྱ་སྟེ། ལྟོས་པའི་རིགས་པ་དང་། བྱ་བ་བྱེད་པའི་རིགས་པ་དང་། འཐད་པས་སྒྲུབ་པའི་རིགས་པ་དང་། ཆོས་ཉིད་ཀྱི་རིགས་པའོ། །དེ་ལ་ལྟོས་པའི་རིགས་པ་ནི་འདུ་བྱེད་རྣམས་འབྱུང་བ་དང་། རྗེས་སུ་ཐ་སྙད་གདགས་པའི་རྒྱུ་གང་དག་ཡིན་པ་དང་། རྐྱེན་གང་དག་ཡིན་པ་སྟེ།

What are the eight types of analytical reasoning? [They are analytical reasoning concerning]: truth, positings, faults, good qualities, modes, engagement, reasoning, and condensing and elaborating.

"Truth is whatever is suchness. Positings are: positing persons; or positing the own-being of the imputational; or positing categorically, making differentiations, or answering a rhetorical question; or positing a position; or positing an answer to the secret and to the differentiated.

"Faults are the disadvantages of afflicted phenomena which I have described in many forms of explanation.[11] Good qualities are the benefits of pure phenomena which I have described in many forms of explanation.[12]

"Modes should be known through six aspects: the mode of the meaning of suchness, the mode of attainment, the mode of explanation, the mode of abandoning the two extremes, the mode of the inconceivable, and the mode of [Buddha's] thought. Engagement [refers to] the three times, the three characters of compounded phenomena, and the four conditions.

"Reasoning should be known in terms of four aspects: analysis of dependence, analysis of performance of functions, analysis of logical correctness, and analysis of reality.

"In regard to 'analysis of dependence', whatever are causes and conditions for compounded phenomena, and their subsequent conventional designations are [the subject matter of] analysis of dependence.[13] Whatever are causes and conditions

དེ་ནི་ལྟོས་པའི་རིགས་པ་ཡིན་ནོ། །ཆོས་རྣམས་འཐོབ་པའམ། འགྲུབ་པའམ། སྐྱེས་པ་རྣམས་ལས་བྱེད་པར་འགྱུར་བའི་རྒྱུ་གང་དག་ཡིན་པ་དང་། རྐྱེན་གང་དག་ཡིན་པ་དེ་ནི་བྱ་བ་བྱེད་པའི་རིགས་པ་ཡིན་ནོ། །སོ་སོའི་ཤེས་པ་དང་། བཤད་པ་དང་། སྨྲས་པའི་དོན་སྒྲུབ་པ་དང་། ལེགས་པར་ཁོང་དུ་ཆུད་པར་བྱ་བའི་རྒྱུ་གང་དག་ཡིན་པ་དང་། རྐྱེན་གང་དག་ཡིན་པ་དེ་ནི་འཐད་པས་སྒྲུབ་པའི་རིགས་པ་ཡིན་ནོ། །དེ་ཡང་མདོར་བསྡུ་ན་རྣམ་པ་གཉིས་ཏེ། ཡོངས་སུ་དག་པ་དང་། ཡོངས་སུ་མ་དག་པའོ། །དེ་ལ་ཡོངས་སུ་དག་པའི་མཚན་ཉིད་ནི་ལྔའོ། །ཡོངས་སུ་མ་དག་པའི་མཚན་ཉིད་ནི་བདུན་ནོ། །དེ་ལ་ཡོངས་སུ་དག་པའི་མཚན་ཉིད་ལྔ་པོ་དག་གང་ཞེ་ན། དེ་མངོན་སུམ་དུ་དམིགས་པའི་མཚན་ཉིད་དང་། དེ་ལ་གནས་པ་མངོན་སུམ་དུ་དམིགས་པའི་མཚན་ཉིད་དང་། རང་གི་རིགས་ཀྱི་དཔེ་ཉེ་བར་སྦྱོར་བའི་མཚན་ཉིད་དང་། ཡོངས་སུ་གྲུབ་པའི་མཚན་ཉིད་དང་། ལུང་ཤིན་ཏུ་རྣམ་པར་དག་པ་གཏན་ལ་ཕབ་པར་བསྟན་པའི་མཚན་ཉིད་དོ། །དེ་ལ་འདུ་བྱེད་ཐམས་ཅད་མི་རྟག་པ་ཉིད་དང་། འདུ་བྱེད་ཐམས་ཅད་སྡུག་བསྔལ་བ་ཉིད་དང་། ཆོས་ཐམས་ཅད་བདག་མེད་པ་ཉིད་འཇིག་རྟེན་ན་མངོན་སུམ་དུ་དམིགས་པ་དང་། དེ་ལྟ་བུ་དང་འཐུན་པ་གང་ཡིན་པ་དེ་ནི་མངོན་སུམ་དུ་དམིགས་པའི་མཚན་ཉིད་ཡིན་ནོ། །འདུ་བྱེད་ཐམས་ཅད་སྐད་ཅིག་པ་ཉིད་དང་། འཇིག་རྟེན་ཕ་རོལ་ཡོད་པ་ཉིད་དང་། ལས་དགེ་བ་དང་། མི་དགེ་བ་ཆུད་མི་ཟ་བ་དེ་ལ་གནས་པའི་མི་རྟག་པར་རིགས་པ་ཉིད་མངོན་སུམ་དུ་དམིགས་པ་གང་ཡིན་པ་དང་། སེམས་ཅན་སྣ་ཚོགས་ལས་སྣ་ཚོགས་ལ་གནས་པ་མངོན་སུམ་དུ

for the attainment of phenomena, their establishment, or their activities are [the subject matter of] 'analysis of performance of functions'.[14] Whatever are causes and conditions for individual understanding, explanation, establishing the meaning of propositions, and comprehension are [the subject matter of] 'analysis of logical correctness'.[15]

"Moreover, in brief, there are two types [of analysis of logical correctness]: pure and impure. The characteristics of the pure type are fivefold. The characteristics of the impure type are sevenfold. The five characteristics of the pure type are: the characteristic of directly observing something, the characteristic of directly observing the basis of something, the characteristic of providing an example of its own type, the characteristic of establishment, and the characteristic of teaching in the manner of delineating very pure scriptures.

"'The characteristic of directly observing something' is direct observation of the impermanence of all compounded phenomena, the suffering inherent in all compounded phenomena, the selflessness of all phenomena in the world, and things concordant with these. 'The characteristic of directly observing the basis of something' is: directly observing the reasoning concerning impermanence, which is based on the momentariness of all compounded phenomena, the existence of a future world, and the non-dissipation of virtuous and non-virtuous actions;[16] directly observing that various sentient beings are based on various karmas; directly observing

དམིགས་པ་གང་ཡིན་པ་དང་། སེམས་ཅན་བདེ་བ་དང་སྡུག་བསྔལ་བ་ལས་དགེ་བ་དང་མི་དགེ་བ་ལ་གནས་པ་མངོན་སུམ་དུ་དམིགས་པ་གང་ཡིན་པ་དང་། གང་གིས་མངོན་སུམ་དུ་མ་གྱུར་པ་ལ་རྗེས་སུ་དཔག་པར་བྱ་བ་དང་། དེ་ལྟ་བུ་དང་འཐུན་པ་གང་ཡིན་པ་དེ་ནི་དེ་ལ་གནས་པ་མངོན་སུམ་དུ་དམིགས་པའི་མཚན་ཉིད་ཡིན་ནོ། །ནང་དང་ཕྱི་རོལ་གྱི་འདུ་བྱེད་རྣམས་ལ་འཇིག་རྟེན་ཐམས་ཅད་ལ་གྲགས་པའི་འཆི་འཕོ་དང་སྐྱེ་བ་དམིགས་པ་ཉེ་བར་སྒྱུར་བ་དང་། སྐྱེ་བ་ལ་སོགས་པའི་སྡུག་བསྔལ་དམིགས་པ་ཉེ་བར་སྒྱུར་བ་དང་། རང་དབང་མེད་པའི་དམིགས་པ་ཉེ་བར་སྒྱུར་བ་དང་། ཕ་རོལ་དག་ན་ཡང་འཇིག་རྟེན་ཐམས་ཅད་ལ་གྲགས་པའི་འགྱུར་བ་དང་། རྒུད་པ་དམིགས་པ་ཉེ་བར་སྒྱུར་བ་དང་། དེ་ལྟ་བུ་དང་འཐུན་པ་གང་ཡིན་པ་དེ་ནི་རང་གི་རིགས་ཀྱི་དཔེ་ཉེ་བར་སྒྱུར་བའི་མཚན་ཉིད་ཡིན་པར་རིག་པར་བྱའོ། །དེ་ལྟར་དེ་མངོན་སུམ་དུ་དམིགས་པའི་མཚན་ཉིད་དང་། དེ་ལ་གནས་པ་མངོན་སུམ་དུ་དམིགས་པའི་མཚན་ཉིད་དང་། རང་གི་རིགས་ཀྱི་དཔེ་ཉེ་བར་སྒྱུར་བའི་མཚན་ཉིད་གང་ཡིན་པ་དེ་ནི་གྲུབ་པར་བྱ་བ་ལ་གཅིག་ཏུ་ངེས་པའི་ཕྱིར་ཡོངས་སུ་གྲུབ་པའི་མཚན་ཉིད་ཡིན་པར་རིག་པར་བྱའོ། །འཇམ་དཔལ་གཏན་ལ་བབ་པར་བསྟན་པ་ཐམས་ཅད་མཁྱེན་པས་གསུངས་པ་འདི་ལྟ་སྟེ། མྱ་ངན་ལས་འདས་པ་ནི་ཞི་བའོ་ཞེས་བྱ་བ་དང་། དེ་ལྟ་བུ་དང་འཐུན་པ་གང་ཡིན་པ་དེ་ནི་ལུང་ཤིན་ཏུ་རྣམ་པར་དག་པ་གཏན་ལ་བབ་པར་བསྟན་པའི་མཚན་ཉིད་ཡིན་པར་རིག་པར་བྱའོ། །དེ་ལྟ་བས་ན་མཚན་ཉིད་རྣམ་པ་ལྔ་པོ་དེ་དག་གིས་རིགས་པ་བརྟག་པ་ཡོངས་སུ་དག་པ་སྟེ། ཡོངས་སུ་དག་པའི་ཕྱིར་བསྟེན་

that sentient beings' happiness or suffering is based on their virtuous or non-virtuous actions; inferring what is not directly observed by means of these; and things concordant with these.

"Know that 'the characteristic of providing an example of its own type' is: providing [examples] of observing disintegration and arising which are well known in all worlds with respect to internal and external compounded phenomena; providing [examples] of observing the suffering of birth and so forth; providing [examples] of observing lack of autonomy; providing [examples] of observing the fortunes and troubles that are known in all worlds as well as in future worlds; and things concordant with these.

"Through ascertaining that [the three]—the characteristic of directly observing something, the characteristic of directly observing a basis of something, and the characteristic of providing an example of its own type—are unitary in terms of establishment, one knows 'the characteristic of establishment'.

"Mañjuśrī, know that the teachings set forth by omniscient persons—teachings such as: 'Nirvāṇa is peace,' and things that are concordant with such teachings—constitute 'the characteristic of teaching in the manner of delineating very pure scriptures'. Thus, by way of these five characteristics, analytical reasonings are purified. Because they are purified, you should rely on them."

པར་བྱའོ། །བཅོམ་ལྡན་འདས་ཐམས་ཅད་མཁྱེན་པའི་མཚན་ཉིད་རྣམ་པ་དུས་རྫོགས་པར་བགྱི་ལགས། འཇམ་དཔལ་ལ་ཞུས་ཏེ། གང་སུ་ཡང་རུང་བ་ཞིག་བྱུང་ན། འཇིག་རྟེན་དུ་ཐམས་ཅད་མཁྱེན་པ་ཉིད་དུ་སྒྲ་རྣམ་པར་གྲགས་པ་དང་། སྐྱེས་བུ་ཆེན་པོའི་མཚན་སུམ་ཅུ་རྩ་གཉིས་དང་ལྡན་པ་དང་། སྟོབས་བཅུས་སེམས་ཅན་ཐམས་ཅད་ཀྱི་ཐེ་ཚོམ་ཐམས་ཅད་གཅོད་པ་དང་། མི་འཇིགས་པ་བཞིས་ཆོས་སྟོན་པའི་དེའི་ཚིག་ལ་ཕས་ཀྱི་རྒོལ་བ་ཐམས་ཅད་ཀྱིས་བརྐལ་དུ་མེད་ཅིང་བརྩད་དུ་མེད་པ་གང་ཡིན་པ་དང་། སྔའི་ཆོས་འདུལ་བ་ལ་འཕགས་པའི་ལམ་ཡན་ལག་བརྒྱད་པ་སྣང་ཞིང་དགེ་སྦྱོང་བཞི་སྣང་བ་ཡིན་ཏེ། དེ་ལྟར་ན་འབྱུང་བ་དང་། མཚན་དང་། ཐེ་ཚོམ་གཅོད་པ་དང་། བརྐལ་དུ་མེད་ཅིང་བརྩད་དུ་མེད་པ་དང་། དགེ་སྦྱོང་དམིགས་པས་ཐམས་ཅད་མཁྱེན་པའི་མཚན་ཉིད་ལྟར་རིག་པར་བྱའོ། །དེ་ལྟར་འཐད་པའི་སྒྲུབ་པའི་རིགས་པ་དེ་ནི་མངོན་སུམ་གྱི་ཚད་མ་དང་། རྗེས་སུ་དཔག་པའི་ཚད་མ་དང་། ཡིད་ཆེས་པའི་ལུང་གི་ཚད་མས་མཚན་ཉིད་ལྔ་པོ་དག་གིས་ཡོངས་སུ་དག་པ་ཡིན་ནོ། །ཡོངས་སུ་མ་དག་པའི་མཚན་ཉིད་རྣམ་པ་བདུན་གང་ཞེ་ན། དེ་ལས་གཞན་དང་འཐུན་པར་དམིགས་པའི་མཚན་ཉིད་དང་། དེ་ལ་གཞན་དང་མི་འཐུན་པར་དམིགས་པའི་མཚན་ཉིད་དང་། ཐམས་ཅད་འཐུན་པར་དམིགས་པའི་མཚན་ཉིད་དང་། ཐམས་ཅད་མི་འཐུན་པར་དམིགས་པའི་མཚན་ཉིད་དང་། གཞན་གྱི་རིགས་ཀྱི་དཔེ་ཉེ་བར་སྦྱར་བའི་མཚན་ཉིད་དང་། ཡོངས་སུ་མ་གྲུབ་པའི་མཚན་ཉིད་དང་། ལུང་ཤིན་ཏུ་རྣམ་པར་མ་དག་པ་བསྟན་པའི་མཚན་ཉིད་དོ། །དེ་ལ་ཆོས་ཐམས་ཅད་ཡིད་ཀྱི་རྣམ

"Bhagavan, by how many aspects are the characteristics of omniscient persons to be known?"[17]

"Mañjuśrī, they are known through five aspects: Suitable persons arise who are proclaimed in all worlds as omniscient; they are endowed with the thirty-two marks of a great being; they eliminate all the doubts of every sentient being through the ten powers; through the four fearlessnesses,[18] the words of their doctrinal teachings are free from the objections and disputes of all opponents; and in their disciplinary doctrine the eight branches of the path of Āryas and the four virtuous practices appear. Thus you should know that arising, marks, elimination of doubts, freedom from objections and freedom from disputes, and observing virtuous practices are the five characteristics of omniscient persons.

"Analysis of logical correctness is purified through: direct valid perception, valid inference, valid believable scriptures, and through these five characteristics [of omniscient persons].

"What are the seven characteristics of impure reasonings?[19] They are: having objects of observation concordant with what is other than that [which one is trying to establish]; having objects of observation discordant with what is other than that [which one is trying to establish]; having objects of observation that are concordant with everything; having objects of observation that are discordant with everything; providing examples of another type; non-establishment; and the teachings of impure scriptures.

པར་ཤེས་པས་རྣམ་པར་ཤེས་པར་བྱ་བ་ཉིད་གང་ཡིན་པ་དེ་ནི་ཐམས་ཅད་འཐུན་པར་དམིགས་པའི་མཚན་ཉིད་ཡིན་ནོ། །རྟགས་དང་ངོ་བོ་ཉིད་དང་། ལས་དང་ཆོས་དང་རྒྱུ་དང་འབྲས་བུ་མཚན་ཉིད་མི་འཐུན་པ་རྣམས་ཀྱི་མཚན་ཉིད་མི་འཐུན་པ་གང་ཡང་རུང་བས་ཕན་ཚུན་མཚན་ཉིད་མི་འཐུན་པར་ངེས་པ་ཉིད་གང་ཡིན་པ་དེ་ནི་ཐམས་ཅད་མི་འཐུན་པར་དམིགས་པའི་མཚན་ཉིད་ཡིན་ནོ། །འཛམ་དཔལ་དེ་ལ་དེ་ལས་གཞན་དང་འཐུན་པར་དམིགས་པའི་མཚན་ཉིད་དཔེ་དང་བཅས་པ་ལ་ཐམས་ཅད་མི་འཐུན་པར་དམིགས་པའི་མཚན་ཉིད་ཡོད་པས་ངེས་ན་དེ་གྲུབ་པར་བྱ་བ་ལ་གཅིག་ཏུ་མ་ངེས་པའི་ཕྱིར་དེ་ནི་ཡོངས་སུ་མ་གྲུབ་པའི་མཚན་ཉིད་ཅེས་བྱའོ། །དེ་ལས་གཞན་དང་མི་འཐུན་པར་དམིགས་པའི་མཚན་ཉིད་དཔེ་དང་བཅས་པ་ལ་ཡང་ཐམས་ཅད་འཐུན་པར་དམིགས་པའི་མཚན་ཉིད་ཡོད་པས་ངེས་ན་དེ་གྲུབ་པར་བྱ་བ་ལ་གཅིག་ཏུ་མ་ངེས་པའི་ཕྱིར་དེ་ཡང་ཡོངས་སུ་མ་གྲུབ་པའི་མཚན་ཉིད་ཅེས་བྱའོ། །ཡོངས་སུ་མ་གྲུབ་པའི་ཕྱིར་རིགས་པས་བརྟག་པ་ཡོངས་སུ་མ་དག་པ་ཡིན་ཏེ། ཡོངས་སུ་མ་དག་པའི་ཕྱིར་བསྟེན་པར་མི་བྱའོ། །དེ་ལྟར་ཤིན་ཏུ་རྣམ་པར་མ་དག་པ་བསྟན་པའི་མཚན་ཉིད་ནི་རང་བཞིན་ཉིད་ཀྱིས་ཡོངས་སུ་མ་དག་པ་ཡིན་པར་རིག་པར་བྱའོ། །དེ་ལ་དེ་བཞིན་གཤེགས་པ་རྣམས་བྱུང་ཡང་རུང་། མ་བྱུང་ཡང་རུང་སྟེ། ཆོས་གནས་པར་བྱ་བའི་ཕྱིར་ཆོས་ཉིད་དབྱིངས་གནས་པ་ཉིད་གང་ཡིན་པ་དེ་ནི་ཆོས་ཉིད་ཀྱི་རིགས་པ་ཡིན་ནོ། །དེ་ལ་བསྡུས་པ་དང་རྒྱས་པ་ནི་མདོར་བསྡུ་སྟེ། ཚིག་གཅིག་གིས་བསྟན་པའི་ཆོས་ཚིག་ཕྱི་མ་ཕྱི་མ་དག་གིས་རབ་ཏུ་ཕྱེ་སྟེ། མཐར་ཐུག་པར་བྱེད་པ་གང་

"[The statement] 'All phenomena are known by the mental consciousness,' is [an example of] 'the characteristic of objects of observation that are concordant with everything'. [The statement] 'Because any discordant characteristic [such as] the discordant characteristics of signs, own-beings, karma, phenomena, causes, and effects is certainly a mutually discordant characteristic,' is [an example of] 'the characteristic of having an object of observation that is discordant with everything'.

"Mañjuśrī, the characteristic of having objects of observation that are discordant with everything exists within examples of 'the characteristic of having objects of observation that are concordant with what is other than that [which one is trying to establish]'. Therefore it is not ascertained as being united with what is to be established. This is therefore [designated as] 'the characteristic of what is non-established'.

"The characteristic of having objects of observation that are concordant with everything also exists in the examples of the characteristic of having objects of observation that are discordant with what is other than that [which one is trying to establish]. Therefore it is not ascertained as being united with what is to be established. Therefore this is also [designated as] 'the characteristic of what is non-established'.

"Because they are non-established, these analyses are impure. Because they are impure, they should not be taught.[20]

"Know that 'the characteristics of the teachings of very impure scriptures' are inherently impure.

ཡིན་པའོ། །ངས་རྣམ་པ་དང་བཅས་པའི་དམིགས་པ་འཛིན་པ་བྱང་ཆུབ་ཀྱི་ཕྱོགས་དང་
འཐུན་པའི་ཆོས་དྲན་པ་ཉེ་བར་གཞག་པ་ལ་སོགས་པ་གང་དག་བསྟན་པ་ནི་དེ་དག་གི་ངོ་
བོ་ཉིད་ཀྱི་མཚན་ཉིད་ཡིན་ནོ། །འཇིག་རྟེན་པ་དང་འཇིག་རྟེན་ལས་འདས་པར་བཅས་པའི་
ཉོན་མོངས་པ་སྤྱོང་བས་དེའི་འབྲས་བུ་འཇིག་རྟེན་དང་འཇིག་རྟེན་ལས་འདས་པའི་ཡོན་ཏན་
མངོན་པར་སྒྲུབ་པ་གང་དག་ཡིན་པ་དེ་ནི་དེའི་འབྲས་བུ་འཐོབ་པའི་མཚན་ཉིད་ཡིན་ནོ། །
དེ་ཉིད་རྣམ་པར་གྲོལ་བའི་ཤེས་པའི་སོ་སོ་ཡང་དག་པར་རིག་པ་གང་ཡིན་པ་གཞན་དག་ལ་
ཡང་རྒྱ་ཆེར་སྒྲོགས་པ་དང་། འཆད་པ་དང་། ཡང་དག་པར་སྟོན་པ་དེ་ནི་དེ་སྤྱོད་པ་རྣམ་
པར་བསྙད་པའི་མཚན་ཉིད་ཡིན་ནོ། །བྱང་ཆུབ་ཀྱི་ཕྱོགས་དང་འཐུན་པའི་ཆོས་དེ་དག་
ཉིད་སྒོམ་པ་ལ་བར་ཆད་བྱེད་པའི་གནས་ལྟ་བུ་ཉོན་མོངས་པ་ཅན་གྱི་ཆོས་གང་དག་ཡིན་པ་
དེ་ནི་དེའི་བར་དུ་གཅོད་པའི་ཆོས་ཀྱི་མཚན་ཉིད་ཡིན་ནོ། །དེ་དག་ཉིད་ལ་གཅེས་སྤྲས་བྱེད་
པའི་ཆོས་གང་དག་ཡིན་པ་དེ་ནི་དེ་དང་རྗེས་སུ་འཐུན་པའི་ཆོས་ཀྱི་མཚན་ཉིད་ཡིན་ནོ། །
བར་དུ་གཅོད་པ་རྣམས་ཀྱི་སྐྱོན་གང་ཡིན་པ་དེ་ནི་དེའི་ཉེས་དམིགས་ཀྱི་མཚན་ཉིད་ཡིན་ནོ། །
འཇམ་དཔལ་རྗེས་སུ་འཐུན་པ་རྣམས་ཀྱི་ཡོན་ཏན་གང་ཡིན་པ་དེ་ནི་དེའི་ཕན་ཡོན་གྱི་མཚན་
ཉིད་ཡིན་པར་རིག་པར་བྱའོ། །དེ་ནས་བཅོམ་ལྡན་འདས་ལ་བྱང་ཆུབ་སེམས་དཔའ་འཇམ་
དཔལ་གྱིས་ཡང་འདི་སྐད་ཅེས་གསོལ་ཏོ། །བཅོམ་ལྡན་འདས་གཟུངས་ཀྱི་དོན་གང་གིས་
བྱང་ཆུབ་སེམས་དཔའ་རྣམས་དེ་བཞིན་གཤེགས་པས་གསུངས་པའི་ཆོས་ཟབ་མོ་རྣམས་
ཀྱི་ལྡེམ་པོར་དགོངས་པའི་རྗེས་སུ་འཇུག་པར་འགྱུར་བ་བྱང་ཆུབ་སེམས་དཔའ་རྣམས་ཀྱི་

"Whether Tathāgatas arise or do not arise, because the Dharma abides, the abiding of the sphere of reality is the 'analysis of reality'.[21]

"'Condensing and elaborating' is summarizing and carefully differentiating the teachings in an orderly manner, in terms of individual doctrinal phrases. It is that which deals with [the teachings] definitively.

"That which I have taught as phenomena in harmony with enlightenment, the [four] mindful establishments and so forth, that apprehend objects of observation together with their aspects are the characteristics of the own-being of those.

"Abandoning the afflictions associated with both the mundane and supramundane manifestly establishes its fruits, which are mundane and supramundane excellent qualities. That is the characteristic of attaining its fruits.[22]

"Comprehending the liberative knowledge of 'just that', one extensively proclaims it, explains it, and perfectly teaches it to others. That is the characteristic of describing the experience of that.

"Afflicted phenomena such as the bases that interrupt the cultivation of phenomena in harmony with enlightenment are the characteristics of phenomena which interrupt that.

"Phenomena that enhance those are the characteristics of phenomena which are concordant with that. Faults that interrupt [those] are the characteristics of disadvantages to that.

མདོ་སྡེ་དང་། འདུལ་བ་དང་། མ་མོ་དེ་དག་གི་གཟུངས་ཀྱི་དོན་མ་ལུས་པ་འདི་ལས་སྣང་
རོལ་པ་རྣམས་དང་། ཐུན་མོང་མ་ལགས་པ་བཤད་དུ་གསོལ། འཇམ་དཔལ་དེའི་ཕྱིར
ཉོན་ཅིག་དང་། འདི་ལྟར་བྱང་ཆུབ་སེམས་དཔའ་རྣམས་ངའི་ལྡེམ་པོ་དག་ལ་འཇུག་པར་བྱ
བའི་ཕྱིར་གཟུངས་ཀྱི་དོན་མ་ལུས་པ་ཁྱོད་ལ་བཤད་པར་བྱའོ། །འཇམ་དཔལ་ཀུན་ནས
ཉོན་མོངས་པའི་ཆོས་གང་དག་ཡིན་པ་དང་། རྣམ་པར་བྱང་བའི་ཆོས་གང་དག་ཡིན་པ་དེ
དག་ཐམས་ཅད་ནི་གཡོ་བ་མེད་པ་གང་ཟག་མེད་པ་ཡིན་ཏེ། དེའི་ཕྱིར་ངས་ཆོས་རྣམས
རྣམ་པ་ཐམས་ཅད་དུ་བྱེད་པ་མེད་པར་བསྟན་ཏོ། །ཀུན་ནས་ཉོན་མོངས་པའི་ཆོས་རྣམས
ཀྱང་སྔོན་ཀུན་ནས་ཉོན་མོངས་པ་ཅན་དུ་གྱུར་ལ་ཕྱིས་རྣམ་པར་བྱང་བར་འགྱུར་བ་མ་ཡིན།
རྣམ་པར་བྱང་བའི་ཆོས་རྣམས་ཀྱང་ཕྱིས་རྣམ་པར་བྱང་བ་ལ་སྔོན་ཀུན་ནས་ཉོན་མོངས་པ
ཅན་དུ་གྱུར་པ་མ་ཡིན་ན། དེ་ལ་བྱིས་པ་སོ་སོའི་སྐྱེ་བོ་རྣམས་གནས་ངན་ལེན་གྱི་ལུས་ལ
ཆོས་དང་གང་ཟག་གི་ངོ་བོ་ཉིད་དུ་མངོན་པར་ཞེན་པའི་བག་ལ་ཉལ་བའི་ལྟ་བ་ལ་བརྟེན
ནས་བདག་གམ་བདག་གིར་འཛིན་ཅིང་། དེས་ན་མཐོང་ངོ་། །ཐོས་སོ། །སྣོམ་མོ། །
མྱོང་ངོ་། །རེག་གོ། །རྣམ་པར་ཤེས་སོ། །ཟའོ། །བྱེད་དོ། །ཀུན་ནས་ཉོན་མོངས་སོ། །
རྣམ་པར་བྱང་ངོ་། །ཞེས་ལོག་པར་མངོན་པར་འདུ་བྱེད་པ་འབྱུང་ངོ་། །གང་ལ་ལ་དེ་ལྟར
ཡང་དག་པ་ཇི་ལྟ་བ་བཞིན་དུ་རབ་ཏུ་ཤེས་པ་དེ་ནི་གནས་ངན་ལེན་གྱི་ལུས་རབ་ཏུ་སྤོང་ཞིང་།
ཉོན་མོངས་པ་ཐམས་ཅད་ཀྱི་གནས་མ་ཡིན་པ། ཤིན་ཏུ་རྣམ་པར་དག་པ། སྤྲོས་པ་མེད
པ། འདུས་མ་བྱས་པ། མངོན་པར་འདུ་བྱ་བ་མེད་པའི་ལུས་འཐོབ་པར་འགྱུར་ཏེ།

"Mañjuśrī, know that concordant good qualities are the characteristics of the benefits of that."

Then Bodhisattva Mañjuśrī again spoke to the Bhagavan: "Bhagavan, please teach the quintessential meanings by which Bodhisattvas enter into the indirect thought of the profound doctrines spoken by the Tathāgata. [Teach] all of the quintessential meanings of the Bodhisattvas' Sūtra discourses, Vinaya, and Mātṛkā that are distinct from those of non-Buddhists."

"Mañjuśrī, listen, and I will explain to you all of the quintessential meanings, so that Bodhisattvas may engage in that which I have spoken of indirectly.

"Mañjuśrī, all afflicted phenomena and purified phenomena are unmoving and without personhood. Therefore, I teach that phenomena are without activity in all their aspects. Further, it is not the case that afflicted phenomena are previously afflicted and subsequently purified. Nor is it the case that purified phenomena have been subsequently purified, after having been previously afflicted.

"Childish ordinary beings, relying on views that predispose them toward exaggerated adherence to the phenomena within the collection of errant tendencies and to an own-being of persons,[23] grasp at 'I' and 'mine'. Due to this, they mistakenly conceive 'I see,' 'I hear,' 'I smell,' 'I experience,' 'I touch,' 'I know,' 'I eat,' 'I act,' 'I am afflicted,' and 'I am purified.'

འཇམ་དཔལ་དེ་ནི་གཟུགས་ཀྱི་དོན་མ་ལུས་པ་ཡིན་པར་རིག་པར་བྱའོ། །དེ་ནས་བཅོམ་ལྡན་འདས་ཀྱིས་དེའི་ཚེ་ཚིགས་སུ་བཅད་པ་འདི་དག་བཀའ་སྩལ་ཏོ། །ཀུན་ནས་ཉོན་མོངས་ཆོས་དང་རྣམ་པར་བྱང་བའི་ཆོས། །ཐམས་ཅད་བྱེད་པ་མེད་ཅིང་གང་ཟག་མེད་པ་ཡིན༑ ༑དེ་ཕྱིར་དེ་དག་བྱེད་པ་མེད་པར་ངས་བཤད་དོ། །དེ་དག་སྡུ་ཕྱིར་རྣམ་པར་དག་དང་ཉོན་མོངས་མིན། །གནས་ངན་ལེན་གྱི་ལུས་ལ་བག་ལ་ཉལ་བ་ཡི། །ལྟ་ལ་བརྟེན་ནས་བདག་དང་བདག་གིར་འཛིན་བྱེད་དེ། །དེས་ན་མཐོང་ངོ་ཟའོ་བྱེད་ཅེས་བྱ་བ་དང་། །ཉོན་མོངས་རྣམ་པར་བྱང་བར་འགྱུར་རོ་སྙམ་པའང་འབྱུང་། །གང་གིས་ད་ལྟར་ཡང་དག་ཇི་བཞིན་རབ་ཤེས་པ། །དེ་ནི་གནས་ངན་ལེན་ལུས་རབ་ཏུ་སྤོང་བྱེད་ཅིང་། །ཉོན་མོངས་གནས་མིན་ཤིན་ཏུ་དག་པའི་ལུས། །སྤྲོས་པ་མེད་ཅིང་འདུས་མ་བྱས་པ་འཐོབ་པར་འགྱུར། །

བཅོམ་ལྡན་འདས་དེ་བཞིན་གཤེགས་པའི་སེམས་འབྱུང་བའི་མཚན་ཉིད་ཇི་ལྟ་བུར་རིག་པར་བགྱི་ལགས། འཇམ་དཔལ་དེ་བཞིན་གཤེགས་པ་རྣམས་ནི། སེམས་དང་། ཡིད་དང་༑ རྣམ་པར་ཤེས་པས་རབ་ཏུ་ཕྱེ་བ་མ་ཡིན་མོད་ཀྱི། འོན་ཀྱང་དེ་བཞིན་གཤེགས་པའི་སེམས་ནི། མངོན་པར་འདུ་བྱེད་པ་མེད་པར་འབྱུང་སྟེ། སྤྲུལ་པ་ལྟ་བུར་རིག་པར་བྱའོ༑ ༑བཅོམ་ལྡན་འདས་གལ་ཏེ་དེ་བཞིན་གཤེགས་པ་རྣམས་ཀྱི་ཆོས་ཀྱི་སྐུ། མངོན་པར་འདུ་བགྱི་བ་ཐམས་ཅད་དང་བྲལ་བ་ལགས་ན། འོན་ཇི་ལྟར་མངོན་པར་འདུ་བགྱི་བ་མ་མཆིས་པར་སེམས་འབྱུང་བར་འགྱུར་ལགས། འཇམ་དཔལ་སྔོན་ཐབས་དང་། ཤེས་རབ་བསྒོམ་པ་མངོན་པར་འདུས་བྱས་པའི་ཕྱིར་ཏེ། འཇམ་དཔལ་འདི་ལྟ་སྟེ་དཔེར་ན།

"Those who understand reality just as it is, having fully abandoned the collection of errant tendencies, have no basis for any of the afflictions. They attain a body that is very pure, free from elaborations, uncompounded, and free from manifest activity. Mañjuśrī, know that this is the entire quintessential meaning."

Then the Bhagavan spoke these verses:

"Afflicted phenomena and pure phenomena
are all without activity and personhood.
Thus I explain that they are without activity:
not purified or afflicted in the past or future.

"Relying on views that predispose one to the
collection of errant tendencies,
one grasps at 'I' and 'mine';
one thinks 'I see,' 'I eat,' 'I act,'
'I am afflicted,' and 'I am purified.'

"Knowing reality just as it is, abandoning the
collection of errant tendencies,
one attains a pure body with no basis for the afflictions,
free from elaborations and uncompounded."

"Bhagavan, how should one know the characteristics of a Tathāgata's mental factors?"

"Mañjuśrī, Tathāgatas are not distinguished by mind, thought, or consciousness. Indeed, you should know that a

གཉིད་ལོག་པ་སེམས་མེད་པ་ལ་ཕྱིར་སད་པར་མངོན་པར་འདུ་བྱ་བ་མེད་ཀྱང་སྔོན་མངོན་
པར་འདུས་བྱས་པའི་དབང་གིས་སད་པར་འགྱུར་བ་དང་། འགོག་པ་ལ་སྙོམས་པར་
ཞུགས་པ་ལ་ལྡང་བར་མངོན་པར་འདུ་བྱ་བ་མེད་ཀྱང་། སྔོན་མངོན་པར་འདུས་བྱས་པའི་
དབང་པོ་ནས་ལྡང་བར་འགྱུར་ཏེ། གཉིད་ལོག་པ་དང་། འགོག་པ་ལ་སྙོམས་པར་ཞུགས
པ་དག་གི་སེམས་འབྱུང་བ་ཇི་ལྟ་བ་དེ་བཞིན་དུ། དེ་བཞིན་གཤེགས་པའི་སེམས་འབྱུང་
བ་ཡང་སྔོན་ཐབས་དང་། ཤེས་རབ་བསྒོམ་པ་མངོན་པར་འདུ་བྱས་པ་ལས་རིག་པར་བྱའོ།།
བཅོམ་ལྡན་འདས་ཅི་ལགས། དེ་བཞིན་གཤེགས་པས་སྤྲུལ་པའི་སེམས་མཆིས་སམ།
མ་མཆིས་ཞེས་བགྱི། འཇམ་དཔལ་སེམས་ཡོད་པ་ཡང་མ་ཡིན། སེམས་མེད་པ་ཡང་མ་
ཡིན་ཏེ། སེམས་རང་དབང་མེད་པ་ཉིད་དང་། སེམས་ཀྱི་དབང་ཉིད་ཡིན་པའི་ཕྱིར་རོ། །
བཅོམ་ལྡན་འདས་དེ་བཞིན་གཤེགས་པའི་སྤྱོད་ཡུལ་གང་ལགས་པ་དང་། དེ་བཞིན་
གཤེགས་པའི་ཡུལ་གང་ལགས་པ་དེ་གཉིས་ལ་ཐ་དད་དུ་བགྱི་བ་ཅི་མཆིས་ལགས།
འཇམ་དཔལ་དེ་བཞིན་གཤེགས་པའི་སྤྱོད་ཡུལ་ནི། དེ་བཞིན་གཤེགས་པ་ཐམས་ཅད་
ཐུན་མོང་བ། ཡོན་ཏན་བསམ་གྱིས་མི་ཁྱབ་པ་དང་། ཚད་མེད་པའི་རྒྱན་བཀོད་པའི་
སངས་རྒྱས་ཀྱི་ཞིང་ཡོངས་སུ་དག་པ་གང་ཡིན་པའོ། །དེ་བཞིན་གཤེགས་པའི་ཡུལ་ནི་
ཁམས་ལྔ་པོ་སེམས་ཅན་གྱི་ཁམས་དང་། འཇིག་རྟེན་གྱི་ཁམས་དང་། ཆོས་ཀྱི་ཁམས་
དང་། འདུལ་བའི་ཁམས་དང་། འདུལ་བའི་ཐབས་ཀྱི་ཁམས་རྣམ་པ་ཐམས་ཅད་དེ། དེ་
གཉིས་ལ་ཐ་དད་དུ་བྱ་བ་ནི་དེ་ཡོད་དོ། །བཅོམ་ལྡན་འདས་དེ་བཞིན་གཤེགས་པའི་མངོན་

Tathāgata's mind arises free from manifest activity; it is like an emanation."[24]

"Bhagavan, if the Dharmakāya of Tathāgatas is free from all manifest activity, in that case, how could there be mental factors in the absence of manifest activity?"

"Mañjuśrī, this is due to the previous manifest activity of cultivating method and wisdom. Mañjuśrī, for example, even though during mindless sleep there is no manifest activity for awakening, due to the force of former manifest activity, one will awaken. Even though, absorbed in cessation, there is no manifest activity for rising from absorption, due to the force of former manifest activity, one will rise. Just as the mind emerges from sleep and absorption in cessation, know that the Tathāgatas' mental factors come from the previous manifest activity of cultivating method and wisdom."

"Bhagavan, do Tathāgatas have emanation minds or not?"

"Mañjuśrī, the minds do not exist, nor do the minds not exist; these minds lack autonomy and are empowered by [the Tathāgatas'] minds."[25]

"Bhagavan, what is the difference between 'the spheres of activity of Tathāgatas' and 'the domains of Tathāgatas'?"

"Mañjuśrī, the spheres of activity of Tathāgatas are the completely pure Buddha fields, arrayed with limitless, inconceivable qualities common to all Tathāgatas. The domains of

པར་རྫོགས་པར་བྱང་ཆུབ་པ་གང་ལགས་པ་དང་། ཆོས་ཀྱི་འཁོར་ལོ་བསྐོར་བ་གང་ལགས་པ་དང་། ཡོངས་སུ་མྱ་ངན་ལས་འདས་པ་ཆེན་པོ་གང་ལགས་པ་དེ་དག་གི་མཚན་ཉིད་ནི། ཇི་ལྟ་བུར་རིག་པར་བགྱི་ལགས། འཇམ་དཔལ་གཉིས་སུ་མེད་པའི་མཚན་ཉིད་ཡིན་ཏེ། མངོན་པར་རྫོགས་པར་བྱང་ཆུབ་པ་ཡང་མ་ཡིན། མངོན་པར་རྫོགས་པར་བྱང་མ་ཆུབ་པ་ཡང་མ་ཡིན། ཆོས་ཀྱི་འཁོར་ལོ་བསྐོར་བ་ཡང་མ་ཡིན། ཆོས་ཀྱི་འཁོར་ལོ་མི་བསྐོར་བ་ཡང་མ་ཡིན། ཡོངས་སུ་མྱ་ངན་ལས་འདས་པ་ཆེན་པོ་ཡང་མ་ཡིན། ཡོངས་སུ་མྱ་ངན་ལས་འདས་པ་ཆེན་པོ་མེད་པ་ཡང་མ་ཡིན་ཏེ། ཆོས་ཀྱི་སྐུ་ཤིན་ཏུ་རྣམ་པར་དག་པ་ཉིད་ཀྱི་ཕྱིར་དང་། སྤྲུལ་པའི་སྐུ་ཀུན་ཏུ་སྟོན་པ་ཉིད་ཀྱི་ཕྱིར་རོ། །བཅོམ་ལྡན་འདས་སྤྲུལ་པའི་སྐུ་ལ་བལྟ་བ་དང་། ཉན་པ་དང་། བསྙེན་བཀུར་བགྱིད་པ་དག་གིས་སེམས་ཅན་རྣམས་བསོད་ནམས་སྐྱེད་པ་དེ་ཅིའི་སླད་དུ་དེ་བཞིན་གཤེགས་པ་ལས་བྱུང་བར་རིག་པར་བགྱི་ལགས། འཇམ་དཔལ་དེ་བཞིན་གཤེགས་པ་ལ་ལྷག་པར་དམིགས་པའི་བྱ་བ་ཉིད་ཡིན་པའི་ཕྱིར་དང་། སྤྲུལ་པའི་སྐུ་ཡང་དེ་བཞིན་གཤེགས་པའི་བྱིན་གྱི་རླབས་ཉིད་ཡིན་པའི་ཕྱིར་རོ། །བཅོམ་ལྡན་འདས་མངོན་པར་འདུ་བགྱི་བ་མ་མཆིས་པར་འདྲ་བ་ལགས་ན། ཅིའི་སླད་དུ་དེ་བཞིན་གཤེགས་པའི་ཆོས་ཀྱི་སྐུ་ཁོ་ན་ལས། སེམས་ཅན་རྣམས་ལ་ཡེ་ཤེས་ཀྱི་སྣང་བ་ཆེན་པོ་འདི་འབྱུང་ཞིང་། སྤྲུལ་པའི་གཟུགས་བརྙན་དཔག་ཏུ་མ་མཆིས་པ་དག་ཀྱང་འབྱུང་ལ། ཉན་ཐོས་དང་། རང་སངས་རྒྱས་ཀྱི་རྣམ་པར་གྲོལ་བའི་ལུས་ལས་ནི་མི་འབྱུང་ལགས། འཇམ་དཔལ་འདི་ལྟ་སྟེ་དཔེར་ན། མངོན་པར་འདུ་བྱེད་པ་མེད་པར་འདྲ

Tathāgatas are the five realms in all of their aspects: the realms of sentient beings, the worldly realms, the realms of phenomena, the realms of discipline, and the realms of the methods of discipline. This is the difference between these two."

"Bhagavan, what are the characteristics of the manifest, complete enlightenment of Tathāgatas, their turning the wheel of doctrine, and their great parinirvāṇa?"

"Mañjuśrī, they are of a non-dual character. They are neither manifestly, completely enlightened, nor not manifestly, completely enlightened. They neither turn the wheel of doctrine, nor do they not turn the wheel of doctrine. They neither have a great parinirvāṇa, nor do they lack a great parinirvāṇa. This is because the Dharmakāya is very pure and the Nirmāṇakāya are fully revealed."

"Bhagavan, how is it that Nirmāṇakāya are known to come forth from Tathāgatas so that sentient beings generate merit through viewing, hearing, and revering them?"

"Mañjuśrī, [a Nirmāṇakāya comes forth] due to intensely observing the Tathāgatas, and also because Nirmāṇakāya are the blessings of the Tathāgatas."

"Bhagavan, if [Tathāgatas] appear to be without manifest activity, why is it that the great light of exalted wisdom arises for sentient beings only from the Dharmakāya of Tathāgatas, and that although incalculable emanations arise [from the

ཡང་འདི་ལྟ་སྟེ། སེམས་ཅན་མཐུ་ཆེན་པོའི་བྱིན་གྱི་རླབས་ཉིད་དང་། སེམས་ཅན་གྱི་ལས
ཀྱི་དབང་ཉིད་ཀྱི་ཕྱིར་ཟླ་བ་དང་། ཉི་མའི་དཀྱིལ་འཁོར་གྱི་ཆུ་ཤེལ་དང་། མེ་ཤེལ་ཕོ་ན
ལས་སེམས་ཅན་རྣམས་ལ་སྣང་བ་ཆེན་པོ་འབྱུང་ལ། དེ་ལས་གཞན་པའི་ཆུ་ཤེལ་དང་།
མེ་ཤེལ་དག་ལས་ནི་མི་འབྱུང་བ་དང་། ནོར་བུ་རིན་པོ་ཆེ་རིགས་དང་ལྡན་པ་དང་། ལས
ཀྱི་བྱི་དོར་ལེགས་པར་བྱས་པ་ལས་རྒྱུའི་གཟུགས་བརྙན་འབྱུང་ལ། དེ་ལས་གཞན་པའི
བྱི་དོར་མ་བྱས་པ་དག་ལས་ནི་མི་འབྱུང་བ་དེ་བཞིན་དུ་དེ་བཞིན་གཤེགས་པའི་ཆོས་ཀྱི་སྐུ
ཡང་། ཆོས་ཀྱི་དབྱིངས་དཔག་ཏུ་མེད་པ་ལ་དམིགས་པའི་ཐབས་དང་། ཤེས་རབ
བསྒོམས་པས་ཤིན་ཏུ་སྦྱངས་པ་བྱས་པ་ལས་ཡང་དག་པར་གྲུབ་པ་ཡིན་པའི་ཕྱིར། དེ་ལ
སེམས་ཅན་རྣམས་ལ་ཡེ་ཤེས་ཀྱི་སྣང་བ་ཆེན་པོ་དང་། སྤྲུལ་པའི་གཟུགས་བརྙན་དཔག་ཏུ
མེད་པ་དག་འབྱུང་གི། རྣམ་པར་གྲོལ་བའི་ལུས་འབའ་ཞིག་དག་ལས་ནི་མི་འབྱུང་ངོ་། །
བཅོམ་ལྡན་འདས་དེ་བཞིན་གཤེགས་པ་དང་། བྱང་ཆུབ་སེམས་དཔའི་བྱིན་གྱི་རླབས་ཀྱི
མཐུས། འདོད་པའི་ཁམས་ཀྱི་མིའི་ལུས་ཕུན་སུམ་ཚོགས་པ་རྒྱལ་རིགས་དང་། བྲམ
ཟེའི་རིགས་ཤིང་སཱ་ལ་ཆེན་པོ་ལྟ་བུ་རྣམས་དང་། འདོད་པ་ན་སྤྱོད་པའི་ལུས་ཕུན་སུམ
ཚོགས་པ་ཐམས་ཅད་དང་། གཟུགས་ན་སྤྱོད་པའི་ལྷའི་ལུས་ཕུན་སུམ་ཚོགས་པ་ཐམས
ཅད་དང་། གཟུགས་མ་མཆིས་པ་ན་སྤྱོད་པའི་ལྷའི་ལུས་ཕུན་སུམ་ཚོགས་པ་ཐམས་ཅད
གདའོ་ཞེས་བགྱི་བ་དེ་ལ་བཅོམ་ལྡན་འདས་དགོངས་པ་གང་ལགས། འཇམ་དཔལ་འདི
ལ་དེ་བཞིན་གཤེགས་པ་རྣམས་དེ་བཞིན་གཤེགས་པའི་བྱིན་གྱིས་བརླབས་ནས། ལམ

Tathāgatas], [emanations] do not arise from the liberation bodies of Śrāvakas and Pratyekabuddhas?"

"Mañjuśrī, for example, though [sentient beings] appear to be without manifest activity, through the blessings of powerful sentient beings and the force of the karma of sentient beings, a great light appears to sentient beings from the water-crystals and fire-crystals of the orbs of the moon and sun. [Illumination] does not arise from other water-crystals and fire-crystals.[26] A jeweler polishes a precious gem and its crystalline pattern emerges. But it will not emerge from the work of others who do not polish in this way. Similarly, the great light of exalted wisdom and innumerable emanations appear to sentient beings from the Dharmakāya because it has been established through training in cultivating method and wisdom which observe the immeasurable Dharmadhātu. However, this [light] does not arise from a mere liberation body."

"Bhagavan, with what thought in mind did the Bhagavan say, 'Due to the power of the blessings of Tathāgatas and Bodhisattvas, there exist the marvelous bodies of humans in the desire realm, such as those of the Kṣatriyas or Brahmans, and those like great śāla trees;[27] all the marvelous bodies of the gods who act in the desire realm; all the marvelous bodies of the gods who act in the form realm; and all the marvelous bodies of gods who act in the formless realm'?"

"Mañjuśrī, having received the Tathāgatas' blessings, Tathāgatas teach, just as they are, the paths and practices for

གང་དང་སྒྲུབ་པ་གང་གིས་ཐམས་ཅད་དུ་ལུས་ཕུན་སུམ་ཚོགས་པ་ཐམས་ཅད་འཐོབ་པར
འགྱུར་བའི་ལམ་དེ་དང་། སྒྲུབ་པ་དེ་ཇི་ལྟ་བ་བཞིན་དུ་སྟོན་ཏེ། གང་དག་ལམ་དེ་དང་།
སྒྲུབ་པ་དེ་སྒྲུབ་པར་བྱེད་པ་དེ་དག་ནི། ཐམས་ཅད་དུ་ལུས་ཕུན་སུམ་ཚོགས་པ་ཐམས་ཅད
འཐོབ་པར་འགྱུར་ལ། གང་དག་ལམ་དེ་དང་། སྒྲུབ་པ་དེའི་ཕྱིར་སྤྲོང་ཞིང་མི་སྙན་པར
བརྗོད་ལ། དེ་ལ་ཡང་ཀུན་ནས་མནར་སེམས་ཀྱི་སེམས་དང་ཁོང་ཁྲོ་བའི་སེམས་དང་ལྡན
ཞིང་འཆིབས་དུས་བྱེད་པ་དེ་དག་ནི་ཐམས་ཅད་དུ་ལུས་ངན་པ་ཐམས་ཅད་ཐོབ་པར་འགྱུར
ཏེ། འཇམ་དཔལ་ལ་རྣམ་གྲངས་དེས་ན་ཁྱོད་ཀྱིས་འདི་ལྟར་ལུས་ཕུན་སུམ་ཚོགས་པ་འབའ
ཞིག་དེ་བཞིན་གཤེགས་པའི་བྱིན་གྱི་རླབས་ཀྱི་མཐུ་ལས་འབྱུང་བ་མ་ཡིན་གྱི། ལུས་ངན
པར་སྐྱེ་བ་ཡང་དེ་བཞིན་གཤེགས་པའི་བྱིན་གྱི་རླབས་ཀྱི་མཐུ་ལས་འབྱུང་བར་རིག་པར
བྱའོ། །བཅོམ་ལྡན་འདས་འཇིག་རྟེན་གྱི་ཁམས་ཡོངས་སུ་མ་དག་པ་དག་ན་གང་ནི་མོད
པ་ལགས། གང་ནི་དཀོན་པ་ལགས། ཡོངས་སུ་དག་པ་དག་ན་གང་ནི་མོད་པ་ལགས།
གང་ནི་དཀོན་པ་ལགས། འཇམ་དཔལ་འཇིག་རྟེན་གྱི་ཁམས་ཡོངས་སུ་མ་དག་པ་དག་ན
དངོས་པོ་བརྒྱད་ནི་མོད་ལ། གཉིས་ནི་དཀོན་ཏེ། འདི་ལྟ་སྟེ་མུ་སྟེགས་ཅན་གཞན་དང་།
སེམས་ཅན་སྡུག་བསྔལ་བ་རྣམས་དང་། རིགས་དང་། རུས་དང་། ཚོ་རིགས་དང་།
འབྱོར་པ་དང་། རྒུད་པ་ཐ་དད་པ་རྣམས་དང་། ཉེས་པར་སྤྱད་པ་སྤྱོད་པ་རྣམས་དང་།
ཚུལ་ཁྲིམས་རལ་བ་རྣམས་དང་། ངན་སོང་རྣམས་དང་། ཐེག་པ་དམན་པ་རྣམས་དང་།
བྱང་ཆུབ་སེམས་དཔའ་བསམ་པ་དང་སྦྱོར་བ་དམན་པ་རྣམས་ནི་མོད་པ་ཡིན་ལ། བྱང

completely attaining all the marvelous bodies, gained by means of such paths and practices. Those who engage in these paths and practices attain all the marvelous bodies in all ways. Whoever abandons and reviles these paths and practices and also whoever holds bitter and angry thoughts regarding them will encounter all kinds of physical woes at the time of death.

"Mañjuśrī, by this form of explanation, know that not only do marvelous bodies arise in this way from the power of the Tathāgatas' blessings, but also the production of physical woes occurs from the power of the Tathāgatas' blessings."

"Bhagavan, in worldly realms that are not completely pure, what things are common, and what things are rare? In completely pure [worldly realms,] what things are common, and what things are rare?"[28]

"Mañjuśrī, in worldly realms that are not completely pure, eight things are common, and two are rare. Tīrthikas; suffering sentient beings; distinctions of lineage, family, patrilineage, wealth, and poverty; practitioners of harmful actions; those of degenerated ethics; bad transmigrations; Hīnayānists; and Bodhisattvas of inferior thoughts and practices are common. But Bodhisattvas who exert themselves in excellent thoughts and practices and the arising of Tathāgatas are rare.

"Mañjuśrī, in completely pure worldly realms, it is the opposite of this. Know that the eight things are rare and the two things are common."

ཆུབ་སེམས་དཔའ་བསམ་པ་དང་སྦྱོར་བ་མཆོག་དང་ལྡན་པ་རྣམས་ཀྱི་སྤྱོད་པ་དང་། དེ་
བཞིན་གཤེགས་པ་རྣམས་འབྱུང་བ་ནི་དཀོན་པ་ཡིན་ནོ། །འཇམ་དཔལ་འཇིག་རྟེན་གྱི་
ཁམས་ཡོངས་སུ་དག་པ་དག་ན་ནི་དེ་ལས་བཟློག་པས། དཀོན་པོ་བརྒྱད་ནི་དཀོན་ལ།
གཉིས་ནི་མེད་པར་རིག་པར་བྱའོ། །དེ་ནས་བཅོམ་ལྡན་འདས་ལ་བྱང་ཆུབ་སེམས་དཔའ
འཇམ་དཔལ་གྱིས་འདི་སྐད་ཅེས་གསོལ་ཏོ། །བཅོམ་ལྡན་འདས་དགོངས་པ་ངེས་པར
འགྲེལ་པའི་ཆོས་ཀྱི་རྣམ་གྲངས་འདིར་བསྟན་པ་འདིའི་མིང་ཅི་ལགས། འདི་ཇི་ལྟར་གཟུང་
བར་བགྱི། བཅོམ་ལྡན་འདས་ཀྱིས་དེ་ལ་བཀའ་སྩལ་པ། འཇམ་དཔལ་འདི་དེ་བཞིན་
གཤེགས་པའི་བྱ་བ་སྒྲུབ་པ་ངེས་པའི་དོན་བསྟན་པ་འདི་དེ་བཞིན་གཤེགས་པའི་བྱ་བ་སྒྲུབ
པ་ངེས་པའི་དོན་བསྟན་པ་ཞེས་བྱ་བར་ཟུང་ཤིག །དེ་བཞིན་གཤེགས་པའི་བྱ་བ་སྒྲུབ་པ་
ངེས་པའི་དོན་བསྟན་པ་འདི་བཤད་པ་ན། བྱང་ཆུབ་སེམས་དཔའ་བདུན་ཁྲི་ལྔ་སྟོང་གིས་
ཆོས་ཀྱི་སྐུ་ཡོངས་སུ་རྫོགས་པ་སོ་སོ་ཡང་དག་པར་རིག་པར་གྱུར་ཏོ། །བཅོམ་ལྡན་འདས
ཀྱིས་དེ་སྐད་ཅེས་བཀའ་སྩལ་ནས། འཇམ་དཔལ་གཞོན་ནུར་གྱུར་པ་དང་། ཐམས་ཅད
དང་ལྡན་པའི་འཁོར་དེ་དང་། ལྷ་དང་མི་དང་ལྷ་མ་ཡིན་དང་། དྲི་ཟར་བཅས་པའི་འཇིག
རྟེན་ཡི་རངས་ཏེ། བཅོམ་ལྡན་འདས་ཀྱིས་གསུངས་པ་ལ་མངོན་པར་བསྟོད་དོ།། ༎
འཕགས་པ་དགོངས་པ་ངེས་པར་འགྲེལ་པ་ཞེས་བྱ་བ་ཐེག་པ་ཆེན་པོའི་ཡོན་ཏན་གྱི་ཚོགས
རྣམ་པར་ངེས་པའི་ལེའུ་ཞེས་བྱ་བ་རྫོགས་སོ། །སྐད་གསར་ཆད་ཀྱིས་ཀྱང་བཅོས་ཏེ་
གཏན་ལ་ཕབ་པ།། ༎

Then the Bodhisattva Mañjuśrī asked the Bhagavan: "Bhagavan, what is the name of this form of Dharma discourse that explains your thought? How should it be apprehended?"

The Bhagavan replied: "Mañjuśrī, this is 'the definitive instruction establishing the deeds of Tathāgatas'. Mañjuśrī, it should be apprehended as 'the definitive instruction establishing the deeds of Tathāgatas'."

When this definitive instruction establishing the deeds of Tathāgatas was explained, seventy-five thousand Bodhisattvas attained correct and perfect knowledge of the perfect Dharmakāya. After the Bhagavan had spoken, the youthful Mañjuśrī, the entire assembly, and the worlds of gods, humans, asuras, and gandharvas praised this teaching of the Bhagavan.

This concludes 'Ascertaining the Tathāgatas' Collection of Qualities', the [final] chapter of the Ārya Saṁdhinirmocana Mahāyāna-nāma Sūtra.

Reference Materials

Notes

Notes to Chapter One

1 The seven precious substances are: gser (gold), dngul (silver), vaiḍūrya (lapis lazuli), spug (a greenish-yellow gem according to W), rdo'i-snying-po (jasper), mu-tig-mar-po (coral), and ke-ke-ru (cat's eye). (B, vol. cho [205]:15.3 and W, vol ti [118]:107.2) For a further discussion of the seven substances, which are difficult to identify conclusively, see S (vol. II, 318) and Rin-po-che-brtag-thabs-mdor-bsdus-nyung-gsal by Ngag-dbang-blo-bzang (Ngag-dbang-blo-bzang-gsung-'bum, Indian blockprint, n.d., vol. ha).

2 "Limitless in reach" (mtha'-yas-pa-rnam-par-gzhag-pa, ananta-vyavasthāna) means that it is "limitless in number and limitless in area," and is "dwelling in a distinctively superior way, or dwelling in various aspects, or abiding limitlessly." (B, vol. cho [205]:16.5)

3 That which "transcends the world" is non-conceptual exalted wisdom (mi-rtog-pa'i-ye-shes, nirvikalpaka-jñāna). (B, vol. cho [205]:18.1) This wisdom "transcends the world" due to completion of causes. The root of supreme virtue that causes the palace to arise is the "non-conceptual exalted wisdom of subsequent attainment" (mi-rtog-pa'i-rjes-thob-ye-shes, nirvikalpaka-pṛṣṭha-labdha-jñāna), which transcends the three worlds. (W, vol. ti [118]:116.5) The palace is a manifestation of the pure mind of the Buddha, and "except for cognition-only (rnam-par-rig-pa-tsam, vijñapti-mātra), the jewels and so forth do not exist." (W 118.2, quoting Nye-ba'i-'od)

4 "One who has mastery" (dbang-sgyur, vaśibhūta) refers to "a yogin who has achieved the [ten] spheres of totality and so forth and who has mastery over all desires for things." (B, vol. cho [205]:19.1. See also S, vol. II, 319)

5 These are advanced Bodhisattvas who have entered into the great stages [probably the eighth stage and above]. (S, vol. II, 319)

6 Devas are the gods of the heaven realms. Nāgas are serpent-like beings who inhabit water-realms. Yakṣas are powerful beings, sometimes beneficent and sometimes malignant, who live on earth, in the air, and in the lower heavens. Gandharvas are celestial musicians who live in the air. Asuras are the opponents of the gods with whom they wage constant war, primarily motivated by intense envy for the superior fortunes of the gods. Garuḍas have eagle wings and lion heads and are the natural enemies of the nāgas. Kiṁnaras are half man, half horse. Mahoragas are large-bellied demons shaped like boas who are lords of the soil. Non-humans are often identified as ghosts or malignant spirits.

7 There are many demons (bdud, māra), whose goal is to tempt beings into ignorance. The four main types of demons are:

demons of the aggregates (phung-po'i-bdud, skandha-māra)
demons of the Lord of Death ('chi-bdag-gi-bdud, mṛtyu-māra)
demons of the afflictions (nyon-mongs-pa'i-bdud, kleśa-māra)
demons who are sons of gods (lha'i-bu'i-bdud, devaputra-māṙa).

Their function is to harm virtuous qualities, and this is why they are called demons. (W, vol. ti [118]:129.7, 193.2)

8 The "jeweled lotuses" (rin-po-che'i-padma, ratna-padma) are "lotuses having the nature of precious jewels." They are characterized as "great kings" (rgyal-po-chen-po, mahārāja) because "they are both great kings of precious jewels and also great kings of lotuses. Alternatively, the jeweled lotuses are the lotuses of the retinue that arise from the Bodhisattvas' blessings. The 'great kings' are the gurus of those Bodhisattvas and so forth. These great kings of doctrine are just those great lotuses that arise from the virtuous roots of Buddhas and Bhagavans." (B, vol. cho [205]:26.1)

9 This list of Buddha qualities also appears in S (vol. II, 134–43). According to S, all the qualities cited are elaborations of the first one: "Buddha's mind of good understanding." "A mind of good understanding is one that understands the varieties of compounded and compounded phenomena and how they actually exist." (B, vol. cho [205]:27.6) The "two [negative] behaviors" are the afflictive obstructions (nyon-mongs-pa'i-sgrib-pa, kleśāvaraṇa) and the obstructions

to omniscience (shes-bya'i-sgrib-pa, jñeyāvaraṇa) that are the behaviors of childish beings and Śrāvakas respectively. (B 28.1)

10 "Abiding in the way that a Buddha abides" means that the Buddha "abides without abiding" (gnas-pa-med-par-gnas-pa). This refers to the non-abiding nirvāṇa (mi-gnas-pa'i-mya-ngan-las-'das-pa, apratiṣṭhita-nirvāṇa) in which Buddhas abide. (W, vol. ti [118]:142.5, citing Vasubandhu's commentary on MS)

11 According to W, this refers to four qualities (although he lists only three): "abiding in the Dharmakāya (chos-kyi-sku-la-gnas-pa); thought (dgongs-pa); and not having discrepancies in performance of actions (phrin-las-mdzad-pa-tha-dad-pa-mi-mnga'-ba)." An explanation from a commentary on MS states that "thought" refers to the Saṁbhogakāya, and "performance of actions" refers to the Nirmāṇakāya. W adds: "In terms of those three, all the Tathāgatas of the ten directions and the three times are similar and non-different; therefore, they have 'attained [sameness with all Buddhas]'." (W, vol. ti [118]: 143.3. See also Bh 6.4)

The "obscurations" are the afflictive obstructions and the obstructions to omniscience, which Buddhas have abandoned "through having cultivated the paths of Āryas." (B, vol. cho [205]:38.2)

12 This refers to "the quality of correctly positing doctrines." Vasubandhu explains that "these correct doctrines that are Sūtras and so forth are immeasurable and inconceivable and are not objects of knowledge by ordinary beings. In dependence upon Buddhas, doctrines that are taught are 'posited'; they are not objects of knowledge by children. Therefore, they are 'inconceivable'." (W, vol. ti [118]:146.4)

13 The embodiment of a Tathāgata is "unimaginable" (rnam-par-ma-brtags-pa, nirvikalpa) because it is free from all elaborations (spros-pa, prapañca), and so cannot be imagined by ordinary beings, whose bodies are produced from conceptual thought and elaborations. "The bodies of ordinary beings arise from conceptuality. Moreover, from elaborations imagination [arises]; from conceptuality actions and afflictions arise; from actions and afflictions a body of suffering is produced. That body is an afflicted body. Because Tathāgatas are free from all elaborations, they do not have conceptuality. Therefore, [Tathāgatas] do not have bodies that are produced by actions and afflictions. Because their unimaginable

embodiments are inconceivable they are distinguished by the quality of appropriating an embodiment that is free from afflictions." (B, vol. cho [205]:32.4)

14 This refers to the non-dual Dharmakāya. (W, vol. ti [118]:155.7, citing Vasubandhu. See also B, vol. cho [205]:33.5)

15 "Just as space is limitless, boundless, inexhaustible, unobstructed, unproduced, unceasing, unchanging, and provides an environment for all physical things at all times, so the Dharmakāya has the characteristic of the continual establishment of help and happiness for all sentient beings." (W citing Asvabhāva, vol. ti [118]:162.5)

16 Śrāvakas constitute one of the three main types of Buddhist practitioners, the others being Pratyekabuddhas and Bodhisattvas. They "are called Śrāvakas ('Hearers') because they hear Buddha's teachings and proclaim them." (B, vol. cho [205]:47.3) "Their minds are liberated because they are free from desire and their wisdom is liberated because they are free from ignorance." (W, vol. ti[118]:173.1)

"Pratyekabuddhas are always solitary, are interested in peace and do not delight in commotion. They completely achieve their endeavors, and they pass beyond the world upon having understood [dependent origination] by themselves, without teachings from a spiritual guide." In seeking exclusively for their own enlightenment, they do not develop the compassionate actions of the Bodhisattva. (W, vol. thi [119]:14.2. See also COM 146 and WE 102–6)

17 The three knowledges (trividyā) are: clairvoyant knowledge that clearly realizes recollections of past states (pūrvanivāsanānusmṛti-sākṣātkāra-abhijñā); clairvoyant knowledge that clearly realizes transmigration and birth (cyutupapāda-sākṣātkāra-abhijñā); and clairvoyant knowledge that clearly realizes the extinction of contaminations (āsravakṣaya-sākṣātkāra-abhijñā). (W, vol. ti [118]:180.7. See also B, vol. cho [205]:53.6 and Kośa VII:45c-d)

18 The "great state" (mahāvihāra) in which they abide is the Mahāyāna. (B, vol. cho [205]:57.2)

19 The five great fears ('jigs-pa-chen-po-lnga, pañca-mahābhaya) are the fears of beginners on the Bodhisattva path: "fear concerning livelihood, fear of disapproval, fear of death, fear of bad transmigrations, and fear that is timidity when addressing assemblies. The

five fears are completely abandoned when one attains the level of surpassing thought (lhag-bsam, adhyāśaya)." (W, vol. ti [118]:195.1)

20 The irreversible stages (phyir-mi-ldog-pa'i-sa, avaivartika-bhūmi) are the eighth through tenth stages, beyond which a Bodhisattva is no longer capable of backsliding. (W, vol. ti [118]:195.3) "When one attains a level on which one is prophesied to omniscience one has progressed to the irreversible stages." (B, vol. cho [205]:60.6)

21 Gambhīrārthasaṁdhinirmocana ('Explainer of the Thought That is the Profound Meaning') is so named because "this Bodhisattva explains by way of the mode of the profound meaning through four [types of] comprehensions." (W, vol. ti [118]:212.2. See p. 181 of this Sūtra for a discussion of how a Bodhisattva comprehends objects.)

Asaṅga quotes chapters one through four of this Sūtra in VS in connection with his discussion of the character of the ultimate (don-dam-pa'i-mtshan-nyid, paramārtha-lakṣaṇa). Asaṅga gives five characteristics of the ultimate: It is (1) inexpressible and (2) non-dual (the main topics of chapter one); (3) it transcends argumentation (the main topic of chapter two); (4) it completely transcends difference and non-difference (the main topic of chapter three); and (5) it is everywhere of one taste (the main topic of chapter four). (VS, P 5539, vol. 'i [111]:47b.6–57b.3)

22 These two terms, "compounded" ('du-byas, saṁskṛta) and "uncompounded" ('du-ma-byas, asaṁskṛta), indicate a common division that includes all phenomena. The compounded is so called because it is produced from the accumulation of many conditions. "Whatever phenomena subsist on the activity of aggregation by causes and conditions and are related with such are compounded." (W quoting the Mahāvibhāṣa, vol. ti [118]:217.6)

"Whatever also appears in terms of production, cessation, abiding, and change is 'compounded'. Whatever lacks production, cessation, abiding, and change is 'uncompounded'." (W quoting AS, 218.1) A commentary on the Perfection of Wisdom provides an alternative explanation: "Whatever is apprehendable is 'compounded'. Whatever is not apprehendable is 'uncompounded'.... Whatever is apprehended in terms of signs is 'compounded'; whatever is not apprehended in terms of signs is 'uncompounded'." One scholar equates the compounded with the own-being of the other-dependent (gzhan-gyi-dbang-gi-ngo-bo-nyid, paratantra-svabhāva), and the uncompounded with the own-being of the thoroughly established (yongs-su-grub-pa'i-ngo-bo-nyid, pariniṣpanna-svabhāva), an explanation W considers to be correct. (W 218.1–219.2)

"The root of compounded phenomena is produced from incorrect thoughts. Due to incorrect thoughts, afflictions are produced. Because of afflictions, karma is produced. Due to karma, ripening [of karma] is generated. Incorrect thoughts arise from apprehending objects. Although these very objects do not truly exist, due to error [ordinary beings] exaggeratedly adhere to them as existent. Because those very objects do not [truly] exist, those incorrect thoughts also do not exist. Since incorrect thoughts do not exist, afflictions are also non-existent. Because afflictions do not exist, karma is also non-existent. Because karma is non-existent, ripening [of karma] is also non-existent. Because even their root is not real, all compounded phenomena are also unreal." (W 220.2)

"Because even the compounded is not compounded, the uncompounded is also similarly not uncompounded. Because they are imputed in this way, 'compounded' and 'uncompounded' are inexpressible." (W 222.3. See also COM 29, 102) The main point in this section is that neither of these designations ultimately reflects the true nature of phenomena. They are merely designated conventionally and have no ultimate validity.

23 An Ārya has attained the path of seeing (mthong-ba'i-lam, darśana-mārga), the third of the Buddhist paths. In Mahāyāna, this means that such a person has had direct experience of śūnyatā. All beings below this level of attainment are referred to as ordinary beings (so-so'i-skyes-bu, pṛthagjana). "'Wisdom' refers to the wisdom of śamatha and vipaśyanā that observes integrated doctrines; this is because it does not have various aspects. 'Vision' is the wisdom of śamatha and vipaśyanā that observes unintegrated doctrines; this is because it has various aspects." (B, vol. cho [205]: 76.4. See also pp. 161–65 of this Sūtra for a detailed discussion of "integrated" and "unintegrated" doctrines.)

24 In the analogy of the magician's illusion, the magician is compared to the basis-consciousness (kun-gzhi-rnam-par-shes-pa, ālaya-vijñāna), which from beginningless time has created things that are unreal. The magician's skillful assistants are compared to the seven collections of consciousness, which are subordinate to the basis-consciousness. The sticks and stones that serve as the basis of the magician's illusory creations are compared to the seeds (sa-bon,

bīja) in the basis-consciousness. The jewels and horses that the audience perceives are like fruits ('bras-bu, phala). (W, vol. ti [118]: 238.3, 239.3) This analogy illustrates the nature of the phenomena of ordinary existence, which is cognition-only. (B, vol. cho [205]:82.2. See also pp. 155 and 342, note 11 of this Sūtra)

25 This verse "indicates the faults of elaborations." (W, vol. ti [118]: 256.1) The statement that they "abide in duality" refers to (the dichotomy of) the compounded and the uncompounded. W's discussion focuses on elaborations of speech (smra-ba'i-spros-pa, vāda-prapañca), which he divides into eight types of conceptions of the unreal. He adds: "Because children are obscured due to differentiating in terms of duality and due to bewilderment with respect to inexpressible objects of activity, they greatly delight in and exaggeratedly adhere to the two types of phenomena—compounded and uncompounded—and to the eight types of elaborations."

W then cites YB: "Because children do not thoroughly understand suchness in that way, on this basis the eight [types of] conceptions arise, whereby the three [types of] phenomena arise and all the worlds of sentient beings and environments are produced. The first of the eight conceptions is conception of own-being: This [refers to] any differentiations of the specific own-beings of all phenomena and conceptions of 'form' and so forth. The second [type] is conception of attributes: This [includes] conceptions [such as], 'This is demonstrable'; 'This is not demonstrable' with respect to those very things that are nominally designated as form and so forth. The third [type] is conception that apprehends wholeness: [conceptions] apprehending self, sentient beings, houses, armies, forests, etc. with respect to those very things that are nominally designated as form and so forth. The fourth [type] is the conception that thinks 'I'. The fifth [type] is the conception that thinks 'mine': [conceptions] apprehending phenomena that are associated with contamination and that are associated with appropriation as 'I' and 'mine'. The sixth [type] is conception of the pleasant. The seventh [type] is conception of the unpleasant. The eighth [type] is conception that is reversed from those two. [The last three] respectively are explained as being 'conceptions arising from things that are beautiful, non-beautiful, and neither of those'."

Hsüan-tsang describes these eight types of conceptions as "undefiled and neutral fruitions that have the nature of knowledges that one is born with. In another way, they have a nature that is conceptual and analytical. With respect to the phrase, 'give rise to three [types of] phenomena': The first three conceptions produce the bases of elaborations of conceptuality and the things that are objects of observation of the six sense powers and the six objects [of their corresponding senses]. The middle two conceptions produce the view of true personhood ('jig-tshogs-la-lta-ba, satkāya-dṛṣṭi) and the pride of thinking 'mine'. The last three respectively produce desire, hatred, and delusion. Because the basis and the object of observation of the sense powers serve as supports they generate the view of true personhood and the pride of thinking 'mine'; and because the view of true personhood and the pride of thinking 'mine' serve as supports one generates desire, hatred, and delusion. Therefore, you should know that the factors of the workings of all the worlds of sentient beings and environments are entirely indicated by these three phenomena." (W quoting Hsüan-tsang, 257.1)

Notes to Chapter Two

1 This Bodhisattva is named Dharmodgata ('Elevated [Through] Doctrine') "because sentient beings vastly increase roots of virtue through [his] teaching doctrines in accordance with their interests." (W, vol. ti [118]:266.4, citing a commentary on the Perfection of Wisdom)

2 Tīrthika (mu-stegs-pa) refers to non-Buddhist schools in general. Five faults prevent Tīrthikas from understanding the ultimate: the fault of being opinionated (kun-tu-tshol-ba'i-nyes-pa), the fault of conceit (mngon-pa'i-nga-rgyal-gyi-nyes-pa), the fault of exaggerated adherence (mngon-par-zhen-pa'i-nyes-pa), the fault of imputation ('dogs-pa'i-nyes-pa), and the fault of argumentativeness (rtsod-pa'i-nyes-pa). (B, vol. cho [205]:89.5)

3 The "ultimate" is that which is uncompounded, lacks production and cessation, and is an object of observation for purification of obstructions. Vasubandhu divides the ultimate into three types: objective ultimate (don-don-dam-pa, artha-paramārtha), e.g., suchness (de-bzhin-nyid, tathatā); attainment ultimate (thob-pa-don-dam-pa, prapti-paramārtha), e.g., nirvāṇa (mya-ngan-las-'das-pa); and practice ultimate (sgrub-pa-don-dam-pa, pratipatti-paramārtha), e.g., a path (lam, mārga). (MV 236–37 [III.11a]. See also EG 47.14 and DLG 47.6)

4 "Through observing the object of suchness with an Ārya's non-conceptual exalted wisdom, [Āryas] manifestly realize their own internal nature." (W, vol. ti [118]:278.4)

5 "[This passage from the Sūtra] indicates that due to the faults of positing—in dependence upon conventions such as seeing and so forth—that living beings and so forth exist, one does not understand the ultimate. [The phrase,] 'in dependence upon conventions such as seeing and so forth' indicates that in dependence upon conventions of seeing, hearing, differentiating distinctions, and consciousness, one posits selves, sentient beings, souls, and persons and so forth as existent due to apprehending [them] as enjoyers and agents. Due to positing [them] as selves one does not understand the ultimate; therefore, this is the fault of positing." (B, vol. cho [205]:91.6)

"Moreover, Dharmodgata, I explain that suchness is the complete elimination of four types of things: seeing, hearing, differentiating distinctions, and consciousness. But conceptuality and analysis arise within observing these four things." (W quoting the Tshig-nges-par-'grel-pa'i-mdo, vol. ti [118]:290.5)

6 "The following five examples are given because there are five types of orientation: limited orientation (sel-bar-mos-pa); orientation toward desire ('dod-pa-la-mos-pa); orientation toward discursiveness (rnam-par-rtog-pa-la-mos-pa); orientation toward conventions (tha-snyad-la-mos-pa); and orientation toward apprehending [the transitory collection of aggregates] as an 'I' and as 'mine' (bdag-gir-'dzin-pa-la-mos-pa)." Each example is posited in terms of a particular type of orientation. (B, vol. cho [205]:93.3)

Regarding the first example, W states: "Just as those persons who partake only of bitter tastes are unable to imagine, infer, or appreciate the taste of honey, so also householders, who abide in cyclic existence for a long time and always partake of the taste of worldly agitation and coarse sufferings, are unable to imagine, infer, or appreciate the very auspicious taste of pure behavior or the bliss of renunciation." (W, vol. ti [118]:307.2)

7 [Belief in] true personhood refers to the aggregates (phung-po, skandha) that we ordinarily view as a real 'I' and 'mine'. (COM 1–22. See also ME 258–59) The nirvāṇa referred to is "the element of a nirvāṇa without remaining aggregates." (B, vol. cho [205]:94.7)

8 This is one of the nine divisions of the world in traditional Indian cosmology. The inhabitants of this country of eternal beatitude are said to have a lifespan of 1,000 years, to be naturally virtuous, and to lead exceptionally pleasant lives. (See VM VII:44; Kośa III:78)

Notes to Chapter Three

1 "Because his correct exalted wisdom and exalted wisdom of subsequent attainment are uncontaminated virtues and free from affliction, he is called Suviśuddhamati ('Very Pure Intelligence')." (W, vol. ti [118]:316.6)

2 The stage of engagement through conviction (mos-pas-spyod-pa'i-sa, adhimukti-caryā-bhūmi) encompasses the first two paths—the path of accumulation (tshogs-lam, sambhāra-mārga) and the path of preparation (sbyor-lam, prayoga-mārga), in which one's practice is motivated by desire to emulate the exalted states of beings on the higher stages. (Geshe Sangyay Samdrup [Georges Dreyfus], oral commentary)

"Since they do not directly realize suchness, in dependence on belief, [Bodhisattvas on this stage] engage in their practices through effort." (W, vol. ti [118]:321.6) They are prevented from understanding the ultimate because of: "obscuration with respect to imputations (gdags-pa-la-shin-tu-rmongs-pa) and obscuration with respect to reasoning (rigs-pa-la-shin-tu-rmongs-pa)." (B, vol. cho [205]:98.5)

3 They are "childish" (byis-pa, bāla) because of having ignorant natures (ma-rig-pa'i-bdag-nyid). They are "obscured" (rmongs-pa) because they are distinguished by their ignorance (ma-rig-pa-las-rnam-par-'byed-pa). They are "unclear" (mi-gsal-ba) because they still have not attained the faculty of knowing all of the unknown. They are "unskilled" (mi-mkhas-pa) because they still have not attained the faculty of omniscience. They are "not properly oriented" (tshul-bzhin-ma-lags-pa) because they still have not attained faculties endowed with omniscience. "Therefore, they have not directly realized the mode of ultimate suchness that is a character which is neither one nor different." (W, vol. ti [118]:325.4. See also Bh 11)

4 In AS (COM 8), Asaṅga indicates that the bonds of errant tendencies (gnas-ngan-len-gyi-'ching-ba, dauṣṭhulya-bandhana) are certain

obstructions of body (lus-sgrib, kāyāvaraṇa) and of mind (yid-sgrib, manas-āvaraṇa). Some dGe-lugs-pa writers add a third type, obstructions of speech (ngag-sgrib, vāg-āvaraṇa).

These errant tendencies are the subtle motivations toward nonvirtuous actions that remain after the passions motivating one to perform them have been overcome. An example of an obstruction of body is seeing a monkey and beginning to jump up and down like a monkey. An example of an obstruction of speech is being verbally abusive to a passer-by, or speaking profanity, but without any harmful intent. (Geshe Sangyay Samdrup, oral commentary)

In SB, Asaṅga writes: "What are the errant tendencies of body and mind that are purified? The arisings of errant tendencies of body and mind [that arise] from physical hardship and physical tiredness are purified through analysis by way of other modes of behavior. And the arisings of errant tendencies of body and mind [that arise] from too much conceptuality and too much analysis are purified through the method of internal mental calm abiding; or they are purified naturally. And the arisings of errant tendencies of body and mind [that arise] from the mind's having been withdrawn and the mind's having become slack due to the entanglements of obscuration and sleepiness are purified through higher wisdom that differentiates phenomena and through very pure mental contemplation; or they are purified naturally. The errant tendencies of body and mind of the class of afflictions from which one has not separated and to which one is always connected due to not abandoning the afflictions are purified through having cultivated a correct path." (NE 4036, vol. dzi:100b.1)

In VS, Asaṅga writes: "In brief, with respect to errant tendencies there are two types: errant tendencies that are contaminated (zag-pa'i-gnas-ngan-len, āsrava-dauṣṭhulya) and errant tendencies that are associated with contamination (zag-pa-dang-bcas-pa'i-gnas-ngan-len, sāsrava-dauṣṭhulya). Because errant tendencies that are contaminated are afflictions that are to be abandoned by [a path of] meditation, Arhats are free from all of them. Moreover, these are simply states that are bad due to their mode of unserviceability with respect to the bodily consciousness as well as latencies (bag-la-nyal, anuśaya). With respect to errant tendencies that are associated with contamination, even though one has eliminated their latencies, they are produced by former contamination and are polluted by contamination. Due to such a mode of unserviceability, they are cases of abiding in a bad way that are naturally very subtle and very miniscule. Errant tendencies that are associated with contamination are 'predispositions of afflictions' (nyon-mongs-pa'i-bag-chags, kleśa-vāsanā). Moreover, Arhats and Pratyekabuddhas have not abandoned them; only Tathāgatas have abandoned them. The complete elimination of these predispositions is an 'unshared quality of Buddhas' (sangs-rgyas-kyi-chos-ma-'dres-pa, aveṇika-buddhadharma)." (NE 4038, vol. zhi:119b.3. See also W, vol. ti [118]:333–37)

5 In this analogy the conch represents the character of compounded phenomena and whiteness represents ultimate truth because it pervades the whole nature of the form [of the conch]. (W, vol. ti [118]:347.3) "The ultimate and conventional exist in mutual dependence" [just as the whiteness of the conch and the conch exist in mutual dependence]. (W 352.1)

6 The vīṇā is a seven-stringed Indian instrument similar to a lute.

7 The agaru tree is Amyris agallocha.

8 Myrobalan arjuna is an important medicinal plant.

Notes to Chapter Four

1 Subhūti, a Śrāvaka, is the main questioner in many Perfection of Wisdom Sūtras, and is praised by the Buddha as the foremost of his disciples in understanding emptiness. (See W, vol. ti [118]:359.5)

2 Conceit (mngon-pa'i-nga-rgyal, abhimāna) is one of seven types of pride. It leads one to imagine that one has attained advanced spiritual states. (Kośa V:10a) Those who are overcome by conceit are ordinary beings, while those who are not are Āryas. (W, vol. ti [118]:360.6, citing Paramārtha's Tshig-nges-par-'grel-pa'i-mdo)

There are three kinds of conceit: conceit of apprehended objects (gzung-ba'i-mngon-pa'i-nga-rgyal); conceit of the apprehending subject ('dzin-pa'i-mngon-pa'i-nga-rgyal); and the conceit of thoroughly differentiating character (mtshan-nyid-rab-tu-dbye-ba'i-mngon-pa'i-nga-rgyal). (B, vol. cho [205]:106.3)

3 These are the five aggregates (phung-po, skandha), the constituents of all phenomena and the basis on which we impute 'I' and 'mine': form (gzugs, rūpa); feeling (tshor-ba, vedanā); discrimination

('du-shes, saṁjñā); compositional factors ('du-byed, saṁskāra); and consciousness (rnam-par-shes-pa, vijñāna). (See VM XIV:33–184, Kośa I:9a–22d, and WE 133–60)

"'Observing the signs of the aggregates' is done from the point of view of thoroughly analyzing their own signs. 'Observing the arising of the aggregates' and 'observing the disintegration of the aggregates' are done from the point of view of general characteristics and thorough investigation. These two indicate the aspects of true sources and true sufferings of the aggregates. 'Observing the cessation of the aggregates' refers to true cessations, and 'observing the actualization of the cessation of the aggregates' refers to true paths." (B, vol. cho [205]:109.4)

4 The sense spheres (skye-mched, āyatana) are the abodes of perception. There is a sixfold enumeration and a twelvefold enumeration of these. W (vol. ti [118]:382.6) indicates that the twelvefold division is being referred to here; see also Kośa I:14a-b, 24; VM XV: 1–16; and WE 170–74. The twelvefold division is:

form (gzugs, rūpa)
sound (sgra, śabda)
smell (dri, gandha)
taste (ro, rasa)
tangible object (reg-bya, sparśa)
phenomenon (chos, dharma)
eye sense power (mig-gi-dbang-po, cakṣur-indriya)
ear sense power (rna-ba'i-dbang-po, śrotrendriya)
nose sense power (sna'i-dbang-po, ghrāṇendriya)
tongue sense power (lce'i-dbang-po, jihvendriya)
body sense power (lus-kyi-dbang-po, kāyendriya)
mind sense power (yid-kyi-dbang-po, mano-indriya).

The twelve links of dependent origination (rten-cing-'brel-bar-'byung-ba, pratītya-samutpāda) are (Kośa III:20a–37b and WE 176–90):

ignorance (ma-rig-pa, avidyā)
karmic propensities ('du-byed, saṁskāra)
consciousness (rnam-par-shes-pa, vijñāna)
name and form (ming-dang-gzugs, nāma-rūpa)
six senses (skye-mched-drug, ṣaḍāyatana)
contact (reg-pa, sparśa)
feeling (tshor-ba, vedanā)
craving (sred-pa, tṛṣṇā)

grasping (len-pa, upādāna)
existence (srid-pa, bhava)
birth (skye-ba, jāti)
old age and death (rga-shi, jarā-maraṇa).

The four sustenances (zas, āhāra) are: material sustenance (khams-kyi-zas, kavaḍīkārāhāra), which is necessary for sustaining the body; sustenance of touch (reg-pa'i-zas, sparśāhāra), which is the sense of mental satisfaction that one experiences when a desire is fulfilled; sustenance of intention ([yid-la-]sems-pa'i-zas, manaḥsaṁcetanāhāra), which is an action (las, karma) that impels the next lifetime; and sustenance of consciousness (rnam-shes-kyi-zas, vijñānāhāra). (Kośa III:38d–41) "Just as the action that impels a future lifetime is called a sustenance, so the consciousness that is imprinted with that action and which will at the time of the effect of that action in the future life be imprinted with other karmas is called a nourisher or sustenance." (Geshe Gendun Lodrö, unpubl. ms., tr. Jeffrey Hopkins. See also VM XI:1–3; W, vol. ti [118]:383.2; and WE 217–18)

5 The four truths (bden-pa, satya) are: the truth of suffering (sdug-bsngal-bden-pa, duḥkha-satya); the truth of the origin of suffering (kun-'byung-bden-pa, samudaya-satya); the truth of the cessation of suffering ('gog-bden-pa, nirodha-satya); and the truth of the eightfold path that overcomes suffering (lam-bden-pa, mārga-satya). (See W, vol. ti [118]:383.5–385.2, and WE 68–76)

6 In the Kośa (I:28a–48d), there are three divisions of constituents (khams, dhātu): (1) a sixfold division: earth, water, fire, air, space, and consciousness; (2) an eighteenfold division: the six senses, their six objects, and the six consciousnesses that arise from them; and (3) a threefold division: form realm, formless realm, and desire realm.

W identifies both the "various" and "manifold" constituents as the eighteen constituents. (vol. ti [118]:385.5, 549.1) Alternately: "The constituents of sentient beings, ranging up to their 80,000 modes of behavior—through modes distinguished as the lineages of Śrāvakas, Pratyekabuddhas, and Tathāgatas and desire and so forth—are called 'various'. . . . With respect to 'observing manifold constituents': If one broadly classifies these various constituents, there are four types: the naturally abiding constituent; the constituent arisen from previous familiarization; the constituent that is suitable as an object of purification. There are also limitless other divisions with respect to each of these." (B, vol. cho [205]:110.2)

EG (p. 6.2) states that the "various constituents" are the eighteen constituents. EG (p. 6.2–.4) and GR (p. 9.4) identify the "manifold constituents" as the six: earth, water, fire, air, space, and consciousness. Tsong-kha-pa states that, although some commentaries explain the "various constituents" and "manifold constituents" differently, he has chosen to explain them in this way in accordance with the seventh chapter of the Saṁdhinirmocana Sūtra, which in many ways parallels this chapter. According to G (86.14–89.10), the reason the Buddha spoke of both eighteen and six constituents is that the eighteen are all-inclusive, but the six are useful in establishing selflessness. He further states (86.14) that the Buddha taught (Dhātubahuka-sūtra, NE 297) that the eighteen constituents and the six constituents are established through their own character as bases of conception of the thought consciousness apprehending them.

7 The four mindful establishments (dran-pa-nye-bar-bzhag-pa, smṛtyupasthāna) are: establishment in mindfulness of body (lus, kāya), feelings (tshor-ba, vedanā), mind (sems, citta), and phenomena (chos, dharma). They "are based on prajña, the discernment of dharmas." (WE 274. See also Kośa VI:14–16, ME 205, and COM 118, 169)

They are called mindful establishments "because wisdom is thoroughly held through the power of mindfulness; thus it is caused to abide continuously." Due to the power of wisdom one gains from cultivating these, mindfulness is able to remain fixed on its objects. (W, vol. ti [118]:387.7, citing bsTan-bcos-yang-dag-pa'i-rig-pa)

There are four "antidotes to the discordances": the antidote of the basis (gzhi'i-gnyen-po, ādhāra-pratipakṣa); the antidote of removal (thag-sring-ba'i-gnyen-po, dūrībhāva-pratipakṣa); the antidote of abandonment (spong-ba'i-gnyen-po, prahāṇa-pratipakṣa); and the antidote of eradication (rnam-par-sun-'byin-pa'i-gnyen-po, vidūṣaṇā-pratipakṣa). (COM 116. See also Kośa V:61a-c) "Increasing and extending" means increasing these antidotes through the power of familiarity and extending them limitlessly." (A 55.2)

8 The four correct abandonings (yang-dag-par-spong-ba, samyakprahāṇa) are:

abandoning non-virtuous phenomena already generated (sdig-pami-dge-ba'i-chos-skyes-pa-rnams-yongs-su-spang-pa, utpannākuśaladharmaprahāṇa) not producing non-virtuous phenomena not yet generated (sdig-pa-mi-dge-ba'i-chos-ma-skyes-pa-rnams-mi-skyed-pa, anutpannākuśala-dharmāropaṇa)

increasing virtuous phenomena already generated (dge-ba'i-chos-skyes-pa-rnams-'phel-ba, utpanna-kuśala-dharmavṛiddhi)

producing virtuous phenomena not yet generated (dge-ba'i-chos-ma-skyes-pa-rnams-bskyed-pa, anutpanna-kuśala-dharma-ropaṇa). (COM 120. See also WE 278–80, 322)

The opposite of the correct abandonings is laziness. (A 55.2–.3)

The four bases of magical abilities (rdzu-'phrul-gyi-rkang-pa, ṛddhipāda) are: aspiration ('dun-pa, chanda); effort (brtson-'grus, vīrya); mental attention (sems, citta); and analytical samādhi (dpyod-pa'i-ting-nge-'dzin, mīmāṁsā-samādhi). W cites the Kośa, which states that they are "bases" "because they serve as bases of extraordinary qualities." (vol. ti [118]:395.1) These "bases" are attained on the great path of accumulation (ME 206) and their discordant factor is distraction. (A 55.2–.3. See also VM XII, Kośa VI:69d–c, and WE 278–79)

Both the powers and forces are fivefold: faith (dad-pa, śraddhā); effort (brtson-'grus, vīrya); mindfulness (dran-pa, smṛti); samādhi (ting-nge-'dzin); and wisdom (shes-rab, prajñā). The powers are attained on the levels of heat and peak of the path of preparation. (ME 206) The discordant factor of the powers is non-interest; that of the forces is little strength of mindfulness and introspection. (A 55.2–.3. See Kośa VI:68b–70, and WE 279–80, 292, 323)

The seven branches of enlightenment (byang-chub-kyi-yan-lag-bdun, sapta-bodhyaṅga) are: mindfulness (dran-pa, smṛti); discrimination of phenomena (chos-rnam-par-'byed-pa, dharma-vicaya); effort (brtson-'grus, vīrya); joy (dga'-ba, prīti); pliancy (shin-tu-sbyangs-pa, praśrabdhi); samādhi (ting-nge-'dzin); and equanimity (btang-snyoms, upekṣā). (W, vol. ti [118]:398.1) These are attained with the path of seeing. (ME 206. See Kośa VI:68b–70 and WE 283)

The eight branches of the path of Āryas ('phags-pa'i-lam-yan-lag-brgyad-pa, āryāṣṭāṇgamārga) are:

correct views (yang-dag-pa'i-lta-ba, samyag-dṛṣṭi)
correct realization (yang-dag-pa'i-rtog-pa, samyak-saṁkalpa)
correct speech (yang-dag-pa'i-ngag, samyag-vāk)
correct aims of action (yang-dag-pa'i-las-kyi-mtha', samyak-karmānta)
correct livelihood (yang-dag-pa'i-'tsho-ba, samyag-ājīva)
correct effort (yang-dag-pa'i-rtsol-ba, samyag-vyāyāma)

correct mindfulness (yang-dag-pa'i-dran-pa, samyak-smṛti)
correct samādhi (yang-dag-pa'i-ting-nge-'dzin, samyak-samādhi).
(W, vol. ti [118]:399.7)

They are attained with the path of meditation. (ME 206. See W 400.1 for a description of these, and WE 75–6, 324–25)

9 "This indicates that thoroughly established suchness, the ultimate, the selflessness of phenomena is everywhere of one taste in the sense of being free from distinctions with respect to all phenomena that are apprehended objects, phenomena that are apprehending subjects, and phenomena that are of thoroughly differentiated characters." (B, vol. cho [205]:111.5. See also Buddhabhūmi-sūtra [ed. Kyoo Nishio, Tokyo: Kokusho Kankokai, 1982, II.2.1])

"The central theme of this chapter is this statement that [the ultimate] is of a character that is everywhere of one taste (ro-gcig-pa'i-mtshan-nyid, ekarasa-lakṣaṇa). This teaching is divided into four parts (B 105.2):

positing the character of conceit (mngon-pa'i-nga-rgyal-gyi-mtshan-nyid-rnam-par-gzhag-pa);

positing the character of the antidotes to conceit (mngon-pa'i-nga-rgyal-gyi-gnyen-po'i-mtshan-nyid-rnam-par-gzhag-pa);

positing the character of examples of those (de-dag-gi-dpe'i-mtshan-nyid-rnam-par-gzhag-pa);

positing the character that subsumes the phenomena that are those (de-dag-gi-dngos-po-bsdus-pa'i-mtshan-nyid-rnam-par-gzhag-pa)."

In this translation of the Sūtra, the first part begins on p. 53 and ends on p. 59, paragraph 2. The second part begins on p. 59, paragraph 3, and ends on p. 63, paragraph 3. The third part begins on p. 63, paragraph 4 and ends on p. 65, paragraph 1. The fourth part begins on p. 65, paragraph 2 and ends with the conclusion of the chapter.

10 "An object of observation for purification has three aspects: It is permanently changeless (rtag-tu-rnam-par-'gyur-ba-med); it has a nature of virtue and happiness (dge-dang-bde-ba'i-ngo-bo-nyid); and it manifestly accomplishes everything (thams-cad-mngon-par-'grub-par-'gyur). (W, vol. ti [118]:406.2, citing the bsTan-bcos-rnam-par-bshad-pa'i-tshig-le'ur-byas-pa)

11 "The suchness that is of one taste is without oneness in the past from the beginning; therefore [the Sūtra says,] 'permanent, perma-

nent time'. It is without oneness in the future; therefore [the Sūtra says,] 'everlasting, everlasting time'." (W, vol ti [118]:416.5) "Because it abides as the reality (chos-nyid) of phenomena in permanent, permanent time and in everlasting, everlasting time, it is uncompounded." (W 567.6) W mentions that someone else equates "permanent, permanent time" with "former, former time." (W 525.6. See also EG 17.10 and 17.18)

12 "With respect to [the example of] space, since it is of a character that is an absence of the own-being of forms, that very absence of the own-being of those is not distinguished with respect to difference in terms of difference from those. The ultimate is also like that." (B, vol. cho [205]:117.6)

Notes to Chapter Five

1 "Because he has no ignorance concerning the various forms of discourse related to the scriptures and commentaries of renunciates and of householders, he is called Viśālamati ('Extensive Intelligence')." (W quoting a Perfection of Wisdom commentary, vol. ti [118]: 422.7) This Bodhisattva is so named "because the objects of activity of [his] wisdom are measureless and limitless." (W 423.1, quoting YB)

This entire chapter is quoted in VS (P 5539, vol. 'i [111]:57b.4–60a.1). Asaṅga states that while the first four chapters concern the characteristics of the ultimate, this chapter concerns the character of mind. According to Asaṅga the function of mind is to act as a support for name and form (nāma-rūpa).

2 In this chapter "mind" (sems, citta) refers to the basis-consciousness (kun-gzhi-rnam-par-shes-pa, ālaya-vijñāna). (B, vol. cho [205]:121.3) The basis-consciousness should be equated with mind "because, having collected the seeds of phenomena, it gives rise to phenomena." (W, vol. ti [118]:421.4) "Thought" (yid, manas) refers to (1) afflicted sentience (nyon-mongs-pa-can-gyi-yid, kliṣṭa-manas), the seventh consciousness in the Yogācāra system, and (2) "a just-ceased consciousness and a consciousness that has been transformed." "Consciousness" (rnam-par-shes-pa, vijñāna) refers to the six collections of operating consciousnesses (i.e., eye-consciousness, ear-consciousness, etc.). (B 121.3. See also W 421.5 and KY 16b.1)

3 The six kinds of beings are: hell beings (dmyal-ba, nāraka); hungry ghosts (yi-dwags, preta); animals (dud-'gro, tiryak); humans (mi, manuṣya); demigods (lha-ma-yin, asura); and gods (lha, deva). (See Kośa III:4a-b; W, vol. ti [118]:447.3–449.7; and WE 208–17. For a detailed discussion of these types of birth see W, vol. ti [118]:449.7–551.7.)

4 These two types of appropriation are "two causes that operate in association with the basis-consciousness and are linked with it. The two types of internal appropriation are: appropriation of physical sense powers associated with a support and appropriation of predispositions to exaggeratedly apprehending imputational natures. Regarding the 'appropriation of physical sense powers associated with a support', those supports of physical sense powers are whatever is counted as the physical aggregates that are apprehended. The 'physical sense powers' are the five physical sense powers." (B, vol. cho [205]:136.6. See also W 457.1–462.2)

"On the occasion of taking birth in those transmigrations, initially when making the transition between lives, the mind that is a consciousness [containing] all seeds ripens." (W, vol. ti [118]:452.3) The mind forms because "at that time, in terms of birthplace, the aspect of the form that is the combination of the semen and blood of father and mother and the basis-consciousness move into a womb and become an establishment and abiding." The mind "develops" "due to continuous operation subsequent to that." Increase takes place "at the time of the arising of the operating consciousness." The mind expands "due to the infusion of predispositions by those operating consciousnesses." (B, vol. cho [205]:138.5)

At the beginning of a new life, a being has the karmic latencies of past lives (referred to as seeds), which begin to manifest themselves in the new continuum. They then grow and develop, and as the new life progresses, they in turn lead to production of new predispositions, and so the process continues and maintains itself.

In a previous discussion of the basis-consciousness, W (441.3) comments: "Due to the basis-consciousness, through the force of maintaining the three types of predispositions, the continuity of the gap between lives is not cut off." According to VJ (478–80), the three types of predispositions are: (1) predispositions of verbalization (mngon-par-brjod-pa'i-bag-chags, abhilāpya-vāsanā); (2) predispositions of apprehending a self (bdag-du-'dzin-pa'i-bag-chags, ātmagrāha-vāsanā); and (3) predispositions of the limbs of cyclic existence ('khor-ba'i-yan-lag-bag-chags, saṁsārāṅga-vāsanā). The first type includes seeds that predispose a person to make differentiations regarding individual compounded phenomena. These are of two types: manifest expressions that define meanings, which are expressions of vocal differentiation with respect to meanings; and manifest expressions that define objects, which are phenomena of minds and mental factors that understand objects. The second type includes seeds that predispose one to incorrectly conceive 'I' and 'mine'. These are also of two types: innate conceptions of self, which are conceptions of 'I' and 'mine' that are objects to be abandoned by a path of meditation; and the imputational conception of 'I', which is a conception of 'I' and 'mine' that is an object to be abandoned by a path of seeing. Due to these two conceptions, sentient beings make distinctions of 'self' and 'other'. The third type of predisposition includes seeds that induce fruition of the three realms of existence. These are also of two types: virtues associated with contamination, which are any actions that induce desirable effects; and non-virtues, which are any actions that induce undesirable effects.

5 It is not twofold because in the formless realm physical sense powers are absent, although predispositions for them are present. (See W, vol. ti [118]:462.2; Kośa III:3a-d, XIII:3c-d; JBW 496–502)

6 "Because it thoroughly holds the seeds of phenomena, thoroughly holds the bases of physical sense powers, and thoroughly holds the connection between lives, it is called the 'appropriating consciousness'." (W citing VJ, vol. ti [118]:462.7. See also JBW 10, 57)

"Why is it called the 'appropriating consciousness'? Because it is the cause of all the physical sense powers and is the support that appropriates all bodies. As long as one is still alive, it holds the five physical sense powers such that they do not disintegrate. Also, when the connection between lives is made, because it appropriates rebirth, the body is appropriated." (S, vol. I, I:5)

7 The existence of the basis-consciousness is established both through reasonings based on the necessity of its existence for continuity and by citations from scriptures that assert its existence (such as the Saṁdhinirmocana Sūtra and the Laṅkāvatāra Sūtra). (See B, vol. cho [205]:125.1–128.1 and W, vol. ti [118]:463.2–466.7, where the functions of the basis-consciousness are described in detail; and Jinaputra's Abhidharmasamuccaya-bhāṣya [P 5554, vol. shi [113]:12a.3–.6], for eight reasonings establishing its existence.)

"If the basis-consciousness did not exist, appropriation of a body would be impossible; initial operation [of consciousness] would be impossible; clear operation [of consciousness] would be impossible; seeds would be impossible; karma would be impossible; bodily feelings would be impossible; meditative absorptions in which mind is absent would be impossible; and transmigration of consciousness would be impossible." (B, vol. cho [205]:124.6)

8 This passage refers to the fanciful etymology of the Sanskrit word *citta* from the verbal root $\sqrt{ci}$, which means 'to accumulate'. Thus, *citta* is what 'accumulates' the predispositions. The basis-consciousness has seeds within it that ripen into eye-consciousnesses. When these become activated, an eye-consciousness results. (KJ 4.12–6.9 and KY 5a, 11b. See also JBW 111–19, 138, 409–20)

9 In other words, this reason alone is not sufficient for Bodhisattvas to merit the designation: "wise with respect to the secrets of mind, thought, and consciousness." They must also directly realize the ultimate in order to be worthy of this designation.

10 "It is deep because it is difficult for its depth to be fathomed by the intelligence even of the wise of the world. It is subtle because it is difficult to know even for Śrāvakas. Therefore, [Buddha] does not teach this [basis-]consciousness to Śrāvakas and the like, because they do not seek extremely subtle omniscience. With respect to [the phrase,] 'all its seeds flowing like a river': Because it continues from one moment to another, it flows without its continuum being cut off, like a river. With respect to [the phrase,] 'I have not taught this to children': It is not revealed to those having a view of self. This is because those who conceive of a self would apprehend [the appropriating consciousness] as being a unitary, unchanging 'self' that exists as long as cyclic existence lasts." (W, vol. ti [118]:489.6, citing Asvabhāva's commentary on MS)

Notes to Chapter Six

1 "With respect to [the name] Guṇākara ('Source of Qualities'): Because [he] has accumulated the causes of [good] qualities for immeasurable eons, this is a case of a designation of a name from a causal point of view. Because [he] has accumulated both types of

bases of [good] qualities—the collections of merit and wisdom—he is [called] Guṇākara." (W, vol. ti [118]:493.5)

This entire chapter is quoted by Asaṅga in VS (P 5539, vol. 'i [111]: 60a.2–62b.2). He states that the subject of this chapter is the character of phenomena (chos-rnams-kyi-mtshan-nyid, dharma-lakṣaṇa).

2 "Why is it called 'imputational' (kun-btags, parikalpita)? Because mental consciousness, having the aspects of immeasurable conceptions, just gives rise to error, [it is termed] 'imputational'. Also because its own character does not truly exist, but is merely perceived conceptually, it is called 'imputational'." (W, vol. ti [118]:496.4, citing MS) "'A character that gives rise to error' means that it has a character of unreal, erroneous objects of observation. 'Its own character does not truly exist' [because] its nature does not truly exist." (W citing Vasubandhu's commentary, 496.7)

"The imputational character is a character that is posited in the manner of names and terminology, but is not posited through its own character. Since it is utterly non-existent in terms of both of the two truths, it lacks own-being due to lacking own-being in terms of character." (B, vol. cho [205]:213.5)

3 "The 'other-dependent (gzhan-dbang, paratantra) character' is the own-being of internal and external phenomena that are dependently arisen through the power of other conditions. Because the own-being of things that are apprehended objects and apprehending subjects are produced due to the power of other causes and conditions, it is the 'other-dependent character'." (B, vol. cho [205]: 187.7) "The other-dependent character is produced by the power of other conditions but is not [produced] through its nature. Therefore—since it exists merely [like] a magician's illusions in terms of conventional truths—it is a lack of own-being due to being a lack of own-being in terms of production. Since it does not have ultimate lack of own-being because it is not an object of observation for purification, it is not an ultimate lack of own-being because it is not an ultimate truth. Therefore, it is a lack of own-being, and the thoroughly established character is the ultimate, and the ultimate is distinguished by being the lack of own-being of all phenomena. Because [the thoroughly established character] is both the ultimate truth and a lack of own-being, it is a lack of own-being due to being the ultimate lack of own-being." (B 213.6. See also pp. 99–105 of this Sūtra)

"Because this exists, that arises" indicates that [effects] arise from conditions unalterably. "Because this is produced, that is produced" indicates that objects are produced from conditions that are impermanent. This is because production of an effect from causes that do not give rise to any phenomenon is not established. The phrase, "due to the condition of ignorance, compositional factors [arise]," indicates that [effects] are produced from conditions that are potencies. Although phenomena are unfluctuating and impermanent, any effect does not arise from any condition. Why is this? Since there are different divisions of potencies of phenomena, it is said that "there are [the links of dependent origination] ranging from the arising of compositional factors due to the power of ignorance up to the arising of old age and death due to the power of birth." "The whole great assemblage of suffering" indicates that there is no beginning or end to the accumulation of suffering. (W, vol. ti [118]: 504–5)

4 "Because [the thoroughly established character] does not change into something else, because it is an object of observation for purification, because it is supreme of all virtuous phenomena, it is called the 'thoroughly established character' in the sense of being supreme." (W quoting MS, vol. ti [118]:499.7) "'Because it does not change into something else' it is not a false phenomenon. It is like a minister who is free from falsity." (W quoting Vasubandhu, 500.1)

"The 'thoroughly established character' is correct knowledge and suchness that are distinguished by having been transformed and by being the suchness of phenomena." (B, vol. cho [205]:187.6)

5 "Clouded vision" (rab-rib, timira) indicates a wide range of visual defects, including occluded or hazy vision, seeing spots or lines in the visual field that may look like a net of hairs, insects, sesame seeds, etc., or perceiving colors incorrectly. (See W, vol. ti [118]:517.4, 518.5; Viṁśatikā-kārikā-vṛtti 161, verse 2 and commentary)

6 Mahānīla (mthon-ka-chen-po) is a blue-colored gem.

7 "In that way, through entering into [understanding of] the character of objects that appear in the manner of mental verbalizations, those Bodhisattvas enter into [understanding of] the imputational character. Through entering into [understanding of] cognition-only, they enter into [understanding of] the other-dependent character. How do they enter into [understanding of] the thoroughly established character? They enter after having reversed even concep-

tions of cognition-only." (W, vol. ti [118]:538.1, citing MS) "At that time, since objects of observation and observers are equalized for those Bodhisattvas, the non-conceptual exalted wisdom of equality arises. Therefore, those Bodhisattvas have entered into [understanding of] the thoroughly established character." (W 538.6)

Notes to Chapter Seven

1 Regarding the name of this Bodhisattva, Paramārthasamudgata ('Exalted by the Ultimate'): "The 'ultimate' is the object to be attained, and it is the object of the supreme exalted wisdom. Therefore it is called 'ultimate'. Because the exalted wisdom that is the means of attainment arises from observing the ultimate, he is 'exalted'." (W, vol. ti [118]:544.7) This chapter explains the meaning of the character of lack of own-being of phenomena. (VS, P 5539, vol. 'i [111]:62b.2)

2 Paramārthasamudgata's question implies that the two sets of teachings (the teachings concerning the aggregates and so forth taught in other Sūtras and the teachings concerning lack of own-being and so forth taught in this Sūtra) are mutually contradictory (phan-tshun-'gal-ba). (W, vol. ti [118]:552.4) Paramārthasamudgata is asking the Buddha to clarify the intentions behind his earlier teachings in light of the teachings being given in this text. According to G (74.6–75.13), Paramārthasamudgata is asking this question not for himself, but for the benefit of others who might have such questions.

3 "That suchness which is the object of the exalted wisdom purifying the two obstructions [i.e., the afflictive obstructions and the obstructions to omniscience] is the thoroughly established nature and is the object of observation for purification." (DLG 48.1)

4 "Lack of own-being in the sense of lack of own-being in terms of character should be understood to be an utter non-existence in terms of both conventional and ultimate truths, like a sky-flower. . . . Like a magical apparition, lack of own-being in the sense of lack of own-being in terms of production and ultimate lack of own-being should be understood as existing only as a conventional truth." (B, vol. cho [205]:187.6) "The similarity of imputational natures with a sky-flower is an example of their merely being imputed by thought and is not an example of their not occurring among objects of knowledge." (EG 13.11)

5 Asaṅga states that when the Buddha said that all phenomena are unproduced and so forth, he was "thinking only of lack of own-being in terms of character." (VS, P 5539, vol. 'i [111]:18a.8)

6 "'Peacefulness' (zhi-ba, śānti) refers to liberation from the afflictive obstructions. 'Proceeds' (bgrod-pa, yāna) refers to the path and the fruit: the path of the Śrāvaka vehicle and the fruit of liberation. 'Solely' (gcig-pu, eka) refers to not attaining the lineage which achieves the conditions for complete transformation into [the state of] unsurpassable enlightenment at that time, and abiding in the partial liberation and nirvāṇa of the Śrāvaka." (B, vol. cho [205]: 239.1. See also Bh 14.5)

"Since the causes of unsurpassed, perfect enlightenment are thoroughly ripening sentient beings and ripening the qualities of a Buddha for oneself, those who do not complete those two [activities] lack the causes of that [i.e., enlightenment] at that time. Moreover, this is merely a difference in practice; it does not come from the nature of the mind. Therefore, [Buddha's] thought is that they are called 'those who proceed solely towards peacefulness' as long as they have not attained the lineage of transformation into unsurpassed enlightenment and do not exert themselves." (B 240.3)

7 "Because Śrāvakas [who evolve with respect to enlightenment] immediately thereafter abide on the eighth Bodhisattva stage, Śrāvakas are also indicated as being among the enumeration of Bodhisattvas." (B, vol. cho [205]:241.2) "When [Śrāvakas] become non-learners [when they reach the path of no more learning of the Śrāvaka vehicle], they turn away from the aspirations of Śrāvakas, and through the Tathāgatas' encouragement they apply themselves to unsurpassed, complete, perfect enlightenment with a body that has a remainder of aggregates [impelled by former contaminated actions and afflictive emotions]." (B 241.3. See also WE 261)

8 "As long as [their enlightenment] is not transformed into unsurpassed enlightenment, they are designated as being of the Śrāvaka lineage." (B, vol. cho [205]:241.4)

9 The "disciplinary doctrine" (chos-'dul-ba, dharma-vinaya) is here understood as "the teaching of the Bhagavan, the Buddha, [which is] endowed with the eight branches of the path of Āryas. Correct views, realization, mindfulness, and samādhi are doctrine. Correct speech, aims of actions, and livelihood are discipline. Correct exertion is

omnipresent. It is 'well taught' since that disciplinary doctrine is explained exceptionally well. It is 'well taught' since it is virtuous in the beginning, virtuous in the middle, and virtuous in the end." (B, vol. cho [205]:242.1) "Because all three scriptural collections [of Vinaya, Sūtra, and Abhidharma] have the capacity to discipline ill deeds, [they are] 'disciplinary'." (W, vol. thi [119]:46.4. See also WE 29–34)

10 "'Having ripened their continuums' [means that] although Bodhisattvas on the occasion of having gained the Bodhisattva lineage abide in the lineage and have thoroughly purified obstructions, due to four causes, they are unable to attain unsurpassed, perfect enlightenment. Due to being free from those four causes indicated earlier, [these Bodhisattvas] have 'thoroughly ripened continuums'. . . . 'Great conviction' [refers to] conviction in the ability to attain the qualities of a Buddha . . . Thoroughly ripened wisdom [is that which] differentiates doctrines and apprehends the ultimate truth. This is indicated by 'they have completed the great accumulations of merit and wisdom.'" (B, vol. cho [205]:244.2)

11 The Buddha's thought differs from what the actual words of his teaching indicate to beings who do not understand this thought. This point is developed at length in EG, especially 3–29, and DLG, especially 8–36. See also JBW 294–97.

12 This is because they do not seek the definitive meaning and the Mahāyāna but adhere to the literal meaning, thus misunderstanding the teachings. (W, vol. thi [119]:61.7) Because they do not seek scriptures of definitive meaning, but grasp at scriptures of interpretable meaning, they hold their own views to be supreme. (W 62.1)

13 The dGe-lugs-pa tradition, beginning with Tsong-kha-pa, interprets this passage to mean that these beings, whom they identify as Prāsaṅgika-Mādhyamikas, think that no object exists by way of its own-character. Thus they fall into the extreme of nihilism. (See EG 13–14) W states that this passage indicates the faults of exaggerated adherence to literal meanings. (W, vol. thi [119]:62)

14 "'They [adopt] the view that all phenomena do not exist' [because] they view the phenomena that lack character, the phenomena of thoroughly afflicted character, and the phenomena of purified character as being equally non-existent. 'They [adopt] the view that character does not exist': They view all imputational char-

acters, other-dependent characters, and thoroughly established characters as equally non-existent. With respect to [the phrase,] 'If other-dependent and thoroughly established characters exist, then the imputational character is also understood': This is because imputation of names and terminology in the manner of own-being and attributes is itself the imputational character. [The phrase,] 'Therefore, they also deprecate all three types of characters' indicates [that they hold] a specific type of belief that arises from little wisdom." (B, vol. cho [205]:252.4)

15 "When dried ginger is put in medicinal powders, they become potent. When one puts these words of lack of own-being and so forth in all Sūtras of interpretable meaning, then one will understand the thoughts [behind] those Sūtras." (W, vol. thi [119]:107.5)

16 Through these examples, Paramārthasamudgata offers four ways of looking at the relation between what the Buddha said in his interpretable teachings and the definitive teachings that state his actual thought. In the first example, the definitive teaching is compared to an ingredient in a medicinal preparation essential to its efficacy. In the second example, the definitive teaching is compared to the background of a painting, which may remain unnoticed, but which provides the basis for the placement of lines and color. In the third example, the definitive teaching is compared to an ingredient in cooking that enhances flavor. In the final example, the definitive teaching is compared to space. Space is all-pervasive, subtle, imperceptible, and generally not noticed, but makes possible the manifestation of physical objects. In the same way, the definitive teaching is said to be subtle, difficult to perceive, and so forth, but is the essence of the explanations given by Buddha in the first two wheels, even when this was not noticed by his audience. (See W, vol. thi [119]:109.2; B, vol. cho [205]:262; and Bh 14–15)

17 "'Surpassable' indicates that there are other Sūtras of definitive meaning that are higher. [They] 'provide an opportunity' [for refutation because they] provide an opportunity for other disputants to find fault with respect to the literal reading of the explicit teaching. . . . [The first wheel] serves as a basis for controversy in that there is a basis for dispute because the Teacher did not differentiate individually in terms of the three characters whether they do or do not exist by way of their own character." (DLG, 29.4)

Notes to Chapter Eight

1 Maitreya is the future Buddha, who presently resides in Tuṣita in preparation for his last rebirth as a fully actualized Buddha. He is called Maitreya ('Love') "because his nature is endowed with love and compassion." (W, vol. thi [119]:174.2)

2 The main topic of this chapter is "the differentiation of the path of śamatha and vipaśyanā, which is subsumed under yoga." (VS, P 5539, vol. 'i [111]:73b.2) This chapter is one of the great scriptural locus classici for śamatha and vipaśyanā in the Mahāyāna tradition. (See also S, vol. II, n12, p. 33 for a bibliography on these topics; W, vol. thi [119]:198–220; and ME 67–114)

3 "Bodhisattvas 'abide in' [this resolution] because they have heard [those doctrines] well, apprehended them well, trained in reciting them, and analyzed them well with their minds, and have realized them through insight. Abiding in [realization of] them, they are not committed to cyclic existence, resources, etc., and they undertake a supramundane path. Therefore, that [resolution] is a cause of undertaking the path of śamatha and vipaśyanā, an abode that has risen above worldlings." (B, vol. cho [205]:275.6)

"[This enlightenment] is 'unsurpassable' in terms of six unsurpassabilities: unsurpassable perception, unsurpassable hearing, unsurpassable attainments, unsurpassable training, unsurpassable religious service, and unsurpassable mindfulness. It is 'perfect' because it is non-erroneous with respect to the own-being of all phenomena. 'Enlightenment' means realization. 'Unwavering resolution' refers to generating, uninterruptedly and continually, from the depth of one's thought, the mind of enlightenment . . ." (B 276.1)

4 In the context of meditation, an 'object of observation' (dmigs-pa, ālambana) is any object that a meditator takes to mind. (See COM 47)

5 "'Conceptual images' are objects of activity imagined by samādhi that are partially similar to things that are objects of knowledge. 'Non-conceptual images' are correct objects that are the focus of samādhi that are partially similar to things that are objects of knowledge." (W, vol. thi [119]:185.7. See also Kamalaśīla's Bhāvanākrama 1–3)

"'Observing the limits of phenomena' refers to observing the relative aspects of existence and the ultimate aspects of existence of all phenomena. 'Relative aspects of existence' refers to the aggregates, constituents, and sense spheres. 'Ultimate aspects of existence' refers to the four noble truths, suchness, the impermanence of all compounded phenomena, the suffering [associated with] all compounded phenomena, the selflessness of all phenomena, [the fact that] nirvāṇa is peace, and to emptiness, wishlessness, and signlessness." (W 180.4) "Accomplishment of the purpose" refers to transformation of the basis (gnas-gyur-pa, āśraya-parāvṛtti) in general, which includes the actualization of the Dharmakāya. (W 180.6. See also B, vol. cho [205]:277–81)

6 "Seclusion" refers to physical isolation (lus-dben-pa, kāya-viveka), and "remaining in seclusion" refers to mental isolation (sems-dben-pa, citta-viveka). There are three aspects of isolation: "an excellent abode, excellent behavior, and excellent isolation." Excellent abodes are of three types: hermitages, places without householders, and roofless dwellings. The third type consists of such places as burial grounds, hermitages, mountain caves, and fields. (B, vol. cho [205]: 302.1) "Genuinely settling the mind inwardly" (nang-du-yang-dag-bzhag) is samādhi. (B 304.6. See also W, vol. thi [119]:195.2)

7 "Pliancy" (shin-tu-sbyangs-pa, praśrabdhi) is one of the ten virtuous mental factors. It "refers to fitness for action that freely applies the full energy of body and mind toward good purposes. This ease comes from relaxing rigidity, and it removes all obstacles." (WE 148) In SB, Asaṅga states: "Pliancy is supreme happiness and joy that is preceded by faith and clarity. Gradually making the mind joyful, pliancy [eliminates] the non-virtuous class of errant tendencies." (NE 4036, vol. dzi:117a.4–.5. See also 147b.6–148a.4; Kośa II:25)

These are called physical and mental pliancy "because there is no physical fatigue and no mental turmoil." (B, vol. cho [205]:308.5)

8 The aspects of the mind (sems-kyi-rnam-pa, cittākāra) that are abandoned are "non-conceptual images, the objects of observation of the path of śamatha." (B, vol. cho [205]:310.4)

9 "'Differentiation' involves differentiation by way of the varieties of existence (ji-snyed-yod-pa-nyid) with respect to objects of observation for purifying behavior, skillful objects of observation, and objects of observation for purifying afflictions. 'Thorough differentiation' involves thorough differentiation by way of how things actually exist with respect to those very objects of activity that serve as objects of observation. 'Thorough investigation' involves thoroughly

investigating those objects of observation—through conceptual mental activity that is endowed with wisdom—after having thoroughly apprehended their signs. 'Thorough analysis' involves thoroughly analyzing those objects of activity that serve as objects of observation at the time of correctly investigating them. The next five are synonyms of vipaśyanā. . . . 'Forbearance' is forbearance in terms of understanding. 'Desire' refers to interest. 'Wisdom' refers to discrimination. 'View' refers to thorough searching. 'Investigation' refers to individual investigation." (W, vol. thi [119]:200.2)

10 "'Perceives [an image]' here refers to a non-conceptual realizational consciousness of a yogi who has vipaśyanā. The 'image that is the focus of samādhi' refers to conceptual and non-conceptual images that are the focus of samādhis of śamatha and vipaśyanā." (B, vol. cho [205]:323.6)

11 This is a key point for Yogācāra writers. "Because that image is of the nature of the mind, it is not different from mind." (B, vol. cho [205]: 324.2) "They are said to be 'not different' because the object is not separate from the mind. The fact that in reality they are neither one nor different destroys the apprehension of them as being different, whereby they are said to be 'not different'." (W, vol. thi [119]:207.5) What serves as an object of observation does not exist when separated from mind: "Whatever is an object of observation by consciousness is explained as appearing from cognition-only." (W 208.1)

In the phrase "Why is it not different?" the word "not" is added in the translation on the basis of the sTog-palace and Them-spangs-ma editions of the Saṁdhinirmocana Sūtra and the commentaries by W and B. The negative particle is not found in the sDe-dge edition.

12 Similar questions, based on observing that an eye cannot see itself, a finger cannot touch itself, and swords cannot cut themselves, have also been raised against the doctrine of cognition-only, but the case of the mind is different from that of the others. (W, vol. thi [119]:208.7) "When an other-dependent phenomenon such as mind is produced, because such images appear, the mind apprehends them as objects." (W 210.3) The mind's perception of objects is not like the rays of the sun illuminating external objects; rather, like an object in a mirror, something appears to be an external object but is only of the entity of mind: "Objects of direct perception arise from the entity of [the consciousness itself]. Thus the Sūtras say that although it is not the case that any phenomenon appre-

hends another phenomenon, at the time when a consciousness is produced it appears as similar in character to those [things]. Therefore it is said that things are apprehended." (W 211.1)

13 "Childish beings who do not perceive suchness, whose vision has degenerated due to faults of vision, perceive external objects as existing although they do not exist." (B, vol. cho [205]:326.5) "Even objects of observation of distracted minds are not separate from the mind, but childish beings' minds are in error, and so they consider objects of observation as external objects." (W, vol. thi [119]:217.5) "When they abandon external objects, then they pacify incorrect minds; when they pacify incorrect minds, then they realize the middle way." (W 218.1)

Asaṅga (MS) states: "When the mind is in meditative equipoise, whatever images that are objects of knowledge—blue and so forth—that are seen, the mind is seen. Blue and so forth are not objects that are different from mind. By this reasoning, Bodhisattvas should infer that all cognitions are cognition-only." (S, vol. I, II:7.2)

14 "At that time, one understands that phenomena do not exist apart from cognition. Having understood that, one also takes suchness to mind." (W, vol. thi [119]:221.6)

15 The three kinds of śamatha refer to a threefold division corresponding to the threefold division of vipaśyanā: śamatha having signs; śamatha of examination; and śamatha of individual investigation. Since there are three kinds of vipaśyanā that observe mental signs, there are three corresponding types of śamatha that observe an uninterrupted mind. (W, vol. thi [119]:226.1)

16 These "signs of the doctrine" (chos-kyi-mtshan-ma, dharma-nimitta) are "signs that are the words, letters, and so forth [of doctrines]." (B, vol. cho [205]:336.4) "These Bodhisattvas obtain śamatha and vipaśyanā in terms of the meaning of the twelve forms of doctrinal teachings [listed on p. 151 of this Sūtra] through wisdom applied to those doctrines that they have previously heard and thought about." (W, vol. thi [119]:247.7)

17 A Bodhisattva who observes integrated doctrines ('dres-pa'i-chos, miśra-dharma) can bring together all the enumerations, characteristics, and contextual etymologies found in various Sūtras and understand that they are all of one taste. (B, vol. cho [205]:339.1. See W, vol. thi [119]:252.6–253.4, and JNG 325a-b)

18 "Transformation of the basis" refers to the fundamental changes that are brought about through the cultivation of method and wisdom. (See p. 341 note 5 of this Sūtra)

"'Nirvāṇa' refers to the sphere of the uncompounded ('dus-ma-byas-pa'i-dbyings) and 'transformation of the basis' refers to the Dharmakāya. 'All these doctrines' refers to all of those doctrines that are of one taste, those countless virtuous scriptural doctrines and realizational doctrines, which, through their manifest expression and their teaching, clarify [meanings] and increase virtue." (B, vol. cho [205]:339.6)

19 "The first, somewhat integrated doctrines, [are so named] because one observes the twelve limbs of teachings in terms of individual differences. The second, highly integrated doctrines, [are so named] because one observes the twelve limbs of teachings collectively. The third, immeasurably integrated doctrines, [are so named] because one observes the twelve limbs of the Tathāgatas' immeasurable teachings as a single collection." (W, vol. di [120]:129.6)

20 The term "conceptual (rtog-pa-dang-bcas-pa, savitarka) samādhi" refers to examination and the term "analytical (dpyod-pa-dang-bcas-pa, savicāra) samādhi" refers to individual analysis. (W, vol. thi [119]: 278.7. See also p. 149 of this Sūtra, and p. 340 note 5, where conceptual and non-conceptual images are discussed; and Kośa VIII:23d-e)

Asaṅga equates non-conceptual samādhi with higher wisdom (adhiprajñā). In his commentary on MS, Vasubandhu states: "Intuitive knowledge [literally, free from concepts] is exalted wisdom. For Śrāvakas, the absence of concepts consists of not imagining any of the four errors; for Bodhisattvas, the absence of concepts consists of not imagining any dharmas. This is the difference between the two absences of concepts." (S, vol. II, 8)

21 "Clear and coarse signs" (mtshan-ma-gsal-zhing-rags-pa, vyakta-sthūla-nimitta) are images on the level of association with conceptuality of the first concentration. (B, vol. cho [205]:346.1) "Coarse signs" include "all signs that are sources of affliction." (W, vol. thi [119]: 441.7)

22 "Sobering phenomena" (kun-tu-skyo-bar-gyur-pa'i-chos, udvegam-āpadyata-dharma) are things such as corpses, specific sufferings, impermanence, etc., that reduce excitement or help one to realize saṁsāric sufferings. "Whatever serves to pacify and isolate the mind through the power of those two types of mental attention [to sober-

ing phenomena and the uninterrupted mind] in that way is a 'cause of śamatha'. "(W, vol. thi [119]:283.5)

23 The term *don* (artha), translated in this section as "objects," could also be correctly translated as "meanings."

24 Jambudvīpa, the southern of the four great land masses of traditional Buddhist cosmology, measures 2,000 yojanas on three sides and three-and-one-half yojanas on its fourth side. (See WE 214)

25 There are fourteen types of resources (longs-spyod): food, drink, vehicles, clothing, ornaments, laughter, singing, instrumental music, perfume, flower garlands, unguents, vessels, exhibitions, and men and women. (W, vol. thi [119]:314.4), citing YB)

26 "Reality-limit" is a synonym for emptiness and the ultimate. (MV 218 [I.14]. See also COM 18–19)

27 See W, vol. thi [119]:319–21.

28 "'Worldly realms' ('jig-rten-gyi-khams, loka-dhātu) refers to limitless worldly realms. These are the environments—limitless in the ten directions and also having limitless names—that are objects for Bodhisattvas to purify. 'The realm of sentient beings' (sems-can-gyi-khams, sattva-dhātu) refers to limitless realms of sentient beings. These are the sixty-four activated and inactivated lineages of sentient beings who are objects for Bodhisattvas to mature. 'The realm of qualities' (chos-kyi-khams, dharma-dhātu) refers to the limitless realms of qualities. These are the realms of sentient beings in the worldly realms that have become afflicted or purified due to virtuous, non-virtuous, and neutral practices that are to be realized by Bodhisattvas. 'The realm of discipline' ('dul-ba'i-khams, vinaya-dhātu) refers to the limitless realms of discipline. These are sentient beings whose lineage has been activated, who are endowed with fortune, are suitable to be liberated from suffering forever, and are to be liberated by Bodhisattvas. 'The realm of methods of discipline' ('dul-ba'i-thabs-kyi-khams, vinayopāyadhātu) refers to the limitless methods of discipline. These are the methods for freeing those sentient beings whom Bodhisattvas instruct." (B, vol. cho [205]:371.7)

29 "They abide in words because wisdom [arisen from] hearing arises due to the power of words. They take them literally because they apprehend these letters according to the literal meanings of the words they comprise. But they do not apprehend the words

through the meaning, as is done by the two [other] wisdoms." They do not understand the intent because they do not fully understand the thought behind the Buddha's scriptures. They do not actualize them because "when they observe such objects, they still do not actualize partially concordant images and do not attain samādhi. They are concordant with liberation because they are concordant with the liberation of nirvāṇa after a long time and because [nirvāṇa] contains both aspects of liberation from compounded and uncompounded phenomena. But they do not thoroughly know liberative objects because they abide in a fluctuating mind and have not abandoned entanglements due to not attaining the cessations." (W, vol. thi [119]:339.2)

30 A standard list of eighteen emptinesses is described in Mahāvyutpatti XXXVII:1–18; W, vol. thi [119]:361–76; B, vol. cho [205]:384–88; and ME 204–5. Sixteen emptinesses are listed in MV 219 (I.16c).

31 "Through having eliminated the two [types of] images that are objects of observation of śamatha and vipaśyanā, there is no manifest grasping of the other-dependent character as the imputational character." (B, vol. cho [205]:388.7. See also W, vol. thi [119]:383.2)

32 "'Views [that overvalue] the body' (lus-la-lta-ba, kāya-dṛṣṭi) are attachments to the internal sense spheres. 'Views [that overvalue] resources' (longs-spyod-la-lta-ba, bhoga-dṛṣṭi) are attachments to the external sense spheres." (B, vol. cho [205]:396.3)

33 "'Abiding in turmoil' refers to physical non-isolation (lus-kyi-mi-dben-pa, kāya-aviveka). 'Being satisfied with inferior [attainment]' refers to mental non-isolation (sems-kyi-mi-dben-pa, citta-aviveka)." (B, vol. cho [205]:396.6. See also p. 341 note 6 of this Sūtra)

34 "'Mental contemplations of the Mahāyāna' are contemplations on the selflessness of phenomena (dharma-nairātmya) and are endowed with the paths and fruits of Bodhisattvas. By contrast, 'mental contemplations of Śrāvakas and Pratyekabuddhas' are contemplations on the selflessness of persons (pudgala-nairātmya) and are associated with abiding on a path of asceticism, and attaining the fruits of asceticism." (B, vol. cho [205]:399.2)

35 "'Signs' are shapes of the forms of men, women, and so forth. 'Conceptuality' refers to the five, conceptuality of desire, harmful intent, and so forth. The 'secondary afflictions' are all the bases that are concordant with making the mind afflicted. 'External objects of

observation' include all aspects of objects. Through these, the mind becomes scattered." (B, vol. cho [205]:399.4)

36 Sentient beings who relish the experience of the four concentrations and the four formless absorptions can attain birth among the long-lived gods. Through this they lose the ability to practice the concentrations and absorptions, and so fall away from benefitting sentient beings. (B, vol. cho [205]:399.6. See also WE 288–89)

37 "With respect to the 'signs of mental appropriation', there are two causes for connecting lives of the basis-consciousness itself: (1) predispositions for manifestly apprehending the imputational character, and (2) appropriating physical sense powers that serve as bases [of consciousnesses]. When viewing the body and establishing mindfulness of the body– the internal body, the external body, and bodies that are both internal and external which are appropriated [through those two causes]–whatever images appear with respect to the body (the impure signs and the signs of suchness that are the focus of samādhi) are the 'signs of mental appropriation'." (B, vol. cho [205]:406.3)

"With respect to 'signs of experience', there is obscuration concerning the self, the view of self, pride of self, and attachment to self of just that mind. When viewing feelings and establishing mindfulness of feelings [produced] by these–the internal feelings, external feelings, and feelings that are both internal and external that are experienced–whatever images appear with respect to feelings (the signs of suffering and the signs of suchness that are the focus of samādhi) are called 'signs of mental experience'." (B 406.5)

"'Signs of cognition' are just that mind's cognitions of objects of observation. Through these, when viewing the mind and establishing mindfulness of the mind–internal minds, external minds, and minds that are both internal and external, which are cognized as just that mind–whatever images appear with respect to the mind (the signs of impermanence and the signs of suchness that are the focus of samādhi) are 'signs of mental cognition'." (B 406.6)

"'Signs of affliction and purification' are the mind's own minds and mental factors. When viewing phenomena and establishing mindfulness of phenomena–in regard to phenomena that are abodes and objects of observation of [those minds and mental factors] that are internal phenomena, external phenomena, and phenomena that are both internal and external–whatever images appear that are the focus of samādhi . . . (the signs of affliction and the signs of the suchness of that and the signs of purification and the signs of the suchness of that) . . . are the 'signs of affliction and purification'." (B 407.1)

"'Internal signs' are aspects involved in realizing the emptiness of the internal. 'External signs' are aspects involved in realizing the emptiness of the external. 'Signs of both' are aspects involved in realizing the emptiness of [both] the internal and external." (B 407.4)

"'Signs involved in thinking, "I must work for the sake of all sentient beings"' are aspects involved in realizing the emptiness of emptiness. One realizes the emptiness of emptiness as an antidote to neglecting the welfare of sentient beings upon having the thought, 'If the internal and the external are both emptiness, then what is to be achieved in emptiness?' One realizes the emptiness of emptiness, thinking, '[I] will apply myself to the welfare of all sentient beings since that emptiness is itself also empty.'"(B 407.5)

"'Signs of knowledge' are aspects involved in realizing the emptiness of the great. This is the realization that all worldly realms in the ten directions are not external or internal things, but are of the nature of consciousness." (B 407.7)

"'Signs of suchness, the truth of suffering, the truth of the source of suffering, the truth of the cessation of suffering, and the truth of the path' are aspects involved in realizing the emptiness of the ultimate." (B 407.7)

"'Signs of compounded phenomena' are aspects that are involved in realizing the emptiness of compounded phenomena. 'Signs of uncompounded phenomena' are aspects involved in realizing the emptiness of uncompounded phenomena." (B 408.1)

"'Signs of permanence' are aspects for realizing the emptiness of what has passed beyond the extremes. One realizes that persons are utterly non-existent in permanent, permanent time and everlasting, everlasting time. 'Signs of impermanence' are aspects for realizing the emptiness of what is beginningless and endless. One realizes the emptiness of impermanent phenomena, [the fact that] compounded phenomena lack a former or later limit." (B 408.2)

"'Signs that have a nature associated with suffering and change' are aspects for realizing the emptiness of the indestructible [i.e., nirvāṇa]. . . . That which has a nature of suffering is the aggregates. That which has a nature of change is also the aggregates. This is because they are true sufferings and because they have an impermanent nature. The aggregates having a nature of suffering and the aggregates having a nature of change are 'what are to be discarded': This is a synonym for the aggregates. The indestructible [literally, 'that which is not to be discarded'] is nirvāṇa, because it is the utter cessation of suffering and has a changeless nature. 'Signs having a nature that is unchangeable' are aspects for realizing what is emptiness by nature." (B 408.3)

"'Signs unlike the characteristics of compounded phenomena' or 'signs of their own characteristics' are aspects involved in realizing the emptiness of character. The different character of compounded phenomena is the uncompounded, the ultimate truth. Their specific characters are compounded phenomena, conventional truths. One realizes that those two characters are empty of being without an inherent nature." (B 409.4)

"'Signs of universality, as in the context of knowing everything as "everything"' are aspects for realizing the emptiness of everything. One realizes that all the phenomena included within [the categories] compounded and uncompounded are empty." (B 409.5)

"'Signs of the selflessness of persons' are aspects involved in realizing the emptiness of the unobservable. One understands persons as being the emptiness of the unobservable." (B 409.6)

"'Signs of the selflessness of phenomena' are aspects involved in realizing the emptiness of non-things. One realizes that phenomena are empty of being non-things. In this way, one enters into suchness, the antidote to all the signs of the other-dependent." (B 409.6. See also W, vol. thi [119]:442)

38 "'Individually and internally' means within the nature of the mind. 'Known by oneself' means that one knows non-dualistically." (B, vol. cho [205]:410.2. See pp. 171–73 of this Sūtra for a list of the seven aspects of suchness.)

39 The term *khye'u* usually means "puppy" or "child." In his Dag-yig-thon-mi'i-dgongs-rgyan (New Delhi, 1969, p. 38), Tshe-brtan-zhabs-drung states that *khye'u* refers to "a small piece of wood that is used to set up and make firm," such as a wooden peg used to hold furniture and so forth together. The example indicates that just as a small nail could be used to expel a much larger one, so this mental contemplation (which at first is weak compared to the afflictions) can be used to eliminate the grossest afflictions at first and then gradually

to eliminate more subtle ones. (See S, vol. II, 219–20 for the same analogy, and W, vol. thi [119]:452.3 for different ways to apply this analogy.)

40 The Bodhisattva's great powers are the power of clairvoyance, the power of doctrine, innate powers, common powers, and uncommon powers. (B, vol. cho [205]:411.7. See also 412–25, and COM 98)

41 In this passage "skillful" refers to "a mind that thoroughly knows" (yongs-su-shes-par-byed-pa'i-sems). (W, vol. thi [119]:457.5)

42 "It is a 'foundation' because it is the appropriating consciousness, which is the abode of the predispositions for afflicted and purified phenomena. It is a 'receptacle' because it is a world that is an environment." (B, vol. cho [205]:425.6)

43 In the Sems-tsam-pa system, "conceptual [consciousness includes] all minds and mental factors of the three realms that have dualistic appearance." (Drang-nges-rnam-'byed-kyi-zin-bris-zab-don-gsal-ba'i-sgron-me, by Ser-shul-dge-bshes, 36a-b)

44 In both Mahāyāna and Hīnayāna systems of meditation, joy and bliss are both present in the first two concentrations. In the third concentration joy is absent but bliss is present. Meditative equanimity is also developed in the third concentration, and is strengthened in the fourth concentration to the point where bliss disappears and is replaced with a pervasive equanimity. Joy and bliss are progressively eliminated because they interfere with mental stability. (See WE 88–90, 287–88; Kośa VIII:2b; *Meditative States,* 92–128)

45 "Faith and so forth" includes the eleven virtuous mental factors, the six contaminated consciousnesses, and the eight uncontaminated consciousnesses associated with those. (W, vol. thi [119]:464.2)

46 "Because the mind's emergence is liberation from the bonds of the other-dependent and the imputational and abides in the suchness of the thoroughly established, in that way consciousness is indicated as being skilled with respect to that. The 'bonds of signs' are signs of the other-dependent character, and the 'bonds of errant tendencies' are predispositions for imputations." (B, vol. cho [205]: 428.7) "Having thoroughly realized, just as it is, the mind that is concordant with non-conceptual exalted wisdom, one renounces the two bonds." (W, vol. thi [119]:465.3)

47 It is called "means" because it induces various qualities, such as the clairvoyances and the absence of affliction. (W, vol. thi [119]:467.1. See also COM 175)

48 "Because they follow from errant tendencies that are seeds of the two obstructions, they are 'errant tendencies that are abodes.'" (W, vol. thi [119]:469.7. See also 470–71 for alternate explanations)

"With respect to awareness of errant tendencies that are abodes: 'abode' refers to the untransformed basis-consciousness itself, because it is the abode of all the phenomena of minds and mental factors and all the predispositions. On this occasion, because one is [at] the level of transformation of the basis into nirvāṇa with a remainder of aggregates, the transformed basis-consciousness abides in non-conceptual exalted wisdom itself." (B, vol. cho [205]:430.2)

The "fruits" of [those tendencies] are the six external objects, which arise through the power of the six internal sense powers and thus are their fruits. Because knowers of objects also arise upon observing those, they are [also] 'fruits'." (W, vol. thi [119]:470.1)

49 "'Awareness of form states' [includes] the seeds of desire realm feelings. 'Awareness of formless states' [includes] the seeds of formless realm feelings. 'Awareness of errant tendencies that have come to fruition' [includes] the seeds that bring forth present results. 'Awareness of errant tendencies that have not yet come to fruition' [includes] the seeds that have not yet brought forth results." (W, vol. thi [119]:471.5) The first is "whatever feelings accompany the five collections of consciousness." The second is "whatever feelings accompany the mental consciousness." These are the physical and mental feelings that are the awareness of present effects produced by past ignorance, motivational factors, and so forth. (W 471.6. See also 491.7)

50 "Should you ask, 'If Tathāgatas pass beyond sorrow in the element of nirvāṇa without a remainder of the aggregates, how then can they work to establish the welfare of others until the end of cyclic existence?' [Their ability to do this] is due to the power of former aspirations: Tathāgatas continually work for the benefit of sentient beings, although they display nirvāṇa." (B, vol. cho [205]:437.7)

Notes to Chapter Nine

1 This great Bodhisattva is named Avalokiteśvara ('The Lord Who Looks Down') "because internally this Bodhisattva is endowed with wisdom and compassion and externally has effortless natural dominion over the three actions of body and so forth." (W, vol. thi

[119]:488.5) Avalokiteśvara is often depicted with a thousand arms, representing his immense capacity for compassionate help.

2 "[On] the fourth stage one abides in surpassing wisdom that is involved with things concordant with enlightenment. [On] the fifth stage, one abides in surpassing wisdom involved with the truths. [On] the sixth stage, one abides in surpassing wisdom involved with dependent origination. [On] the seventh stage, one abides in signlessness with exertion. [On] the eighth stage, one abides in signlessness without exertion. [On] the ninth stage, one abides in correct individual knowledge. [On] the tenth stage, one abides in the excellences and thorough completions of Bodhisattvas. The eleventh stage is the state of a Tathāgata." (W, vol. thi [119]:493.6)

"Pure thought" refers to "surpassing thought." (W, vol. thi [119]: 489.7) According to a commentary on MS it refers to "the nature of non-conceptual exalted wisdom," but according to YB it refers to "the nature of belief." According to Asvabhāva and Vasubandhu it refers to "the nature of faith and aspiration." (W 490.4) Through this attitude one overcomes the afflictions, secondary afflictions, and all activities of Māra; one thinks to control one's own mind; one considers the faults of compounded phenomena; considers the benefits of nirvāṇa; thinks to constantly engage in meditative cultivation of virtuous phenomena concordant with enlightenment; thinks of the isolation [of body and mind] concordant with that cultivation; thinks without regard to worldly things, renown, goods, and services; one thinks to realize the Mahāyāna upon having abandoned the Hīnayāna; and one thinks to bring about the welfare of all sentient beings. (W 491.4)

3 "'Limb' (yan-lag, aṅga) means 'state' (gnas)." (W, vol. thi [119]: 494.6)

4 The ten aspects of doctrinal practice are: "(1) causing beings to copy Sūtras that are included in the Bodhisattva canon and that contain Mahāyāna doctrines; (2) memorizing them; (3) venerating them; (4) giving them to others; (5) honoring them when they are taught and listening to them; (6) reading them oneself; (7) likewise receiving an oral transmission for realizing them entirely; (8) extensively reciting those for which oral transmission has been received; (9) extensively teaching them to others; (10) having gone into seclusion, engaging in contemplating them, comprehending them, realizing them, and meditating on them." (W, vol. thi [119]:497.2, citing YB)

5 "When one thoroughly passes beyond preparation due to the power of the causes and conditions of the ten doctrinal practices and so forth, one enters into the faultless reality of the first stage. Due to those causes and conditions, one thoroughly completes those limbs. 'Reality' (yang-dag-pa-nyid) refers to the uncontaminated path of the Āryas, which is called 'reality' because due to it one turns away from error." (W, vol. thi [119]:498.5)

6 On the first Bodhisattva stage Bodhisattvas are not endowed with advanced abilities, so they do not understand habituation to subtle faults of faulty ethics. "This inability is due to three obscurations: (1) ignorance of faults that are subtle infractions; (2) ignorance of various types of actions; and (3) 'fruition of an errant tendency', which is whatever is associated with what is manifested due to connection with those very ignorances. Through abandoning these three obscurations, one engages in correct effort. Having abandoned these three obscurations, one enters the second stage and attains eight pure qualities: pure thought, pure love, pure compassion, pure perfections, pure perception with respect to performing the activities of a Buddha, pure ripening of sentient beings, pure power, and pure qualities. From the first stage up to the Buddha stage these eight qualities become progressively greater and more advanced." (W, vol. thi [119]:502.3, citing YB)

7 "They are called 'absorptions' (snyoms-par-'jug-pa, samāpatti) because they are final states that are devoid of laxity and excitement. This is because they are final states of pacification and isolation.... They are referred to as 'worldly' ('jig-rten-pa, laukika) [samādhis] because they are associated with contamination and because they are 'engagers'." (W, vol. thi [119]:503.3. See also WE 287–90)

"To retain" (gzungs, dhāraṇī) "has the nature of memory and wisdom." (W, vol. thi [119]:507.3) There are four types of retention: "retention of doctrines, retention of meanings, retentions that are secret mantras, and retentions that are means of attaining the forbearances of Bodhisattvas." (W 507.4, citing YB) Samādhi and absorption are the causes of wisdom [arisen from] meditation, and retention is the cause of wisdom [arisen from] listening and reflecting. (W 508.4)

8 To enter into the fourth stage, one must cultivate dispassion toward meditative states. (W, vol. thi [119]:509.6) The causes of not completing the limbs of the fourth stage are: "not abiding according to one's wish in [contemplation of] things concordant with enlight-

enment that one has attained; and not being able to abide in thoroughly pure mind after having abandoned craving for absorptions and for doctrine. (W 510.3, quoting MS)

9 They are not dispassionate toward saṁsāra and nirvāṇa "because they have not attained the path of non-difference of saṁsāra and nirvāṇa." (W, vol. thi [119]:511.5)

10 "The sixth stage is not attained for two reasons: [Bodhisattvas] are unable to individually realize, just as it is, the reasoning of dependent origination with respect to involvement in cyclic existence; and they are very discouraged about suffering and the afflictions that are the sources [of suffering]." (W, vol. thi [119]:513.3)

11 On the first five stages one mainly practices meditation associated with signs and practices only a little signless meditation. On the sixth stage, however, the situation is reversed, and one mainly meditates on signlessness. Until Bodhisattvas are able to perform this meditation continuously and uninterruptedly they cannot progress to the seventh stage. (W, vol. thi [119]:514.5, citing VJ)

12 "Due to inability to abandon exertion with respect to abiding in signlessness and inability to also attain mastery with respect to signs, seventh-stage Bodhisattvas do not complete the eighth limb." (W, vol. thi [119]:516.2)

13 "'Enumerations' are objects of the comprehension of doctrine. 'Characteristics' are objects of the comprehension of meanings. 'Etymologies' are objects of the comprehension of etymologies. 'Attaining mastery in teaching the doctrine in all its aspects' is the object of the comprehension of meditation. Mastery of these is the precondition for entering the ninth stage." (W, vol. thi [119]:517.3. See also W, vol. di [120]:13.1)

14 Ninth-stage Bodhisattvas gain mastery over the four comprehensions. (W, vol. thi [119]:518.1. See also p. 181 of this Sūtra) Ninth-stage Bodhisattvas do not have the capacity to perfect the Dharmakāya that teaches doctrine thoroughly and cannot attain the unhindered and unobstructed wisdom of the six clairvoyances. (W, 519.7, citing a commentary on MS)

15 On the tenth stage there are three obstructions to entering the Tathāgata stage: ignorance in terms of very subtle attachments to all objects of knowledge; ignorance in terms of very subtle obstruc-

tions from all objects of knowledge; and errant tendencies that arise from those. When one overcomes these three, "one enters the Tathāgata stage, attains seven superior purities and purity that is free from birth. One perfects the Dharmakāya and also attains unattached and unobstructed insight and wisdom." (W, vol. thi [119]:521.5, citing a commentary on MS)

16 "In the first moment, due to actualizing a path of an uninterrupted vajra-like samādhi, one abandons the most subtle seeds of the two obstructions simultaneously. Because one abandons the afflictive obstructions, one is 'unattached'. Because one abandons the obstructions to omniscience, one is 'unimpeded'. In the second moment, one actualizes a path of liberation and becomes completely enlightened with respect to all aspects of objects of knowledge." (W, vol. thi [119]:542.1)

17 "Because [the obscurations] are ignorances, they are a class discordant with liberative wisdom. The eleven discordant classes of errant tendencies are connected with each of the eleven stages. Because they are predispositions, they are a class discordant with liberation of mind." (B, vol. cho [205]:520.3. See also W, vol. di [120]:3.2)

18 "Those who cultivate generosity, ethics, and patience on the first, second, and third stages are similar to worldly [beings]. Those on the fourth stage attain qualities concordant with enlightenment and pass beyond the mundane, completely conquering the two views of belief in true personhood [as constituting a real 'I' and 'mine']." (W, vol. di [120]:9.1)

19 "On the fifth stage, through meditating on the four truths, one enters a path that is without the differentiation of the causes and effects of affliction and purification with respect to the four truths. Therefore, one abandons the great obscurations of turning away [from saṁsāra] and toward [nirvāṇa]." (W, vol. di [120]:10.1, citing VJ)

20 "'The obscuration to manifestly realizing the operation of compounded phenomena' refers to considering afflictions as existent; this is because the operation of compounded phenomena is part of the class of afflicted [phenomena]. 'The obscuration of the arising of many signs' involves considering purification as existent; this is because one grasps at the signs of purified [phenomena]. . . . [Because of the first,] one conceives [true] sufferings and [true] sources as the approach to entering saṁsāra. [Because of the sec-

ond,] one conceives [true] cessations and [true] paths as the approach to the characteristics of purification." (W, vol. di [120]:10.4, citing VJ)

21 The first obscuration involves "conceiving beings as existent." The second type involves "conceiving negators as existent." This involves conceiving as existent the arising of the subtle signs of production and cessation due to one type of innate karma of the obstructions to omniscience. (W, vol. di [120]:11.2, citing VJ. See also VJ 649–50)

22 On the seventh stage one continually, uninterruptedly engages only in signlessness, but this requires exertion. On the eighth stage, one overcomes the need for exertion and engages in this meditation effortlessly, thus attaining mastery with respect to signless meditation and mastery with respect to signs. (W, vol. di [120]:12.4)

23 Mastery of "fearless inspiration" (spobs, pratibhāna) is "comprehension of fearless inspiration, because one understands the faculties [of other sentient beings] well and is skilled in teaching doctrine." Fearless inspiration enables Śrāvakas and Bodhisattvas to correctly and fearlessly preach doctrine. (W, vol. di [120]13.4)

24 "'The obscuration of very subtle attachment to all that is knowable' is a subtle obstruction to omniscience. 'The obscuration of very subtle obstacles' refers to all the seeds of naturally operating afflictive obstructions." (W, vol. di [120]:14.5, citing VJ)

25 "Bodhisattvas have six kinds of skill in means by which they ripen other sentient beings: Bodhisattvas cause small virtuous roots of sentient beings to bring about limitless effects; with little difficulty they produce and establish vast and limitless roots of virtue; they eliminate the anger of those who wish to harm Buddha's teachings; they cause ordinary [beings] to enter [into the path]; they thoroughly ripen those who have entered; and they liberate those who have been ripened." (B, vol. cho [205]:544.2) Through compassion "Bodhisattvas take rebirth in order to protect sentient beings." (W, vol. di [120]:37.3, citing YB)

26 "All the Bodhisattvas' aspirations can be condensed into five types: aspiration for bodhicitta, aspiration for births [that benefit sentient beings], aspiration for [auspicious] objects of activity, correct aspirations, and great aspirations." (B, vol. cho [205]:545.1) Bodhisattvas have "extensive aspirations" because they have extensive objects of observation [i.e., all sentient beings]. Their aspirations are

"auspicious" because they seek enlightenment, an auspicious state of perfection. (W, vol di [120]:38.7)

27 "Because they aspire toward the Bodhisattva emptiness, they are not frightened by nirvāṇa, whereby they perceive the benefits of nirvāṇa and do not abandon the faith and belief that perceive the benefits existing in it. Due to this, they have previously completed the accumulations [for] nirvāṇa, and so they are 'skilled regarding the blissful state of nirvāṇa'." (B, vol. cho [205]:547.1)

28 "When Bodhisattvas apply themselves through the aspiration toward [realization of] emptiness, because they understand cyclic existence as it really is they are able to enter into surpassing equanimity of mind with respect to all afflictions, desire, and so forth." (B, vol. cho [205]:547.3) "When applying themselves to [realization of] emptiness, Bodhisattvas will not quickly pass beyond sorrow in seeking nirvāṇa. Because they do not pass beyond sorrow, they ripen the qualities of a Buddha and ripen sentient beings." Although there are many sufferings in cyclic existence, "their minds do not become depressed by cyclic existence." (B 547.5) "They do not pass beyond sorrow because they constantly generate great compassion." They aspire to benefit sentient beings despite the tribulations of cyclic existence because they have completely pacified desire. (W, vol. di [120]:39.7)

29 These are the six perfections. "They are called 'perfections' because their time and nature are pure, and through them one attains supreme results." (W, vol. di [120]:41.6, citing YB)

30 "Effort is 'omnipresent' (kun-tu-'gro-ba, sarvatraga) because [effort] is of the nature of applying oneself to all virtuous qualities."(B, vol. cho [205]:566.5)

31 "Spiritual guides" (dge-ba'i-bshes-gnyen, kalyāṇa-mitra) are those who abide in the ethics of the Bodhisattva vows. (W, vol. di [120]:58.2, citing YB) Applying themselves to a virtuous course, literally "virtuous class" (dge-ba'i-phyogs, kuśala-pakṣa), involves "completing the cultivation of the six perfections in a manner that is constant, continuous, and uninterrupted." (W 59.3, quoting MS)

32 These four types are the perfection of skillful means, the perfection of aspiration, the perfection of power, and the perfection of exalted wisdom.

33 The four means of gathering disciples (bsdu-ba'i-dngos-po, saṁgraha-vastu) are methods used by teachers to attract students: giving both teachings and material goods, speaking pleasantly, engaging in beneficial activities, and making one's actions accord with one's words. (See Mahāvyutpatti XXXV:1–4)

34 "'Giving material things' involves giving what is good, what is clean, and what is suitable after having eliminated the stains of miserliness and the stains of hoarding wealth. 'Giving the Dharma' involves engaging in teaching doctrine non-erroneously, in teaching logically, and in causing [others] to take up the bases of training." (W, vol. di [120]:78.2, quoting YB) "Granting fearlessness" consists of "protection from the conditions of suffering, protection from loss of life, and protection from the continuum of cyclic existence." (B, vol. jo [206]:7.7. See also VJ 620)

35 "Patience that endures injury" means that when harmed, "a Bodhisattva trains [in thinking]: 'This is a result of my own actions, and thus I am undergoing the fruits of suffering from non-virtuous actions that I myself have done.'" ... "Patience that does not consider one's own suffering at all" is the patience of a Bodhisattva who trains correctly and encounters suffering but is able to endure even great suffering that seems meaningless. (W, vol di [120]:81.3–.4, citing YB) "'Patience in discerning the Dharma' has three aspects: not being frightened by emptiness, not being attached to the two extremes, and being firm with respect to engaging in asceticism." (B, vol. jo [206]:8.6)

36 "'Effort that is armor' has three aspects: putting on the armor of great love, the steady force of great compassion, and the steady force of great effort. 'Effort applied to virtue' also has three aspects: relying on meaning with great faith, engaging in virtue with great practice, and infusing [all] sentient beings with great dedications. 'Effort applied for the welfare of sentient beings' also has three aspects: making unexcelled effort [to develop] equanimity and ethics; laboring to establish [others] in the meaning of doctrines through the four means of gathering [disciples]; and endeavoring [to practice] skillful means with undaunted wisdom." (B, vol. jo [205]:9.2. See also W, vol. di [120]:83.2–.7 and VJ 622)

37 "'The samādhi of blissful abiding' has three aspects: mind that does not conceive doctrine, doctrine that does not conceive mind,

and a concentrated mind that does not conceive either. The 'samādhi that manifestly achieves good qualities' has three aspects: that which establishes bodily qualities, that which establishes qualities of exalted wisdom, and that which establishes qualities of the powers and so forth. The 'samādhi that manifestly achieves the welfare of sentient beings' has three aspects: samādhis that are dedications, pervasive samādhis, and unchangeable samādhis." (B, vol. jo [205]:9.6. See also W, vol. di [120]:85.1)

38 "'[Wisdom] focusing on conventional truth' has three aspects: skill with respect to the characteristics of compounded phenomena, skill with respect to the continuum of cyclic existence, and skill with respect to turning away from the continuum of cyclic existence. '[Wisdom] focusing on ultimate truth' also has three aspects: It is non-abiding due to emptiness, non-conceptual due to signlessness, and non-attached due to wishlessness. '[Wisdom] focusing on the welfare of sentient beings' has three aspects: It is [wisdom] that is applied through samādhis to inherent suffering, [wisdom] that eliminates the suffering of compounded phenomena through antidotes, and [wisdom] that completely liberates one from the suffering of doubt." (B, vol. jo [205]:10.2)

39 The first purity entails not seeking fame or profit from others because they have practiced the six perfections. The second refers to practice in terms of the three wheels of purification, i.e., viewing action, agent, and recipient as lacking self. The third indicates the strength of their belief. The fourth indicates that they do not praise themselves and do not despise others, because these would be "serious faults." The fifth is due to being free from laziness. The sixth entails not being satisfied with inferior attainments because they engage in extensive practices and are without discouragement. Regarding the seventh: "Since Bodhisattvas practice doctrine themselves, when they perceive others who also practice, they do not engage in miserliness or jealousy with respect to material things or doctrine." (W, vol. di [120]:108.5)

40 Giving gifts, having purified faults, is giving with "purity of ethics." Not apprehending that "I am the giver and that what is given is mine" and so forth is "purity of view." Giving gifts with compassionate intention is "purity of mind." Giving gifts with an honest face and speaking straightforwardly is "purity of speech." Giving gifts with the correct name, nature, and so forth of the gift is "purity of knowl-

edge." Giving gifts after having abandoned the defilements of laziness, desire, hatred, obscuration, and so forth is "purity from defilements." (W, vol. di [120]:110.2)

41 "A Bodhisattva who suspects that an enemy is about to harm that Bodhisattva quickly goes to that enemy and confesses. [The Bodhisattva] does not wait for the other [i.e., the enemy] to come to him." (W, vol. di [120]:116.1) "When others harm them, they do not retaliate, they do not become angry, they do not even conceive of the idea of an enemy." (W 115.5)

42 The first is "samādhi that understands well the signs of conventional truths." The second is "samādhi that observes an object that is complete suchness." The third is "samādhi that observes both conventional and ultimate objects." (W, vol. di [120]:120.7)

43 "'Exaggeration' is apprehending the non-existent as existent. 'Deprecation' is denigration of the existent as non-existent. Imputations are only exaggerated and are without denigration, because they are completely non-existent. Other-dependent phenomena are not exaggerated, because their natures exist. They are not deprecated, because they exist only as conceptualizations of the unreal. Thoroughly established natures are not exaggerated because they exist in reality. [With respect to them] there is only deprecation." (W, vol. di [120]:123.4, quoting Asvabhāva's commentary on MS)

44 Conventional truths (kun-rdzob-bden-pa, saṁvṛti-satya) include "whatever is produced from conditions, exists only imputedly, arises from conceptuality like illusory things, is expressible in words, and is like a dream." (W, vol. di [120]:126.7, quoting the bsTan-bcos-shin-tu-rgyas-pa-brgya-pa) The five topics of knowledge (rig-pa'i-gnas-lnga, pañca-vidyā-sthāna) are philosophy, logic, grammar, medicine, and knowledge of crafts. (See W 127.3)

45 These are the "individual capabilities of the five aspects of characteristics" that the Buddha describes in his answer to this question. (W, vol. di [120]:130.2–133)

46 In the analogy comparing sentient beings with hungry ghosts, water is analogous to the resources of Bodhisattvas. Due to the Bodhisattvas' great compassion and merit, these resources are pure and vast. But the karma of sentient beings distorts the Bodhisattvas' beneficial gifts, just as the karma of hungry ghosts is said to cause them not to see refreshing water or to misperceive it as something

unclean. (W, vol. di [120]:144.2. See also W 141–45 for a lengthy discussion of this passage; WE 212; and S, vol. II, 250–51)

47 All afflictions fall within two categories: (1) innate (lhan-cig-skyes-pa) and (2) arisen from imputations (kun-brtags-las-byung-ba). Innate afflictions are "afflictions that are objects to be abandoned by [a path of] meditation." Afflictions arisen from imputation are "afflictions that are objects to be abandoned by [a path of] seeing." [The "assistors that are completely destroyed" mentioned in this passage in the Sūtra are "arisen from imputations."] Prior to the first Bodhisattva stage these two types of afflictions accompany one another, but when one attains the path of seeing the non-innate afflictions are completely destroyed. (W, vol. di [120]:156.1)

48 "Errant tendencies that are like something on the outer layer of skin are abandoned on the first [Bodhisattva] stage. Those that are like something existing in subcutaneous skin are abandoned on the eighth stage. Those that are like something existing in the marrow are abandoned on the Tathāgata stage." (B, vol. jo [206]:37.3)

49 According to one explanation, one abandons errant tendencies that are like something existing on the outer layer of skin during the first period of incalculable eons; during the second period one abandons those that are like something existing in subcutaneous skin; and during the third period one abandons those that are like something existing in the marrow. (W, vol. di [120]:170.2) According to another explanation, one abandons the first type during the first two periods of incalculable eons, abandons the second type during the third period of incalculable eons, and abandons the third type after having entered the Tathāgata stage. The second explanation accords with the words of the Sūtra. (W 170.5)

50 "This is because they generate afflictions having understood the faults of the afflictions. This is called 'the characteristic of absence of affliction'." (W, vol. di [120]:178.3)

51 "[Bodhisattvas] have afflictions but are not overcome by them. Thus the afflictions cannot generate suffering, and so these [Bodhisattvas] are called faultless." (W, vol. di [120]:178.7) "Although these Bodhisattvas have not abandoned the afflictions, the harmful consequences of the afflictions are not generated, like poison that has been overcome through mantras and medicine." (W 179.1, quoting AS)

Bodhisattvas on the first through seventh stages "generate afflictions so that they can overcome and eliminate them in order to gain mastery over their own consciousnesses." Because they are motivated to help sentient beings, they are able to turn even afflictions to their advantage. (W 180.4)

52 "Collective stages" include the four purities and eleven limbs. "Collections of discriminations" ('du-shes-bsdus, saṁjñā-saṁgraha) is the name of the eleven stages mentioned previously, and "discriminations" are "names." The "discordances" of the stages refer to the twenty-two obscurations and the eleven errant tendencies. The "distinctive arisings" refer to "the distinctive superiority of Bodhisattvas' births." "Aspirations" refer to the three aspirations. The "trainings" of the stages include "the various doors [of training] in the perfections." (W, vol. di [120]:187.2)

Notes to Chapter Ten

1 This great Bodhisattva is named Mañjuśrī ('Soft Glory') because "his mind [that realizes] the truth of suchness is permanently peaceful and isolated, benefits all enemies and friends, and does not harm them." (W, vol. di [120]:193.6) He is "endowed with the meaning of 'glory' because he is revered and worshipped by all worldlings and is praised by everyone." (W citing a commentary on the Buddhabhūmi-sūtra) "In reality this Bodhisattva is a Tathāgata, but in order to teach Buddha's doctrine he displays the form of a Bodhisattva." (W 194.1) Considered an embodiment of wisdom, Mañjuśrī is strongly associated with the Perfection of Wisdom Sūtras and is often an interlocutor in them.

2 "Well-established transformation of the basis" (gnas-gyur-pa-yang-dag-par-grub-pa, āśrayaparāvṛtti-samudāgama) refers to Tathāgatas, "who are of the character of the Dharmakāya, which is thoroughly established in the sense of being an exalted wisdom of reality and suchness that is unerring and changeless." (B, vol. jo [206]:48.3)

Asaṅga (AS, ed. Pradhan, 76.9–.11) states that there are three types of transformation of the basis: transformation of the basis of mind (cittāśraya-parivṛtti), transformation of the basis of path (mārgāśraya-parivṛtti), and transformation of the basis of errant tendencies (dauṣṭhulyāśraya-parivṛtti). According to Jinaputra's commentary on this passage (Abhidharmasamuccaya-bhāṣya, ed. Tatia, 93.15), the first involves freeing the mind (which is of the nature of clear light) from all adventitious afflictions. The second involves transforming mundane paths into supramundane paths. Through this process, one transforms the basis, which is the path, and brings the path to completion. The third type involves transforming consciousness in the sense of eliminating the obstructions to omniscience. (See also S, vol. II, 261–65 and COM 138)

3 The Dharmakāya is "inconceivable" (bsam-gyis-mi-khyab-pa, acintya) because it is free from elaborations (i.e., arising, cessation, and so forth), and because "that character of transformation of the basis of the Dharmakāya is free from all obstructions, permanently abides in suchness, and is changeless. Therefore, it lacks the manifest activity of actions and afflictions." (W, vol. di [120]:197.1)

"'Freedom from elaborations' (spros-pa-med-pa, niḥprapañca) has the following aspects: It is without cessation, birth, permanence, and annihilation; it is not of diverse meanings or one single meaning; and it is without coming and going." (B, vol. jo [206]:50.6)

"Elaborations" refer to "the four types of elaborations of existence, non-existence, and so forth [i.e., the tetralemna or catuṣ-koṭi]; and to elaborations such as, 'Everything is permanent,' '[everything] is impermanent' and so forth." (W, vol. di [120]:196.7)

4 "Liberation bodies" (rnam-par-grol-ba'i-lus, vimukti-kāya) are "bodies liberated from the arising of afflictive obstructions." (B, vol. jo [206]:52.3) Asvabhāva states that liberation bodies result from mere separation from the bonds of the afflictions. He compares this to a common person who, upon being released from shackles, experiences the cessation of the suffering they had caused. By contrast, the Dharmakāya is compared to a prince who, upon being released from prison, not only experiences the cessation of suffering, but is also crowned king and obtains dominion over the entire kingdom. (commentary to MS I.48, P 5552, vol. li [106]:262b.6–263a.2)

"The Dharmakāya, which has immeasurable distinctively superior qualities, is not to be known through examples and so forth." (W, vol. di [120]:201.1) Because the Dharmakāya is incomparable, nothing else remotely resembles it. (B, vol. jo [206]:52.7)

5 "When previously abiding in the practices of the [Bodhisattva] stages, Tathāgatas achieved various types of qualities for the sake of

sentient beings. They completed the cultivation of these qualities and achieved the powers resulting from them." Through cultivating immeasurably good qualities and great power, they achieved the ability to benefit sentient beings by taking limitless forms appropriate to the training needs of sentient beings. (W, vol. di [120]:203.1)

In Hsüan-tsang's Chinese translation of this Sūtra, the phrase "The characteristics of the Nirmāṇakāya have birth and arising" is found before "The Dharmakāya has no genesis." (See W 203.5)

6 "It is called 'skillful' because the three types of charismatic actions (phrin-las) that arise from exalted wisdom that accomplishes activities are in accordance with the faculties of sentient beings. It is called 'method' because application is continuous." (W, vol. di [120]:204.1, citing a commentary on the Buddha-bhūmi-sūtra)

7 The first category refers to obtaining the twelve forms of doctrinal teachings (see p. 151 of this Sūtra). The second refers to taking refuge in the Buddha, Dharma, and Sangha. The third category refers to training in ethics, samādhi, and wisdom. The fourth refers to the enlightenments of the three vehicles. (W, vol. di [120]:228.7, citing a commentary on the bsTan-bcos-rnam-par-bshad-pa)

8 The first category refers to phenomena that are included among compounded phenomena, such as the five aggregates, the constituents, and the sense spheres. The second refers to the twelve links of dependent origination. "Them" refers to just the five aggregates. The third and fourth categories refer to conceptions of true existence: "Due to these very conceptions, through the power of conceiving the afflicted aggregates as having a self [of persons] and conceiving them as having [a self of] phenomena, this serves as a cause of engagement with cyclic existence in the future." (W, vol. di [120]:232.6) These first four members are "categories of pure worldly phenomena," and the next twenty-five are "categories of pure supramundane phenomena." (W 233.6)

9 The fifth category refers to "wisdoms [arisen from] hearing that belong to the desire realm. These are mental designations with respect to teachings. They are also mental designations with respect to the meaning of what is expressed and objects of mindful establishments."

The sixth category "indicates the category of wisdoms [arisen from] reflection. This is taking to mind these very objects of wisdom [arisen from] hearing with ardent effort after having perceived them in terms of unitary truth."

The seventh category "indicates the samādhi of application. This is mentally abiding in the samādhi of application through the power of wisdom [arisen from] reflection."

The eighth category "indicates actual samādhi. This is abiding blissfully in this life after having attained the six clairvoyances."

The ninth category "indicates the twenty-one categories of types of things that transcend the world."

The tenth category has three aspects: "comprehending the basis [of suffering], beginning with error; comprehending the basis [of suffering caused by] mistaken establishment with respect to external sentient beings, beginning with conceiving them as sentient beings; and comprehending the basis [of suffering] due to separation from internal conceit."

"The category of the basis of meditation, the category of actualization, and the category of meditation [11-13] respectively indicate teachings concerning the categories of abandonment of [true] sources [of suffering], actualization of [true] cessations, and cultivation of [true] paths. Moreover, because true sources [of suffering] are the two afflictions that are discordant with meditation, this is the category of the basis of meditation. Because true cessations are uncompounded, this is the category of actualization. The paths of the Āryas [comprise] the category of meditation."

The next four categories (14-17) refer to teachings about the paths of seeing. The fourteenth refers to "correct paths" "because through the power of seeing the path as it really is, one does not degenerate from the two types of paths of seeing: (1) correct, and (2) having signs." The fifteenth refers to "a path of seeing having signs." The sixteenth refers to "the category of objects that are objects of observation of a path of seeing having signs." The seventeenth refers to "individually analyzing in terms of abandoning afflictions that are objects to be abandoned by a path of seeing that has signs; and afflictions not yet abandoned that are objects to be abandoned by [a path of] meditation."

The next six (18-23) refer to teachings about paths of meditation. There are differing explanations with respect to each of these: With respect to "the category of being distracted from that [meditation]," one scholar's opinion is that from the time of having passed beyond the path of seeing up to the time of entering the path of meditation, one can become mentally distracted although one is not afflicted. With respect to categories nineteen and twenty: "These are activities of exertion that abandon afflictions that are to be abandoned by a path of meditation in the desire realm when one abides in samādhi." The twenty-first category refers to "unobstructed paths abandoning afflictions that are to be abandoned by [paths of] meditation in the form and formless realms." The twenty-second category refers to uninterrupted paths and paths of release that abandon afflictions that are to be abandoned by form realm [paths of] meditation." The twenty-third category refers to "an uninterrupted path that abandons afflictions that are to be abandoned by a formless realm [path of] meditation: the vajra-like samādhi."

The next three categories (24–27) refer to "teachings concerning paths of no more learning." The twenty-fourth includes "exhaustible and unproduced knowledges that are included among correct exalted wisdoms." The twenty-fifth includes "exhaustible and unproduced exalted wisdoms that apprehend [their objects] by way of exalted wisdoms of subsequent attainment." The twenty-sixth refers to "meditation on suchness when one is close to entering a [nirvāṇa] without remainder." The twenty-seventh refers to "the thorough passing beyond sorrow of basis-consciousness itself through meditative absorptions that are cessations—due to former meditative absorptions that are cessations—when one is close to entering a [nirvāṇa] without remainder."

The twenty-eighth and twenty-ninth respectively refer to "distinctive superiority and absence of distinctive superiority." The "disciplinary doctrine that has been well explained" refers to the teachings of the three baskets (sde-snod-gsum, tripiṭaka, i.e., Vinaya, Sūtra, and Abhidharma). "Discipline" ('dul-ba) refers specifically to Vinaya. (W, vol. di [120]:234.3–241.3)

10 These bases of defeat (pham-pa'i-gnas, pārājāyika-sthāna) are the four root offences resulting in expulsion from the monastic order: non-celibacy, taking what is not given, killing, and lying. Citing YB, W gives a different fourfold list: "attachment to property and respect and elevating oneself and deprecating others; not giving material goods and doctrine to sentient beings due to miserliness; beating and speaking harsh words to sentient beings with a belligerent mind; and deprecating the Bodhisattva canon and teaching false

doctrines." They are called bases of defeat "because when the faults of these four weighty [offences] arise, without question those [who commit them] come under the influence of afflictions that defeat them and overpower Bodhisattvas." (W, vol. di [120]:247.6)

11 "Faults" refers to teachings concerning the three contaminations, the four fetters, the causes of thorough entanglements, the ten complete bindings, and so forth. (W, vol. di [120]:260.4)

12 "Good qualities" (yon-tan, guṇa) refers to teachings concerning qualities such as clairvoyances, liberations, samādhis, powers, fearlessnesses, and so forth. (W, vol. di [120]:260.6)

13 "Compounded phenomena are not autonomous with respect to production and subsequent designation of conventions. Indicating their dependence upon causes and effects—by way of dependence upon cause and effect and their arising and subsequent conventional designations—is 'analysis of dependence'." (B, vol. jo [206]:271.4) "An example is a sprout arising in dependence upon a seed, season, water, and a field, or a consciousness arising in dependence upon a sense power, an object, and a [former moment of] mind." (W, vol. di [120]:309.5)

14 "Analysis of performance of functions" refers to "indicating the functions of phenomena." (B, vol. jo [206]:271.2) "What are the characteristics of analysis of performance of functions? Whatever are the causes and whatever are the conditions—in terms of which the attainment or birth of phenomena function—are [the subject matter of] analysis of performance of functions. 'Attainment or non-establishment' are just differentiations of agent. . . . Attainment refers to both acting in order to gain something—obtaining a mere seed—and attaining the entity of the fruit. What is obtaining a mere seed? It is [obtaining] the virtuous roots for attaining the level of an Ārya and its fruits; performing meritorious activity, which leads to attainment of the happinesses of men and gods; moral wrong-doing, which leads to experiencing the sufferings of bad transmigrations; and causes that are concordant with what is neutral and whatever has the predispositions that are seeds of those. . . . Whatever is indicated as being the performance of functions of phenomena is [the subject matter of] 'analysis of performance of functions'." (B 279.5)

15 "Analysis of logical correctness" involves "indicating the reasonings that establish individual meanings through the correctness of

the three valid cognizers [tshad-ma, pramāṇa, i.e., direct perception, inference, and believable scriptures]." (B, vol. jo [206]:271.2)

16 One directly observes the reasoning concerning impermanence through reasonings concerning the impermanence of a basis. One realizes what is subtle based on understanding what is coarse with respect to a particular basis. Thus, one understands subtle impermanence in dependence on first understanding coarse impermanence; one understands that there will be effects of karma in the future due to observing the varieties of suffering that are present now; and one understands subtle selflessness in dependence upon understanding coarse selflessness. (W, vol. di [120]:281.5)

17 "The masters of this country . . . state that whatever is an exalted wisdom that observes suchness is 'omniscience' (thams-cad-mkhyen-pa, sarvajña). Whatever is exalted wisdom that abides in conventions is an 'exalted knower of all aspects' (rnam-pa-thams-cad-mkhyen-pa, sarvākāra-jñatā). (W, vol. di [120]:284.7)

"'Omniscience' refers to the general characteristic (spyi'i-mtshan-nyid), and 'exalted knower of all aspects' refers to the specific characteristic (bye-brag-gi-mtshan-nyid). The first is cause, and the second is effect. Also, the first refers to 'destruction of ignorance that obscures all phenomena', and the second refers to 'destruction of ignorance in terms of individual analysis of various types of phenomena'." (W 288.5, citing another scholar's position)

18 "The four fearlessnesses are: fearlessness with respect to being manifestly and completely enlightened with respect to all phenomena; fearlessness with respect to knowing that all contaminations have been extinguished; fearlessness with respect to teaching definitive scriptures that are uninterrupted and [contain] unchangeable doctrines; and fearlessness with respect to the nature of the path of renunciation on which one attains all wonders." (B, vol. jo [206]:318.1. See also S, vol. II, 286, 298 and COM 169)

19 The "seven characteristics of impure reasonings" are rarely described in Buddhist literature. W gives a technical discussion of them too lengthy and complex to reproduce here. Note, however, that unlike the "pure reasonings" that rely on "direct valid cognition," the "impure reasonings" rely on various types of "objects of observation." One cannot prove what one is trying to establish through these impure reasonings. "Because these seven character-

istics have faults, they are 'impure'." (W, vol. di [120]:296.6. See also Khri-srong-lde-btsan's bKa'-yang-dag-pa'i-tshad-ma-las-mdo-btus-pa, NE 4352; and Mahāvyutpatti CC:6–12)

20 "Because they are discordant with the mode of the meaning of suchness, their characteristics are not established." (B, vol. jo [206]: 347.3) This means that they are not renowned in the world; they contradict common sense; and they also contradict believable scriptures. Thus they are worthless as reasonings, are discordant with correct reasonings, and should not be used. (W, vol. di [120]:305.6)

21 "The analysis of reality" (chos-nyid-kyi-rigs-pa, dharmatā-yukti) refers to analysis of what is known from beginningless time as the nature of phenomena abiding in specific and general characteristics. An example is stating that fire burns, water moistens, and wind moves. (W, vol. di [120]:310.1)

22 "The qualities of overcoming afflictions through mundane paths, nirvāṇa that achieves complete abandonment of afflictions through supramundane paths, and compounded qualities that are manifestly established by those [constitute] the 'characteristic of attaining its fruits'." (W, vol. di [120]:311.5)

23 "Predispose" (bag-la-nyal, anuśaya) refers to the "seeds" (sa-bon, bīja), specifically seeds of the two types of mistaken apprehension: apprehension of a self of persons and apprehension of a self of phenomena. These are the two types of obstructions: afflictive obstructions and obstructions to omniscience. (W, vol. di [120]:317.7)

24 "Mind" refers to the basis-consciousness. "Thought" refers to afflicted thought. "Consciousness" refers to the six consciousnesses: the five sense consciousnesses and mental consciousness. (W, vol. di [120]:322.6) "Tathāgatas do not have conceptual mental activity, but—due to the power of wisdom from the previous causal period—mental phenomena arise without exertion: like emanations, for instance. [Tathāgatas] manifest [whatever is suitable] in accordance with their thought due to the power of samādhi, and not due to the power of conceptual mental activity." (W 324.1)

25 It is not suitable to say that these emanations have minds, and it is not suitable to say that they do not. That they are not autonomous means that they arise in dependence upon the seeds of types of views of different sentient beings in accordance with their natures. According to YB, the Sambhogakāya and Nirmāṇakāya manifesta-

tions do not have real minds and mental factors, but do have phenomena that appear like minds and mental factors. The emanations of Tathāgatas are like things having minds, but the minds controlling them are external to them, and so the emanations themselves cannot be said to have real minds. They are also not said to be actually existent "because they lack the abilities of physical faculties of emanations and faculties in terms of phenomena that are minds and mental factors and so forth." (W, vol di [120]:330.4)

26 According to ancient cosmology, fire-crystals are radiant, hot and clear, and produce the light of the sun. Water-crystals produce the light of the moon and are cold and clear. (See Kośa III:60b and W, vol. di [120]:339.7)

27 "Kṣatriyas or Brahmans, and those like great śāla trees" refers to humans who are well-endowed with wealth, fame, and attractiveness. (W, vol. di [120]:341.7. See also Kośa IV:108c-d)

28 These pure realms are not included among the three realms, but are realms that transcend them and are produced from unsurpassable virtuous roots. (W, vol. di [120]:345.3) "In these pure lands the three bad migrations do not exist, nor does [there exist] anything called 'the three poisons', 'the two [lesser] vehicles', or 'man' and 'woman'. The Buddhas of these pure lands have the thirty-two marks of a great being and appear in worldly realms through the power of their luminescence, emanate innumerable bodies in each moment, benefit sentient beings in worldly realms more numerous than the sands of the Ganges river, and then return to their former abodes." (W 345.3, citing a commentary on the Perfection of Wisdom)

Abbreviations

A Drang-ba-dang-nges-pa'i-don-rnam-par-'byed-pa'i-bstan-bcos-legs-bshad-snying-po'i-dka'-'grel-rin-chen-sgron-me by A-khu-blo-gros-rgya-mtsho

AS Abhidharmasamuccaya by Asaṅga

B Ārya-saṁdhinirmocana-sūtra-vyākyāna by Byang-chub-rdzu-'phrul (Cog-ro-klu'i-rgyal-mtshan). Page numbers are referenced to the Karmapae Choedhey edition of the sDe-dge bsTan-'gyur.

BCLS *Bulletin de la Classe des Lettres et des Sciences Morales et Politiques, Académie Royale de Belgique*

Bh Ārya-saṁdhinirmocana-bhāṣya by Asaṅga, in *Two Commentaries on the Saṁdhinirmocana-sūtra,* translated by John Powers

COM *La Compendium de la Super-Doctrine d'Asaṅga,* the Abhidharmasamuccaya, translated by Walpola Rahula

DLG Legs-bshad-snying-po'i-dka'-'grel-bstan-pa'i-sgron-me by dPal-'byor-lhun-grub

EG Legs-bshad-snying-po by Tsong-kha-pa, Sarnath edition

G Drang-nges-rnam-'byed-kyi-dka'-'grel-rtsom-'phro by Gung-thang-dkon-mchog-bstan-pa'i-sgron-me

GR Drang-nges-rnam-'byed-legs-bshad-snying-po-dka'-gnad-rnams-mchan-bur-bkod-pa-gzur-gnas-blo-dga'-ston by Geshe Rabten

JBW *The Meaning of Mind in the Mahāyāna Buddhist Philosophy of Mind-Only,* includes the Kun-gzhi-rtsa-ba by Tsong-kha-pa, translated by Joe B. Wilson

JNG	Ārya-saṁdhinirmocana-sūtreārya-maitreyakevala-parivarta-bhāṣya by Jñānagarbha, in *Two Commentaries on the Saṁdhinirmocana-sūtra,* translated by John Powers
KJ	Kun-gzhi-rtsa-'grel by Tsong-kha-pa
Kośa	Abhidharmakośa-bhaṣya by Vasubandhu, translated by Louis de la Vallée Poussin
KY	Kun-gzhi'i-yig-cha by Gung-thang
ME	*Meditation on Emptiness* by Jeffrey Hopkins
MS	Mahāyānasaṁgraha by Asaṅga
MV	Madhyāntavibhāṅga-ṭīkā by Vasubandhu, in *Seven Works of Vasubandhu,* translated by Stefan Anacker
NE	Nyingma Edition of the sDe-dge bKa'-'gyur and bsTan-'gyur. The text numbers cited from the Nyingma Edition are equivalent to Tohoku Catalogue text numbers.
P	Peking Edition of the bKa'-'gyur and bsTan-'gyur
S	*La Somme du Grand Véhicule d'Asaṅga,* the Mahāyāna-saṁgraha, translated by Étienne Lamotte
SB	Śrāvakabhūmi by Asaṅga
T	Taishō Edition of the Buddhist Canon
VJ	Vijñaptimātratāsiddhi by Hsüan-tsang in *Vijñaptimātratā-siddhi: La Siddhi de Hiuan-tsang traduité et annoté,* translated by Louis de la Vallée Poussin
VM	Visuddhimagga by Buddhaghosa, in *The Path of Purification,* translated by Bhikkhu Ñāṇamoli
VS	Viniścaya-saṁgrahaṇī by Asaṅga
W	Ārya-gambhīra-saṁdhinirmocana-sūtra-ṭīkā by Wonch'uk. Page numbers are referenced to the Karmapae Choedhey edition of the sDe-dge bsTan-'gyur.
WE	*Ways of Enlightenment*
WZ	*Wiener Zeitschrift für die Kunde Süd- und Ostrasiens*
YB	Yogacaryābhūmi by Asaṅga

Bibliography

Editions of the Saṁdhinirmocana consulted for this translation:

sDe-dge edition: Nyingma Edition of the sDe-dge bKa'-'gyur and bsTan-'gyur, vol. 18, text 106. Berkeley: Dharma Publishing, 1980.

sTog Palace edition: *The Tog Palace Edition of the Tibetan Kanjur,* vol. 63: 1–160. Leh: Smanrtsis Shesrig Dpemzod, 1975–1978.

Them-spangs-ma edition: Photocopy of the edition brought to Japan by Ekai Kawaguchi, now kept in the Tōyō Bunko Library in Tokyo.

Peking edition: vol. 29, text 774. Tokyo: Tibetan Tripiṭaka Research Institute, Suzuki Research Foundation, 1958.

Lhasa edition: vol. mdo nga. Microfiche distributed by the Institute for Advanced Studies of World Religions.

sNar-thang edition: vol. 51. Microfiche distributed by the Institute for Advanced Studies of World Religions.

Co-ne edition: vol. 5, Kanjur. Microfilm copy from the Library of Congress, Washington, D.C.

Viniścaya-saṁgrahaṇī (P 5539, vol. 110: 233–vol. 111: 61; vol. 111: 63–121; NE 4038), quotes most of the Sūtra.

Stein Tib. 194, Tun-huang manuscript in the old translation style containing most of the seventh chapter.

Stein Tib. 683, Tun-huang manuscript in the old translation style containing a portion of the seventh chapter.

Chieh-shen-mi-ching, the Chinese translation by Hsüan-tsang, T 676.

Shen-mi-chieh-t'o-ching, the Chinese translation by Bodhiruci, T 675.

Chieh-chieh-ching, the Chinese translation by Paramārtha, T 677.

Canonical Commentaries on the Sūtra

Asaṅga. Ārya-saṁdhinirmocana-bhāṣya ('Phags-pa-dgongs-pa-nges-par-'grel-pa'i-rnam-par-bshad-pa). P 5481, vol. 104: 1–7; NE 3981. In *Two Commentaries on the Saṁdhinirmocana-sūtra,* translated by John Powers. Lewiston and Queenston: The Edwin Mellen Press, 1992.

Byang-chub-rdzu-'phrul (Cog-ro-klu'i-rgyal-mtshan). Ārya-saṁdhi-nirmocana-sūtra-vyākhyāna ('Phags-pa-dgongs-pa-nges-par-'grel-pa'i-mdo'i-rnam-par-bshad-pa). Delhi: Delhi Karmapae Choedhey, 1985, vol. cho [205]–vol. jo [206]; NE 4358; P 5845, vol. 144: 191–vol. 145: 89.

Jñānagarbha. Ārya-saṁdhinirmocana-sūtreārya-maitreyakevala-parivarta-bhāṣya ('Phags-pa-dgongs-pa-nges-par-'grel-pa'i-mdo-las-'phags-pa-byams-pa'i-le'u-nyi-tshe-bshad-pa). P 5535, vol. 109: 196–211; NE 4033. In *Two Commentaries on the Saṁdhinirmocana-sūtra,* translated by John Powers. Lewiston and Queenston: The Edwin Mellen Press, 1992.

Wonch'uk (Tibetan: Wen-tshegs; Chinese: Yüan-ts'e). Ārya-gambhīra-saṁdhinirmocana-sūtra-ṭīkā ('Phags-pa-dgongs-pa-zab-mo-nges-par-'grel-pa'i-mdo'i-rgya-cher-'grel-pa). Delhi: Delhi Karmapae Choedhey, Gyalwae Sungrab Partun Khang, 1985, vol. ti [118]–vol. di [120]; NE 4016; P 5517, vol. 106: 1–345.

Works by Indian Authors

Asaṅga. Abhidharmasamuccaya (Chos-mngon-pa-kun-las-btus-pa). P 5550, vol. 112: 236–72; NE 4049; *Abhidharmasamuccaya of Asaṅga,* edited by Prahlad Pradhan. Santiniketan: Viśva-Bhāratī Studies #12, 1950; *Le Compendium de la Super-Doctrine d'Asaṅga (Abhidharma-samuccaya),* translated by Walpola Rahula. Paris: Publications de l'École Française d'Extrème-Orient, LXXVIII, 1971; reprint 1980.

——. Bodhisattvabhūmi (Byang-chub-sems-pa'i-sa): Yogacaryā-bhūmau-bodhisattvabhūmi, P 5538, vol. 110: 131–232; NE 4037.

——. Mahāyānasaṁgraha (Theg-pa-chen-po-bsdus-ba): P 5549, vol. 112: 215–36; NE 4048. In *La Somme du Grand Véhicule d'Asaṅga (Mahāyānasaṁgraha),* translated by Étienne Lamotte. 2 vols. Louvain: Université de Louvain, 1938.

——. Śrāvakabhūmi (Nyan-thos-kyi-sa): Yogacaryābhūmau Śrāvakabhūmi, P 5537, vol. 110: 35–130; NE 4036.

——. Viniścaya-saṁgrahaṇī (rNam-par-gtan-la-dbab-pa-bsdu-ba): Yogacaryābhūmi-viniścaya-saṁgraha, P 5539, vol. 110: 233–vol. 111: 61; vol. 111: 63–121; NE 4038.

——. Yogacaryā-bhūmi (rNal-'byor-spyod-pa'i-sa). P 5536, vol. 109: 211–vol. 110: 33; NE 4035.

Buddhaghosa. Visuddimagga. In *The Path of Purification*, translated by Bhikkhu Ñāṇamoli. 2 vols. Berkeley & London: Shambhala, 1976.

Jinaputra. Abhidharmasamuccaya-bhāṣya (Chos-mngon-pa-kun-las-btus-pa'i-bshad-pa). P 5554, vol. 113: 83–141; NE 4053. *Abhidharmasamuccaya-bhāṣyam*, edited by Nathmal Tatia. Patna: K. P. Jayaswal Research Institute, 1976 (Tibetan Sanskrit Works Series, #17).

Kamalaśīla. Bhāvanākrama. NE 3917. *Bhāvanākrama III*, edited by G. Tucci, in *Minor Buddhist Texts*, Part III. Rome: Instituto Italiano per il Medio ed Estremo Oriente (Serie Oriental Roma), 1971.

Mahāvyutpatti. NE 4346. *Mahāvyutpatti*, prepared by R. Sakaki. 2 vols. Tokyo: Suzuki Research Foundation, 1916.

Sthiramati. Madhyāntavibhāṅga-ṭīkā (dBus-dang-mtha'-rnam-par-'byed-pa'i-'grel-bshad). P 5534, vol. 109: 136–96; NE 4032.

Vasubandhu. Abhidharmakośa-bhāṣya. NE 4090. *Abhidharmakośabhāṣyam*, translated by Louis de la Vallée Poussin, English translation by Leo M. Pruden, 4 vols. Berkeley: Asian Humanities Press, 1988.

——. Madhyāntavibhaṅga-ṭīkā (dBus-dang-mtha'-rnam-par-'byed-pa'i-'grel–pa). P 5528, vol. 112: 121–33; NE 4027. In *Seven Works of Vasubandhu*, edited and translated by Stefan Anacker, 191–286 and 424–63. Delhi: Motilal Banarsidass, 1984.

——. Mahāyānasaṁgraha-bhāṣya (Theg-pa-chen-po-bsdus-pa'i-'grel-pa). P 5551, vol. 112: 272–307; NE 4050.

——. Triṁśikā-kārikā (Sum-cu-pa'i-tshig-le'ur-byas-pa). P 5556, vol. 113: 231–33; NE 4055. In *Seven Works of Vasubandhu*, edited and translated by Stefan Anacker, 181–90 and 422–23. Delhi: Motilal Banarsidass, 1984.

——. Trisvabhāvanirdeśa (Rang-bzhin-gsum-nges-par-bstan-pa). P 5559, vol. 113: 236–37; NE 4058. In *Seven Works of Vasubandhu*, edited and translated by Stefan Anacker, 287–98 and 464–66. Delhi: Motilal Banarsidass, 1984.

——. Vādavidhi. "Vasubandhu's Vādavidhi," edited and translated by Erich Frauwallner. WZ 1 (1957): 104–34. See also *Vasubandhu: Three Aspects,* translated by Stefan Anacker, 87–98. Doctoral dissertation, University of Wisconsin. Ann Arbor: University Microfilms, 1969.

——. Viṁśatikā-kārikā and Viṁśatikā-vṛtti (Nyi-shu-pa'i-tshig-le'ur-byas-pa and Nyi-shu-pa'i-'grel-pa). P 5557, vol. 113: 233–34; NE 4056 and 4057. In *Seven Works of Vasubandhu,* edited and translated by Stefan Anacker, 157–80 and 413–21. Delhi: Motilal Banarsidass, 1984.

Works by Tibetan Authors

Khri-srong-lde-btsan. bKa'-yang-dag-pa'i-tshad-ma-las-mdo-btus-pa. NE 4352.

Gung-thang-dkon-mchog-bstan-pa'i-sgron-me (Gung-thang). Kun-gzhi'i-yig-cha. *Collected Works,* vol. 2. New Delhi: Ngawang Gelek Demo, 1972.

——. bsTan-bcos-legs-bshad-snying-po-las-sems-tsam-skor-gyi-mchan-'grel-rtsom-'phro-rnam-rig-gzhung-brgya'i-snang-ba. *Collected Works,* vol. 1: 725–876. New Delhi: Ngawang Gelek Demo, 1975.

——. Drang-nges-rnam-'byed-kyi-dka'-'grel-rtsom-'phro. Sarnath: Guru Deva, 1965.

Tāranātha. rGya-gar-chos-'byung. *Tāranātha's History of Buddhism in India,* translated by Lama Chimpa and Alaka Chattopadhyaya. Simla: Indian Institute of Advanced Studies, 1970; reprint Calcutta: K. P. Bagchi and Co., 1980.

dPal-'byor-lhun-grub, gNyal-ston. Legs-bshad-snying-po'i-dka'-'grel-bstan-pa'i-sgron-me. Buxaduar: Sera Monastery, 1968.

Blo-bzang-phun-tshogs, Ser-shul-dge-bshes. Drang-nges-rnam-'byed-kyi-zin-bris-zab-don-gsal-ba'i-sgron-me. Mysore: Sera Byes Monastery, n.d.

dBus-pa-blo-gsal. Grub-pa'i-mtha'-rnam-par-bshad-pa'i-mdzod. In Blo gsal grub mtha', edited and partially translated by Katsumi Mimaki. Kyoto: Zinbun Kogaku Kenkyūshō, 1982.

Tsong-kha-pa-blo-bzang-grags-pa. Kun-gzhi-dka'-'grel. Sarnath: Gelugpa Students' Welfare Committee, Central Institute of Higher Tibetan Studies, 1984.

——. Kun-gzhi-rtsa-'grel. Sarnath: Pleasure of Elegant Sayings Printing Press, 1984.

——. Kun-gzhi-rtsa-ba. In *The Meaning of Mind in the Mahāyāna Buddhist Philosophy of Mind Only,* translated by Joe B. Wilson. Doctoral dissertation, University of Virginia. Ann Arbor: University Microfilms, 1984, DER 85-03465.

——. Legs-bshad-snying-po. Sarnath: Pleasure of Elegant Sayings Printing Press, 1979. In *The Central Philosophy of Tibet,* translated by Robert A. F. Thurman. Princeton: Princeton University Press, 1991.

Rabten, Geshe (Tre-hor-dge-bshes-rta-mgrin-rab-brtan). Drang-nges-rnam-'byed-legs-bshad-snying-po-dka'-gnad-rnams-mchan-bur-bkod-pa-gzur-gnas-blo-dga'-ston. Delhi: lHun-grub-chos-grags, 1978.

bSod-nams-grags-pa, Paṇ-chen. Legs-bshad-snying-po'i-dka'-gnad-dogs-gcod. Indian blockprint, n.d.

A-khu-blo-gros-rgya-mtsho. Drang-ba-dang-nges-pa'i-don-rnam-par-'byed-pa'i-bstan-bcos-legs-bshad-snying-po'i-dka'-'grel-rin-chen-sgron-me. Delhi: Kesang Thabkhes, 1982.

Work by Chinese Author

Hsüan-tsang. Ch'eng wei shih lun (Vijñaptimātratāsiddhi). T 1585. *Vijñaptimātratāsiddhi: La Siddhi de Hiuan-tsang traduité et annoté,* translated by Louis de la Vallée Poussin. 2 vols. Paris: Paul Geuthner, 1928; *Ch'eng wei shih lun: The Doctrine of Mere Consciousness,* translated by Wei Tat. Hong Kong: Dai Nippon Printing Co., 1973.

Works by Contemporary Scholars

Davidson, Ronald Mark. *Buddhist Systems of Transformation.* Doctoral dissertation, University of California, Berkeley. Ann Arbor: University Microfilms, 1986, DES 86-09992.

de la Vallée Poussin, Louis. "Le Petit Traité de Vasubandhu-Nāgārjuna sur les trois natures" *(Trisvabhāvanirdeśa). Mélanges Chinoises et Bouddhiques* 2 (1933): 147–61.

———. "Vasubandhu l'Ancien." *BCLS* 16 (1930): 15–39.

Demiéville, Paul. "Le Chapitre de la *Bodhisattvabhūmi* sur la Perfection du Dhyāna." *Rocznik Orientalistyczny* 21 (1957): 109–28; in *Choix d'Études Bouddhiques, 1929–1970:* 300–319. Leiden: Brill, 1973.

———. "Review of Étienne Lamotte, *Saṁdhinirmocana-sūtra*." *Journal Asiatique* 228 (1936): 645–56.

Eckel, Malcolm. *Jñānagarbha's Commentary on the Distinction Between the Two Truths.* New York: State University of New York, 1987.

Frauwallner, Erich. *On the Date of the Buddhist Master of the Law Vasubandhu.* Rome: Instituto Italiano per il Medio ed Estremo Oriente (Serie Orientale Roma), 1951.

———. "Landmarks in the History of Indian Logic." WZ 5 (1961): 129–32.

Guenther, Herbert V. *Philosophy and Psychology in the Abhidharma.* Delhi: Motilal Banarsidass, 1978.

Hakamaya, Noriaki. "A Consideration of the *Byams shus kyi le'u,* from the historical point of view." *Indogaku Bukkyō-gaku Kenkyū* 14.1 (Dec. 1975): 20–30.

———. "The Old and New Translations of the *Saṁdhinirmocana-sūtra:* Some Notes on the History of the Early Tibetan Translations." *Komazawa Daigaku Bukkyō-gakubu Kenkyūkiyō* 42 (1984): 1–17.

Honda, Megumu, with Johannes Rahder. *Annotated Translation of the Daśabhūmika-sūtra.* New Delhi: International Academy of Indian Culture, 1968 (Śatapiṭaka Series #74).

Hopkins, Jeffrey. *Compassion in Tibetan Buddhism.* London: Rider, 1980.

———. *Meditation on Emptiness.* London: Wisdom Publications, 1983.

———. with Geshe Lhundup Sopa. *Practice and Theory of Tibetan Buddhism.* New York: Grove Press, 1976.

Iida, Shotaro. *The Great Silla Monks of Korea.* Seoul: Yemun Ch'ulp'ansa, 1988.

———. "The Three Stūpas of Ch'ang An." *Papers of the First International Conference on Korean Studies,* 484–97. Seoul: The Academy of Korean Studies, 1980.

——. "Who Can Best *Re-turn* the Dharma-cakra: A Controversy Between Wonch'uk (623–696) and K'uei-chi (632–682)." *Indogaku Bukkyō-gaku Kenkyū* 34.2 (1986): 948–51.

Inaba, Shōju. "On Chos-grub's Translation of the *Chieh-shen-mi-ching-shu.*" In *Buddhist Thought and Asian Civilization,* edited by Leslie S. Kawamura and Keith Scott, 105–13. Emeryville, CA: Dharma Publishing, 1977.

——. *Restoration of Yüan-tse's Chieh-shen-mi-ching-shu Through Its Tibetan Counterpart.* Kyoto: Hierakuji, 1972.

Jaini, Padmanabh S. "On the theory of the two Vasubandhus." *Bulletin of the School of Oriental and African Studies* 21 (1958): 48–53. Summarized in *Proceedings of the International Congress of Orientalists* 24, vol. 1 (Munich, 1957): 552–54.

Kiyota, Minoru, ed. *Mahāyāna Buddhist Meditation.* Honolulu: University of Hawaii Press, 1978.

Lalou, Marcelle. *Inventaire des Manuscrits Tibétains de Touenhouang conservés à la Biblioteque Nationale,* 139. I. Paris: 1939.

Lamotte, Étienne. "L'ālayavijñāna (Le Réceptacle) dans le *Mahāyānasaṁgraha.*" *Mélanges Chinoises et Bouddhiques* 3 (1934–35): 169–255.

——. "The Assessment of Textual Interpretation in Buddhism," translated by Sara Boin-Webb. In *Buddhist Hermeneutics,* edited by Donald S. Lopez, 11–27. Honolulu: University of Hawaii Press, 1988.

——. *History of Indian Buddhism,* translated by Sara Boin-Webb. Louvain-la-Neuve: Université Catholique de Louvain, 1988.

——. *Saṁdhinirmocana-sūtra.* Louvain and Paris: Université de Louvain & Adrien Maisonneuve, 1935.

——. "Les Trois Caractères et les Trois Absences de Nature-propre dans le Saṁdhinirmocana-sūtra, Chapitre 6." *BCLS* (1935): 289–303.

Lancaster, Lewis. "The Oldest Mahāyāna Sūtra." *Eastern Buddhist,* vol. 8 #1 (1975): 30–41.

——. *Prajñāpāramitā and Related Systems.* Berkeley: Berkeley Buddhist Studies Series, 1977.

Mejor, Marek. "A Contribution to the Biography of Vasubandhu from Tibetan Sources." *Tibetan and Buddhist Studies Commemorat-*

ing the 200th Anniversary of the Birth of Alexander Csoma de Körös 2 (1984): 159–74.

Murti, T.R.V. *The Central Philosophy of Buddhism.* London: 1955.

Nagao, Gadjin. "The Buddhist World-View as Elucidated in the Three-Nature Theory and its Similes." *Eastern Buddhist* 16 (1983): 1–18.

——. *Madhyamaka and Yogācāra* (English translation of *Chūkan to Yuishiki*), translated by Leslie S. Kawamura. Albany: State University of New York, 1989.

——. "Vasubandhu" in *Encyclopedia of Religions,* edited by Mircea Eliade, 191ff. New York: Macmillan, 1987.

——. "What Remains in Śūnyatā: A Yogācāra Interpretation of Emptiness." In *Mahāyāna Buddhist Meditation,* edited by Minoru Kiyota, 66–82. Honolulu: University of Hawaii Press, 1978.

Nakamura, Hajime. *Indian Buddhism: A Survey with Bibliographical Notes.* Hirakata: Kufs Publications, 1980.

Péri, Nöel. "À Propos de la date de Vasubandhu." *Bulletin de l'École Française d'Extrême-Orient* 11 (1911): 339–90.

Powers, John. *The Concept of the Ultimate (don-dam-pa, paramārtha) in the Saṁdhinirmocana Sutra: Analysis, Translation, and Notes.* Doctoral dissertation, University of Virginia. Ann Arbor: University Microfilms, 1991, 92-21104.

——. *Hermeneutics and Tradition in the Sūtra Explaining the Thought.* Leiden: E.J. Brill, 1993 (Indian Thought and Culture Series, #5).

——. "Lost in China, Found in Tibet: How Wonch'uk Became the Author of the *Great Chinese Commentary.*" *Journal of the International Association of Buddhist Studies,* vol. 15.1 (1992): 95–103.

——. "The Term *'Saṁdhinirmocana'* in the Title of the Saṁdhinirmocana-sūtra." *Studies in Central and East Asian Religions,* vol. 4 (1992).

——. "The Tibetan Translations of the Saṁdhinirmocana-sūtra and Bka'-'gyur Research." *Central Asiatic Journal,* vol. 37 (3/4) (1993): 198–224.

——. *The Yogācāra School of Buddhism: A Bibliography.* Metuchen, NJ: Scarecrow Press, 1991.

Rahder, Johannes. "Daśabhūmikasūtra." *Le Muséon* 39 (1926): 125–252.

——. *Daśabhūmikasūtra et Bodhisattvabhūmi: Chapitres Vihāra et Bhūmi.* Paris: Paul Geuthner, 1926.

——. "*Daśabhūmika-sūtra,* Seventh Stage—Sanskrit Text Including Translation of Vasubandhu's Commentary." *Acta Orientalia* 4 (1925): 214–56.

Rahula, Walpola. "Ālayavijñāna." *Mahabodhi* 72 (1964): 130–33.

——. "Asaṅga." *Encyclopedia of Buddhism* 2.1, edited by G. P. Malalasekhana, 133–46. Columbo, Sri Lanka, 1966.

Ruegg, David S. "An Indian Source for the Tibetan Hermeneutical Term *Dgoṅs Gzi* 'Intentional Ground'." *Journal of Indian Philosophy* 16 (1988): 1–4.

——. "On the Knowability and Expressibility of Absolute Reality in Buddhism." *Indogaku Bukkyō-gaku Kenkyū* 20.1 (1971): 1–7.

——. "Purport, Implicature, and Presupposition." *Journal of Indian Philosophy* 13 (1985): 309–25.

——. *La Théorie du Tathāgatagarbha et du Gotra.* Paris: Publications de l'École Française d'Extrême-Orient, LXX, 1969.

Schmithausen, Lambert. *Ālayavijñāna.* 2 vols. Tokyo: The International Institute for Buddhist Studies, 1987.

——. "Der Nirvāṇa-Abschnitt in der *Viniśacayasaṁgrahaṇī* der *Yogācārabhūmiḥ.*" Wien: Veröffentlichungen der Komission für Sprachen und Kulturen Süd- und Ostasiens, Heft 8, 1969.

——. "On the Problem of the Relation of Spiritual Practice and Philosophical Theory in Buddhism." *German Scholars on India,* vol. 2. Bombay: Nachiketa Publications, 1976.

——. "On the Vijñaptimātra Passage in *Saṁdhinirmocana-sūtra* VIII.7." *Acta Indologica,* vol. VI (1984): 433–55.

Shukla, Karunesha. "Asaṅga in Buddhist Literature." *Journal of the Ganganatha Jha Research Institute* 27.1–2 (1971): 17–22.

Sponberg, Alan. "Dynamic Liberation in Yogācāra Buddhism." *Journal of the International Association of Buddhist Studies* 2.1 (1979): 44–64.

——. "The Trisvabhāva Doctrine in India and China." *Bukkyō Bunka Kenkyū-jo Kiyō* 21 (1982): 97–119.

Steinkellner, Ernst. "Who is Byaṅ-chub-rdzu-'phrul?" *Berliner Indologische Studien* (1989): 229–51.

Takakusu, Junjiro. "The Date of Vasubandhu." *Indian Studies in Honor of Charles Lanman,* 78–83. Cambridge, MA: 1929.

——. "The Life of Vasu-bandhu by Paramārtha." *T'oung Pao,* ser. II, #5, 269–96; reprint Leyden: E.J. Brill, 1904.

——. *Records of the Buddhist Religion by I-tsing.* Oxford: Clarendon Press, 1896.

——. "A Study of Paramārtha's Life of Vasubandhu and the Date of Vasubandhu." *Journal of the Royal Asiatic Society* (1905): 33–53.

Takasaki, Jikidō. "The Date of Vasubandhu the Great Buddhist Philosopher." *Indian Studies in Honor of Charles Lanman,* 79–88. Cambridge, MA: 1929.

Takeuchi, Shōkō. "Phenomena and Reality in Vijñaptimātratā Thought." In *Buddhist Thought and Asian Civilization,* edited by Leslie S. Kawamura and Keith Scott, 254–67. Emeryville, CA: Dharma Publishing, 1977.

Thurman, Robert. "Buddhist Hermeneutics." *Journal of the American Academy of Religion* 46.1 (1978): 19–39.

Tola, Fernando, and Carmen Dragonetti. "The *Trisvabhāva-kārikā* of Vasubandhu." *Journal of Indian Philosophy* 11 (1983): 225–66.

Tucci, Giuseppe. "Idealistic School of Buddhism." *Dacca University Bulletin* 12 (1926): 1–16.

——. *Pre-Dignāga Buddhist Texts on Logic From Chinese Sources.* Baroda: Gaekwad Oriental Series #49, 1929.

——. *On Some Aspects of the Doctrines of Maitreyanātha and Asaṅga.* Calcutta: 1930.

Ueda, Yoshifumi. "Two Main Streams of Thought in Yogācāra Philosophy." *Philosophy East and West* 17 (1967): 155–65.

——. "Two Views on Vijñāna—The View that Vijñāna Develops and the View that Vijñāna Knows." *Yūki kyōju shōju kinen bukkyō shisōshi ronshū (Essays on the History of Buddhist Thought Presented to Professor Reimon Yūki)*, 211–22. Tokyo: Daizō Shuppan, 1964.

Warder, A. K. *Indian Buddhism.* Delhi: Motilal Banarsidass, 1970.

Wayman, Alex. *Analysis of the Śrāvakabhūmi Manuscript.* Berkeley: University of California Publications in Classical Philology #7, 1961.

——. "Nescience and Insight According to Asaṅga's *Yogācārabhūmi.*" In *Buddhist Studies in Honour of Walpola Rahula,* edited by S. Balasooriya, 251–66. London: Gordon Fraser; Sri Lanka: Vimamsa, 1980.

——. "The Rules of Debate According to Asaṅga." *Journal of the American Oriental Society* 78 (Jan.-March, 1958): 29–40.

——. "Yogācāra and the Buddhist Logicians." *Journal of the International Association of Buddhist Studies* 2.1 (1979): 65–78.

Ways of Enlightenment. Berkeley: Dharma Publishing, 1992.

Weinstein, Stanley. "The Ālayavijñāna in Early Yogācāra Buddhism: A Comparison of its Meaning in the *Saṁdhinirmocana-sūtra* and the *Vijñaptimātratāsiddhi* of Dharmapāla." *Kokusai Tōhō Gakusha Kaigikiyō* #3 (1959): 46–58.

——. "The Concept of Ālaya-vijñāna in pre-T'ang Chinese Buddhism." *Yūki kyōju shōju kinen bukkyō shisōshi ronshū (Essays on the History of Buddhist Thought Presented to Professor Reimon Yūki),* 38–51. Tokyo: Daizō Shuppan, 1964.

Willis, Janice Dean. *On Knowing Reality.* New York: Columbia University Press, 1979; reprint Delhi: Motilal Banarsidass, 1982. A translation of the *Tattvārtha* chapter of the *Bodhisattvabhūmi.*

Zahler, Leah, ed. *Meditative States in Tibetan Buddhism.* London: Wisdom Publications, 1983.

Glossary

Abhidharma teachings of the Buddha that emphasize training in wisdom

Affliction (kleśa) obscuration based on emotionality and ignorance

Arhat one who attains realization by breaking through the bondage of the emotional obscurations, i.e., kleśas

Ārya a realized one who has attained the path of seeing

Bhagavan a respectful epithet used to refer to the Buddha

Bodhisattva a Mahāyāna practitioner who aspires to become enlightened for the welfare of all sentient beings

Desire realm one of three saṁsāric realms of existence (desire, form, and formless); includes the domains of the desire realm gods, humans, animals, hungry ghosts, and hell beings. In this realm beings are dominated by attachment to the senses.

Dharma the teachings of the Buddha; also signifies truth or reality, or (lower case) 'phenomena' or 'thing'

Dharmadhātu 'Dharma realm'; the suchness of phenomena

Dhyāna meditative concentration

Form realm a saṁsāric realm of existence that includes many of the heavenly spheres and is characterized by temporary bliss and peace

Formless realm a saṁsāric realm of existence whose inhabitants dwell in states of meditation

Hīnayāna the vehicle of realization for those who seek release from saṁsāra for themselves alone, including Śrāvaka and Pratyekabuddha practitioners

Karma voluntary action producing consequences that determine the conditions and circumstances of sentient beings

Mahāyāna the Great Vehicle of realization, which emphasizes the Bodhisattva's great compassion and culminates in the state of a fully enlightened Buddha

Māra the lord of illusion and death, ruler of the desire realm, whom the Buddha defeated before attaining enlightenment

Nirvāṇa the extinction of saṁsāra

Prātimokṣa precepts for ordained and lay people found in the Vinaya teachings

Pratyekabuddha a Dharma practitioner who realizes dependent origination and the selflessness of phenomena, but who is without the great compassion of the Bodhisattva

Samādhi state of concentration and meditative absorption

Saṁsāra cyclic existence: the cycle of frustration and suffering kept in motion by actions based on ignorance

Śrāvaka one who practices the Dharma by focusing on impermanence, the reality of suffering inherent in saṁsāra, and the non-existence of an independent self

Suchness (tathatā) the inexpressible, inconceivable reality of phenomena inseparable from emptiness

Sūtra a discourse of the Buddha

Tathāgata a perfectly realized being; an epithet for the Buddha

Tīrthika a follower of extreme views such as nihilism or eternalism that are not conducive to enlightenment

Tripiṭaka the three collections of the teachings of the Buddha: Sūtra, Abhidharma, and Vinaya.

Vinaya the Buddha's teachings which focus on mindfulness and ethical behavior

Yogācāra one of two main philosophical schools of Mahāyāna Buddhism. The Saṁdhinirmocana Sūtra is one of the principal scriptural sources for the Yogācāra school.

Index

Śrī Vaiśravaṇa

[illegible]